Also by Tahir Shah

In Arabian Nights
The Caliph's House
House of the Tiger King
In Search of King Solomon's Mines
Trail of Feathers
Sorcerer's Apprentice
Beyond the Devil's Teeth
The Middle East Bedside Book

Travels With Myself

"Each story in this book is a fragment of a journey, a memory of happiness or hardship. It is a kaleidoscope of adventure, a lens held over humanity and oddity, and the ordinary as well"

Tahir Shah

⊗ SILVERSEA

The Tale *of* Tales

Travels With Myself

Collected Work

TAHIR SHAH

MOSAÏQUE

Travels With Myself, Collected Work

First Published in 2011 by Mosaïque Books

Copyright © Tahir Shah, 2011
All rights reserved

ISBN 978-1-4478-0582-3

Set in Goudy, 11.5 on 14.5

www.mosaiquebooks.com
www.tahirshah.com

For Rachana, with much love
and twenty years of memories together.

Contents

ONCE UPON A TIME there was a little boy who loved picking up pebbles on the beach.

No journey was complete until he'd spent time selecting the very choicest pebble, and stuffed it in his pocket. As soon as he got home, he put the pebble on his bedroom window ledge.

Some of the pebbles in the collection were smooth, cool and black, others were jade-green, more still were coarse and, yet more, seemed to smell of a secret island far away.

As the years passed, the little boy took comfort in his pebble collection. In times of sadness they were there for him, a reminder of happier days – triggering memories of a beach, of rolling waves, or of the setting sun.

One day, the little boy grew up.

It was time to leave home. He longed to leave on a journey in search of the Mango Rains. But, before setting out, he packed up all his belongings in tea crates, and put most of them into a storage locker, an eternity of waiting for things he once had loved.

Before clearing his bedroom, he went over to the pebble shelf, stroked a hand over one or two of the stones, breathed in deep. Then, taking a battered old shoebox from under his bed, he laid out the collection in nests of crumpled newspaper.

Twenty years passed.

The box was never opened, not once. The little boy, now a man, kept it locked up in a cupboard. He never forgot it was there, and would take comfort that it was with him.

The pebbles had been chosen at random over so many years, selected then studied, turned into the light, and observed from every angle once again. As the years passed, the types of stones he chose differed depending on his mood or age, the latter ones being quite different from the first one of all.

The stories in this book are like the pebbles in the little boy's collection. They're all different shapes and styles, and come from all corners of the world. Some will satisfy the curiosity of a select few, while others will appeal to all. I hope that the words will remind you of encounters you have had yourself, and stimulate thoughts you have never entertained before.

The common thread, if there is one, is fascination.

I've written about people, places, and things that have had a genuine and even mesmerizing grip over me. Whether they be the women on America's death row, or the thousands who live in Cairo's cemeteries, or portraits of lands through which my feet have strayed.

For me, this is a collection of work that exemplifies travels through many realms – north, south, east and west. Each story is a fragment of a journey, a memory to me of happiness or hardship. Designed to be opened at random, this book will, I hope, be a companion on a journey or in an idle moment at home. Although in random order, the styles and the quality of the writing vary – a reflection of my own journey on the writer's path.

The collection is a kaleidoscope of adventure, a lens held over humanity and oddity, and the ordinary as well.

As for the little boy and his precious collection of pebbles, he's now living in Casablanca, and has a little boy of his own.

Yesterday I took him down to the beach just before dusk. Together, we watched the sun slip down into the calm waters of the Atlantic. When it was gone, we stood there in the twilight in silence. After a long while he asked:

'Shall we go home, Baba?'

I tapped a hand down to the beach.

'Pick up a pebble,' I said.

'But why?'

'Because it's time you started a collection of your own.'

India's most exclusive train

Battlements of the Meherangarh Fort, Jodhpur

Aboard the Maharajah Express

A WILD RUMPUS of Indo-Gothic style, Mumbai's CST station stands as a glorious monument to the excesses of the British Raj. The evening's rush hour is well underway amid its turrets and spires, great sprawling domes, leering gargoyles and, of course, the towering statues of Imperial Britannia.

Moving at break-neck speed through the building's cavernous heart, the oceans of commuters make a beeline for the waiting trains. Once the blur of humanity is safely aboard, with many more clinging to the outside, there's a whirring of diesel engines. A jolt, then another, a grinding of steel, and the packed carriages heave away into the night.

India's rail network is vast and efficient, but low on frills.

It's all about getting a whole lot of people across town – or across the country – with the least amount of fuss. The network has more than sixty-four thousand kilometres of track, fourth most in the world.

Despite the faded grandeur of its exterior, CST station has a stripped-down functionality, catering to more than three million passengers each day.

In their rush to get home, most of the commuters don't notice the commotion at the far end of the terminus.

On the last platform, well away from the crowds, there's the distinct whiff of luxury, on a scale that would have impressed even the British Raj.

A small army of staff are rolling out a lengthy red carpet – up the steps from the VIP parking and along the platform. As soon as it's laid, a bearer sprinkles it in pink rose petals, while another steps forward with a silver salver laden with flutes of chilled Champagne.

A moment later, a brass band is in position. And, as they begin to play, the sleek crimson carriages of India's most luxurious train, the Maharajah Express, glide into place.

Then, right on cue, the passengers arrive.

Hailing from the United States, Europe, and from India itself, they are soon festooned in fragrant garlands, symbolic red *tikka* dabbed onto their foreheads, their fingers washed in rose water. And, while they admire the spotless livery of the train that will be their home for the next week, the hospitality staff lead them aboard to their cabins.

I boarded along with about seventy guests. To accommodate us, the Maharajah Express had sixteen guest carriages, two restaurants, two bars, and dozens and dozens of staff.

The cabin assigned to me was in a carriage called 'Katela', located about halfway down the train. Adorned with sumptuous fabrics and with mahogany furniture, it was panelled in teak, bathed in old-world charm. Best of all – even better than the fact there was WiFi everywhere – was the en suite bathroom. I'm a sucker for fabulous bathrooms. Ornamented with marble and with silver fittings, it boasted a flush-toilet and a power-shower. The larger cabins were even more decadent still, with roll-top baths.

As I stood there admiring the details, my valet – named Vikram – introduced himself. Turbanned, ever smiling, and exquisitely polite, he begged me to ask him for even the most insignificant request. As I was to soon find out, he lived in little more than a cupboard in the corridor. Whenever he heard me approaching, he'd dart out. And, standing to attention, he would await orders, grinning like a Cheshire cat.

A few minutes after boarding, the Maharajah Express slipped out of CST station on a schedule all of its own. As it did so, I tasted real luxury – a world in which the train waits for the passengers to be ready for it to leave.

Pushing out through Mumbai's endless suburbs and slums, there was a sense of awkwardness at first. It was as if I was separated from appalling poverty – that was inches away – by nothing more than a pane of glass.

On the first evening I took dinner in the Rang Mahal restaurant. Beneath a hand-painted ceiling – a gold floral motif on vermillion – the dining car was beyond opulent. The plates were Limoges edged with gold, the glasses finest crystal, and the flatware monogrammed with the letter 'M'.

With an entire carriage devoted to the kitchens – packed with chefs, equipment, and the freshest supplies, the two restaurants serve cuisine from both East and West. The beverage list, too, features a tremendous range of wines and Champagnes from France, the New World, and India as well – there's even a sommelier to help you choose.

Sitting there, as I watched the slums give way to countryside, I found myself thinking of the Maharajahs and their obsession with locomotives.

With the coffers of the Princely States filled to bursting, funding railways between their dominions wasn't held back by the usual constraints. Vying with each other to create the most over the top carriages, the Maharajahs installed salons and billiard rooms, private suites, and even air-conditioning – made from electric fans and blocks of ice.

The Nizam of Hyderabad's carriages were said to be the most opulent of all. They were adorned with ivory and 24-carat gold. But the prize for sheer bling-bling surely went to the Maharajah of Vadodara. He had a throne installed aboard his royal train.

Coincidentally, it was along his stretch of track that the Maharajah Express took us first. The next morning we awoke to find ourselves in the city of Vadodara, capital of Gujarat.

Stepping down onto a red carpet once again, we were serenaded by musicians, and then led on a tour of the ancient Gaekwad culture. And with it, came the first of a royal flush of palaces – a banquet at the Jambughoda estate at lunch, and another at the awe-inspiring Laxmi Vilas Palace at dusk.

There, in the great durbar hall, the royal band was positioned on a low dais. With a full retinue of staff and factota, the Maharajah could have commanded anything in terms of musical entertainment. And so I appreciated all the more what had been laid on. A pair of musicians was strumming simple stringed instruments, with a third playing about forty soup bowls filled with varying levels of water, with the end of a spoon.

During the night the train roved northward, reaching the Rajasthani city of Udaipur as I took my last bite of toast.

One of the great treasures of India, Udaipur has palaces aplenty, each one more astounding than the next. At the centre of it all is the Lake Palace, floating like a magical marble island amid the serene waters of Lake Pichola. Famously, it featured in the 1980s James Bond film *Octopussy*. From a vantage point high above, we were given a private reception in the sixteenth century City Palace, in which the Maharajah and his family still reside.

On once again through the night to Jodhpur, Rajasthan's 'Blue City'. Set on the edge of the Great Thar Desert, Jodhpur bustles with life, with wares, and with a kaleidoscope of colour. Many of the buildings are dyed blue with indigo, signifying the homes of aristocracy.

During a famine in the 1930s, the Maharajah there commissioned the Umaid Bhavan, a vast Art Deco palace, to give the starving populace paid work. The colossal dome was only accomplished by the ingenuity of a local engineer. The stones fitted together so tightly that there was no space for them to be pushed into position by hand. The engineer came up with a brilliant solution. The giant corner stones were placed on blocks of ice. As the ice melted, the stones dropped slowly into place.

On the evening of our visit to Jodhpur, we were treated to a banquet on the battlements of the colossal Meherangarh Fort, itself one of my most memorable experiences of recent years.

Yet, on the Maharajah Express there was almost no time to stop and ponder the wonders, which were coming thick and fast.

The red carpet was awaiting us once again.

Climbing back aboard, we sped northward once more, this time to the city of Bikaner.

The next afternoon was spent touring the exquisite Lalgarh Palace, its red sandstone structure adorned with sublime filigree work. Then, just before nightfall, we mounted a convoy of camel carts and trouped into the Thar Desert. A banquet had been prepared under the stars, Rajasthani tribal dancers and campfires illuminating the night.

Another day, and another city.

This time, the crème de la crème – Jaipur. Capital of Rajasthan, it's a raw and regal fusion of medieval and modern. One of the must-visit destinations for anyone, the 'Pink City' is steeped in nostalgia and in a dazzlingly vibrant charm unlike anything else.

The highlight of the entire journey came for me that afternoon. Having reached the Jai Mahal Palace, we were invited to take part in the sport of kings – a match of 'elephant polo'.

Mahouts steer the elephants, while the riders lean down with their mallets, in a desperate attempt to knock a football into the goal. Quite unlike the rip-roaring speed of equestrian polo, the game played on elephant back is sedate to put it mildly – the overwhelming problem being that the elephants tend to burst the ball by treading on it.

After Jaipur, the Maharajah Express rumbled on to the tiger reserve at Ranthambore, one of the only sanctuaries of the noblest of cats left on the Subcontinent. And on again to the deserted Mughal city of Fatehpur Sikri. Constructed by Emperor Akbar, it's a UNESCO World Heritage Site, and remains as pristine as the day it was built four centuries ago.

The following morning, we reached the most famous landmark of all – the Taj Mahal. Lost in an eerie mist, the Taj is one of those buildings whose chilling beauty can grasp even the most wayward attention for hours at a time. That the Maharajah Express should deliver us so close to such a jewel of human endeavour seemed like the ultimate perfection.

Late that afternoon, the bubble of opulence that we all now regarded as our home, chugged through an eternity of slums, the lead up to any sprawling Indian city. And, eventually, we came to a halt on a platform at Delhi's Safdarjung station just in time for the evening rush. By now, there was a definite sense that it was our train, just as the thought of leaving it was almost too much to bear.

Before stepping down onto the red carpet for the last time, my valet, Vikram, eased himself out from his cupboard in the corridor and saluted me. Then he shook me by the hand.

'Very sad you leaving, Sahib,' he said.

I thanked him. He shook my hand a second time, and saluted again for good measure.

A moment later, I was just another lost soul adrift on a sea of commuters. I glanced back at the platform. The Maharajah Express had vanished.

I wondered if it had ever been there at all.

A Conversation Paid for in Postage Stamps

HICHAM HARRASS LIVES in a one-room shack he built himself on the western-most edge of Casablanca.

The walls are made from third-hand breeze blocks and the roof is laid with rusting tin. His home does not have an address, but it does have a number. It is number 2043. All around it there's a jumble of other shacks, each with their number daubed on the wall in dripping red paint. If you turned up at the *bidonville*, the shanty-town, you'd have no hope in finding Hicham's place in the maze of alleyways. But ask for him by name and every man, woman and smallest child, will jab a finger towards his door.

I met Hicham because of his passion for postage stamps.

Our house is half a mile from the Atlantic. Its gardens are an oasis of date palms and mimosa trees, and are surrounded on all sides by the breeze block shanty-town. When we first moved into the house I must admit I was anxious. We had no idea how our neighbours would greet us, whether they could get used to a family of foreigners living in their midst.

One morning during our first week in Casablanca, there was a tap at the door. I went to open it, and found an elderly man standing in the frame. His skin was the colour of roasted almonds. He had a long shiny face with a scrub of white beard at the end of his chin. He wore a frayed black and white wool *jelaba*, and old yellow *baboush* slippers on his feet.

Before I could ask how I could help him, the man extended a hand, smiled, said his name was Hicham, and that he collected postage stamps.

'Do you have any to spare?' he enquired politely. 'I could pay you money for them, a few dirhams.'

I thought for a moment.

'We haven't received any mail yet,' I replied. 'We've just arrived.'

Hicham's smile melted. I told him to come back in a week.

'Will you forget?' he asked.

I promised not to.

A week later Hicham was at the door again. I had collected five British stamps, all bearing the Queen's head. I handed them over, and a remarkable friendship began.

After that I collected all the stamps on my letters and gave them to Hicham. He was a proud man and insisted on paying me, although he had almost no money at all. I didn't want to offend him by refusing payment, and so we came up with a solution.

We agreed to meet at his home at the same time each week. I would pass over the postage stamps and, in return, he could tell me about his life.

Hicham Harrass was born in a village three days' walk from the southern city of Agadir. His father had been a farmer, with half an acre of dusty land. Along with five brothers and a sister, he grew up in a house made from flotsam, gleaned from the Atlantic waves.

When Hicham was seven years old, a *sehura*, a witch, came to the house and declared that he would drop dead within the next cycle of the moon. The only way to avoid such a fate, she said, was for Hicham's parents to give the boy away to a stranger. The family was very upset but, believing the witch's prediction would come true, they gave him to the next man who came into the village. Fortunately for Hicham, that man was a trader, a man called Ayman.

'He needed a boy to help him,' said Hicham, 'and so I travelled around Morocco with him and his cart, buying and selling scrap metal as we went. On the long journeys between small towns he taught me,' Hicham continued. 'He taught me about life, and how to live it.'

I asked what he meant.

The old man's wife flustered over with more mint tea.

'Ayman taught me to be selfless,' he said. 'That means giving more to the people you meet than you take from them. And it means walking softly on the Earth.'

As the years had passed, Ayman and the young Hicham crisscrossed the Kingdom again and again. They travelled from Agadir to Essaouira, from Marrakech to Fès, from Tangier to Casablanca, always on the donkey cart piled high with scrap metal.

'We visited places that aren't on any maps,' said Hicham. 'It was adventure. Real adventure. You can't understand what it was like – it was like waking from a dream! Every mile that we travelled, Ayman would talk. Every mile was a lesson. He taught me about honour, and to tell the truth. It's because of Ayman that I cannot lie. Truth is the backbone of my life. It's my religion.'

'But Islam is your religion,' I said.

'It's the same thing,' said Hicham. 'Islam is Truth. It's the truth to believe in yourself, in those around you, and in God.'

Almost every week for a year, Hicham and I met and talked and talked, in conversation paid for in postage stamps. There are so many memorable conversations in my head, but few have ever been quite so revealing as those with Hicham. Over the months, I found myself grasping the basics of what must surely be real Islam.

One afternoon, Hicham invited me in, served me a ubiquitous glass of steaming mint tea, and said:

'You are young, your eyes are wide open, your mind is clear. But you must take care to understand.'

'To understand what?'

'To understand the right Path.'

Hicham called out the door to his wife, who was chatting to a neighbour in the street. He apologized.

'I'm sorry,' he said, 'she forgets the duty of honouring a guest with food.'

I asked about the Path.

'To understand the right Path,' Hicham said, stroking his tuft of beard, 'you must understand what it is not. It's easy. It's a lesson in life. Islam is not complicated, or cruel, or unfair. Anyone who cannot describe it in the most simplistic way is telling falsehoods. He's telling lies. He's as bad as the fanatics.'

I asked about the fanatics – about Al-Qaeda, and other radical groups.

Hicham rubbed his eyes.

'They pretend that what they are doing is in the name of Allah, but it's in the name of Satan,' he said very softly. 'They are hijacking our religion. Open your eyes and see it for yourself! Islam teaches tolerance and modesty. It doesn't tell people to fly passenger jets into skyscrapers, or to strap plastic explosives to the waists and to slaughter innocent women and children. These people must be stopped.'

The next week, I handed over a fresh crop of postage stamps.

As always, the old man spent a few moments poring over them, commenting on each one. His favourites were from England but, 'not those silly ones with the Queen,' he would say. 'I like the big, more unusual ones. They hint at the society, the tradition.'

I steered the conversation away from postage stamps, and onto the problems of the world. I asked Hicham how Islam could stop Al-Qaeda. He didn't say anything at first; he was too busy sorting through the stamps.

'I'll tell you,' he said at length. 'You have to starve them of publicity. That's what to do. Don't report their misdeeds. Ignore them. Pretend they don't exist.'

'Won't that just make them wilder for publicity?'

Hicham laughed. He laughed and he laughed until his old sagging cheeks were the colour of beetroot.

'Of course it would,' he said. 'But it doesn't matter how angry they get, so long as we rise up tall and spread the truth about Islam. We must tell people the facts, the real facts. That's what I'm saying.'

'What are the real facts?'

'Tell them that Islam doesn't order women to veil,' he said. 'The tradition was copied from the Christians of Byzantium. And tell them that Islam doesn't say you cannot drink wine – it just says you can't become intoxicated. And,' Hicham went on, his voice rising in volume, 'you can tell them that Islam says that all Muslims are equal. We are brothers. That means an imam or a religious scholar is equal to us. He can't tell us what to do!'

Three weeks ago I flew to London for a few days, leaving my wife and the children at our oasis in the shanty-town. On the evening I returned to Casablanca, there was a knock at the door.

'That will be Hicham,' I said to my wife, 'he'll be wondering where I have been.'

I opened the door, expecting to see the old man's face. But it wasn't him. It was his wife, Khadija. She was crying.

'My husband died three days ago,' she said. 'He told me if anything ever happened to him, that I should give you this.'

The old woman was holding a box. She held it out towards me. I thanked her. A moment later she was gone. I went inside to my desk, turned on the lamp, and opened the box.

In it were Hicham's stamp albums. I sat down in the dim light. I was sad to have lost a wise friend, but at the same time I was happy – happy that we had found each other at all, and had so many good conversations, each one paid for in postage stamps.

A Labyrinth in Fès

THEIR HOOVES STUMBLING over the flagstones, a procession of clove-brown pack mules lurch downhill into the ancient labyrinth.

Laden with tanned sheepskins and sacks of cement, with soap powder and TV sets in crates, the mules ply a route trodden by animals and men for a thousand years and more.

The Fès medina is a vast sprawling honeycomb of interwoven lanes, many of them no wider than a barrel's length. They form a kaleidoscope of life that's changed little in centuries, the spiritual heart of Morocco. Wander the streets and you're cast back in time as your senses are overpowered. The pungent scent of lamb roasting on spits, the muffled sound of hammers striking great sheets of burnished brass; the sight of camel heads hanging outside butchers' stalls.

In recent years it's Marrakech that's attracted the bulk of Morocco's tourists. But, as that city inches ever closer to becoming a Disneyland distortion of reality, it's Fès that stands as a beacon for the genuine article – without doubt the only medieval Arab city on Earth left almost completely in tact.

Moroccans regard Fès as nothing short of a sacred treasure trove. In whispers they describe the dark authenticity which doesn't exist anywhere else. It's true that some visitors find the medina's labyrinth bewitching, even unsettling, but all who reach out and grasp it, are mesmerized by what they find.

Founded in the year 789 by King Idriss I, on the river whose name it bears, Fès has been a centre of culture and learning since the days of Harun ar-Rachid. Once part of a network of interconnected cities, spread throughout the Islamic world, Fès was linked by pilgrimage routes to Cordoba, Baghdad, Cairo and Samarkand. At the forefront of knowledge, and home to the greatest thinkers of its day, it was a city where breakthroughs were made – in science and technology, in

The great doors of a courtyard home in the medina of Fès

literature and the arts.

But time is a great leveller.

For centuries Fès lay asleep – its palaces, fondouks, medrasas and mosaic fountains, each one a jewel of craftsmanship, hidden beneath a veil. Although proud of their city, the rich gradually moved away to the new town, or to Casablanca – the kingdom's economic hub – leaving the ancient medina to languish.

Only now is the veil being lifted.

And, nowhere is the change faster than on Talaa Kebir. A main thoroughfare bustling with people and animals, feet and hooves jostling for space, the street almost defies description. Angled steeply downhill, (its name translates as 'great climb'), it snakes down all the way to the ancient Karaouiyine Mosque.

Beginning at the fabulous arched blue gate of Bab Boujloud, Talaa Kebir runs deep into the rabbit warren of alleyways and lanes, spanning centuries of life. To stroll down it is to strip away the layers of humanity towards its medieval core.

Every inch of the way, it's packed with action.

There are street stalls heaped with melons, pomegranates and prickly pears. Fish sellers, their battered old carts serenaded by cats. Knife sharpeners grinding away at rusty blades, barbers and blind men, merchants, musicians and mendicants. Either side of the street, there are stalls piled high with ordinary wares – flour sieves, sneakers and underpants, bunches of fresh mint furled up in newspaper, loofahs and Man United football strips.

While there's an abundance of tourist kitsch, most of the stuff on offer is aimed at ordinary Moroccans – in a way the magic of the place. And, as if the daily bustle weren't enough, weaving through the crowds like shuttles on a loom are the pack mules. Almost everything on sale is heaved into the medina on their trusty backs.

But centuries of slumber have taken a heavy toll on Talaa Kebir, a theatre of the ordinary – and extraordinary. The wooden shop-fronts are rotting, their foundations battered by the elements – searing summer heat and austere winter cold. Most of the merchants can't afford to make repairs. They struggle to make a living as it is.

Fortunately though, UNESCO spearheaded an international

campaign, adding the ancient medina to its roll call of World Heritage sites. Although not actually paying for repairs – which were funded by the Moroccan government under the auspices of the King – UNESCO made a master plan for the old city's revival. The first job undertaken was to erect wooden scaffolding around more than a thousand buildings regarded as in danger of collapsing.

One of the most prominent success stories – not to mention one of the greatest architectural masterpieces in Fès – is the Bouinania Medrasa, the celebrated religious school. Found on Talaa Kebir, it's recently been restored, and offers a window into a medieval realm that has vanished throughout the Arab world. Get there early, stand in the central courtyard, and you can't help but travel back in time.

Another renovated marvel, a stone's throw from the central thoroughfare, is the Fondouk el-Nejjarine, a fabulous galleried caravanserai. Nearby it is the Attarine Medrasa, yet another newly-restored tour de force of culture, built seven centuries ago.

Spend a little time traipsing through the medina, and you come to realize that it's all about detail. Wherever you look, it's there: A pattern sculpted into the plaster frieze above a doorway, a tarnished appliqué lamp that's a work of art in its own right; a mosaic fountain at which a pack mule is pausing to slake its thirst.

And, according to some of the foreigners obsessed by Fès, it's the attention to detail that makes all the difference.

An American scholar who's lived in the medina for more than a decade, David Amster is one of them. He believes in 'guerilla restoration' on a micro scale. Whenever he's raised a little money through his tiny 18th century guest house, called Dar Bennis, David ploughs the funds into hiring a team of master craftsmen. Often working at night when the streets are empty, they restore the ancient zellij mosaic fountains, and repair centuries-old walls with *medluk*, a traditional lime rendering.

'The work isn't fast,' says David over a glass of tar-like morning *café noir*, 'but what's important is getting it right.' He fumbles in his coat pocket and pulls out a crumpled twist of iron. 'Look at this nail,' he says dreamily, 'it was handmade three hundred years ago by someone who cared about detail. If he cared so much about a single insignificant nail like this, imagine how much he cared about an entire building!'

Half way down Talaa Kebir, opposite the Bouinania Medrasa, is a small alley, beneath what's left of the medieval water clock. Venture down it and, as it telescopes into nothingness, take a left again. You emerge into a small courtyard, once a home and now the celebrated Café Clock.

The Clock, as it's known by all, is set over half a dozen levels, and is one of the medina's most lively oases – popular with locals and foreigners alike. Serving up a mélange of Moroccan and continental dishes, it's the brainchild of Englishman and former *maitre d'*, Mike Richardson.

Decorating a camel burger with a little garnishing as it leaves the kitchen, Mike flutters a hand out towards the labyrinth through which Talaa Kebir wends a path. 'It takes time to understand Fès,' he says. 'And in some ways you're more baffled the longer you stay here. I can't claim to be an expert, but I admit that the city has seeped into my blood. Now I've lived here I don't know if I could ever put roots down anywhere else. Look around you – Fès is a splinter of Paradise!'

Arranged inwards around central courtyards, many cooled by fragrant orange trees, traditional Moroccan architecture tends to be hidden from an outsider's view. Roam the lanes of the medina and you can find yourself desperate to glimpse the jewels that lie behind firmly bolted doors.

A tip for anyone eager to peek inside – go in search of your very own home in Fès. Instantly, the arched cedar portals are pulled open from within, and you find yourself ushered in. It's the best way to conjure the doors to open.

For the last five years, Fred Sola has been finding homes for foreigners and assisting them in renovations. A Frenchman born in Casablanca, he's the owner of the palatial Riad Laaroussa, and has an eye for a home with potential. 'House hunting in Fès is like nowhere else,' he says, his eyes ablaze with delight. 'This is the only city I know where you can find a palace for the price of a terraced house anywhere else...'

Pausing in mid-conversation, Fred Sola stares out at the street. He squints, then smiles gradually, as a bridal party pushes through. With much whooping and trumpeting, the bride is borne forwards waist-height on a dais. The Frenchman combs a hand back through his hair.

'You really must believe me,' he says gently, 'life just doesn't get any better than this.'

A Price on Their Heads

EVER SINCE MY AUNT lifted me up to a glass case at the back of Oxford's Pitt Rivers Museum, at the impressionable age of eight, I have been hooked on shrunken heads.

Like so many schoolboys before me, my lower jaw dropped as I gazed in awe at the array of miniature human heads, correctly known as *tsantsas*. There was something wholly captivating about their gnarled features, the sewn lips, little hollow necks and manes of jet black hair.

I longed to learn the secret processes, known to a tribe deep in the South American jungle, which enabled decapitated human heads to be shrunk to the size of a grapefruit.

Despite an ongoing debate about whether museums should harbour human remains, the Pitt Rivers Museum still holds five, and the British Museum has at least ten. Interest in the gruesome exhibits remains strong. A roaring private trade in the illicit handicraft has developed, with heads being snapped up by wealthy collectors, many from the Far East and Japan.

The genuine article comes from the Upper Amazon, a region on the Pastaza river between Peru and Ecuador.

For thousands of years a tribe called the Shuar (misnamed by Western observers as Jivaro, meaning 'savage'), shrunk the heads of their slain enemies. Although historically dozens of tribal societies have taken trophy heads, only the Shuar ever came up with the curious idea of reducing these trophies in size. One possible exception is the ancient Nazcan and coastal civilizations of the Atacama desert, with whom the Shuar share a common ancestry.

The Shuar's victims were subject to swift and brutal attacks. During surprise raids on enemy villages, warriors would hack off as many heads as they could. The *tsantsa* raids were their raison d'etre. They proved a warrior's bravery and the community's superiority.

20

Ramon, the Shuar shaman, the Upper Amazon, Peru

Retreating into the jungle with their fresh harvest of heads, the Shuar would immediately begin work on their trophies. They believed that humans have three souls. One of these – the *musiak* – is charged with avenging the victim's death. The only way of pacifying the enraged soul was by shrinking the head in which it lay.

During decapitation, a knife was used to peel back the victim's skin from the upper part of the chest, the shoulders and the back. Then the head was chopped as far as possible, close to the collar bone using a stone-edged knife. The warrior would remove his own headband and thread it through the neck and out of the mouth, making it easier to carry, slung over the shoulder.

The face was literally peeled off the skull, before being sewn up into a neat pouch of skin. This was steeped in hot water for a few minutes. Baked pebbles were then placed in the pouch, causing it to shrivel and shrink, taking great care not to damage the features. When the pouch was too small for pebbles, hot sand scooped from a riverbank was carefully swished about inside.

Next, the lips were sewn tightly shut with a strand of twine. A machete's blade was heated and pressed against the lips to dry them. Then the facial skin was repeatedly rubbed with charcoal. Sometimes a large red seed was placed beneath the eyelids, filling the hole, preventing the *musiak* from peering out.

Between four and six days of treatment were needed for the basic *tsantsa* to be completed, at which time it was about the size of a man's fist. A hole was made at the top of the head and a string attached to it, so that the warrior could wear it around his neck for the celebratory *tsantsa* feast.

As far as the Shuar people were concerned, the *tsantsas* had no intrinsic value, and they were merely tossed back into the jungle as soon as the avenging souls had been appeased. But once Victorian trailblazers got their hands on the curious trophies, a thriving market began.

Search the Internet and you come across plenty of examples. Most of them are fakes, or made for the tourist trade, and are often fashioned from plucked goat skin, which has overly large pores. Genuine *tsantsas* have delicate nasal hair, and a light oily shine to the skin. Only a finished one will have twine hanging from the lips, which signifies that three enormous feasts have been held in honour of the head.

On the Internet you can find black, white, and even Chinese shrunken heads. They are outright fakes – generally made in Guatemalan workshops at the turn of the last century. The Shuar would never have any cause to shrink a foreigner's head, because they don't believe that outsiders have souls.

On one expedition to the Upper Amazon, I hired a ramshackle boat and made for the remote Pastaza in search of the Shuar. My guide was a veteran of the USA-Vietnam war who told me that the Shuar tribe, 'made the Viet Cong look like pussy cats'. Everyone en route warded us away. 'The Shuar will chop off your heads,' they told us, 'and drink your blood and eat your brains.'

When we finally reached Shuar territory late in the evening, a man ran down to greet our boat and present me with a gift of a roasted monkey. In the background we could hear singing, which I was sure was the ancient ballads of the Shuar. Shrunken heads would be nearby.

In the dawn light we climbed the steep bank up to the village, where the chief was waiting. He plied us with a strange white creamy beverage, called *masato*.

Only later did I realize how it is made.

Manioc roots are boiled up and mashed with a stick. As they mash, the makers grab handfuls of the goo, chew it, and spit it back into the bowl. The enzymes in their saliva start off the fermenting process.

After downing a third bowl of *masato*, I asked the chief if he had problems with the neighbouring villages. I motioned the shape of a small head with my hands.

'We love our neighbours,' said the chief, 'they are our friends. We all pray together when the people in the flying boats come.'

'Flying boats?'

The chief nodded.

'The friendly people from Alabama. They bring us tambourines and little pink pills – but best of all, they brought us Jesus.'

'What about war? What about heads?' I asked.

'Why do we need to kill or shrink heads when we have the son of God?' he replied.

In little more than a generation the ancient ways of the Shuar have been changed forever. Small-scale petroleum projects in the deep jungle are one reason for this. But the overbearing responsibility must be assumed by a variety of missionary groups who have sought to cast the Shuar into the modern world, and to save their souls.

Landing in remote jungle enclaves in 'flying boats', the white man has wrought change on an unprecedented scale. The Shuar peoples have also been devastated by the measles, tuberculosis, venereal diseases and the common cold. The cures no longer come from traditional plant-based medicines but by handfuls of 'little pink pills'. The only positive factor in terms of population is that the cessation of *tsantsa* raids has led to a reduction of death through warfare.

After a tour of the village, the chief invited us to the makeshift church, built by the missionaries from Alabama. The proud former head-shrinkers stood in neat rows. As the noises of the jungle night echoed around us, the villagers sang Onward Christian Soldiers, translated into Shuar.

But although most of the villagers were keen to sing hymns and show off their Shuar Bibles, one man – the village shaman – was less happy.

'The missionaries don't understand what their religion has done,' he explained. 'Head-hunting was a brutal practice, but it was our culture. It developed over a very long time, and had meant much more to us than Jesus and the Bible.'

The shaman lit a home-made cigar of *mapacho*, black jungle tobacco, as thick as his wrist. His eyes seemed to glaze over.

'Head shrinking gave reason to our existence,' he went on, exhaling a plume of pungent smoke. 'Without the head-raiding parties our lives have changed, we are not the same people as we were in our fathers' time. We are weaker. We are timid now. But worst of all, we have lost our honour.'

Brazil's Sanctuaries From Abuse

IT'S LIKE ANY OTHER Saturday night in São Paulo's infamous Pedreira slums.

Music blares out from a line of makeshift bars. Dark brown bottles clang together as neighbours celebrate the end of another week. The air is filled with cheap cigar smoke and with laughter. A young couple is samba dancing in the muddy main street. Everyone, it seems, is in a jubilant mood. But away from the revelling drinkers the atmosphere is far less cheerful.

Martina Alberto, a young mother of two, sits on her bed waiting for her husband's return. For Martina, surviving unscathed until Sunday morning is always an achievement. Her husband, Rogerio, an unemployed labourer, bursts in soon after midnight. In one hand is a bottle of home-brewed cane liquor, and in the other there's a carving knife.

In a fit of drunken rage Rogerio swears that he'll chop up their two small daughters. Weeping hysterically, Martina pleads with him to take his fury out on her rather than the children. Eagerly, he agrees. An hour later and Martina has been kicked, beaten, stabbed with the knife, and raped.

With her eyes swollen, her body bruised from the kicks, and her face badly cut, Martina runs from the house. It's three a.m. Clutching her daughters, Andresa, six months, and Paola, three years, she staggers through São Paulo's dark streets. The sound of singing from the back-street bars has now been replaced by high-pitched police sirens and sporadic exchanges of gunfire. The only men still out are drunks, and the only women, prostitutes. Calming her daughters as best she can, Martina heads for a large, modern building at Campo Grande, a sprawling suburb in São Paulo's south zone. This, the 9th Police Precinct, is located at the violent heart of Brazil's largest city.

With determined strides, Martina hurries her daughters inside. She heads straight for a stark waiting-room. She knows the way well. Since her marriage to Rogerio, she's been a regular visitor there.

It looks like any other precinct, but this is a police station with a difference. Named *Delegacia de Policia de Defesa da Mulher*, the station is run by women officers, for women in trouble. The imposing size of the building hints at the number of women in the community who need police help. There are more than a hundred and twenty similar stations in São Paulo alone. *Delegacia*, which were first established in Brazil in the 'eighties, play an important role in the war against household violence.

From the outset, the stations were an instant success, taking seriously battered women's pleas for help. Like much of Latin America, Brazilian society suffers from machismo syndrome, a society that closes ranks to protect abusive men.

Before there were *Delegacia*, women reporting domestic violence, even rape, were usually chased away from regular police stations. For the few sympathetic male officers, domestic violence was a matter beyond their jurisdiction.

More than three hundred thousand women take refuge at *Delegacia* across Brazil each year. Most of them, like Martina, are too terrified at first to report their spouses' crimes. But genuinely fearing for their lives, and those of their children, Martina and thousands like her have no other choice.

Waiting for her name to be called, Martina glances around the room. About two dozen other women sit about on red plastic chairs. Some are weeping. Others nurse fresh wounds, or comfort their children. A teenage mother sitting beside Martina holds a bloodied bandage to her thigh. The early hours of Sunday morning are always the most eventful at São Paulo's *Delegacias*.

At six a.m., Martina is still waiting.

Her baby daughter is crying for food. The officer, a tall middle aged woman wearing a dark blue uniform, leads her to an interview room. Staring at her across the desk, Martina says simply: 'I want him put in jail. You must do it. Please help me.'

In charge of the 9th Women's Division, Detective Katia Marinelli notes down the complaint and sighs deeply. 'We will do all we can to help you,' she replies, 'but will you assist us this time, by taking him to court?' Staring blankly into space, Martina nods her head, and is taken away by a clerk for an examination.

Detective Marinelli rubs her eyes and looks at her watch. It's almost six-thirty. 'Tonight we've had about seventy women here,' she explains. 'We often get many more than that. The worst is when "Corinthians" – one of the most popular soccer teams in São Paulo – have lost their game. I'm not a follower of football, but I always pray that the Corinthians win.'

The detective pauses to sign an official document, 'Most of the women we get here are in their twenties,' she continues, 'but an increasing number are teenage wives. Those are the saddest cases. They've usually been made pregnant and have got married to abusive, alcoholic men. Most don't have a clue what they've got themselves into. For them, this is an escape from Hell.'

Next door, Martina is being examined by Roseli, a clerk of about the same age. Roseli lifts up the blood-splattered blouse to examine the mass of plum-coloured bruises. The cut on Martina's face and another on her forearm are scrutinized. Then Roseli types in the statement at a computer terminal. With its details of drunken debauchery, rape and stabbing, the report is so usual that Roseli feels as if she knows it by heart.

'When I first met Rogerio,' Martina says softly, 'I knew he was an ex-convict. But I was in love with him and he seemed intent on bettering his life. Soon after our marriage he lost his job. Then he started drinking heavily. Now I want him in jail, otherwise he will kill me and the kids. He's already sworn to cut off their fingers when I bring them home.'

Martina puts her signature beneath the printout of her statement, and wonders what to do next. She is too afraid to return to their home. 'I think I will go and stay with a cousin in Belo Horizonte,' she says. 'I'll have to find a job. I never want to see Rogerio again.'

The *Delegacia* has a special shelter for women too afraid to go home. The *abrigos*, shelters, support homeless and vulnerable women and their children for up to three months. The details of such safe houses are kept secret, for fear that a violent husband would come to get revenge on his wife.

At nine a.m. officer Marinelli is still at her desk.

Sunlight is streaming in through the window. 'All the drunks will be sobering up by now,' she says weakly, 'getting ready for another evening of drinking. At least ninety-nine per cent of the cases we deal with involve alcohol. Illegal cane liquor is cheap and strong. They should put a warning in the bottle: drinking it won't just damage your health, but the health of your family.

'We always try to reconcile the parties involved,' continues Marinelli. 'Slamming an abusive husband in jail may get rid of him, but it often leaves a family without a breadwinner.'

When Governor Franco Montoro originally decreed that women-only police stations were to be built, the idea was met with a mixed reception. Pressure groups insisted that special treatment was necessary for women in such a macho society. But the powerful male lobby greeted the proposal with skepticism. Nowhere else in the world had women's police stations, they said, so why did they need them?

Brazil's first all-woman police station was at Parque de San Pedro, a run-down area near São Paulo's long distance bus terminal. From the first day, the office was over-flowing with female victims. In the years since, the *Delegacia* have spread like wildfire through Brazil's major cities and beyond. Now they are not only found throughout Brazil, but across Latin America, from Argentina to Venezuela. Dozens of other countries around the world now are calling for their own forms of *Delegacia* as well.

Inspector Maria Valente has been with the *Delegacia* project right from the start. From her spacious ninth floor office at the Public Security Headquarters Building in downtown São Paulo, she controls more than a hundred women's police stations across the city and its state.

São Paulo, which is regarded by the United Nations as one of the world's most dangerous places to live, boasts an average of forty murders each weekend. The majority of the city's twelve million inhabitants live below the poverty line. For many men, unemployment is a reality they bear uneasily. Large numbers turn to alcohol, drugs, and wife battering to alleviate the frustrations of poverty.

Facing domestic violence head on, Inspector Valente and her team are used to the tales of savage attacks and stabbings, rape, and even incest.

'Beating up women is as old as history and happens everywhere,' says Valente sharply. 'Of course we register more wife abuse amongst the poor, simply because there are more poor than rich in Brazil. Rich men do terrible things to women too, but they have money to pay good lawyers when a case gets to court. We had one case where a wealthy businessman smashed his wife's head against a wall for dropping a plate of food; and another where a teenage girl came to us, made pregnant by her father – himself a pillar of society.'

For Valente and her staff, the problem of getting women to come forward to testify in court against their spouses, is a vexing one. 'Women are terrified that if the husband gets off, he'll hunt them down and kill them. It's that simple,' she says.

In a society where beating up your wife is sometimes almost seen as a man's birthright, his prerogative, the challenge is breathtaking. To meet that challenge at hand, Inspector Valente and her colleagues look for female officers who have what it takes to deal with the traumas of the job. 'Most of the officers we recruit are aged below thirty,' says the Inspector, as she stares out across São Paulo's rooftops. 'They can empathize with the young mothers who seek our help. We need women who are patient, caring, and who are unlikely to be deterred by the sight of blood, or by the intimate details of a rape.'

Officers working at the *Delegacia* encounter a wide range of frustrations every day. 'One of our biggest problems,' continues Valente, 'is that when battered women arrive here, they're often hysterical. They beg us to throw their violent husband in prison and throw away the key. Unfortunately, we have to act according to the law. That's one reason why officers are advised to avoid striking personal friendships with the victims, even in the most heartbreaking cases.'

With a view to reconciliation, the *Delegacia* often summon the husbands to explain themselves. 'When men turn up to give their side of the story they can behave very arrogantly,' explains Sandra Claro, a new officer at the 9th Precinct. 'They swear and jeer at us, but soon they realize that although we're women we are police officers, like any others. It's then that they get nervous at the prospect of a spell in jail.'

Back at the reception of the 9th Precinct a steady stream of assaulted women have wandered in during the day. As usual, the waiting-room is full to capacity. Some of the tired, frail figures sitting there refuse to file complaints. Too fearful to formally document the crimes, they come in to have a chat with the officers, and to pause for breath in the security of the station.

Deputy Sandra Claro is dealing with a typical case in interview room Number Three. A young woman called Olivia is sitting across from her. Married just three weeks before, Olivia, who's only nineteen, has seen her husband's true character revealed for the first time. 'On Friday night he went out with his friends. At two in the morning he came back... and he brought another woman with him. I found him with her on the couch,' she says. 'When I asked him what was going on he slapped me on the face and said that he'd bite off my nose if I didn't leave him alone.'

Olivia's statement is typed out and presented for her signature. An illiterate, she whispers for an ink pad. Then, almost ceremonially, she adds her thumbprint at the end of the document and bursts into tears.

Two doors down, in another interview suite, Marcia is telling her tale. 'My husband doesn't drink much,' she explains. 'But he's addicted to heroin. It's always in the morning when he's craving the drug he gets so violent. We have no money. We can't pay the rent. And now he threatens to pour gasoline over me when I'm asleep and set me alight, unless I go out and steal to pay for his addiction. I don't know what to do.'

Marcia stares at the young female officer beside her, tears rolling down her face. 'I'm so frightened, can you please, please help me?'

When an abusive husband refuses to make an appearance at the *Delegacia* Precinct, officers are sent on a mobile patrol to investigate the situation. The 9th Precinct's territory covers all kinds of areas, ranging from millionaires' mansions to the perilous shanty-towns of south São Paulo.

Silvia Rodrigues has been with the all-female police force for six years. Carefully checking her .38 calibre black service revolver, she prepares for an investigation along with her partner, Vera Lucia. 'Most men don't believe it when we turn up and ask them to accompany us to the Precinct,' she says. 'For archetypal Brazilian macho males, the ultimate humiliation is to be arrested by a woman. When we handcuff the suspect and lead him away, a crowd often gathers. Then the gossip spreads – everyone recognizes us and our vehicle. They know why we've come.'

'We do get shot at from time to time,' says Vera Lucia. 'We've had to wrestle men to the ground so many times. I'd never go on patrol without my .38. You see, especially in the slums some men think they're gods. They're worshipped by everyone. Our job is to make it known that there's only one God, and it's not them. We want to increase the equality level between men and women. Equality between the sexes is something that just doesn't exist in Brazil. When we enter poor neighbourhoods we're greeted by the women and children with great respect.'

It's evening again at the 9th Precinct. The waiting-room is packed with familiar faces. Detective Marinelli is in a sombre mood. Her worst nightmare has been realized – the Corinthians have just lost their game.

'You better put some extra chairs in the waiting-room,' she says to her assistant. 'It looks as if things will get really busy here tonight.'

Buying A Home in Morocco

THE SMELL OF PAPRIKA, cardamom, rose water, of freshly tanned leather; the braying of donkeys and the shrill echo of the *muezzin's* call to prayer ringing over the high flat roofs, are seared into my memory. In a childhood of conventional English life, our journeys to Morocco were a time to escape, to dream, and to slip into the *Arabian Nights*.

Three decades passed and I found myself living in a microscopic London flat, with a toddler and an expectant wife. I felt deceived, bitter at myself for not achieving more. Then I remembered Morocco. I thought back to the scent of spices, to the blazing light, to the intoxicating blend of cultural colour. In a moment of high drama, I stood on a chair, punched the air, and yelled:

'We're moving to Morocco!'

Sometimes the best way to realize your dream is to go at it headlong, without thinking about it very much. That was my approach to buying a *riad*, a traditional home, in Morocco. I knew that if I listened too much to my family or friends, the momentum would be lost and I would never break free. I had heard that Marrakech was the place to go, and so I flew down and had a look.

It seemed that most Moroccans living in the old city had the same ambition – to sell their ancestral home and to move to the new town. I could find no formal estate agents, but every second barber's shop and fruit stall seemed to double as a makeshift one.

My advice to anyone searching for a Moroccan dream home is firstly to look at dozens of houses. That way you get a feeling for what is good and what is questionable or downright rotten. And look at houses that have been renovated as well, as they'll boost your morale. Secondly, talk to people who have bought and renovated homes of their own. Learn from the communal melting pot of mistakes.

Living in the medina is like living in the corner of a great sprawling

One of the magnificent mosaic fountains at Dar Khalifa

honeycomb. So when you look at a house, you must take into account what else is around it. Is there an abattoir uncomfortably near, or a leather tannery (both of which stink in the summer heat), or is the local mosque's loudspeaker poking into your bedroom window? How far is the house from a road which is accessible by car? It can be expensive to cart rubble and bricks to and from a main road. Another downer is that a *riad* four centuries old may have its walls inside covered with modern factory-made tiles, or its floor concealed in lino. It can make for a depressing sight. But the great joy of Morocco is that the same work is being done today as it was five hundred years ago – which means you can renovate (and affordably so) with the very finest crafts. Better still is that the current boom in restoration has kick-started and strengthened workshops producing exquisite mosaic, terracotta tiles, carved plaster and wood.

Early on my quest for a Moroccan home I was fortunate to meet a local businessman named Abel Damoussi, who had spent twenty years in London, before returning to his native Marrakech. His dream was to buy and then restore a *kasbah*, a fortress home, outside the city. Looking back at the 'before' photos of his now magnificent luxury hotel Kasbah Agafay, you can only admire the man.

The fortress was being used as a barn for livestock when he found it. To look beyond what was a derelict building, took indefatigable willpower and the ability to dream. Abel was a fountain of advice. He told me to look beyond what was obviously apparent, and to concentrate on what you could not see.

'When you buy a place in the medina,' he said, 'you have to ask yourself first what shape the houses around you are in – they're more than just neighbours. Their houses are a part of your home. Look after their houses before you even think about your own.' Abel's shrewdest advice was on the subject of sewers. 'Don't start working on the house itself,' he warned, 'until you've opened up the sewers and shored them up.'

Traditionally, most *riads* had a single toilet, if they had one at all. The modern craze of renovating medina homes has meant that luxury-hungry foreigners want each bedroom to have an en suite bathroom. The sheer number of toilets and baths, coupled with the fact that Marrakech's sewers were designed before the invention of toilet paper, can lead to an overwhelming stench, especially in the blazing summer heat.

On my own quest for a home in Morocco, I started by looking at about seventy Marrakech *riads* – some no more than a crumbling shell, others palatial, and way beyond my budget. And I toured houses which had been restored to a high standard, to get an idea of what work could be done. Prices in the medina have risen sharply over the last few years and well exceed traditional homes elsewhere in the country.

It so happened that I was eventually offered a magnificent rambling villa in Casablanca. The house had been empty for almost a decade and was in need of tremendous repairs. I decided to use traditional Moroccan crafts, and to source the majority of the artisans from Marrakech and from Fès.

Dozens of workmen arrived, and most of them lived in the house. They would sleep in the sitting-room, and cook their meals on a small brazier there. The advantage was that while they were there they worked hard and as fast as they could. You have to remember that traditional Moroccan crafts are executed almost entirely by hand. You never hear the whirr of a Black & Decker drill, or an electric saw. The downside is that, as a result, the work can seem to take forever.

But as with anything else Moroccan – a little faith and, with time, even the most exacting of problems melts away.

Café Clock Cookbook

MY EARLIEST MEMORIES are tinged with the scent of Moroccan cuisine.

I was born in England and subjected to a childhood of grey school uniforms, even greyer skies, and to food so bland that it tasted of almost nothing at all. But, unlike my friends in the playground, I was certain the real world was out there – somewhere. It was a fantasy, a Promised Land, a realm of rich textures and dazzling light, a place where the air was fragrant with spices, and the kitchens abundant with the most magical ingredients.

This secret knowledge came about because of my family's love affair with Morocco. My first journeys there were made as a small child in the early 'seventies – a time when the kingdom was awash with stoned-out hippies, tie-dye and bongo drums, VW Combis, and Rolling Stones' songs. I didn't quite understand how a place could be so different from the world in which I lived. It was so utterly mesmerising, vibrant, and so culturally colourful.

I can remember the pungent, intoxicating scent of orange blossom on Tangier's rue de la Plage, and the taste of summer melons in Marrakech. My tongue still tingles at the thought of the warm almond pastry passed to me one balmy September afternoon in Chefchaouen. And, as for my first sugar-sprinkled *pastilla* – it stole my heart.

Then decades passed.

My feet traipsed through forgotten corners of the world, but never found their way back to my first true love – Morocco. Sometimes on my journeys I would close my eyes and be transported back – to the windswept sea wall of Essaouira, or to Marrakech's Jma el Fna square, or to the twisting, labyrinthine streets of medieval Fès. With eyes closed as if in a dream, I would breathe in deep and sigh, feasting on the smells and on the memories.

Then, one morning, living in an East End flat no bigger than a postage stamp, I had a *Eureka!* moment. It was so obvious. We would embrace the land of my fantasy: we'd go and live in Morocco.

And we did.

It was like stepping through a keyhole into a world touched by a magician's wand. In the years we have lived here, we have glimpsed an unbroken circle of life that's been eroded and disjointed elsewhere. It's a world dominated by values – by chivalry and honesty, by charity and, above all, by a sense of family.

And at the same time, it's a world dominated by food.

Anyone who has ever spent time in Morocco has been charmed from the first meal by the kingdom's astonishing range of cuisine. Through succulent flavours, textures, ingredients, and through sheer artistry – they go together to form an ancient kind of alchemy all of their own.

One of the first things I learned while living here is that most Moroccans prefer eating their own cuisine at home. A meal, especially one prepared for guests, is a sumptuous blend of hospitality and abundance, and is about honouring the invited as much as it is about feeding them. The dishes presented tend to be enjoyed communally, eaten from a central platter or *tagine*. And, of course, each home has its own carefully-guarded recipes, passed on through centuries from mother to daughter.

Like most of my Moroccan friends, I too am sometimes reluctant at eating in restaurants. As with them, I know that what we have at home is superior to almost anything found outside.

But there are exceptions.

When I first heard that an Englishman had given up a promising culinary career in London's West End, swapping it for the Fès medina – where he planned to start afresh – I rolled my eyes. Then I put my head in my hands. It sounded like a recipe for catastrophe.

But, stepping across the threshold of the Café Clock, I was utterly enthralled. Not only was its founder, Mike Richardson, a man of magnetic charm, but he had conjured a spellbinding ambience in the heart of a city I hold so dear.

And, as for the food... it's the exception to the rule. At last there is a restaurant that equals the cuisine found in Moroccan homes.

Café Clock's success lies in the subtle flavours of a culinary tradition which itself stands at a crossroads of geography and culture. It's made possible by seasonal foods, by spices, and by raw ingredients that have found their way to the medieval city through centuries, along the pilgrimage routes. After all, for more than a thousand years, Fès has been connected to the farthest reaches of the Islamic world, to destinations as variant as Seville, Cairo, and Timbuktu, Bokhara, Kabul, and Samarkand.

With time, Café Clock has become far more than a place to dine well. In the tradition of the ancient caravanserais, once found in every town and city between it and Mecca, and beyond, it's a place where people gather. Some are locals, while many more are travellers, gorging themselves on the intensity of Fès for the first time. Together, they swap stories, talk, listen, laugh, and learn from the endless range of cultural events laid on in the crucible that is Café Clock.

Just as I had been anxious at hearing of an Englishman opening a restaurant in Fès, I had wondered a little anxiously how the Café Clock's cookbook might look. Making the shift from the experimental fluidity of a kitchen, to the restricted world of the printed page, is not easy. It's a realm in which too many talented food writers have failed.

But what strikes me squarely between the eyes is how the author, Tara Stevens, has approached this project. From the outset she's harnessed an astonishing perspicacity, and a clear sense of observation. Through watching, tasting, and, above all, through listening, she has brought to this book's pages a rare and comprehensive culinary experience.

At the same time, Tara has explained how and where specific ingredients are sourced, and has clarified the ways in which they are used in the kitchens of Café Clock.

The result is far more than a cookbook. It's a key. Immerse yourself in its pages and, in return, it will unlock a domain that's more usually cloaked in mystery, and quite off limits to the outside world. Study the pages well, and the ancient alchemy is revealed.

N.B. *Clock Book*, published by 33books, 2010.

A child rides his trike at his home in one of the tomb complexes at Cairo's City of the Dead

Cairo's City of the Dead

MUSTAPHA SITS IN THE SHADE of a sprawling fig tree, listening to the birdsong and whisking away the flies with the end of his scarf.

Every day he sits there, in a chair he made himself from old scraps of wood, just as he's done since his childhood seven decades ago. From time to time one of his grandchildren hurtles out of their imposing stone home, whooping and hollering into the light. The scene is so usual that it could be anywhere in Egypt, or in any corner of the Arab world. But it's made unique by the fact that Mustapha and his family live not in a residential street, but in Cairo's vast cemetery, Al Qarafa, The City of the Dead.

No one's quite sure how many people live there in the sprawling burial grounds among the graves. The number banded around is anything between five hundred thousand and five million. But to the people who make it their home, the numbers don't really matter. For Mustapha and the other families, it's a place where they can live quietly without the outside world intruding on their lives.

Drawing a wrinkled hand over his face, Mustapha sighs.

'I have seen a universe of life,' he says, 'right here in the cemetery. Birth, life, and of course I have seen death. Plenty of it. They are all parts of the same thing, a cycle that never ends.'

Asked how it feels to live amongst the dead, the old man shrugs.

'The dead have been truer friends to me than many of the living I've known,' he says breaking into a smile, 'and in any case, they don't have tongues wagging nonsense and lies.'

Spend a little time in the cemetery and you realize that the title 'City of the Dead' is something of a misnomer. In Cairo there's not just one main burial ground, but five – the Northern and Southern Cemeteries, the Bab el Wazir and the Bab Nasr, and the Cemetery of the Great.

Viewed from a distance, and from the comfort of the city's highways, the most impressive is the Northern Cemetery. It stretches out in a honeycomb of sand-coloured shacks. Every so often there's a fabulous dome sticking out, hinting at a grand mausoleum hiding in the jumble of more ordinary tombs. Visitors to Cairo could be excused in thinking the expanse of buildings is just another quarter of the old city. And in a way they'd be right.

Cairo's great cemeteries were developed at least a thousand years ago in the Fatimid era, if not before, at the time of the Arab Conquest. Egypt is of course well-known for its burial traditions. After all, the Pyramids up the road in Giza are arguably the most celebrated tombs ever created by Man. Some believe that certain beliefs dating back to Pharaonic Egypt may have survived, most notably the way that Egyptians perceive death. For many, death is not regarded as the end but the beginning, and cemeteries are not places to be avoided or dreaded, but visited and respected.

The tradition of travelling to a family grave on certain days during the calendar, and on Fridays, is a part of Egyptian culture, and in part it's a reason that so many people live in the burial grounds. The tombs of the rich or powerful have always had guardians who attend to their families when they visit the deceased, and during the forty days of mourning after a death. Many others look after the pilgrims who flock to the city's Sufi shrines, and to the graves of members of the Prophet's family.

Centuries ago when the cemeteries were first established, they were far from the medina of medieval Cairo. But as the city's urban sprawl has raged forwards like wildfire, the City of the Dead finds itself as being remarkably central. Free from the press of tenement blocks, and choking traffic, the vast burial grounds are not such a bad place to live. It's true that the plumbing is almost non-existent, and the lack of sewerage leads to the insufferable stench during the summer heat, but there is often electricity, and a few mod cons as well.

Mustapha's little home has a battered old television and, his pride and joy, a Chinese-made refrigerator. Keen to show them off, he pours from a two-litre bottle of Coca Cola. As elsewhere in the Arab world, hospitality to a guest is taken very seriously indeed.

'I can keep drinks cool for days,' he says enthusiastically.

'Where do you buy the drinks?'

The old man waves a hand towards the end of his lane.

'Down there... haven't you seen all the shops?'

Far from being a place of just desolation and death, parts of the cemetery are alive with the most vibrant life. There are cafés and small restaurants, where skewers of lamb are being grilled for lunch, food stalls, barbershops and, of course, there are thousands and thousands of homes. Some people even come from outside the cemetery to buy fruit and veg, declaring that the prices are lower because there are none of the overheads that there are elsewhere.

Around the corner from where Mustapha lives, at the end of a narrow alley, thick with dust, Fatima is hanging out the laundry in the blazing spring sunshine. She seems oblivious to the fact that there are three elaborate marble headstones a few feet away, or that the skeletons of an entire family lie beneath her feet.

'I've lived here all my life,' she says, reaching for another clothes' peg, 'and there's nothing usual about the cemetery. If you ask me, it's the safest place in Cairo to live. The people are good here. There's plenty of space, and a sense of right and wrong.'

Fatima nudges a hand towards her little son, Yussef, who's trundling about on his trike.

'If we lived anywhere else we would not have a yard like this, a place where the children can play safely. I thank God for providing us with this.'

The laundry dripping in the sun, Fatima leads the way into her home, a squat cinderblock shack on the west side of the yard. Her father is lying in bed in the small sitting-room, squinting at a soap opera on the TV.

Fatima brews up a pot of tea, pours it out, steam billowing from the spout.

'My husband has a cart from which he sells sweet yams,' she says. 'He makes enough for us to live. And besides, we get a little money for guarding this ancestral tomb. The relatives live far from here and so they rely on us to make sure the place is kept in order and clean.'

While there are now many times more people living in the cemetery than ever before, the tradition is one that goes back centuries.

Some of the mausolea found in the City of the Dead are imposing structures, built during the Mameluk and Ottoman times. A great number of them contain precious details of ornamental art. Wary of thieves, the rich have always employed guardians to watch over their family graves. It's a system that suits everyone. The families can rest assured that the graves are kept free from desecration, and the guardians can be sure that their own families have somewhere safe, central, and affordable to live.

According to Islamic tradition, bodies are usually not covered with earth as in the West, but wrapped in muslin and lain out on their sides, facing toward the holy city of Mecca. The entrance and the staircase into the vault are concealed by a series of stone slabs. Above ground, the site is marked by a tombstone, set within a courtyard or covered by a mausoleum.

Large Egyptian tombs often have one or more outhouses for use by visiting relatives or caretakers. Some of them have sets of chairs kept in storage to be laid out on days when the entire family is there.

A short distance from where Fatima lives, is a dusty lane which ends in the grand nineteenth century mausoleum of a Pasha. Half way down the lane is a less opulent building, a rough brick dwelling in which a young woman is sitting on an upturned packing crate. Her name is Hasna, and she has lived in the cemetery for three years, since her husband died in a car crash.

'After my husband's death,' she says, 'my in-laws threw me out of the house. They said I brought shame on the family, because I was unable to have children. I had a friend who lives here and she told me to come. She said it was safe, that it was a place where others do not judge you, where they leave you alone. And she was right. The people who live here are mostly good, the kind of people who work hard and are pious. They respect the fact that I am alone, and they have become my family.'

From time to time Hasna gets some work sewing clothes, and sometimes cleans apartments on the other side of the city. She says she dreams of a time when she'll be reunited with her husband. When asked if she will ever marry again, she wipes a tear from her eye.

'I don't ever want to be married again,' she says solemnly. 'Anyway, who would marry a widow?'

I ask Hasna of her greatest fear. Her faces freezes and she glances down at her lap.

'Every day people come here and ask if there's any space. They come from the countryside, and know that the cemetery is a cheap place to live. My great worry is that the man who rents this little room to me will throw me out onto the street, or put up the rent. If that happened, I don't know where I would go.'

Hasna touches a hand to her headscarf and sighs.

'Thank God most people forget that we are here,' she says.

Hasna might be surprised if she knew the irony of her remark. In recent years foreigners visiting the Egyptian capital have become increasingly fascinated with the City of the Dead, itself a uniquely Egyptian phenomenon. Although still limited in number, a few tour operators offer visits to groups of two or three tourists at a time through the cemetery maze, so that they can see it for themselves.

Not far from Hasna's home, a young Australian couple, Jack and Marty, are taking one such tour. Both towering and blonde, they look a little incongruous, as if they made a wrong turn on the way to the Pyramids. But they're savouring the experience.

'When we saw the City of the Dead from a distance,' says Jack, 'we just assumed it was low-income housing. And when we realized it was the cemetery, we never imagined there'd be so much life here. I've even seen cyber cafés. Imagine that – surfing the Internet in a cemetery! It's as if we're seeing a side of Cairo that's very traditional – very Egyptian – but one that's been hidden and inaccessible until now. I'd recommend this to anyone who wants a new take on one of the oldest cities on Earth.'

Back in his courtyard, Mustapha is hammering a nail into his homemade chair. He hits his thumb by mistake and curses.

I ask if he's seen the tour groups in his neighbourhood. He shakes his head, glances at his injured thumb.

'That is absurd,' he says. 'What kind of a fool would want to take a tour of a cemetery?' Mustapha smiles again. 'But I suppose it isn't quite so foolish... after all I bet you they charge more to see the Pyramids.'

One of Casablanca's fabulous junk shops

Casablanca Junk

Saïd ben Saïd sits in a pool of sunlight at the front of his shop and waits for the rush of customers, a rush that never comes.

In the darkness behind him is a treasure hoard worthy of Ali Baba. Stacked up on shelves and piled high in orderly heaps, lies an assortment of antique wares – brown Bakelite radios the size of suitcases, gramophone players and gilt clocks, graceful bronze statuettes, espresso machines, vintage posters and chamber pots. What makes the collection unusual is that it comes, almost in entirety, from the Art Deco glory days of Casablanca. The city, created as a showcase of French Imperial style and might, boomed from the 'twenties until the 'forties, when began its gradual and ignominious decline.

The little junk shop owned by Saïd ben Saïd sits at the far end of a labyrinthine flea-market in the working class quarter of Hay Hasseni, on the western edge of Casablanca. With almost no tourists attracted to the city, and few Moroccans interested in anything second hand, Ben Saïd is glum.

His passion for Art Deco tends to be met with scorn from his peers, and has certainly not made him rich.

'Everyone here has the same dream,' he says, wiping a hand over three days' of grey stubble, 'they dream of living in a new house, filled with brand new things. They look at the treasures I have collected, and they laugh!'

Soon after moving to a ramshackle mansion in Casablanca, I discovered the junk yards in nearby Hay Hasseni, and found myself drawn into a dream world of bargains. A shameless hoarder, I snapped up what others considered to be worthless junk – aspidistra stands, tea caddies and porcelain urns, all decorated with zigzag lines, silver sets of cutlery, posters, cocktail shakers, ice buckets, and tin-plate toys.

But the *objets d'art* are only the start.

One morning I was bemoaning the low quality of new washbasins to Saïd ben Saïd. He shook his head in despair.

'The stuff you find downtown in the fancy shops is all rubbish,' he said. 'You'd better go out back behind the flea market.' I followed his advice and came across a place with a striking resemble to the end of the world. There were heaps of twisted scrap metal fifty feet high, mountains of third-hand bricks, mahogany doors and battered window frames, and an ocean of what we might call 'architectural salvage'.

In the middle of it all I found a lovely roll-top bath, cast iron with ball and claw feet. Inside it was a huddle of newborn puppies. Nearby there were more than a dozen enormous Art Deco washbasins, ripped out from a villa in the nick of time, before the building was torn down the week before.

As the months passed, I sniffed out Casablanca's other affordable antique shops. There must be a dozen or so, scattered across the city, most of them hidden down back streets, awaiting the intrepid. It's true that the arrival of a fresh-faced foreigner tends to nudge the prices up. But, in time-honoured Moroccan tradition, a little hard bargaining or feigned disinterest, can have a magical effect.

Corrosion from the Atlantic breeze, and cowboy repair jobs has taken a toll on some of the more fragile pieces. But I am constantly surprised at what has survived, and the general good condition of it all. There's plenty of less than perfect bric-à-brac, as well as toe-cringing reproductions of Louis XIV but, for all of that, there are museum-quality gems.

Tucked away in the textile market of Derb Omar is a new and rather well-heeled gallery named *Memo-Arts*. The showroom has a few exquisite pieces, including a rosewood writing desk with ormolu legs, a davenport, and a pair of Art Nouveau bronze nymphs. In the middle of the room sits a magnificent grand piano from about 1925, crafted in by the celebrated Parisian house of Erard.

In the last two or three years a few high-end antique galleries have sprung up. Like *Memo-Arts*, or the impressive *Galerie Moulay Youssef*, they cater to the richest Moroccan clientele. You tend to get the feeling that people buy from them in a perverse show of wealth, rather than for their fondness of antiques. The same can be said for the two or three new auction houses, established for the local market, where the rich delight in publicly flashing their cash.

Most visitors find Casablanca bewildering in its size and scope, and few bother to spend any time there, except to change trains or to visit the great Mosque of Hassan II. On the surface, the city can seem overly European, after all it was built largely by the French. But just under the surface, there's Morocco's ubiquitous blend of vibrant colour, rich aromas and sounds – donkeys braying, dogs barking, and the clamour of water-sellers pushing through the traffic.

And there is of course the allure of the Bogart and Bergman, and their *Casablanca*. Rick's Café does exist, having opened recently for tourists not far from the Port. But the real flavour of that time is kept alive in the flea-markets, the junk yards and antique shops in town. Tracking them down is a way of seeing the city, and exploring hidden corners to which tourists rarely venture.

Back in the labyrinth at Hay Hasseni, Saïd ben Saïd is asleep with a newspaper over his face. He stirs at the sound of footsteps, the prospect of a customer. When asked if he can acquire a grand piano at flea-market prices, he shrugs.

'I have a friend with a warehouse full of grand pianos,' he says absently. 'You can find them in any size. When the French ran away from Morocco, they left them behind in their hundreds. But who would ever want one?'

'I would,' I said.

The shopkeeper scratched a thumbnail to his neck, and glanced back into his Aladdin's den.

'Well you are wise,' he said. 'If there were others like you, I would be a far richer man with a far happier wife.'

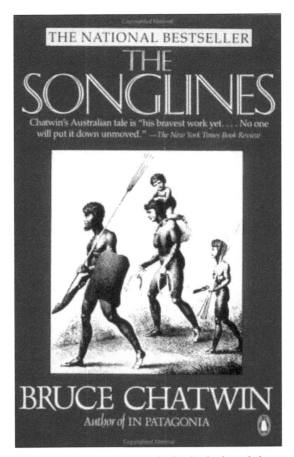

Bruce Chatwin's masterwork, the book which made him
a best-selling author

Chatwin and *The Songlines*

ONCE IN A VERY LONG TIME you come across a book that is far, far more than the ink, the glue and the paper, a book that seeps into your blood.

With such a book the impact isn't necessarily obvious at first... but the more you read it and re-read it, and live with it, and travel with it, the more it speaks to you, and the more you realize that you cannot live without that book. It's then that the wisdom hidden inside, the seed, is passed on.

The Songlines first appeared more than twenty years ago. It was the book that made British travel writer Bruce Chatwin a bestselling author. And it is the book that established him as an oddball genius, a giant of the travel genre, and a writer whose works commented on the human condition as much as they did on the lands which passed beneath his feet.

During his short life, Chatwin published only a handful of books. Some were fact, others fiction, and all were a blend of both. They were the kind of books that many people had waited a lifetime to read: pithy, lyrical, and capable of easing the reader down through layer after layer until they hit raw metal, a mirror in which they saw themselves.

The Songlines is Chatwin's masterwork. I remember the day I first saw it.

I was standing outside a bookshop in Nairobi, staring in at the window display of titles I couldn't afford. A man sidled up, nudged me in the ribs, and jabbed a thumb at the hardback book:

'That's a cracker,' he said.

'I can't afford it,' I replied. 'I've only got enough cash for lunch.'

The man nudged me again.

'Go hungry,' he said.

I handed over my money and entered a world where the sharpest realism touches far-flung fantasy. Since then I have carried the book with me on almost all my journeys. It's always there, at the bottom of my bag, a trusted friend that can be opened at random and can pacify me in moments of solitude.

My copy has been through the Namib Desert and the Sahara, across the Amazon, twice, over the Himalayas, and through the Madre de Dios cloud forest in Peru, where I was almost tempted to trade it for an exquisite macaw-feather crown. It has been a pillow, and a fly-swat, and entertainment in a small Ethiopian village when I had the runs, for days. And, it was one of two books I was permitted in my cell during the weeks I spent in solitary confinement in a Pakistani prison.

The Songlines is about the Australian Outback and the Aboriginals, who, through history, have roamed the vast, desert region, walking softly on the Earth. It is a journey of sorts, and a catalogue of meetings with ordinary people and eccentrics, each of them making do in the furnace of central Australia. It is about the essence of humanity, the lust of a nomadic existence, and about rejecting a world of materialism, a world that Chatwin must have suspected he might soon depart. While writing it, he had already been diagnosed with HIV.

Chatwin's career began in the art world. He used to say he picked up the skill of writing detailed descriptions while working at Sotheby's, where he had been made the youngest partner in the firm's history. It's a skill that resonates through all his writing, no more brilliantly than in this book. The initial character descriptions in particular are works of art.

The Songlines kicks off with Chatwin meeting Arkady Volchok, an Australian of Russian heritage, whose father was a Cossack. For Chatwin there was nothing so irresistible as a person found in a habitat that was at odds to the one from which he had come. *He* was of course a character for his collection, as was Arkady, who was surely an extension of himself. The people he collected were woven into his books, and described, turned into the light, and described again. None of them do very much in *The Songlines*, except to spit out a few succinct lines of words; but their appearance is enough – gems glinting for our delight.

No one fascinated Chatwin more than polymaths, people with a diverse range of knowledge and experience. He was one himself, of course, as was Theodor Strehlow, the character whose book *Songs of Central Australia* first activated his interest in so-called Songlines. Strehlow was an anthropologist of Austrian extraction, who had spent years in the Outback, and was adopted into an Aboriginal clan, the elders of which had entrusted him with their secrets. In his youth, he had been schooled in the Aboriginal dialect Aranda, as well as in Classical Greek, Latin, German and English, while raised at a Lutheran mission: all of it food for Chatwin's vivid imagination.

Strehlow recorded the native Australian concepts of Songlines, and Dreamtime, and he mapped out a kind of blueprint that may have been a template for all primitive man. Chatwin was hooked from the start, and must have found in Strehlow's work, as his biographer Nicholas Shakespeare puts it, 'a structure on which to hang not only his nomad theories, but more or less everything else in his notebooks…'

Then, a little over half way through the narrative, the reader hits just that – a long italicised section labelled 'From The Notebooks'. It's something that even divides diehard fans of the Chatwinesque: a collection of aphorisms, ideas, and obscure details of culture and history. For my money, it's the icing on the cake, the treasury of a short but brilliant life of observation. The section reflects Chatwin's essence. It covers a world of obscure destinations – Kabul, Omdurman, Yunnan and Timbuktu. And it shines a beam of light onto aspects of human belief from which we have become distanced or removed.

Since his death early in 1989, Chatwin has been feted for his good looks, his love of distinguished company, and for his personal life. An enormous amount has been written on him, not least by his official biographer Nicholas Shakespeare, whose warts-and-all life story is two inches thick.

Sometimes you get the feeling that Chatwin is famous for being famous, that people are so caught up with him as an icon, that they forget to read his books. They pore over his private life, tracing his long-lost love affairs, and searching for skeletons in closets that I believe would best be left alone. Or they waste their time in dissection – trying to work out where the fact comes to an end and where the fantasy begins. For me, that's all nonsense: Chatwin ought to be remembered instead as the pre-eminent storyteller, the raconteur, the man whose prose has perfect rhythm, and whose books walk the fine tightrope between fact and fantasy.

The Songlines works so powerfully, because in the native *Aboriginals of the Outback* Chatwin found himself. He was drawn to their gentle interpretation of the world, and to the way their dreamtime ascended far above the black and white world in which our own lives are sometimes confined.

Literary reviewers may have attacked Chatwin for over-romanticizing his subject, but they were not the only critics. The Aboriginals themselves felt short-changed by the way they were depicted in the book – fodder for Chatwin's theories on nomadic life. And some found it odd that for a book on Aboriginal belief, the author spent such little time actually with Aboriginals, and so much with the wacky cast of immigrants who people the Outback.

As for my own travels with the book, the most touching moment came in Senegal. One night in the capital, Dakar, I was sitting in a café waiting for the sun to go down. The heat was terrible, and the place was packed with *femmes de la rue* parading themselves, hoping to attract a fresh infection-free clientele. I was alone, and ferreted *The Songlines* from the bottom of my bag. The waiter slapped down a glass of *café noir* and looked at me sideways.

'He came here once,' he said.

'Who did?'

'That man?'

'Who?'

'The blonde one,' he said, pointing to the author photo on the back of the book.

'Chatwin?'

'Yes.'

'Did you talk to him?'

'Yes I did.'

'Do you remember the conversation?'

'Yes I do.'

'What did you talk about?'

The waiter looked out at the road, and wiped a hand across his mouth. 'We spoke about silence,' he said.

He wafted away. I opened *The Songlines* at random, and my eyes found a Moorish proverb favoured by Chatwin:

'He who does not travel does not know the value of men.'

Chefchaouen

A WAITER IN FÈS first directed me to the small town of Chefchaouen, nestled in the foothills of the Rif Mountains.

I had praised a bowl of delicious *harira*, the wholesome soup Moroccans love to eat through the winter. He told me that the recipe had been prepared by his family for eight centuries at their home in Chefchaouen.

'If you go there,' he said, his eyes welling with tears, 'your heart will dance with delight.'

The idea of my heart dancing with delight was far too good to pass up. I set off from Fès next morning, drove north across the agricultural heartland, through forests of cork oaks, and up into the Rif.

Northern Morocco couldn't make for a sharper contrast from the deserts of the south. There were small rocky fields, scattered with cactus and sheep, wizened men perched on donkeys, their wives in conical straw hats, orange groves and farmsteads, and translucent winter streams.

The first view of Chaouen, as locals call it, sends a tingle down the spine. It sits cradled between two summits (from which it gets its name, meaning 'two-horned'), above the Oued Laou Valley, gleaming white in the blazing afternoon sun. Entering it, is like stepping into a lost piece of Andalucian Spain. Chaouen was built as a secure citadel for the Islamic faith, a bastion from which the Muslim refugees pouring out from southern Spain, could regroup and plan their assault on Portugal, the rising power. It was founded in 1471 by an Idrissid prince, Cherif Moulay Ali bin Rachid, and was populated largely by Andalucian Muslims from Granada.

The town's architecture, cuisine, and its unlikely Mediterranean feel are results of its curious Spanish heritage. Until 1920, when Spanish troops occupied northern Morocco, Chaouen was cut off from the Christian world. The invading Spanish found a time capsule of their own culture. They heard spoken a form of tenth century Catalan – a language brought by the Andalucian Jews – which had died out on the Iberian peninsula four centuries before. And they found Granada leatherwork, pottery, and other crafts long extinct from their native Iberia.

Chefchaouen provides a welcome break from the profound grandeur of the Imperial cities of Fès, Mèknes and Marrakech. It tends to feel more like a big walled village than a town. The streets are steep and cobbled, shaded by trellises erupting with clematis, the houses whitewashed or rinsed with indigo, their doors studded, their roofs tiled with terracotta. As you stroll up and down the alleys of the medina, what strikes you is the tranquility. It's as if the outside world is still out there, somewhere, but you have broken free.

The first thing you notice is the absence of cars. There are almost none at all. Without them, the air is clean and crisp. Visitors amble about over the cobbles with a glazed look in their eyes, sustained by the thought they have discovered a little-known Moroccan jewel. They tour the fifteenth century *kasbah*, clambering along the battlements, examine its rank dungeons, and marvel at the Grand Mosque with its spectacular octagonal minaret.

Chaouen is popular with visitors from Spain, who come to peer into the looking-glass of their own history. There's not a sense though that the town is overrun with tourists. Instead, there's a sleepy innocence, a feeling that the locals are happy to share their world. And, of course, the visitors snap up bargains at the multitude of shops and stalls found throughout the medina. All sorts of merchandise is on sale, from the Andalucian-style pottery with its characteristic glazes, to the wide conical hats with wool bobbles worn by the women in the Rif.

There are rugged mountain tapestries, too, and stalls awash with musical instruments – *ouds*, goat-skin tambours, and giant metal castanets. And in the narrow passages veering steeply down the hill, you can find delicate homemade jewellery on sale, woollen sweaters, boxes inlaid with camel bone, and rock crystals cut from quarries in the Rif.

In the heart of the old town is the plaza of Uta el-Hammam, lined with trees, paved with pebbles, and the perfect place to flop down and watch life. The cafés there vie for your attention and your business, waiters fanning menu cards at passing visitors. The food on offer ranges from succulent *pastilla* (a savoury-sweet pie made with chicken or pigeon), to mouth-watering *tagines*, such as lamb stewed with apricots, to couscous served with seven vegetables, and *harira*, the robust winter soup which is a meal in itself. There are western delicacies too, especially dishes from Spain, such as paella, tortilla, and grilled fish caught in the local river.

In the labyrinth of backstreets that make up the medina, there are a wide number of small hotels and hostels, most of which fall into the 'affordable' category. There are one or two larger hotels, too, such as the Parador, which has a pool and bar. Elsewhere alcohol is not widely served, for Chaouen is regarded as a holy city of Islam. But some drinkers are prepared to forego their tipple, in the light of another vice.

The Rif's rugged landscape has always been a hardship for those who farm the sheering mountain slopes. Few crops flourish there, few except for marijuana. The illicit crop may explain why there are so many imported foreign sports cars trundling on the open roads in the north, wealth gained from *kif*. On the drive up from Fès, I stopped in the middle of nowhere to relieve myself, and staggered into the undergrowth, only to realize it was an ocean of marijuana plants five foot high.

The upper floors of some cafés in Chaouen are smoking rooms for those with an affection for the weed. Although illegal, smoking *kif* seems to be tolerated. But visitors would be extremely unwise to take away what they could enjoy in the town.

Outside one of the smoking haunts, I came across a baby-boomer from San Francisco who had followed Jimi Hendrix to Morocco, as a groupie back in the summer of '69. He was tall, a little hunched and spoke very slowly, as if the forbidden fruit had taken a severe toll. He held out his arms.

'Welcome to Paradise,' he said, lighting the end of a joint. 'The home of Free Love.'

The pace of life in Chefchaouen is so serene that you forget about the pressures of checking email and chatting on a mobile phone – for me the test of a town's true charm. Whether you venture there as a place to relax and regroup, or as a starting point for hill walking in the Rif, Chefchaouen is the kind of place one stumbles upon very rarely. As I took to the road once again, and headed north towards the nearby waters of the Med, I thought of the waiter who had directed me to his home town. Chaouen was as wonderful as he had described. And, just as he promised, it made my heart dance with delight.

The Royal Bombay Yacht Club, established in 1846

The verandah of Mumbai's prestigious Willingdon Club

Colonial Clubs of India

To stand at the crossroads near Mumbai's Haji Ali's Tomb is to witness a slice of modern India at its most vibrant.

Giant-sized billboards loom down over the seething traffic, alluring the nouveau riche with the latest in must-have fashions and all mod cons.

Down below, reclining primly in their chauffeur-driven cars, this new self-made class do their level best to block out reality, a realm that's never more than a pane of glass away. They seem immune to the incessant hooting, the droves of beggars, the eunuchs, and the street hawkers, all of whom glide through the gridlock like sharks hunting prey.

Spend a little time out in Mumbai's human stew, and you feel yourself being poached alive. But salvation is at hand – to a privileged few at least.

A stone's throw away from the traffic jam, there's a gentle haven of calm, a throwback to another time – a world that couldn't be more incongruous if it tried. Drive in through the solemn silver-painted gateposts, and you enter a kind of fantasy island, albeit one adrift on turbulent seas.

Inside, there are sprawling verandas cooled by ancient swirling ceiling fans, manicured lawns, and waiters dressed in starched white shirts and little black bow ties. There are crustless sandwiches as well, and scones and lemon tea, chit books, jam tarts, and miniature brass bells for summoning the legions of staff.

A bastion of propriety and good form, The Willingdon Club is part of a legacy which dates back to the earliest days of the British Raj. It's a lost shard of a world in which old-fashioned values diehard. In a country more often regarded for its own blend of perfected chaos, The Willingdon, and other clubs like it, are run with almost military efficiency. Membership is valued as the epitome of social status, the dividing line between old wealth and the rising nouveau riche.

In the heyday of colonial rule there were many dozens of such clubs, found across the subcontinent, the Far East, and Africa. Established for the droves of bureaucrats who powered the colonial machine, they were as ruthless in their rules and membership requirements as any club on Pall Mall. Their drawing rooms were where colonial policy was thrashed out, and where the Raj's secrets were circulated among the privileged elite. It was a domain in which the old boy network thrived, one reserved for British gentlemen alone.

During the Raj, each club catered to a specific social strata. A tradesman or low-ranking bureaucrat would never have aspired, for example, to membership of Calcutta's exalted Bengal Club. And, membership for top-notch clubs had waiting lists so long that applicants often perished from consumption much before they ever came up for membership at all.

When the British set sail for home after Independence, sixty plus years ago, there could have been few who would have imagined that the colonial clubs could endure. After all, they were a symbol of decadence and, of course, of the despised British rule.

But endure they have.

Almost every major Indian city has at least one club. Mumbai has half a dozen, Delhi has several, as does Chennai, and as do the hill stations like Simla, Darjeeling and Dehradun.

The most snobbish and historical of all are the clubs in Calcutta, the capital of India under the Raj until 1911. The sniffiest of them all is the Bengal Club. Founded in 1827, with waiting lists that run into decades, its ambience has to be experienced to be believed. The highlight is the 'Reynolds Room', a salon whose walls are adorned with murals inspired by the painter's life work. Its great rival is The Tollygunge Club, known by all as 'The Tolly', an oasis even now of decorum and stiff upper lip. Laid out over a hundred acres of former indigo plantation, once owned by Tipu Sultan himself, the clubhouse is more than two centuries old.

With the financial explosion gripping modern India, the clubs are a sure fire way for the old elite to set themselves apart. Basking effortlessly on the white-washed verandas or, playing bridge in the card rooms, the landed gentry manage to assert their social status by membership to a closed world. It's the perfect way of distancing oneself from the growing swathes of society who are cash-rich but culture-poor. Membership subscriptions aren't usually cheap, but it's not about money. It's about being approved.

As soon as I was married into a known Mumbai family, my in-laws put me up for The Willingdon Club. In the years that I've had membership, I have been enthralled by a system that, despite all odds, has managed not only to survive, but to thrive. What impresses me is the way that there's almost no slack in the system. The rules, committees, and sub-committees, maintain a state of blissful harmony, and keep the prevailing state of mayhem outside the gates at bay.

Founded by the Marquess of Willingdon, in 1917, the club was supposedly established after the peer was refused entry for his guest, an Indian Maharajah, at the nearby Bombay Gymkhana. (According to legend, that club had a sign at its gates, bearing the slogan, 'No dogs or Indians allowed'). Needless to say, membership there was, like everywhere else at the time, restricted to whites. Incensed, the Marquess, later to become Viceroy, set up the first club with the radical new vision of membership for all.

But open membership doesn't mean for a moment the lowering of standards. Even now, Bollywood actors don't have a hope in getting their names onto the list. Nor do those who flout its rulebook. In a famous Mumbai moment, the celebrated artist M. F. Husain, who never wore shoes, was refused entry for arriving barefoot. (The rules also stipulate that rubber sandals or bedroom slippers are unacceptable).

Set in acres of greenery in the middle of the city, The Willingdon's land value runs into billions of dollars. All around it, fashionable tower blocks are rising up, swish homes to the newly arrived.

As with many of the clubs established during the Raj, The Willingdon is predominantly a sports' club. A little further south, in Colaba, is another – the Royal Bombay Yacht Club. Overlooking the Gateway of India, and next door to the Taj Mahal Hotel, the Yacht Club is set in a hulking Indo-Gothic building. One of the oldest of all Indian clubs, it was founded in 1846, and was awarded royal patronage by Queen Victoria.

For foreign visitors to India, temporary membership to a wide number of clubs is possible. The easiest way is to track down a local member to vouch for you. But if you can't find one, there are other ways of slipping in under the net. The Royal Over-Seas League in London's St. James's, for instance, has reciprocal membership to a plenty of old colonial clubs across India and the Commonwealth, and it is forthcoming to new members.

Before being married I used to stay at the Yacht Club, in the grandest chambers imaginable. They were vast, had a view right over the Gateway of India, and they came with a manservant who was meek, fawning, and ever available. He even offered to dress me once, and did a great job killing the cat-sized rats that infested the upper floors. I used to spend months there at a time, fraternizing with characters straight out of a Graham Greene novel, and forgetting my responsibilities elsewhere.

In the evenings the resident members would congregate in the bar, its walls adorned with ensigns and naval insignia. Over pegs of whisky, they would swap tall tales from the high seas. The most colourful character of all was an Irishman. An Honorary Consul, who had managed to arrange for himself a grand apartment on the first floor, he was known to all as 'Callaghan of India'. A friend of his, an impeccable old member and former admiral in the Indian navy, once told me of the time during the monsoon that a sea of rats swarmed up from the sewers and into the Yacht Club.

'They were simply everywhere,' he said dreamily.

I asked what was done to quell them. The admiral shrugged.

'One of chief members was a Jain,' he replied, 'and refused to allow them to be poisoned. So we just put up with them. A lot of them are still here.' The old admiral sipped his Scotch. 'I fear they outnumber the members six to one.'

Although a great many of the colonial clubs now find themselves in the middle of sprawling cities across the Subcontinent, many more are tucked away in small towns and hill stations. In their ceaseless search for cool climes, the British would decamp *en masse* from the cities each summer, and move to higher ground. Hidden in the Nilgiri Hills is the hill station of Ootacamund (known as 'Ooty' by all). A bastion even now of English decorum, Ooty traditions die hard. There's still fox-hunting in red jackets, even though there are no foxes at all. And, right at the centre of Englishness, is the Ootacamund Club.

Entering into the clubhouse is to step back into a sepia-tinted world right out of *The Far Pavilions*. The walls are hung with game trophies, the antique furniture carved from rosewood, mahogany and teak. The reading room has an imposing portrait of Queen Empress Victoria, and all around there are pictures of the Hunt.

Founded in the first half of the 19th century, the Ooty Club is a nugget of real England, albeit one far away from home.

There's English fare (Spotted Dick and Yorkshire Pudding), snooker, croquet, and rigid codes of dress. But, most English of all is the weather. Indeed, the English must have been in seventh heaven there. Discovering the Nilgiri Hills for the first time, in 1819, Lord Lytton wrote home to his wife:

'Such beautiful English rain and English mud!'

Damascus

SALIM THE SON OF SULEIMAN was reclining on an ancient Damascene throne at the back of his shop.

His eyes were closed, the face around them lined with creases, its cheeks obscured by a week's growth of tattered grey beard. As he slept off a lunch of mutton kebabs, his fingertips caressed fragments of ivory inlaid on the throne's regal arm. Lost in the shadows between the front door and the chair, lay a treasury of objects, a spider's web of clutter gleaned from centuries of Damascus life.

There were Crusader battle standards blackened by fire, tortoise shell jewel boxes, and Qur'an stands carved from great slabs of teak, epaulettes and chamber pots, fountainheads fashioned in the form of gazelles, mosque lamps and astrolabes, vast gilt mirrors, and bull elephant tusks.

Before leaving home I had found a visiting card from the very same antique emporium, in a file packed with my grandfather's papers. An Afghan writer and savant, he had visited Damascus seventy-five years before me, and had written a book about the journey, entitled *Alone in Arabian Nights*. I was pleased to not only see the shop still standing, but to find it filled with such a treasure trove of wares.

At the sound of a customer's feet, Salim opened an eye. He scanned the room, jolted up, and let the kitten curled on his chest tumble to the floor.

'Can I interest you in an amulet?' he said with a grin, 'to keep you safe on Syrian roads.'

'I don't believe in all that,' I replied.

The shopkeeper's smile melted away.

'Shhhh!' he hissed. 'You mustn't say such things.'

'Why not?'

'Because *He* is listening!'

We both cocked our heads to look at the ceiling, and I changed the subject. I asked the price of a fabulous ceremonial axe that had caught my eye. Its blade was crafted from watered steel, inscribed with a spell.

Suleiman wagged a finger in my direction.

'Everything is for sale *except* that,' he said.

'Why's it different?'

'I cannot tell you.'

Salim the son of Suleiman brewed a pot of tea, and sat in silence, while I begged him to sell me the axe. The more I implored, the more he shook his head. After an hour of sweet tea and failed persuasion, I strolled out into the thin winter light, feeling as if somehow I had been robbed of the opportunity of parting with my money.

Visit the old city of Damascus and it's impossible not to be struck by a sense of living antiquity, and by the gems that fill the emporia hidden within its shadows. Explore the teeming souqs and you descend down through layer upon layer, onion-skins of life, stretching back twenty centuries, and more.

I have never been in a place where the antiques and bric-à-brac fit so squarely against the backdrop of humanity.

Trawl through the loot on sale, and the waves of past invaders stare you in the face. The Greeks were there, and after them the Romans and Byzantine Christians. Then came the Umayyed Caliphate, its empire stretching from India to Islamic Spain and, after it, the Abbasids, the Fatimids and the Seljuq Turks. The Crusades gave way to Mameluk rule, itself followed by the conquest of Tamerlane, the Ottomans and, after them, the French.

Mark Twain was spot on when, in the 1860s, he wrote, 'To Damascus, years are only moments, decades are only flitting trifles of time. She measures time not by days, months and years, but by the empires she has seen rise and prosper and crumble to ruin.'

The American author's visit to Damascus coincided with the great Victorian preoccupation for all things Arabian. The interest was partly fuelled by the translation of *A Thousand and One Nights*, which made the Orient fashionable. European parlours were suddenly awash with exotic furniture, tiles, and silks from the Arab world. By far the best of it came from Damascus, where the remnants fill the antique shops today, and where the craftsmen still toil away making merchandise that has changed little in design in over a thousand years.

In the 1800s, intrepid adventurers like Twain visited Damascus and were awed by it, while others swapped their prim London townhouses for palaces hidden in the depths of the Old City.

The most famous of the Orientalists was Sir Richard Burton. He arrived on January 1st 1870, shortly after Mark Twain had passed through. Employed as British Consul, Burton found himself in a melting pot of ancient and modern, a rare blend of Arab life that he regarded as utter Paradise. It's easy to imagine his delight, after all his Consulate was housed in one of the grandest palaces of all, the fabulous Bait Quwatli. Now divided into homes and storerooms, and in a terrible state of repair, the interior harks back to a time when the Syrian capital was one of the grandest, most sophisticated cities in existence.

For me, a journey to Damascus is an amazing hunt from beginning to end, a slice through layers of history in search of treasure. Seeking out the palaces – ruined and restored – is a great way to glimpse at centuries past. Some buildings have sadly been destroyed, and others have had their beauty savaged by botched restorations, but there are riches awaiting anyone with a sense of adventure.

Look for the old palaces and, when you find them, there aren't any turn-styles or tourist lines – just a watchman if you're lucky to open the door. The ceilings may have fallen in, and the frescoes might be cracked, but squint a little, use your imagination, and it all comes vibrantly to life. Very soon you can hear the sound of music and staccato conversation, and smell the scent of *fleurs d'oranges*, as the hostess sweeps through the room.

A Damascene mansion's reception rooms were designed to astonish visitors, aweing them with a sense of wonder. Such buildings tended to be the property of powerful political families, rather than successful merchants. And so the mansions themselves were an expression of political power and aspiration. Of them all, the most extraordinary, and the easiest to visit now, is the eighteenth century Beit Nizam, located on a narrow residential lane off Straight Street.

From the outside nothing at all is given away. It looks quite unremarkable. But ring the bell, and wait for the guardian to get up from his afternoon siesta, and you enter a dream world of Arabian fantasy.

The house boasts three sprawling courtyards and many reception rooms as grand as any. There are alabaster colonnades and marble floors inset with quartz, octagonal fountains and lavish gilded doors, fabulous painted ceilings and stained glass, turquoise Iznik tiles, exquisite mosque lamps, and murals festooning the walls.

The house is silent now except for birdsong in the orange trees, the stillness bridging the century and a half since the mansion was a hub for high society. Stroll the courtyards and it's easy to picture the exiled Algerian leader, Abd al-Qadir, sitting in the shade, chatting with Burton, or their scandalous friend Lady Jane Digby revealing her latest love affair.

But the longer you spend in palaces like Beit Nizam, the more you find yourself touched by melancholy. A sense of sadness is somehow reflected in it all, as if the bandwagon rolled on.

As I traipsed around the Old City, marvelling at the shattered time-capsules of splendour, I got a sense that no one really cared – except me. The guardians were blasé to the grandeur, as were the ubiquitous families of cats perched on the rooftops; and the local Damascenes were too busy struggling with the present to give much care to the past.

The most poignant example of this sense of sorrow surrounds the home of Jane Digby. An English socialite and aristocrat, she had exiled herself to Damascus at the age of forty-five. It must have been the one place she could think of where her reputation had not yet reached.

In Europe, the drawing-rooms of high society resounded to gossip of her indecent liaisons. She had been married young to an English Baron, before being divorced by him after a slew of scandalous affairs, including one with her own cousin. Freed from marriage, she embarked on a catalogue of liaisons with numerous nobles, including King Ludwig I of Bavaria and, after him, with his son, King Otto of Greece.

Lady Jane spent half the year near Palmyra in goat hair tents, with her lover, a Bedouin sheikh twenty years her junior. The other six months was passed in Damascus, in a house that lies just outside the walls of the Old City.

I had heard that the building had been rediscovered by Lady Jane's biographer, Mary Lovell, a few years ago. With time to spare, I went in search of it for myself. The trouble was that no one in the Syrian capital was interested in a European woman who lived more than a century ago, and one celebrated for her promiscuity. I had inexact directions, which were of little use until, that is, I came across a little shop where electrical motors were being repaired.

Mohammed, the owner, was having lunch at a workbench strewn with wire, dismembered fans, and grease. As I entered with my makeshift map, he insisted I join him. In the Arab world, a visitor must be received with hospitality irrespective of circumstance.

Lunch was followed by tea and conversation mostly about Chinese-made fans, and a blow by blow account of Mohammed's youth. After that, he guided me through an album of pictures of his extended family, and served yet more tea. Three hours after my arrival, I inquired politely if he might show me the house of Lady Jane. He seemed confused, then smiled.

'Follow me,' he said.

We left the workshop and went round the corner and down an alley no wider than a man. Mohammed rang a bell high on the doorframe. After some time, an old woman poked her veiled head out and I was ushered quickly inside. The palace of Beit Nizam had impressed me for its sheer grandeur and indulgence, but rarely have I been touched as I was by the home of Lady Jane.

In the many decades since her death, the house has been divided up among as many as thirty families, but the famous octagonal parlour remains in a near-perfect state. The walls are still covered with the original handmade paper, brought from London by Lady Jane herself. Fitted cupboards stand in each corner, their doors inlaid with delicate filigree. The ceiling – alas partly concealed by a crude mezzanine floor – is octagonal, its central medallion ornamented with little mirrors.

Three generations of a family live in the two rooms now. They were clustered on vinyl couches with bouquets of plastic flowers all around, watching *Baywatch* on an old Japanese TV. Before leaving, I took a mental snapshot, and found myself wondering what the scandalous Lady Jane might have made of the scene.

Back in the covered bazaar, the traders were getting ready for the evening rush, when Damascenes take a stroll before dinner. Brisk business was being done in saffron, mothballs and in underpants, in pumice, plastic buckets and olive oil soap.

One shop was far busier than all the rest.

Its back wall was lined with jars filled with curious ingredients – sulphur, dried chameleons, oak apples and antimony. Dangling from a string near the light was a clutch of tortoise shells, eagles' wings, and a glass box filled with salamander's tails. I watched as veiled women would wander over one by one. They would hand a scribbled list to the apothecary who, in turn, would weigh out a handful of roots, damask roses, poppy seeds or a dried starfish.

In a narrow alley a stone's throw away, a hunched old craftsman was hammering a strand of steel beside a forge. His workshop was blackened with soot, his hands as coarse as glass-paper. The swordsmith paused to greet me, and held the blade into the light for me to examine his work. Damascus was once famed for so-called 'watered steel', a technique which leaves a fluid-like grain on the metal. Blades of astonishing sharpness were fashioned until about 1700, when the technique was lost.

Nearby, in Souq al Khayyatin, the tailor's bazaar, I came across a series of chambers where red and white *kafir* headscarves were being woven on great cast iron looms, imported from France more than a century ago. The chambers were vaulted, their frescoed walls hinting at the former use of the place, as a hammam. The brocade spinners now populate the magnificent central steam room, its ceiling crowned by an octagonal cupola, songbirds tweeting in their cages all around.

Inspired by the ruined bathhouse, I decided to follow Arab tradition and visit a hammam. Bathing is extremely popular across the Islamic world, and is a way for friends to spend time together relaxing, as much as it is a means to get clean. The hammams of Damascus are legendary, many dating back more than a thousand years.

I had been recommended the Al Selsela, which lies close to the ancient Umayyed Mosque. Its owner, another Mohammed, was slouched on a chair near the doorway, watching an Egyptian soap opera on a portable TV.

'A clean man has a pure heart,' he whispered as I entered, quoting a favoured Syrian proverb. His family had run the establishment for generations, he said, and he knew all the customers by name. Some of them were lounging about in the central salon, chatting, smoking *shisha*, and drinking sweet tea.

Wrapped in a towel, I shuffled past them into the blistering steam room. The chamber was illuminated by shafts of natural light, pinpoints of radiance, like a night sky. After being scalded then scrubbed down to the bone with a hunk of pumice, I shuffled out again squeaky clean. As I changed, I found myself pondering how the Occidental world could have lost the tradition of communal bathing – one of the pillars on which the Arab world was born.

Mohammed spat out another proverb as he took my money: 'Clean feet leave no footprints,' he said. Then he directed me to the famous Nawfara Café on the other side of the Umayyed Mosque. He said that if I heard the storyteller there, I would be the happiest man alive, a prospect too good to let go by.

Out on the street, I made my way through a river of Shi'a pilgrims, most of them women, furled from head to toe in black. There were men, too, beating their chests rhythmically as they went. They come each winter in their thousands from Iran, to pray at the shrine of the daughter of Imam Husain.

I carried on down the lane.

Even before I had turned the corner and descended the steps, I smelled the scent of apple *shisha* on the breeze.

The Nawfara Café is an institution in Damascus. You get the feeling that entire lives have been swallowed up there, a ritual of conversation, tobacco, and the bitter Arabica blend.

Inside, a waiter hurried around replenishing the *shisha* with burning coals. In the middle of the room, propped against the wall was a kind of raised throne. Perched on it sat a grey-haired man. He was wrapped in a black robe, its lapel trimmed with gold. Nestled on his lap was a book filled with tight black handwriting. He was shouting out, waving a sword.

But no one paid any attention at all.

The reason for the lack of interest was a widescreen TV on the adjacent wall. Chelsea was playing Arsenal. Everyone in the room, except for me and the storyteller, was glued to the game.

Throughout history, Damascus has been famed for its *hakawatis*, storytellers, a tradition that was celebrated until as recently as a decade ago. But the ubiquitous satellite channels and televisions have killed the ancient Arab art of conversation. The result – a world in which storytellers are a dying breed.

And there is none in the Arab world more respected than Rachid Abu Shadi.

Silently, he finished the tale, put down the sword and the book, and slipped off his throne. The room was filled with applause, but it was not for the storyteller. No one noticed him leave, because Arsenal had just scored.

I invited Abu Shadi to join me for a cup of coffee.

'When I was young,' he said, a glint in his eye, 'my father used to bring me here and I would listen for hours on end – to the tales of Antar and Abla. You see here at Nawfara there's a tradition. Only the tales of Antar, the most famous Arab hero, are told.'

I asked about *Alf Layla wa Layla, A Thousand and One Nights*. The *hakawati* lit a Turkish cigarette and drew the smoke through his clenched fist.

'They were told elsewhere,' he said, 'you see, each café had its own repertoire, but all that's now gone. I am the last of my kind.' He wiped his eye. 'One day the television will break,' he said darkly, and then they will remember me, not because of the stories, but because of the silence there will be without me, and without that vile contraption that hangs up there on the wall.'

The next day I awoke with Lady Jane on my mind.

I had dreamt of her octagonal parlour and wanted to see Palmyra for myself, where she lived half the year with her beloved sheikh. Standing two hundred kilometres to the north-east of Damascus, Palmyra once boasted a vast community, poised on the caravan routes between Persia and the Mediterranean.

Travelling there in the 1930s on camel, my Afghan grandfather was astonished by the Classical ruins. He wrote, 'To set eyes on this remote oasis is to be reminded that, however mighty an empire imagines itself to be, it is as fragile as a child's toy.'

The scale of the ruins at Palmyra are truly awe-inspiring. They stand like an ancient movie back-lot, all ruined and bleak like the end of the world. But it is the silence that made the strongest impression on me. I found myself picturing both Lady Jane and my own grandfather listening to it, and to the infrequent blasts of wind ripping across the plains. It was as if the breeze were singing a warning, that civilizations crumble and fall as sure as they take seed and flourish.

Still known to the Arabs by its pre-Semitic name, *Tadmor*, Palmyra was once a place of decadence and wealth. Walk the ruins and you get a sense of the power of the culture that shaped it.

There are vast colonnaded streets, temples and theatres, ceremonial arches and elaborate tombs, replete with exquisite funereal busts. It's all fashioned from sumptuous honey-yellow stone, built with a confidence that must have defied anyone who questioned such a metropolis could exist in the desert. But then of course, the landscape has changed dramatically in the forty centuries or more since its founding. Palmyra's name, meaning 'the City of Palms', hints at the fertility of the oasis long gone.

Not quite so certain are the origins of this now-desolate commercial and cultural outpost of antiquity. Its name appears on stone tablets dating to the nineteenth century before the birth of Christ, and is apparently the place mentioned in the Bible's *First Book of Kings*, as 'Tamor', a city founded by Solomon. More clear is the Roman Empire's delight at capturing the oasis, which they regarded as almost without equal. When Hadrian visited in 129 AD, he renamed it *Palmyra Hadriana*, and proclaimed it a free city.

Sitting among the ruins in the fading light of dusk, the image of Lady Jane Digby was irresistible. I could see her quite clearly in desert robes, strolling in the long shadows thrown by towering colonnades. Like me, I am sure she was taken by the romanticism of it all, and by the desperate beauty that is so alluring as to defy accurate description. By visiting Palmyra, I understood Damascus a little better, reminded that the circle of life stops for no man.

On arriving back in the capital, I paid Salim the son of Suleiman another visit.

As before, he was asleep, the tabby kitten curled up on his chest. In the background was the rumble of a generator, the sound drowning out the *muezzin*'s call to prayer.

When Salim was awake, and tea had been brewed and served, I brought up the subject of the ceremonial axe. The shopkeeper smiled.

'You have earned it,' he said.

'What do you mean?'

'An object as special as that isn't for the first day,' he said, 'the fact you came back means that the axe was in your dreams. You can have it half the price.'

Desert Stopover

MY JOURNEY BEGAN three weeks ago at Tangiers.

There's no city like it: a heaving emporium of woollen *jelabas* and yellow *baboush* slippers, dark veiled faces, incense and antimony, spices and fruit. It is a place of sheer anticipation, where the ancient and modern mix, the point at which East meets West.

I was following a childhood dream, a trail southwards venturing from the north-west corner of Africa, south to Timbuktu. My budget was limited and so I opted to travel by local bus. A few miles from this town to that, squashed up at the back with live chickens, spare tyres, and baskets of fish. After all, real travel is not about luxury, but about endurance, and looking on all that passes with fresh eyes.

The vivid colours of Moroccan life were blinding. Every fruit stall, every kiosk was a blaze of reds and blues, dazzling pinks and sun-ripe yellows. But the colour was eventually traded for the stark desert. Dry terracotta browns, patches of withered maize, parched scrub... and then all of it replaced by a sea of rippled dunes.

The road became a track no wider than the bus. The sun arched west, and disappeared over the baked sand horizon. Coolness. Then the dark; the moon no more than a sliver of ivory in an ink-black sky. The other passengers and I breathed easy for the first time in as many hours. It was late – ten or eleven. And it was cold. I pulled on my filthy jacket and tried to sleep. We were running hours late, the dilapidated vehicle having overheated in the afternoon just before crossing the border into Mauritania.

I slipped into sleep, and gradually the discomfort melted away. An hour must have passed.

Then... BANG!

A jerk of tremendous force. The sound of glass shattering. The stench of dust and smoke. The bus was on its side. There was screaming and panic in the dark. Instinct took over. I clambered out of what was left of my seat, and crawled from the wreckage. One or two others had managed to do the same. They huddled on the ground, all in shock. Then the petrol tank erupted – a volcano of fire illuminating the night. I thanked fortune for sparing me, and covered my nose. My jacket was drenched in what I assumed at first to be sweat. But I realized it was blood, flowing from a gash on the side of my head.

It was then that I heard a voice, that of a man. He was calling out to me.

'I am alive,' I said, breaking into tears. 'I am alive.'

The voice spoke again. It was nearer, and a moment later a hand was pressed on my shoulder. I saw the face in the reflection of the inferno. A furrowed brow above and scattered grey bristle below. The man tugged me away from the fire.

'Come,' he said, 'I help you.'

We crossed a low ditch and traipsed over barren fields and sand. I was still dazed, shaking, my ears ringing. It was impossible to make out very much in the dark. The man might have slit my throat right then but I was too confused to care. I walked with my hand as a fist, and tried to prepare myself for danger.

'Where are we going?'

'To my home.'

I must have passed out. Because I can't remember anything more. Suddenly it was day, bright light, scorching heat. I was lying on a mattress on a cracked mud floor. I could make out the muffled sound of a goat bleating outside, and of a child singing. The singing stopped and the child began to weep. A moment later the old man from the night before was crouching over me. I strained to open my eyes and saw him, a blur of features and yellow teeth. He offered me a tin cup filled with cool water. Struggling, I gulped down the liquid.

'I am Hakim,' he said.

'Where is my rucksack?'

'Destroyed,' said the man. 'The fire. Everything was destroyed.'

'But my passport, my money…?'

'All gone.'

'What can I do?'

Hakim swept a hand over the stubble on his face.

'Rest, and your fever will go.'

I lay back and the fever took hold again. It felt as if I was adrift on an ocean of sweat. As I prayed for salvation, my ears filled with the mumbled hum of the *muezzin* reciting the call to prayer far away.

Time passed.

Night, day, night, day, cold interleaved with heat.

From time to time I would break free from the delirium, just long enough to hear snatches of the world outside. The girl would be singing, or laughing, amidst a backdrop of farmyard sounds. The sounds couched in my desperate thirst.

It was dark again, and cold, and I was shaking, waiting for the old man or his wife to stumble in and fill my cup. I heard a fruit bat high up in the trees, and a dog worrying the goat. Then the sound of the old man's voice.

'We must do it,' he said.

There was a pause, and the woman replied:

'Let him live a few more days. There's no need to slaughter him yet.'

'No,' said Hakim. 'I will do it tonight.'

My body was suddenly charged with an almost primeval sense of fear. I was alert. Sweating like a madman, but alert all the same. My mind was racing. I jerked up off the mattress and searched for my clothes. They weren't there. I scanned the room in which I had been recovering. I hadn't really noticed it before. It measured about twelve feet by six, the walls made from hand cut planks, and the roof a sheet of crumpled tin. One corner was piled high with sacks of dried maize. There was a single window, glazed with a scrap of polythene, and one doorway. That was the obvious route of escape.

I moved over to it and listened hard. It led into another room, I supposed the kitchen. I could make out the girl singing softly to herself. There was a sense of peace. Then I made out the sound of the man's feet entering the kitchen.

'We will kill him tonight,' said Hakim. 'It is a matter of honour.'

The girl did not reply. Instead she broke into tears and seemed to run from the house. I could hear her bare feet darting over the baked mud. The old man must have been standing on the other side of the door. I could feel him there, weight balanced evenly over his feet, thinking, waiting. I felt a wave of fever rolling towards me again, swelling with force as it neared. My eyes watered. I struggled to keep still, and forced myself to think.

Travel far enough from home and you enter the real world, a realm where life and death are two inseparable facets of the same thing. I had not yet reached my goal, Timbuktu, but I was staring death in the eyes.

It was very real, cold, clinical.

Ten seconds later, the Hakim had shuffled outside. Taking my chance, I flung the door open and charged out into the night. I was naked, but for a pair of sweat-drenched boxer shorts, running on bare feet. Which way to go? God knows. It's all pitch black. I hurtled towards the horizon, into the dark. There were shouts behind me, and the sound of a dog raising the alarm. I charged on, running for all I was worth. Running for my life. The shouting grew more muffled, and I felt the night air pressed on my back. It was cool. Pleasing.

I ran and ran like never before.

I hoped I would find a road, but this was wilderness. Thorn trees silhouetted by the full moon. I would have felt pity for myself, but I was too weak, too confused. Eventually I lay down at the foot of a gnarled tree and passed out.

The dawn touched my face, a blush of pink, gentle, innocent light. I strained to open my eyes, and glanced around fretfully. Lacerated feet, unclothed, lost in a wasteland of nature. The sun soared up overhead, and began to roast me alive. I cursed myself for setting out in search of adventure in the first place. Then I wondered how it might all end. I sat there crouched for most of the morning, unable to decide what to do, or in which direction to trudge.

Late that afternoon something remarkable happened.

On the horizon, I saw an object moving. It was low and black, and was too far away to make any noise. I waited and watched, and the object – a vehicle – moved closer. Half and hour passed and it closed in, wheels spinning, churning up the dust. I waved as vigorously as I could. The vehicle, a battered grey Land Rover, rolled to a halt beside the thorn tree under which I had been crouching. I heard the handbrake being pulled on hard.

A white man clambered out.

He was tall, young, and almost athletic, dressed in khaki, with an impressively wide canvas hat.

'You've got to cover your head in this heat,' he said, in a clipped English accent.

'Someone was trying to kill me,' I said feebly.

The Englishman peered at me, said his name was Rick. He kept a distance, didn't even step over to shake me by the hand.

'Oh,' he said.

'I was in a bus crash. There was an explosion. Then the man who saved me was going to kill me. I managed to escape.'

I hoped for pity. Rick broke into a grin. His teeth reflected the sunlight. He waved to the car.

'You'd better get in,' he said.

I climbed into the passenger seat and, before I could slam the door shut, we were hurtling forward at an alarming pace, jolting up and down and from side to side.

'You've gotta be careful out here,' shouted Rick over the noise of the engine.

Five minutes later I spotted a group of shacks, tall straight plank walls, roofed in crumpled tin. They were familiar. I felt a pang of fear shoot down my back.

'I can't go there!' I shouted. 'This is where they were keeping me. They were going to kill me.'

I tried to open the car door, but we were still moving too fast.

Rick slammed on the brakes, and looked me in the eye.

'These are my friends,' he said. 'They sent their son to find me. He walked for two days to get to me. And he came to me because of you.'

A moment later, Hakim came rushing out. He looked concerned, confused. I shied away when he neared me.

'I know your plan,' I said bitterly.

'What plan?'

'I heard you... heard you plotting with your wife. Plotting to slit my throat.'

The old man peered at the dry mud beneath his feet. He didn't reply at first. His head was drooped in thought. Then I saw the faintest glimmer of a smile at the corner of his mouth. A second later it had swept across his face. A moment after that he was roaring in laughter. He said something fast and Rick began to laugh as well.

I stood there, shirtless, shoeless, sunburned.

'You don't understand,' said Hakim.

'Yes I do,' I said. 'You were going to take advantage of me. You were going to *kill* me.'

'Not you,' said he replied. 'We were not going to kill *you*, but the goat… in honour of you, our guest.'

That night we feasted on goat stew.

For me it was a celebration of a kind. I was thankful for having survived my partly self-made ordeal. The next morning, Rick drove me to the next town, gave me a little money, and waited with me for the local bus to arrive. I had changed my plan, a detour to Mauritania's capital to obtain a new passport. The bus eventually rolled up. Rick, the Englishman, shook my hand hard and wished me luck.

'The less wealth a man has to give,' he said, as I clambered aboard, 'the greater the depth of his heart.'

N.B. This piece is fiction.

Essaouira, A Portrait

ON MY FIRST NIGHT IN ESSAOUIRA a man tried to sell me a ghost.

We were sitting on the ramparts facing the sea, the searing winter wind on our faces, sipping our *café noir*. The man, a local, with a Portuguese name held a clenched fist in my direction.

'It's in here,' he said.

'What is?'

'The ghost.'

'How much is it?'

'A hundred dirhams.'

'Why's it for sale?'

The vender frowned.

'I've no need for it,' he said.

'Well, what use is it to me?'

'Believe, really believe,' he said, 'and this ghost will be the keyhole into your dreams.'

There is something about Essaouira, the former Portuguese city clinging to Morocco's Atlantic coast, which touches all who venture there. It's a hybrid, a meeting point of East and West, one of those rare destinations where you never quite know who you'll meet. The only certainty is that you will leave it different from when you came.

In atmosphere, Essaouira is quite unlike the imperial cities of Morocco's interior. It's magically desolate, almost like a forbidden enclave perched at the end of the world. The buildings are stone: thick grey walls, standing proud to the wind and to the freezing Atlantic waters. They form a stark and alluring canvas for a thousand colours – carpets hanging for sale in the souqs, skeins of wool dripping with dazzling dyes, panniers of glinting red mullet being hauled up from the port.

Spend a few days there, traipsing up and down the ramparts with their weatherworn Portuguese cannons, or down the orderly stone

81

streets laid out by the French, and you forget that the rest of Morocco – or the rest of the world – exists. For me, that's the extraordinary power of the place, a power that's lured visitors for centuries.

The Phoenicians moored their ships at Essaouira in the seventh century BC. Five hundred years after them, the Romans arrived under Juba II. They used their base there as a manufactory for Tyrian purple dye, a colour derived from murex sea snails, prized for dyeing the Senatorial robes. Then came the Portuguese in the fifteenth century. They christened the city 'Mogador' and, after them, Essaouria became a haven for pirates, who plied the Atlantic waters raiding European ships. The medina was laid out in about 1760, by French engineers, on the orders of the Alaouite Sultan Mohammed III. Having glimpsed the natural strategic position, he built a naval base there, and one devoted to trade.

I myself was first drawn to Essaouira by the scent of the wood. The narrow lanes of the lime-washed media are packed with tiny workshops, carpenters busy in the shadows of each. They are master craftsmen, *moualems*, creating marquetry boxes, carved from the aromatic *thuya* tree, whose gnarled roots are harvested from the surrounding region. I first smelled the fragrance when taken there as an infant. Essaouira was a destination then on the hippy trail: VW combos, tie-dye and the fresh memory of Jimi Hendrix, who'd just swaggered out of town. Smell those roots, get their aroma deep into your chest, and they lure you back like the scent of lotus flowers on the wind.

The baby-boom hippies may be gone now, but you can still feel their presence. I am never sure whether they came to Essaouira because of the community's free-thinking attitudes, or if they actually changed the place.

Go down to the beach and you'll find surfers aplenty, some of them the children of hippies who were here a generation ago. They come from all over the world to do battle with the ferocious winter waves. And in the narrow streets of the old city, tie-dye, dreadlocks, and illicit tobaccos are also in plentiful supply.

As the severe winter chill melts into spring, Essaouira's atmosphere transforms like a chameleon. The skies turn indigo blue, daubed with wisps of cirrus, the sharp light radiant against white-washed walls. And as spring slips into summer, the city is charged with electric anticipation at the annual Gnaoua Festival, held each June.

An ancient mystical fraternity with their roots sunk deep in African lore, the Gnaoua conjure music that's a powerful blend of African and Arab, a bridge between this and the spirit world.

Sit at one of the medina cafés and from a distance you hear the distinctive clatter of *qarkabeb*, the oversized iron castanets, symbol of the Gnaoua. As they come closer, their rhythm shaking the soul, they have the power to send locals and foreigners into trance.

On the night I was offered a cut-price ghost, a group of four Gnaouas swept into the café in which we were sitting. The clatter of their iron castanets was like an exorcism rite, chasing out the demons.

The man beside me held his fist above his head.

'They can smell it,' he said.

'Smell what?'

'The ghost, the gnaoua… look at them!'

I turned in time to see one of the troupe collapse to the floor. He began writhing, his eyes rolled back.

'It's quite normal,' said the man, darkly.

'Are you sure?'

The ghost-seller nodded.

'I speak the truth,' he said. 'I swear it, on all I hold sacred.'

Fès

LYING BEHIND A PLAIN STEEL DOOR on a dusty lane in Fès, stands one of the most unexpected treasures of North Africa – the Glaoui Palace.

To cross the threshold is to enter a medieval Twilight Zone, one touched by the fantasy of the *Arabian Nights*. It's a place where straightforward questions posed by the Western mind go unanswered, and where visitors find themselves changed by the experience. A vast sprawling labyrinth of interlocking courtyards, the Glaoui is a jewel of the faded grandeur at Morocco's secret heart.

Perched on a broken chair in the shade of an immense galleried courtyard, is Abdou, the guardian. He's cloaked in a voluminous sky blue Tuareg desert robe, and is drowsy, having just stirred from a mid-morning siesta. He smiles, his lips framing a clutch of infirm teeth, as he struggles to stand.

Abdou has lived at the Glaoui for as long as he can remember. If you ask him whether he was born there, or if he actually owns the palace, he looks away, stares across the heat haze, and widens his eyes. He gives the same response when you ask him what its future might bring, or why the courtyard is filled with ducks and geese. After visiting Abdou, as I have done over the years, I've come to learn that the best way to appreciate his home is to forget the questions that an Occidental education teaches us to ask, and to listen to the pearls of wisdom that tumble from his lips.

'Fès is the heart of this kingdom,' he says in a voice moulded by a fondness for Turkish tobacco, 'and this is one of the hearts of Fès. It's a place of secrets, of mystery, a home that has known love and betrayal, poverty and wealth.'

A single drop of perspiration wells up on Abdou's brow and rolls down his dark cheek, evaporating before reaching his chin. The afternoon is swelteringly hot – the high thirties. The geese and ducks

The medieval dyeing pits in Fès

Abdou in the harem of the Glaoui Palace

are flapping about because their basin of filthy water has dried up, turned into sludge. Abdou doesn't seem to care. He lurches forwards in slow motion and leads the way down a dark, dank corridor running off the central courtyard.

A moment later we find ourselves in a kitchen that's like something out of Henry VIII's Hampton Court. A colossal chimney stands at the far side of the room. Beneath it there's a clutter of cauldrons, ladles the size of spades, battered old kettles, and a mountain range of empty tin cans. Abdou flicks his fingers towards the inch-thick dust as if to excuse his disapproval for housework.

'Come this way,' he says in a whisper.

Another twist to the right and one to the left, and we're in another courtyard. Smaller than the first, the walls are ornamented in *zelij*, mosaics in white and black. Above the mosaics, and the towering colonnades, there's an upper terrace adorned fabulously with painted wood, all of it about to collapse from rot.

'This is the harem,' says Abdou dreamily. 'Beautiful ladies guarded by eunuchs. Close your eyes, breathe in deep, and you can smell them!'

A little imagination goes a long way in Fès.

Do as Abdou suggests – close your eyes, take a deep breath – and you find yourself catapulted back through centuries. There's the clatter of mules clip-clopping up the narrow alleyways, the scent of lamb roasting on spits, and the muffled sounds of bustle from the souq.

Fès is without doubt the greatest medieval Arab city still intact anywhere. To wander its streets is to be part of a way of life that has become fragmented or has disappeared entirely elsewhere across the East. Describing it to someone who's not been there, is like trying to describe a computer circuit to a blind man. However hard you try, you just don't know where to start.

One of my earliest memories is of arriving at the great city walls of Fès at dusk. I was only five or six, but I can vividly remember it. We had driven from London, and on reaching Fès it felt as if we had arrived at a citadel poised at the very end of the world. We spotted a group of old men huddled in their *jelabas* near the great Boujloud gate.

I asked my mother who they were.

'They're gamblers,' she snapped disapprovingly.

'They are not,' my father corrected, 'they are part of an ancient tradition that stretches back a thousand years. They are the storytellers,' he said.

That first journey was like stepping through an aperture into a magical realm, where the senses came to life, touched by a frenzy of cultural colour. The vibrant sights, intoxicating sounds, delicious tastes and smells changed me, right deep down.

Everyone who journeys to Fès is affected in a similar way. Whereas Marrakech has become a Disneyland version of the *Arabian Nights*, Fès is the real thing.

Some visitors find it uncomfortable, even a little sinister. And in a way it is. The city is a religious centre, a place that's content to have tourists but that's quite nonchalant at the same time. You can't escape the dark heart, or the city's bewitching soul. It's everywhere – in the rambling labyrinth of streets, where pack-mules stumble forward, laden with freshly-dyed skins from the tanneries; and in the ancient medrasas, in the palaces, and the simple courtyard homes.

Talaa Kebir, the main thoroughfare that runs downhill from Bab Boujloud, has more life on it than entire cities I have seen. There are a few emporia touting the usual tourist kitsch, but what's so wonderful is that most of the shops are selling stuff for the locals – rip-off Nike sneakers and blue fluorescent bras, flour sieves and camel heads for boiling into soup, David Beckham football strip, candyfloss, and chicks dyed pink.

And with every step you hear the sound of artisans, hidden in the maze of workshops that back onto the main street. Some of them are carving appliqué designs from sheets of burnished brass, others sculpting cedar-wood, blowing glass, or weaving cloth for *jelabas* on enormous homemade looms.

Many of the wares on sale in Marrakech and other Moroccan cities are actually made in Fès where, for centuries, craftsmen have passed on secret techniques from father to son. As well as goods for the tourist emporia, most of Morocco's mosaics and ceramic tiles are made near the city as well. The kilns are on the outskirts of town and are well worth a visit. They are fired with burning olive stones, and stacked by hand by the youngest apprentices, in a system that's endured since

Roman times.

While Europe languished in its Dark Ages, Fès was already a bustling centre of intellect and commerce. Linked to the great cities of the emerging Islamic world through ever-expanding pilgrimage routes, it found itself connected to Seville and Cordoba, to Cairo, Baghdad, Delhi and Samarkand.

The immense Haj caravans which crossed North Africa and Asia formed a kind of medieval Internet, and brought some of the most celebrated scholars of the age to Fès. Among them, men like the Sufi mystic Ibn Arabi, the scientific polymath Ibn Khaldun, and the Jewish scholar Maimonedes. Their work led to breakthroughs in science and urban planning and directly influenced the city that became their home. It boasted a state of the art sewage system, schools and universities, community hospitals, fountains, and even public water clocks.

Exploring Fès today, it's quite challenging at times to imagine when the city was at the cutting edge of technology – a time when the mosaic fountains ran with water and were not just used as communal garbage bins, and a time when the delicate wooden shop façades weren't all rotten, as they often are today. Even for diehard lovers of the city, people like me, there's a sadness in the medina, a kind of melancholy. The wealthy merchants departed for the new town and for Casablanca decades ago. These days anyone still to be found in the labyrinth has been left behind. Many of them dream the same dream – to sell their homes and shops to rich foreigners, and to buy apartments with all mod cons in the *ville nouvelle*.

Thankfully, the love affair with Fès touches a great many Moroccans and foreigners as well. It's something that none of us can really explain. When we meet, we mumble about details of ornaments and fragments of the city's soul, in conversations that must mystify those who don't share our obsession.

One man bitten deeply by the Fès bug is the American-born scholar David Amster. He moved to the medina more than a decade ago, and knows the twists and turns of the nine thousand streets as well as any child playing marbles in the shadows of the Karaouiyine Mosque.

Amster is a connoisseur of the kind of detail that tends to go unnoticed by the untrained eye. He has a passion for the handmade nails and hinges that once adorned every Fassi door. He waxes lyrical about the traditional *medluk*, a lime rendering which allows the ancient buildings to breathe (cement is the curse of renovation as it suffocates the walls); and he speaks of his dream with a glint in his eye – a time when all renovation is done with obsessive care and age-old skill.

Each month, David Amster's small team of master craftsmen, known as *moualems*, restore a stretch of neglected street, or a fountain filled with trash. It's a kind of guerrilla restoration on a micro scale that's often done at night when everyone else is tucked up in bed. Amster pays for it all himself by renting out to foreigners a small *riad* he owns.

Even visitors who stay in the medina sometimes complain of how difficult it is to get under the skin of the city. Once you stray off the main streets, the arteries, you can find that the ever-narrowing web of alleyways are dark and even a little imposing. You quickly get the feeling that all kinds of life is going on behind the battered old doors, but as an outsider you can't peer in to what is a secret world. A good way of getting instant access is to hint that you want to buy a little house, or even a palace, a dream home conjured from the pages of *A Thousand and One Nights*. The *immobiliers*, estate agents, are only too happy to take you round as many homes as you want to see.

In my experience, there's no better way of getting a cross section of medina life – kitchens with grandmothers toiling away at the dishes and the couscous, laundry dripping in the sun, children scampering about on their trikes, families gripped in front of interminable Egyptian soap operas, and caged chickens up on the roof waiting to become lunch.

A few months ago I was shown a palace for sale with magnificent cedar ceilings, painted in fabulous geometric designs. An elderly craftsman lived in its great salon with a dozen white doves and a ferocious-looking cat. He spent his days cutting leather sandals from animal hides, and told me that he'd been born in the corner room eight decades before.

He looked me straight in the eye.

'Some of my ancestors are buried in the basement,' he said.

Nearby, I was taken to another a home at Bab Er-rsif, the most historic area of the medina. Its owner showed me the title document, a scroll twenty feet long. He said his family had lived there for many generations, and that the foundations had been laid at least five hundred years ago.

When I sighed loudly, exclaiming that I simply didn't have the funds to buy it, the owner smiled. It was a wry, toothless smile of an old man with a plan.

'Do not worry about money,' he said dreamily, 'because there is a secret, and I will tell it to you.'

I asked what it was.

'Under the floor,' he went on, jabbing a thumb at the exquisite ancient glazed terracotta tiles, 'there's a treasure. It's vast and worth many times the price I am asking for the house.'

I thought for a moment, and then posed the obvious question:

'If there is indeed a treasure under this floor,' I said, 'why have you not dug it up yourself?'

The owner wiped his eyes with the sleeve of his *jelaba*.

'Do you have any idea,' he said slowly, 'what problems a treasure like that would give to an old man like me?'

In the end I didn't buy the house, even though the lure of treasure was strong. But plenty of foreigners have bitten the bullet and snapped up houses – treasure or no treasure – most usually as second homes. There's a small Anglophone community living permanently in the Fès medina. Of them all, the most indefatigable and offbeat is certainly Mike Richardson.

Mike was a *maitre d'* at London's swish Ivy Restaurant, and at the Wolseley on Piccadilly.

'One day I was at a party and I overheard someone talking about Fès,' he says. 'It sounded absolutely glorious. Before I knew it, I'd moved here, bought a little house with my savings, and opened the Café Clock.'

Lodged in a narrow alley opposite the medieval Medrasa Bouinania, 'The Clock', as it's known to all, is spread out over several levels and is immensely popular. Clambering up and down to all the terraces is such a strain on the legs, that Mike hired a waiter with a penchant for mountain-climbing.

In a back room off the staircase, the chef's assistant is adding a pinch of dried damask rose petals and a handful of secret ingredients to a fresh batch of minced camel meat. After searching his entire culinary career for the perfect hamburger meat, Mike found it in Fès. As he says – 'Camel meat sits so nicely on the bun.'

Another European to have realized his dream in Morocco's secret heart, is Fred Sola, a Frenchman who was actually born in Casablanca. A few years ago he bought Riad Laaroussa, a seventeenth century palace, once owned by the Moroccan Minister for War. His intention was at first to have it as a private home.

The colossal property was in a terrible state of repair, and required renovation on a grand scale. It was so big that when it was finally done, Fred felt lonely. So he started inviting people to stay. Today, it's an exclusive *riad* hotel with just eight sumptuous suites. There's a serenity about the place that soothes everyone who steps across its threshold.

As you sit in the shade of the central courtyard, you're lulled by the sound of birdsong, and water issuing gently from a marble fountain. The air is still, scented by orange blossom, the sky above indigo blue.

'The secret of Fès is not to be in a hurry,' says Fred, lounging back on a chaise longue, 'if you hurry, all sorts of obstacles appear as if by magic. We had about fifty craftsmen working with us for a year and a half. They were so incredibly skilled, doing work that relies on pure expertise and not on power tools as is so often the case in the West. When we finished Riad Laaroussa I didn't want to lose the craftsmen, and so we now renovate homes for other people who, like me, have been bewitched by the spell of Fès.'

A few streets away, back at the Glaoui Palace, Abdou is lowering his eyelids for a second siesta of the day. The only sound is the honking of the geese in the background and the muffled call to prayer far away. One day, Abdou's home will surely be transformed into a name-brand chain hotel, the rot, old tin cans, and the geese long gone. There'll be bell boys in smart little uniforms, piped music, and plumbing that actually works.

My own dream is that Fès – Morocco's Sleeping Beauty – dozes off again like Abdou, and that the future waits a while longer to arrive.

Friendship, Morocco

A POPULAR MOROCCAN PROVERB goes, 'A man without friends is like a garden without flowers'.

It was told to me in the first week I arrived to live in Casablanca, by a plumber who had turned up to clean out the drains. He seemed distraught that I could have moved to a new home in a foreign land where I knew no one at all. I told him that it felt liberating.

'I don't have to avoid people any more,' I said, beaming.

The plumber wiped a rag over the crown of his bald head.

'But how will you live if you don't have friends?' he replied.

Looking back to that first week, I now understand what he meant. For us in the West, friends are sometimes little more than people we go to the pub with so we aren't there alone. That may sound bitter, I know. But in Morocco, friendship is quite a different thing. It's a support structure par excellence, a system by which the old values of chivalry and honour are passed on. But more than that, it's something that's actively nurtured and raised, like a seedling in a garden.

My story is not unusual.

I had been lured to Morocco from London, to escape the damp grey sky and the exorbitant British living costs. My dream involved buying a rambling mansion, renovating it, and learning to live again.

Move to a new country and you quickly see that visiting a place as a tourist, and actually moving there for good, are two very different things.

Over the first year we renovated the house, exorcised the wayward Jinns who supposedly inhabited it, and battled the waves of conmen who beat a path to our door. At times I would find myself wondering if I would ever find anyone I could trust, a real friend.

Then, one Spring morning I met Abdelmalik.

I was having my hair cut in a rundown barber's shop near to my house, when a tall, suave man strode in and sat on the chair beside mine. He asked for a shave. A pair of dark glasses were worn like a tiara across his slicked back hair. He smiled a great deal. I supposed he was in his late thirties. While the barber sharpened the cut-throat razor on a leather strop, the man made conversation.

He asked me if I missed England.

'How do you know I've come from England?' I asked.

'Because you look too pale to be Moroccan and too content to be French.'

The man's cheeks were shaved, and anointed with a home-brewed Cologne. He pressed a coin into the barber's hand.

'I will wait for you at the café opposite,' he said.

I was still unfamiliar to Moroccan society and wondered if I should accept the invitation. But unable to resist, I crossed the street and found the man, Abdelmalik Leghmati, sipping a *café noir*. We both sketched out the broad details of our lives – wives, children, work, and exchanged telephone numbers. He expressed his great love for Arab horses, and his lifelong dream of owning one.

It was an interest we both shared.

We chatted about horses and life for an hour or more. Then Abdelmalik glanced at his watch.

'We will be friends,' he said firmly, as he left.

From then on the suave clean-shaven Moroccan swept into my life. He saw it as his duty to solve every one of my abundant problems and to help me settle in. First, he taught me local etiquette – how to be regarded as a local, how to receive and entertain a Moroccan guest, and how to prepare the sweet mint tea which everyone drinks constantly.

From the outset, Abdelmalik stressed again and again that I could ask anything of him. As my friend, it was his duty to be there for me. I found it strange at first that someone would make such a point about friendship, rather than just letting it develop as we do in the Occident. We would meet at least every two days on the terrace of Café Lugano, near Casablanca's coast road, where we always sat at the same table. At the other tables the same people were usually seated as well. I commented on this, that the same people were always in position.

'Of course that's how it is,' said Abdelmalik. 'You see they are friends.'

In Morocco there is no occupation more honourable for a man that to be seen with his pals sitting at a café, drinking sweet mint tea. In the West, we might frown on spending so much leisure time in such a way. But, for Moroccans, time spent working on a friendship in public is extremely important indeed.

When I told an expatriate acquaintance about Abdelmalik, he waved his arms in caution.

'Beware!' he shouted. 'Before you know it, this man will be demanding you to repay his kindness. What happens if he gets into a family feud?' The expatriate paused. 'You could find yourself at war,' he said. 'All because you're his friend.'

After we had known each other for a month, Abdelmalik invited me to his apartment. It was small, cosy, and dominated by a low coffee table. On the table were laid at least ten plates, each one laden with sticky cakes, biscuits and buns. I asked how many other people had been invited.

'Just you,' replied my host, confused.

'But I can't eat this much,' I said.

Abdelmalik grinned like a Cheshire cat. 'You must try to eat it all,' he lisped.

A few days later, he called me and announced he had a surprise. An hour later, I found myself in the steam room of a hammam, a Turkish style bath. For Moroccans, going to the hammam is a weekly ceremony. Abdelmalik taught me how to apply *savon noir*, and the ritual of *gommage*, scrubbing myself down until my body was raw. In the scalding fog of the steam room, he presented me with an expensive wash-case packed with the items I would need. When I choked out thanks, embarrassed at the costly gift, he whispered:

'No price is too great for a friend.'

Months passed, and I found myself waiting for Abdelmalik's ulterior motive. I felt sure he would eventually ask me for something, some kind of payment for our friendship. Then, one morning, after many coffee meetings, he leant over the table at Café Lugano and said:

'I have a favour to ask you.'

I felt my stomach knot with selfishness.
'Anything,' I mumbled, bravely.
Abdelmalik edged closer and smiled very gently.
'Would you allow me to buy you an Arab horse?' he asked.

Gendercide

AMBIKA RECLINES ON A STRETCHER as Dr. Gupta applies a patch of sticky gel to her stomach.

She lies quite still, staring up at the makeshift clinic's bare lightbulb. The doctor gazes into a computer monitor as he runs an electrode across her belly. Then, as if peering deep into a crystal ball, he searches for an answer. Ambika clenches her fists and waits.

Suddenly the physician moves over from the machine, looks at Ambika, and shakes her head from side to side.

She is pregnant with a female foetus – a daughter.

Ten minutes later, Ambika, who had her twenty-first birthday a week before, is undergoing a termination.

Ambika lives in the small town of Sirsa, in north-west India. Under pressure from her husband and his family to a produce a son, she is one of millions of women in India whose families consider bearing a daughter to be a disgrace, especially when there's no male heir.

India's ancient custom decrees that, when wed, the bride's family must pay a dowry to the groom's – meaning that girls are far less wanted than boys.

For centuries female infanticide has been quite common in India. But, now, advanced technology is enabling women to determine the gender of the foetus during pregnancy. The result: hundreds of thousands of female foetuses are aborted each year in India alone.

Ambika is no newcomer to Dr. Gupta's infamous surgery.

The waiting area with its aborted female foetuses preserved in formalin (proof to clients that females are being hunted down and disposed of) no longer impresses her. For she's undergone five abortions already. Each abortion followed a brief scan using state of the art Ultrasound equipment.

Billboards all over Sirsa remind people about the joys of bearing a son, and they give details of clinics which will help mothers realize their dream. At least five thousand female foetus' are estimated to be aborted in Sirsa (a town of about 120,000 people) each year.

Across the Indian subcontinent, often with only the most rudimentary training, doctors are purchasing Ultrasound diagnostic equipment, and setting themselves up in business.

Since the mid 1980s Ultrasound equipment has been filtering into India. Making use of bank loans to buy the apparatus, unscrupulous physicians can recoup the initial expenditure in a matter of weeks, or even days. For those who can't get a bank loan, companies across India lease out advanced Ultrasound units.

At least two electronic corporations are known to be manufacturing Ultrasound diagnostic equipment in India. Groups such as the Mumbai-based Forum Against Sex Determination believe that this will lead to less control in the standards and quantity of units being produced.

The Forum seems to be fighting an uphill battle.

Mumbai's state, Maharashtra, was the first in India to proclaim S.D.T. (Sex Determination Tests) illegal. Far from reducing the Ultrasound testing, the ban has merely driven such clinics deep underground. The billboards have been taken down, but the surgeries are still booming. Diagnostic testing is far from a lower or middle class phenomenon. High society requires male heirs for its business empires. Women come from across India and even from abroad (particularly the Arab Gulf), to have S.D.T. in Mumbai. Ultrasound equipment in the city is probably the best on the Indian Subcontinent.

Chaitna, a twenty-three year old mother living near the southern city of Bangalore, has two daughters and has been trying to conceive a son. When she gave birth to a third daughter, her husband's mother fed the baby the sap of the lethal Errukum plant mixed with milk. Death came instantly. The next time Chaitna was pregnant she solicited the services of a surgeon who arrived at her village with mobile Ultrasound unit – powered by a generator. The scan was done. Chaitna was assured that the foetus was female. She opted for abortion: which was performed a few minutes later. Only then was it discovered that the foetus had in fact been male.

Misinterpretation of Ultrasound images is extremely common. Most systems are completely operator dependent. When in the hands of an inexperienced user, the results can be anything but accurate. If in doubt, doctors generally maintain the foetus is female – so curtailing the chance of a daughter being born. Other, even more dissolute physicians are known to assert that the foetus is female when it is not, thus assuring themselves extra business: through abortion.

Despite its relatively short history in India, Ultrasound sex testing is having a devastating effect on the ratio between men to women. A recent census found there were 929 females to 1,000 males in India. Ten years before, there were 972 females to 1,000 males. Across the nation there's a distinct lack of girls aged twelve or below.

During a meeting in one reputable clinic, in the southern city of Chennai, the telephone rings. On the line is a pregnant woman who wants to know if she's carrying a son. The doctor shakes his head wearily, and replies:

'Why do you want to know? Why? This is God's greatest surprise to you, why do you want to kill that joy?!'

One state in southern India, Tamil Nadu, openly acknowledges that female foeticide is a major problem. In October last year, the state government launched a 'cradle scheme'. Now, every state hospital or clinic has to provide a cradle – often just a cardboard box – outside its doors, twenty-four hours a day, so women can anonymously leave their unwanted daughters. These girls are sent to the main hospitals for medical check-ups before being sent to orphanages. Later, the fortunate ones are adopted. Although not providing a solution, this system at least gives the girls a chance to live a life that's otherwise denied to them.

Goldeneye

In a sprawling apartment block, a stone's throw from Oxford Street, half a dozen well-dressed Arab men are crammed into a tiny office.

Mobile phones pressed tight to their cheeks, they are all calling out numbers, frenetically bidding in auctions around the world. Stacked all over the desks, the floor, and the shelves, are hundreds of auction catalogues. From this office one of the men peers nervously towards a spacious sitting-room decorated with indigo silk curtains, exquisite red leather chairs, and dotted with simple pieces of modern art.

One wall is covered with bookshelves; another is taken up with three large glass tanks, each containing brightly coloured Amazonian poison-arrow frogs. Every few minutes the door swings open and a courier staggers in with crates of fine art. In the hallway a dealer waits patiently to show off his wares. In the background there's the constant buzz of telephones ringing, and feet hurrying across the polished parquet.

Watching the frenzy of activity from the far corner of this room, swishing a set of tiger's eye worry beads, is Sheikh Saud bin Mohammed bin Ali Al-Thani. At thirty-seven, he has already overwhelmed the art world with his astonishing buying power.

He is in a restless mood.

One of his team is bidding for an important piece of Islamic glasswork. The price is going up and up. The sheikh swishes in anticipation. He crosses the room and peers into one of the tanks at the turquoise frogs, but his mind is on the sale. Just as the tension becomes almost too much, the aide puts down his mobile phone. He nods to his master.

Success.

Five years ago Sheikh Saud slipped quietly on to the international art scene and began to buy. It takes a great deal to stir the restrained world of fine art and no one took much notice of the softly spoken collector – not at first, anyway.

But auctioneers and dealers have realized that this buyer is different. His pockets are very deep indeed. With unprecedented zeal he has bought and bought: Mughal treasures and Islamic art, royal French furniture and vintage cars, statues, leather-bound libraries, even dinosaur skeletons. But what the dealers have also seen is that the mysterious Arab, widely regarded as the biggest buyer of fine art in modern times, has more than money. He has an eye for artistic excellence, and he has vision.

The sheikh has attained near legendary status as a collector, for the quantity of high-quality art he has procured on behalf of his country, Qatar. His buying power is so great that many established foundations and private collectors have been driven off. They just can't compete.

Dealers all tell the same tale: if Sheikh Saud wants something, he will buy it, irrespective of the price.

At some auctions he has been known to acquire almost everything. Yet, remarkably for such a dominant force in the art world, Saud remains an enigma. Almost nothing has been written about him as little is known. Until now, he has never given an interview.

Born into the ruling family of Qatar, the tiny oil-rich peninsula in the Persian Gulf, he is first cousin to the country's Emir, Sheikh Hamad bin Khalifa Al-Thani. Educated in Doha, the capital of Qatar, where he is based with his wife and their three young children, Saud never studied antiquities or art. He's self-taught.

Only now is the extent of the dream that lies behind his buying spree becoming clear. Backed by the Emir himself, he plans to put the fabulously wealthy nation of Qatar firmly on the cultural map, with the capital becoming the chief artistic and architectural centre for the Persian Gulf.

Sheikh Saud is in charge of building half a dozen museums and a national library, as well as a new residence for himself. Once they are finished, he is going to fill them all with treasures. Many of the world's foremost architects and artists are already involved.

The architect I. M. Pei has been commissioned to design the National Museum of Islamic Art; Santiago Calatrava (who built the Dallas/Fort Worth International Airport) is planning a photographic museum; and Arata Isozaki is working on the National Library of Qatar, as well as the sheikh's private villa. This will have a sculpture garden, with major pieces by Richard Serra, Jeff Koons and Eduardo Chillida (the veteran Spanish sculptor has produced his largest piece ever, which will stand seven metres high and weigh more than a hundred tons). David Hockney is said to be in discussions over designs for the swimming pool.

Qatar is lodged between the ancient traditions of the nomadic Bedouin people and the trappings of the modern world. The population of about three hundred thousand Qatari Arabs is easily outnumbered by migrant workers, largely from India and Pakistan. Islam is the bedrock of the society. Alcohol is forbidden, and most of the Arab women choose to wear the veil. In this tiny country, the size of an English county, crime is virtually unknown, the skies are crystal clear, and there's almost no income tax to pay.

Until oil was discovered in the 1930s Qatar was a quiet, impecunious Emirate, famous for its pearls, tribal handicrafts and Arab hospitality. The peninsula has been ruled since the mid-1800s by the Al-Thani family. It formed part of the Ottoman Empire and became a British protectorate before gaining full independence in 1971. The reigning Emir overthrew his father in a bloodless coup in 1995, and has recently launched a major industrial modernization drive. The new commercial agenda has been accompanied by considerable cultural growth. Much of the money Sheikh Saud spends, is on behalf of the Qatari government.

The morning after my arrival in Doha, a sleek black Mercedes pulls up at my hotel and whisks me down avenues lined with whitewashed date palms. We drive due west from the capital. The city's skyscrapers and luxurious villas die away as we enter the pancake-flat expanse of desert. The only road signs warn of wandering camels. After thirty minutes we veer off the highway and are soon poised outside a high wall.

As if by magic, the steel gates slide open electronically.

We have arrived at Al Wabra, Sheikh Saud's desert retreat. It is here that he holds court, plans projects and enjoys some of the treasures he has bought. A flock of pink flamingos and grey pelicans preen themselves on the manicured lawns. Peacocks can be heard screeching in the distance. Sprinklers are working overtime to ensure the grass is kept alive in the scorching desert climate. Behind the pelicans stands a gleaming white building.

An aide runs up and ushers me in.

The audience hall is lit by three crystal chandeliers, its walls hung with Islamic textiles, and the floor covered by oriental rugs. At the far end of the hall, a slim man in Arab dress is hunched forward, his fingertips pressed together in thought. It's Sheikh Saud. His features are prominent, piercing eyes radiating a calm confidence. A wisp of moustache hides his upper lip, mirrored by a hint of beard on his chin. *Kafir* and *agal*, the traditional headdress of Qatar, obscure his hair, and a finely woven white cotton robe runs down to his sandals, its French cuffs pinned neatly with small diamonds. The sheikh rises to greet me, welcoming me with a smile to his country and his home.

Miniature glasses of sweet tea are brought, and I enter the mysterious world of Sheikh Saud Al-Thani. At his feet a dozen catalogues from international auction houses are scattered, their pages marked thickly with yellow Post-it notes. Each is a sale of the superlative: 'Important' furniture, 'Fine' jewellery, 'Exceptional' carpets, 'Rare' clocks. There are loose colour photographs of valuable objects as well, offered by dealers from around the world.

The collections he has put together encompass many quite different and wide-ranging areas. Although each is important in its own right, the Islamic collection stands out as the most remarkable – virtually unequalled in terms of quality. Even so, it's just one of several diverse collections.

The sheikh has assembled a comprehensive assortment of antique photographic equipment as well, and an astounding collection of photographs. The natural history collection comprises rare fossils, dinosaur skeletons, minerals and taxidermy; and the military collection boasts early cannons, muskets, armour and Napoleonic uniforms. The furniture covers a wide range of eras and styles, including Louis XV and Baroque, Regency and Art Deco. As well as the main collections, there are textiles, wrist-watches and woodworking tools, jewellery, glassware, statues and sculpture.

The sheikh leafs through auction catalogues and piles of

photographs as he talks, sometimes stopping in mid-sentence to stare sharply at the picture of a particular object. An assistant in orange overalls staggers in under the weight of a wooden crate. He prises off the lid and removes its contents, a piece at a time. The first object is a narrow black leather shoe.

'Look at this,' says Sheikh Saud enthusiastically. 'It was worn by Napoleon III. Can you see his monogram and the eagle crest on the sole? I bought the pair from one of his descendents living in Switzerland.'

Half a dozen more wooden crates are ferried into the meeting room. The sheikh's latest acquisitions are unpacked and presented. There are early botanical illustrations, dervish hats and headdresses, an assortment of Leica cameras and glass mosque lamps, aspidistra stands, Ottoman textiles, fossils and uniforms, sporting trophies and dozens of antiquarian books.

'Money isn't everything,' he says, sipping his tea. 'The problem is getting extraordinary pieces: you see, the greatest objects are already in museums. And museums or entire collections rarely come up for sale.'

This may be true, but Saud has sometimes managed to use his position in the market to buy entire collections. His photography collection, for example, has been built by acquiring two extremely important groups. The first, the Bokelberg Collection, was amassed over more than twenty years by one man, the German Werner Bokelberg. The collection is not large – no more than about 150 images – but it is improbable that there is another that charts the history of photography so accurately, through such perfect and rare images. It includes the very best examples of Fox Talbot's work, as well as some of the finest prints by Man Ray. Among those is the famous 1920s image of Man Ray's mistress, Kiki de Montparnasse, with an African mask. The print, complete with Man Ray highlights, was the one originally made for *Vogue*.

Sheikh Saud added to the Bokelberg photographs by buying the key works from the Jammes photographic sale in 1999, which included a number of pioneering images by Gustave Le Gray, taken during the 1850s. The photographs are complemented by a dazzling array of rare cameras, many acquired from the Spira collection, itself regarded as one of the most comprehensive collections of photographic equipment in existence.

Photography, which Sheikh Saud so admires as an art form, may have been the inspiration behind his dream in the first place.

A few years ago he saw a photograph of an Indian prince taken by Man Ray. The prince, Rao Holkar, the former Maharaja of Indore, bore a striking resemblance to the sheikh.

An aesthete, and great collector in his own right, Holkar commissioned the German designer Eckart Muthesius in the 'thirties to build his new palace, and decorate it with Art Deco furniture and works of art. Some have suggested that the Maharaja's photograph started off the sheikh's quest for a complete artistic lifestyle.

While Holkar was photographed by Man Ray, Saud has sat for Henri Cartier-Bresson and Irving Penn, Richard Avedon, Helmut Newton, David Bailey and Bruce Weber.

Whenever he is in Qatar, Sheikh Saud spends the scorching afternoons on the desert estate listening intently as his assistants' report. Every detail of every project is cleared by him directly just as he selects each item to buy himself.

At the far end of the estate stands a pair of giant steel-sided warehouses, easily mistaken for grain silos or barns. But as you draw closer to the compound, you see the high wall, the razor wire, and the reinforced gate, which rolls back automatically as you approach.

Behind these walls another team of men in overalls is unpacking more wooden crates, hauling out statues and carved stone blocks. Some of the stones have already been reassembled, forming elaborate porticoes, marble fountains and an entire terrace replete with balustrades.

An Indian curator begins the tour of the treasures, kept in the cavernous, air-conditioned warehouses. Most objects still have their auction lot numbers attached. The curator points out the most unusual pieces. First there's a pair of immense eighteenth century globes by Coronelli, sitting on carved walnut bases. They stand more than fifteen feet tall and five feet wide. Beside them is a Louis XV gilt wood screen and next to that is an Italian Baroque-style throne, painted gold.

We walk on past an Italian crib carved in the shape of a gondola, a clutch of mammoth tusks, a long narwhal's tusk and skull, and a shoal of prehistoric fish. Next come petrified tree trunks from the Upper

Triassic period, a complete triceratops dinosaur skeleton (labelled 'Willy'), dozens of insects trapped in amber, and 'an extremely rare nest of raptor eggs'.

We push ahead through a maze of bookshelves filled with oversized leather-bound volumes, all in mint condition. Sheikh Saud has a great interest in the large folio of works of natural history produced in the late eighteenth and early nineteenth centuries. He has assembled a complete set of John Gould's works on ornithology. Numbering more than forty volumes, they include some three thousand hand-painted lithographic plates. Saud has also acquired the Marquis of Bute's copy of Audobon's *Birds of America*, described as 'a monumental masterwork'; as well as his personal favourite, *Les Roses*, the late eighteenth-century volume of floral prints by Pierre-Joseph Redoute.

We carry on, past marble benches and more fountains, carved alabaster panels from Mughal India and a set of massive wrought-iron gates with matching urns. And on again, past a giant silver birdcage, dozens of muskets, pouches of mammoth fur and a fossilized walrus skull found in a cave in Alaska.

Then we cross the courtyard into the second hangar-like warehouse. Inside it is a whole variety of different forms of transport. There is a magnificent Louis XV carriage with original lacquered paintings on the exterior panels, numerous three-wheel Messerschmitt cars, as well as E-type Jaguars, a Jaguar racing car and a 1911 Rolls-Royce Silver Ghost. The warehouse is packed with bicycles, too, including some of the rarest ever made: such as the 'Hobby Horse', a bike with a solid wood frame from 1820, and a four-seater model from about 1910.

Sheikh Saud suddenly whooshes in on an early form of penny-farthing, his robes billowing out behind.

'I will show you some of the animals,' he calls, cycling over to a chauffeured Mercedes.

He enjoys his antiques, but you get the feeling his real passion lies with the thousands of rare and exotic creatures which live on the desert estate.

The Mercedes limousine crawls out of the warehouse courtyard and on to one of the tree-lined paths. The driver is cautious: if he goes too fast the sheikh's tumbler of iced Pepsi might spill on to the cream suede seats.

Even though he may be a man of few words, you can always sense Saud watching everything. He watches the peacocks as they scurry into the shade, and the migrating hoopoes in the alfalfa grass, the pens of long-horned gazelle from the Hindu Kush, and the cheetahs pacing in their pens. He watches the birds of paradise, too, and the Peruvian cocks-of-the-rock in their air-conditioned cages. He pauses to ask the team of German zoologists a few technical questions. As with his other collections, the sheikh likes to be well briefed. He can name many of the estate's 1,700 species by their Latin names, and is a recognized authority on the gazelle: Al Wabra has about twelve hundred species of them alone.

'We are keeping the genetic species apart as much as possible to avoid mixed breeding,' he explains as the car rolls ahead at walking pace.

'Soon we'll start building a modern animal hospital here, complete with operating theatre and quarantine unit. Our target is to play a part in taking rare animals off the endangered list.'

There is a staff of more than twenty looking after the animals, the bulk of the feed is shipped in from Germany every few months, and the zoologists here share their research with San Diego Zoo and other major animal centres worldwide.

We roll on past a colossal flight cage for cockatoos which, when finished, will have a computerized watering system. Next stop is a series of large conservatories where the Sheikh is nurturing dozens of species of rare palm trees.

Far from the trees and rare animals of Al Wabra, Sheikh Saud's most important project is gathering pace. The jewel in Qatar's cultural crown will be the Emirate's new Museum of Islamic Art. When he was initially approached to design the complex, I. M. Pei declined, explaining that he had retired. But Sheikh Saud who had been greatly impressed by his Miho Museum in Kyoto, decided he would do all he could to talk Pei into accepting the commission. What finally convinced Pei was when the Sheikh showed him some of treasures to be kept in the museum.

Before Pei began the designs, he spent months studying the region's culture and its own Gulf architecture. The result is a unique blend of traditional and contemporary styles, which will be set out in the water and overlooking Doha's corniche. The museum will house some of the world's most important objects of Islamic culture.

The collection was founded with a rare bronze fountainhead in the form of a hind, crafted in tenth century Cordoba. The piece, described by dealers as 'massively important' established Sheikh Saud and Qatar as key players on the world art scene. All the major areas of Islamic art are represented in the collection, which contains treasures such as the fourteenth century glass Cavour Vase. Once owned by Count Cavour and Queen Margaret of Italy, it is considered to be the best piece of Mameluk enameled glass known. The ceramics include a spectacular tenth century epigraphic dish from Nishapur (in what is now Iran), inscribed with a proverb in Kufic script.

Among the scientific instruments, there is one of the two most important astrolabes in existence, dating from tenth century Baghdad. There are early illustrated Islamic texts, too, such as the *Book of the Fixed Stars*, by Abd al-Rahman al-Sufi, one of the eminent Arab astronomers of the early Islamic era. The armoury has the yataghan of Sultan Bayazid II (the earliest Imperial Ottoman sword of its kind), which is regarded as one of the greatest pieces of Islamic weaponry in existence. The metalwork collection boasts a unique pair of door knockers with interlacing arabesques, from a thirteenth century Iraqi mosque; and among the Mughal treasures there's a rare jade *huqqa* (water pipe) base, set with rubies, gold and lapis lazuli, once owned by Emperor Quinlong of China. When asked if he has enough pieces for the Museum of Islamic Art, Saud replies with characteristic tenacity,

'We are not filling the shelves of a supermarket,' he says. 'A single outstanding object would be enough.'

The tradition of the museum will be balanced by the modern style of the Sheikh's new villa. Before commissioning Arata Isozaki the distinguished Japanese architect, to design the building, Saud took him to India to see the great monuments such as the Taj Mahal and Fatehpur Sikri.

Isozaki is responsible for building the Museum of Contemporary Art in Los Angeles, the Disney Building in Lake Buena Vista, Florida, and the New Tokyo City Hall. After discussing the way the Mughal architects used empty spaces within buildings, they used similar techniques as they collaborated on the design for the villa. The residence will exhibit work by prominent artists such as Ellsworth Kelly, Antoni Tapies and Anish Kapoor. The bathrooms are being designed by Philippe Starck, and Saud has commissioned architect Santiago Calatrava to design a special set of cutlery for the house.

Spend a little time in Sheikh Saud's company and you wonder what drives him. Some say members of his family die young, that the source for his restlessness is a desire to fulfill his dreams while there's still time. As those who know him confirm, he's not interested in the price he has paid for a work of art itself. Whatever fires him, Saud is a collector on a grand, Victorian scale. He has grown up with great wealth, but seems not to be obsessed by money. Some of his offices and private apartments are decidedly modest.

In any other country, Saud's buying potential would probably make him far more conspicuous, but Qatar is a land where vast personal wealth is not rare. Many young Qataris are preoccupied by the latest mobile phones, foreign sports cars and drive-in fast food restaurants. They relish a lifestyle that their nomadic ancestors would have found bewildering. Most of Sheikh Saud's peers seem perplexed by his collecting. They don't understand what he is doing. When the subject is raised the young Sheikh answers,

'We are trying to create collections that will last and will add to the heritage of Qatar. What we are doing here may not be understood for generations to come.'

Sokha Tun holding a defused PNM-2 landmine, used in training

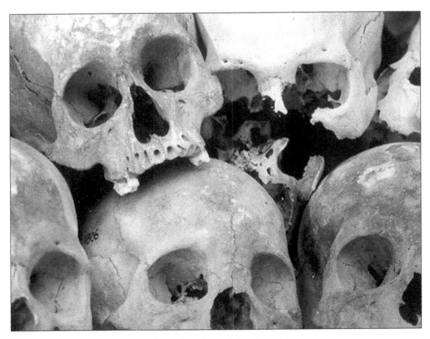

Victims of the Khmer Rouge rule in Cambodia's Killing Fields

In Cambodia's New Killing Fields

LYING ON HER STOMACH with her legs spread far apart, Sokha Tun gently probes the clump of tall grass before her, using the blade of a bayonet.

With a fixed stare of concentration, as beads of sweat run down her face, Sokha cuts the grass away a stalk at a time. Clothed in a navy blue Kevlar bullet-proof vest, with a steel helmet protecting her head, she takes a long, deep breath in the suffocating humidity. Then, wiping the perspiration from her right hand, she pauses for a moment. At the base of the tuft of grass, six inches from her visor, sits a green plastic disc – no larger than a hockey puck.

The disc, a 72B type Chinese-made landmine, designed to maim rather than to kill, will explode if tilted through more than ten degrees. Sokha cautiously checks for booby-traps wired into the base of the mine. One careless movement, and her arms will be blown clean off.

Widowed four years ago, when her husband stepped on a landmine in the fields nearby, Sokha lives with her mother and three young children in Battambang Province, western Cambodia. With her husband dead, Sokha and her family had faced starvation. The choices for the region's thousands of widows are stark: sell vegetables in the market, resort to begging, or turn to prostitution.

But eight months ago, as the future looked increasingly hopeless, Sokha got a job with a British-based organization. Now, together with a small team of other women, she clears landmines for a living.

This time last year, she was barefoot, dressed in rags, and had no home. With her children huddled around her, she slept in a doorway. But a year on, and her life has changed for the better. Sokha now makes $160 a month – an enormous wage, when compared with other local salaries in rural Cambodia.

Sokha, who has rented a large house in an affluent part of Battambang, can suddenly afford to ride to work on her new Honda motorcycle. She and her children are dressed in clean new clothes and, next month, she plans to buy the ultimate status symbol – a colour TV.

Once regarded as among the most fertile farmland in the Far East, Cambodia's rural areas became known as the 'Rice Bowl of Asia'. But two decades of conflict have left the nation's fields, forests and hillsides, desperate and depleted of vegetation. The war with the Khmer Rouge may be over, but the enemy is still there, invisible and ever-present. For the people living in Cambodia's countryside, simple daily tasks – fetching water and firewood, or planting rice – constantly expose them to the hidden foe which awaits them in the tall grass.

The British-based Mines Advisory Group (MAG) first came to Cambodia four years ago. After isolating the most afflicted areas, the charity began training teams of local people to clear landmines. Their three-month course offers a grounding in detecting and destroying all twenty-eight types of landmines commonly found in Cambodia.

From the outset, MAG was eager to employ people whom had been directly affected by mines. They created a team of amputee de-miners, all of whom had lost limbs to landmines. And, in a society where a woman's place is more usually in the home, they established the first all-female mine clearance unit in the world.

The twenty-six women in the team are widows, their husbands all slain by landmines. Aged between twenty and thirty-five years, the women are playing a frontline role in tackling Cambodia's overwhelming landmine problem. Accurate statistics are vague, but there's at least one mine for every man, woman and child in the country. Each day, more than ten Cambodians lose one or more limbs when they tread on a mine; and every year hundreds of children are killed. Clearing the estimated ten million mines, a process which may take generations, is a necessity if any kind of development or normal life is to be achieved.

Chris Horwood, director of MAG's project in Cambodia, oversaw the establishing of the first all-female de-mining team.

'We thought there would be enormous pressure against the idea from the local community,' he says, 'we expected that, by sending young women out into an active minefield, we would be harshly condemned. But the project has been a massive success. So much so that we're just about to hire another thirty women de-miners. And, from now on, we're planning to actively recruit amputee women to clear mines. The mine clearance instructors continually report how studious and careful the women are – far more so, it seems, than the men.'

The struggle to clear landmines from rural Cambodia is likely to be longest war the country will ever face and, until the mines have been destroyed, Cambodia hangs in a state of limbo.

'People can't get to their fields, to their water sources, or to their schools,' says Horwood, 'while major roads, temples, and areas of housing, lie abandoned for fear of hidden explosives. Landmines, have almost single-handedly brought Cambodia to a standstill. It's hard to imagine a more toxic form of pollution. Mines are "poverty creating": once you're in the poverty cycle, you're forced to carry out highly hazardous risk-taking activities to break out of that cycle. So, although you know there are mines in the forest, you have to cut wood there – or else you starve.'

Like other humanitarian groups working to clear the world's hundred million landmines, MAG practices what they call 'humanitarian mine clearance'. Quite different from military de-mining (which recognizes that casualties are an inevitability of war) the humanitarian approach strives for a hundred per cent clearance with no civilian casualties.

'Military de-mining', Horwood continues, 'is only ever conducted to create a path through a minefield to get to the enemy. Fatalities are expected. But, our units have to ensure that each mine, every fragment of metal, is cleared from the ground – whether it be on a hillside, in woodland, or in rice fields. Conventions of war do state that minefields must be mapped – but, in Cambodia, such maps are unreliable or entirely non-existent.'

The women clearing mines near Battambang – Cambodia's second largest town – perform their de-mining work as well as attending to their endless household chores. Until recently, women in rural communities would tend to the family and raise the children, rarely holding down anything more than the most menial paid jobs. But the huge loss of male workers has led to rapid change. For the first time, Sokha Tun, and other young women like her, are finding themselves at the head of their extended families. As the sole breadwinners, they are winning new respect, and are gaining unprecedented levels of emancipation.

When Sokha first saw the advertisement for women to become de-miners pasted to a wall, she quickly walked away.

'My husband was killed by a landmine,' she says sombrely, 'so I didn't want to have anything to do with explosives. But we were very poor, and my children were going hungry. I would sell fruit at the market. On some days I made as much as 1500 riels (25 pence). Without my husband life was very hard. When my family heard that I was thinking of clearing landmines, they said it was very dangerous, and they tried to discourage me. But I thought very hard about it. We all know so many people here who have been killed or wounded by mines. I wanted to help rid Cambodia of this curse – so that my children could play in the fields.'

Sokha applied, was accepted into MAG's first six-woman team, and was sent to Phnom Penn for a month for training.

'It was so exciting,' she whispers, 'I had never left Battambang before. We were trained at the Cambodian Mine Action Centre and were taught about all types of explosives. There are many different types of landmines in Cambodia – made in the former USSR, Vietnam and China, as well as Czechoslovakia, Belgium, and even America. We had to learn about the problems that each kind of mine poses, and about booby-traps.'

The second stage of training took place beside a live minefield, in Battambang Province itself. It's there that the women practiced using high-tech metal detecting equipment.

'When I started the training course,' says Sokha, I met Sophia Sien. She became my partner, and we're now best friends. Working in a minefield teaches you to trust, and rely on your partner totally: we've become closer than sisters.'

Landmine clearance teams are subject to a series of rigid, unyielding rules designed to minimize risk, and to keep members alive. Danger is ever-present and can strike with the smallest lapse of concentration. When preparing to clear a new tract of ground, the team – which is always split into pairs – cordon off a 'safe lane'. The lane, one metre wide, is cleared first. It is via this corridor that the de-miners enter the minefield.

Each morning, before setting out into the cordoned zone, the de-mining teams are given a briefing by their supervisors. They're continually cautioned about safety, and warned about ground conditions: the level of moisture in the soil alters the sensitivity of the metal detector. After the briefing, the teams assemble their detecting equipment. Austrian-made Schiebel AN-1912 detectors are used, selected for their simplicity and general ruggedness. The units can detect metal down to fifteen centimetres, depending on the type of ground and the conditions. The morning ritual of testing the metal detectors is conducted with great care. A plastic testing block containing just seven millimetres of metal is used to check that all the detectors are in prime working order.

When working in the minefield, the de-miners scan the ground an inch at a time. They are trained to watch out for the latest generation of blast-mine, for some of the world's most lethal, yet undetectable landmines lie in Cambodia's new killing fields. The modern breed of minimum metallic mines can contain no more metal than the tiny ball at the tip of a Bic biro.

Sokha and her partner Sophia, take it in turns to enter the minefield. Sophia goes in first, holding the detector at arm's length ahead of her. As she sweeps the circular twelve-inch head of the unit slowly across the ground, she listens out for the detector's piercing screech. No sound is overlooked. It may be a harmless bottle top, but is just as likely to be a POMZ fragmentation mine – powerful enough to tear her body apart. When a metallic object has been isolated, Sokha puts on her RBR Kevlar jacket, and helmet. A bayonet in one hand, and a pair of gardener's secateurs in the other, she approaches the suspect device.

The threat of distraction is a constant worry for Russell Bedford, MAG's director at Battambang. Like the other ex-British army instructors working in Cambodia, Bedford has seen casualties arise from momentary lapses in concentration.

'There's always the danger that a de-miner will lose an arm, a leg or, will be killed,' he says, 'if he or she stops concentrating. We supervise the teams closely and have regular rest breaks. It's important to switch round jobs often, if you want to keep concentration levels at a peak.'

And, when a mine is located, no risks are taken.

'We never remove mines from the ground,' says Bedford, 'we always destroy them in situ. What's the point of putting someone's life on the line to disarm an explosive device? Worse still is the possibility of a disarmed mine being re-armed and laid again. There's always the chance that the landmine is booby-trapped. Small mines can be linked to a much larger explosive charge – like an anti-tank mine. Remove an anti-personnel mine and you could trigger the anti-tank mine: so increasing the danger radius, and widening the killing zone.'

Freeing Cambodia from the scourge of landmines is an unrelenting, pitifully slow, and expensive task. A team of thirty de-miners can take a month, or longer, to clear a single acre of land. The cost to seek and destroy each landmine is put at between $250 and $1000. Ironically, mass production of anti-personnel mines make them one of the cheapest and most effective military tools available.

Although they often kill children, landmines tend to injure adults rather than kill them, burdening an army on the move. Wounded soldiers need transport and medical attention, and the constant fear of mines lowers overall morale. A 72A type mine is thought to cost less than two dollars to manufacture and lay. But, for Russell Bedford and the other supervisors, the speed and cost of de-mining is irrelevant.

'We're returning land to the community, so it can be used for housing and be farmed,' he says, 'so that it doesn't lie as a permanent killing ground. So what if it takes a month to clear a square metre? At least that one square metre is positively a hundred per cent clear – it's far better than clearing ten thousand square metres to ninety per cent safety levels!'

A shift clearing mines in western Cambodia is one of seven strenuous hours in asphyxiating tropical heat. But, for Sokha, Sophia, and the other widows who work for MAG, the day starts long before they arrive at the minefield. Sokha's day begins at 4.20 a.m. with the sound of her Chinese-made alarm clock ringing in the darkness. After washing with a bucket of cold water, she puts on the pair of light green army fatigues and matching green jacket. Then, having stoked the fire, she cooks a small meal of rice and fish. Her children, fast asleep under a billowing mosquito net – a great luxury in Cambodia – are reluctant to get up.

'They're very lazy in the morning,' Sokha grins, 'they don't like getting ready for school. When they're older, I will tell them about my work in the minefields. At the moment, they are still too young to understand.'

At six a.m., Sophia arrives at Sokha's large, thatched house, which is built on stilts. In a country where women are rarely seen riding a motorcycle, Sokha's brand new Honda is an impressive status symbol.

Each morning, she and Sophia make the hour-long ride together, out through some of Cambodia's most magnificent scenery to the minefield. When the de-mining shift is over, and all the equipment is dissembled, the couple rides back to Battambang together. Sokha's afternoon is filled with chores as well. She shops for groceries at the market; washes her uniform and her children's clothes; cooks an evening meal; cleans the motorcycle; supervises her eldest daughter's homework; and studies English, before going to bed, at midnight.

Most evenings, Sophia's two daughters come to play at Sokha's house. The two women have become inseparable. As widows, it's unlikely that they will ever get married again. Not because they don't want to, but because teenage brides are generally preferred.

'If anything ever happened to Sokha in the minefield,' Sophia says tenderly, 'I would be devastated. We try not to think of accidents, but of course we know that the danger of triggering a mine is always there. Nothing matters to us more than clearing Cambodia of the mines. It hurts me to forbid my children from playing out in the fields. How can they understand what a PNM-2 blast-mine is capable of doing to them?'

Sophia is angry at the Khmer Rouge for laying the mines so densely. But she apportions equal blame to the companies that manufacture anti-personnel mines.

'Dozens of countries are getting rich by developing new and more terrible kinds of landmine,' she says, as she loosens the laces of her hobnailed boot, 'sitting in their offices in England or China, the arms' makers haven't seen what their weapons are doing! They're maiming our children and killing innocent people.'

Leng works in the same unit as Sokha and Sophia. When her husband was killed by an anti-personnel mine while searching for firewood, she thought she and her baby daughter would starve to death.

'There's almost no work for a widow in Battambang,' she says despondently, 'times are very hard, and women are generally thought to be too stupid to do a technical job. People used to say that I was *just* a woman, so I ought to sell bananas in the market.'

Leng now makes more money than almost anyone else in her community.

'I support my family, and take care of my parents, who are very old,' she says. 'They rely on me totally. My salary pays for our rent, for our food, clothes and firewood. My parents worry continually for my safety, but I worry about getting sick myself – that would mean I'd be unable to work. Losing my job would effect us all.'

Leng's partner in the minefield, is Sabun. Taking turns in sweeping with the detector, and prodding for booby-traps, they have a lot of time to mull over the life-threatening nature of their work.

'When I get up and leave for work,' says Sabun gingerly, 'it's still very early and my three children are still asleep. I look at them each morning all curled up together and, before I close the door behind me, I realize that I may never come home that evening.'

Surprising the widowed de-miners of MAG's female unit is no easy task. Each of them has become an expert on the main types of landmine and unexploded ordinance. They can tell the difference between a Chinese 72A & a 72B type anti-personnel mine (the former is virtually undetectable, while the latter is fitted with a distinctive tilt-switch mechanism). They know the dangers of a Soviet-made PNM-2 model (which tends to lead to an above-the-knee amputation). And, they're wary of anything unusual in the field: a cigarette packet, a discarded tin can, or a child's toy may be a booby-trap. They know too that, if they survive, theirs is a profession with considerable longevity.

Cambodia is a country where one of the most booming industries makes artificial prosthetic limbs. The country claims the prize for having the largest minefield on Earth. Stretching for six hundred kilometres along the south-western coast and up the Thai border toward Laos, the *Kor Bram*, or K5 Barrier Belt, is said to contain no fewer than three million anti-personnel mines. With the technology for detecting mines about twenty-five years behind the technology which is creating them, Cambodia's new killing fields are set to kill and maim many, many more innocent civilians.

Although the NATO, the UN, and even NASA, are said to be developing anti-landmine equipment, the results so far have been unimpressive. Mine clearance devices may look fine on paper, but they rarely take into account the varying types of minefield encountered. There is no quick, cheap way of destroying mines. It's not as easy as setting fire to a mined area. A partially burned, or 'deflagrated' mine, is extremely dangerous, as is any ordinance that's been left exposed to the elements for years on end.

Amazingly, it seems that only now we are discovering what a long term problem landmines can be. Areas of the Libyan Desert in North Africa are still heavily mined from World War II. In Flanders, there are tracts of land still sealed off because of unexploded ordinance, a legacy of the First World War. And, in Laos, BLU 3/B fragmentation mines, scattered from aircraft by American forces over forty years ago, are still very much alive.

As MAG, Greenpeace, and the United Nations, call for a moratorium on the production of landmines, two million new anti-personnel mines continue to be deployed each year, with many more millions being produced and stockpiled.

'The situation we have right now is absurd,' says Paul Davies, author of *War of the Mines*. 'Landmines don't recognize cease-fires: so when the heavy weapons of war have been carted off, they remain in the ground, praying on innocent civilians for decades to come. And, with each new generation of landmine far superior to the last, the future for Cambodia and other countries like it, is set to be a turbulent one.'

Far from the wrangling of diplomats at the UN and from the high-level talk of moratoria, the female de-mining unit near Battambang continues with its work. As a detonation charge is attached to Sokha's most recent find – the 72B anti-personnel mine, the women rest in the shade of a sprawling apple tree.

'This was once a beautiful orchard,' declares Sokha, 'but for twenty years the apples have rotted. No one has dared to pick them. Now that the area is almost cleared, a new village will be built here. There will be houses, a new temple, a school and a market. But best of all,' says Sokha softly, casting an eye across the minefield, 'children will play in this orchard safely once again.'

Frank Hayter, who claimed to have located King Solomon's Mines

In Search of King Solomon's Mines

AN INKY HAND-DRAWN MAP was hanging on the back wall of Ali Baba's tourist shop, deep in the maze of Jerusalem's Old City.

Little more than a sketch, and smudged by a clumsy hand, the map showed a river and mountains, a desert, a cave, and what looked like a trail between them. At the end of the trail was an oversized 'X'.

'Is it a treasure map?' I asked.

Ali Baba, an old man with a pot-belly, glanced up from his newspaper.

'It shows the way to the fabled gold mines of Suleiman,' he said.

After an hour of negotiation, I slid a wad of Israeli shekels across the counter and left with the map. Anyone else may have scoffed at the object, or laughed at my gullibility. After all, Jerusalem's Old City is cluttered with Holy Land bric-à-brac. I had a feeling from the start that Ali Baba's map was suspect, for it had no place names or co-ordinates.

But to me it symbolized a family obsession.

In the 1920s my grandfather, Sirdar Ikbal Ali Shah, an Afghan traveller and scholar, searched for King Solomon's mines in southern Arabia. He felt certain that Solomon had acquired his gold in what is now Yemen. He was forced to cut his expedition short after being accused of spying. Thirty years later, my father carried on the search, scouring the Red Sea coast of Sudan. He found no gold either, but did come across a great labyrinth of what appeared to be ancient mine shafts.

Not long before his death, my father cautioned me not to continue the search, declaring it to be a waste of time and money. I had never given much thought to carrying on the family tradition, but Ali Baba's map changed all that.

I spent almost two years researching the mines, turning to texts like the Septuagint, the oldest known version of the Old Testament. It describes the magnificent temple that Solomon constructed in Jerusalem, near to where the Dome of the Rock now stands. The building's interior was overlaid with the purest gold, supposedly brought from the mysterious land of Ophir.

The Bible suggests that Ophir was a source of exotic merchandise, brimming with peacocks and apes, frankincense, ivory, silver and gold.

I realized that if I were to have a hope of discovering the source of Solomon's wealth, I needed to find Ophir, a land searched for by scholars and adventurers for almost three millennia.

Ptolemy said it lay near the Straits of Malacca (off the Malaysia peninsula); Christopher Columbus was sure he had found it in modern-day Haiti; while Sir Walter Raleigh thought it was hidden in the jungles of Suriname. Others have said it was in India or Madagascar, China or even in Peru.

Eventually, in the 1880s, amid the gold and diamond bonanza in southern Africa and the discovery of the 'Great Zimbabwe' ruins, the Victorians felt that they had at last solved the mystery. The young writer Henry Rider Haggard capitalized on the hysteria, and his rattling novel King Solomon's Mines first appeared in 1885.

As my research progressed, I became sure that Ptolemy, Columbus, Raleigh and Rider Haggard – not to mention my own father and grandfather – had all been looking in the wrong place.

They should have been searching in Ethiopia.

We know that the Israelites gained their knowledge of mining and working gold from the Egyptians, during their slavery under the Pharaohs. We know, too, that the Egyptians mined their gold in Nubia, near Ethiopia's western border (*nub* meant gold in ancient Egyptian).

The imperial family of Ethiopia claims descent from the child born to King Solomon and the Queen of Sheba. But, most significant of all, Ethiopia has an abundance of pure gold which – unlike in other parts of Africa – is close to the surface and can easily be mined.

So I packed a Bible, some old clothes, hiking boots, and Ali Baba's map. Then I bought myself a Gold Bug metal detector, and a cut-price ticket to Addis Ababa.

As the plane landed at the Ethiopian capital, I was overcome with fear. I sensed my father and grandfather peering down at me, shaking their heads in disappointment.

When I was sitting comfortably at home in London, it was easy to talk about searching for King Solomon's mines. But the task at hand was impossibly difficult: a foreigner travelling in Ethiopia with a metal detector and gold-mining manuals is immediately suspected of being a spy. I had to keep the real reasons for my journey a secret.

Then I met a young taxi driver called Samson.

It turned out that he had worked as a miner in the illegal gold mines of southern Ethiopia. He spoke several tribal languages, and had secretly studied the country's history during the oppressive Derge regime (1974 – 1991). Taking one look at Ali Baba's map, he cackled in laughter. It was complete rubbish, he said.

Impressed by his candidness, I hired him on the spot.

I had heard that an important manuscript was preserved at a monastery in the extreme north of the country. My informant said that the text – known as the Kebra Negast (meaning 'The Glory of Kings') – contains clues to the whereabouts of the mines. So we travelled northward, through the highlands and over the Simien Mountains, to a cliff face called Debra Damo.

The monastery, which is perched at the top of a precipice, is home to three hundred priests. No women or female creatures of any kind are permitted to ascend.

At the base of the cliff, we deliberated how we could scale it. As we stood there, gazing up, a plaited leather rope was lowered down. I wrapped it around my waist, tied it in a reef knot and, as if by magic, I was pulled upward.

An elderly monk led us through dark cloisters, thick with the smell of incense. Sweeping a scarlet cloth away from a lectern, he revealed a very large book: the Kebra Negast. Handwritten in Ge'ez, the ancient language of Ethiopia, it recounts in detail the story of Solomon and Sheba. The monk translated some of the text in a whisper. I asked him if it gave the exact location of Solomon's gold mines. He narrowed his eyes, and barked at Samson ferociously in Amharic.

'What's he saying?'

Samson replied: 'He says that the book does have the answers, but we're not to reveal them to foreigners like you, or else you'll steal all the gold for yourself!'

I pressed the monk with more questions about the gold, but Samson was growing nervous. He nudged me, insisting that we leave immediately. It was maddening, especially as I thought I was on to something with the ancient manuscript. Samson told me later that the monks at Debra Damo had a direct line to God. As far as he was concerned their wishes had to be respected.

We negotiated the cliff face once again, and beat a retreat.

Samson suggested we head to the south, where he'd mined gold for eight years. The journey took many days, taking us through some of the most dramatic landscape on the African continent. There were great expanses of farmland, endless forests, and rivers seething from heavy winter rain.

In the West, our impressions of Ethiopia have been moulded by television images of drought and starvation, yet much of the country is lush, and utterly breathtaking in its beauty. In a land where poverty is endemic, the illegal gold mines near the small town of Shakiso offer a chance of escape.

Nothing could have prepared me for the mines.

They were like a scene from a Hollywood epic of the Old Testament: hundreds of men, women and children drenched in mud, digging the ground, many with their bare hands. They had excavated a crater the size of a football pitch. At the bottom of the pit was alluvial silt, which Samson told me contained the gold dust. The silt was scooped onto rounded wooden pans and hurled to the surface in a relay.

The mine is one of many to have sprouted up in southern Ethiopia over the past fifty years. The alluvial seam probably wasn't worked in ancient times, as it would have been entirely depleted. But what was so interesting was that the mining techniques were almost identical to those devised five millennia ago by the Egyptians.

Solomon's slave labour mined tons of gold in the same way – using wooden trays, sluices and panning pools. The big difference was that the people I saw mining near Shakiso were not slaves. They were working for themselves.

Life is cheap there, especially for the fraternity of young miners, many of whom worked in tunnels, digging down to the seam. In the rainy season, when the ground is soft, fatalities are common. The tunnels collapse, burying brave men alive.

The risks may explain the miners' way of life. In the makeshift village adjacent to the pit they spend their money as fast as they earn it. All kinds of illicit services are available in the dark grass-roofed shacks – including gut-rot *araki*, gambling and prostitution.

I was impressed that Samson had broken free from such a destructive existence. One morning, he told me, he had glanced into a sliver of broken mirror and seen not himself, but the Devil.

He fled to Addis Ababa to begin a new life.

Although I'd hoped at first that these mines could be those once worked by Solomon, I realized there was little real chance of that. Yet, as we left the mines and continued westward following another lead, I was buoyed by having seen such ancient methods in action.

In the 1920s an eccentric Englishman called Frank Hayter claimed to have found a cave on a remote mountain near the border with Sudan. There, he said, he came upon a cache of gold and precious stones. He thought the find was somehow connected to King Solomon's mines.

In western Ethiopia we hired a herd of mules. They were savage, resented having to work, and bit anyone who got near them. They bucked, too, tossing both Samson and me to the ground.

We made the long trek to the mountain, through forests and stretches of deep mud, in search of Hayter's cave. It rained non-stop for a week. I kept the muleteers going with handfuls of monosodium glutamate powder.

We scoured the mountain for days, but the only cave we came to ended after a few feet in a natural stone wall. If the cave was indeed there it eluded us, yet I felt certain that we were close to where Solomon mined the gold for his temple.

By the time we finally reached the main road, morale was very low, made worse by mule bites and the constant downpour. Samson and I hitch-hiked towards the capital. We stopped for the night in the small town of Nejo and put up at the only hotel which wasn't a brothel.

Its Ethiopian owner, Berehane, overheard us talking of gold and Solomon's mines. It turned out that his grandfather was an Italian prospector called Antillo Zappa. I knew from my research that Zappa had been a friend of Frank Hayter, and had mined gold nearby.

Next morning Berehane led us out of the town and across open fields. There, on an exposed hillside, we came to a series of pits. They had evidently once been much larger, but had been filled in over the centuries by natural erosion. Berehane said that local people often found shards of pottery here, and that his grandfather believed the pits were ancient.

Given the location and abundance of pure gold in the area, I think there is a strong possibility that these pits once formed part of Solomon's mines. It is impossible to say for certain without mounting a full-scale archaeological dig, and to this end I have approached the British Museum and several biblical and archaeological foundations in the United States. If all else fails, it may eventually fall to my own children to raise the funds, and thus continue the family obsession with King Solomon's mines.

In the Scorpion Palace

THE EXTRAVAGANCE OF THE Nizams of Hyderabad needs no introduction.

Until losing power at India's Independence, their Princely State endured for two centuries, presiding over a huge chunk of the Deccan. A byword for profligacy and for spending on a truly lavish scale, the Nizams' dynasty rivalled large countries in terms of its wealth.

Of the seven Nizams, who governed Hyderabad State from 1720 until 1948, the richest of all was the last – Mir Osman Ali Khan. Regarded as the wealthiest man on Earth, his portrait graced the cover of Time Magazine and, as recently as 2008, he was rated fifth highest on the Forbes' 'All Time Wealthiest List' (Bill Gates ranked 20th).

He had his own mint, printing his own currency, the Hyderabadi rupee, and a vast private treasury. Its coffers were said to contain £100 million in gold and silver bullion, and a further £400 million worth of jewels. Among them, was the fabulously rare Jacob Diamond, valued some £60 million today, and used by the Nizam as a paperweight. There were pearls, too – enough to pave Piccadilly – hundreds of race horses, thousands of uniforms, tons of royal regalia, and Rolls Royces by the dozen.

But it was the Nizams' great love affair with palaces that cost more than anything else to maintain. They owned more than a handful in Hyderabad alone, staffed by many thousands of servants, retainers, bodyguards, eunuchs and concubines.

The favourite of all was the Falaknuma.

Set on a hillock with sweeping views across Hyderabad below, the Falaknuma Palace was laid out in the shape of a scorpion with a double stinging tail. Known as 'Mirror of the Sky', it was constructed in the classical style from Italian marble, with hints of Art Nouveau. No expense was spared to create it, a European masterpiece on the plains of central India.

The magnificent Falaknuma Palace, Hyderabad

The entrance hall of the Falaknuma

It was actually the Nizam's Prime Minister, Viqar ul Omra, who conceived the palace as a lavish residence for himself. The foundation stone was laid in 1884, but the building wasn't completed for almost another decade. In that time, the Prime Minister was forced to borrow increasing funds to finish it – money that even he had no chance of ever earning.

The story goes that to save face his wife suggested a wily plan. Inviting his master, Mehboob Ali Pasha, the sixth Nizam, to stay, the Prime Minister waited to be extolled for creating such a glorious pleasure dome. And, when the praise was lavished, Viqar ul Omra offered the building to the Nizam as a gift. Accepting graciously, the ruler reimbursed the full cost – a pittance to man of such colossal wealth. With so many homes already, he used it as a residence for his most distinguished guests.

The palace soon became a great favourite with royal visitors, among them King George V, Queen Mary, Edward VIII, Tsar Nicholas II, and a kaleidoscope of European aristocracy. It was for them an illusion of Europe in a principality whose affluence exceeded their wildest dreams. But, with the withdrawal of the privy purse, and the subsuming of Hyderabad into Independent India, the billionaire lifestyle came to an abrupt end.

The palaces were boarded up, their doors fastened with wax seals by order of the courts. And, for decades they slept, like something from a child's fairytale. The Falaknuma was no exception. For thirty years or more almost no one was permitted entry, and the place went from rack to ruin.

Yet, just before reaching the point of no return, Princess Esra, the Turkish-born former wife of the current Nizam (he has the title but nothing else), stepped in. Realising the terrible loss about to occur, she brokered a deal that would save not only the Falaknuma, but other properties once owned by the Nizams.

For an extendable lease of thirty years, the Falaknuma has been signed over to the Taj Group. As part of the arrangement, the luxury hotel chain agreed to foot the jaw-dropping bill for renovations. Every detail was overseen by Princess Esra herself, in a transformation that took more than a decade to complete. Once again sparing no expense, the Princess brought in experts from all over world, each one charged with the solemn duty of returning the apple of the Nizam's eye to its original state.

And the result is a royal palace fit for a Nizam again.

As the standard bearer leads the way up the great bowed staircase, the thing that strikes you first is the silence. There's nothing for miles around and, in India, such seclusion is itself a symbol of wealth.

Inside, there's a vestibule, its walls and ceilings adorned with lovely frescoes, Greek urns and alabaster nymphs. There's no reception desk, no concierge, none of the trappings of a luxury hotel. Rather, there's a sense that you are a guest in the Nizam's own home.

Step through into the main body of the palace, and you enter a world that disappeared half a century ago. In the distance there's the delicate chiming of a Louis XIV timepiece and, nearer by, a row of liveried factotums are standing to attention, awaiting instructions.

Once welcomed in whispers, and suitably indulged with refreshments, I was taken to my suite in the Zenana wing, where my luggage had already been unpacked by a valet. While lavish, the sixty or so rooms and suites of the Falaknuma exude the kind of understated luxury that only true prosperity can provide.

A little later the palace historian, Prabhakar Mahindrakar, took me on a palace tour. A towering figure of a man, dressed in a flowing black *sherwani*, he walks softly over the rosewood parquet.

We stroll into the ballroom, with its great Venetian chandeliers, gilt ceiling, teak and walnut furniture, and miles and miles of silk.

'Before Princess Esra saved the palace,' says Prabhakar, 'I thought it would simply crumble into dust. You should have seen it. In this very room the curtains were rotting, the upholstery eaten away by termites and ants. There were cobwebs everywhere, rats the size of cats, and unimaginable amounts of dust.'

He leads the way out onto the landing, illuminated by Carrera marble lamps, and adorned with portraits of the Nizams looming down in giant rococo frames. Next door is the Jade Room. *Haute Chinoiserie* in style, it's festooned with *objets d'art*, with yet more magnificent chandeliers above, and an intricate geometric parquet under foot.

Prabhakar paces softly through to the Hukka Lounge, replete with its multi-stemmed water pipe, chaise longues, and embossed leather walls. There's a vast billiard table too, made by Burroughes & Watts of Soho Square and, beside it, a rack of ivory-tipped cues. And, slipping through a small doorway to the left, we emerge into the cavernous dining-room. Running down the centre is one of the longest dining tables in the world. Thirty-three metres in length, fashioned from teak and rosewood, it can seat one hundred and one guests, and was once laid with the Nizam's solid gold cutlery and plates.

He may have owned the palace, but it was his Prime Minister, Viqar ul Omra, whose monogram is all over it. Just about everything from the dining chairs to the stained glass bears his initials – 'V.O.'

Even the library ceiling is monogrammed. Inspired by the one at Windsor Castle, the room has six thousand rare volumes, including a series of oversized leather-bound tomes, entitled *Glimpses of the Nizam's Dominions*. Flicking through them, you get a sense at the limitless power and wealth held by the Nizams – power and wealth that's long gone.

The palace historian, Prabhakar, suddenly seems overcome with melancholy. Kissing his fingers, he touches them gently to the book.

'We're all equal now,' he says, 'but I must admit I wish the old days would come back if only for a while.'

The Islamic Legacy of Timbuktu

THE CARAVAN OF SULTAN MANSA MUSA, ruler of the Mali Empire, snaked its way through the scorching heat of the central Sahara on its long return from the pilgrimage to Mecca.

The year was 1324.

Eight thousand soldiers, courtiers and servants – some say as many as sixty thousand – drove fifteen thousand camels laden with gold, perfume, salt and stores of food in a procession of unrivaled size.

Their destination was the newly conquered city of Gao, on the Niger River. From there, they turned toward another metropolis recently added to the Mali Empire, one surrounded by unrelenting dunes, a fabled oasis city on which Mansa Musa had longed to make his mark – Timbuktu.

No word in English connotes remoteness more than that city's name. Thanks to the astonishing wealth that Mansa Musa had displayed on his visits to Cairo and Mecca, it suggests riches too. For eight centuries, Timbuktu captured the imaginations of both East and West, albeit for very different reasons. In 1620, the English explorer Richard Jobson wrote:

> The most flattering reports had reached Europe of the gold trade carried on at Timbuktu. The roofs of its houses were represented to be covered with plates of gold, the bottoms of the rivers to glisten with the precious metal, and the mountains had only to be excavated to yield a profusion of the metallic treasure.

Other reports said that rosewater flowed in the city's fountains, that the sultan showered each visitor with priceless gifts. Europe's greatest explorers set out to risk their lives in search of the riches of the fabled Timbuktu.

Exploration and travel societies sponsored competitions, with prizes for the man who reached there by the most difficult route. Most

European travellers perished long before they ever saw the city rise above the desert horizon, and those who did get there found that the tales they had heard had missed the point.

Muslim travellers – most notably Ibn Battuta and Hasan al-Wazan, also known as Leo Africanus – were no less eager to visit the city, but for them, and a host of rulers, dignitaries and scholars from Morocco to Persia, the remote city held riches of another sort.

Timbuktu was the starting point for African pilgrims going on the Haj, a centre of some of the finest Islamic scholarship of the Middle Ages.

Located in modern Mali, just eight miles north of the Niger flood-plain along the southern edge of the Sahara, Timbuktu today is little more than a sleepy, sweltering stop on the adventure-tourism trail. Most visitors fly in and out in a single afternoon. The city's days as a caravanserai and desert *entrepôt* are long gone.

A more purposeful visit, however, has its rewards.

There is much to see as one strolls about the stark streets, lingers, looks beyond the soft-drink stalls and engages in casual conversation here and there. Although Timbuktu has been conquered over and over by many powers, absorbed into one empire after another, none ever sacked or looted it.

As a result, traces of its Islamic legacy appear at almost every turn. Qur'anic inscriptions decorate doorways. The tombs of hundreds of famous scholars and teachers dot the town – some unremembered, some within the knowledge of local guides. Most noticeably, a handful of fabulous mosques reel upward into the brilliant African sky and constitute the anchor points of the city's plan.

Set on the Islamic world's southwestern edge, Timbuktu was the product of an eclectic mixture of West African and Arab influences that found in Islam a common denominator. Its peoples often saw themselves as the faithful pitted against the pagans lurking beyond the city's walls. Tuareg, Fulani, Berbers, Soninke and Songhoi lived side by side, in peace, bound together by their belief in God, their acceptance of the Qur'an, and their familiarity with Arabic.

Because the city lay on the periphery of the kingdoms that ruled it – and was left to its own devices by most of them – the community of Timbuktu was forced through isolation to look inward. This introspective attitude influenced all aspects of Timbuktu's society, and nowhere did this become more apparent than in its pious pursuits.

Barely two centuries after being founded as a small Tuareg settlement around 1100, Timbuktu had earned its reputation as the most important Islamic centre in West Africa. Its quiet rise to high regard – against enormous odds of geography and climate – is quite remarkable. Equally astonishing is that Timbuktu also prospered economically, seemingly beyond reason, as if to spite the adversity of its surroundings.

At its height during the mid-sixteenth century, the city had a population of about sixty thousand. A prime caravan stop and centere of manufacturing, it dominated West Africa in trade and exports. Al-Wazan wrote that:

The rich king of Tombuto keeps a magnificent and well-furnished court. The coin of Tombuto is gold. There is a most stately temple to be seen, the walls of which are made of mortared stone; and a princely palace also built by a most excellent workman of Granada. Here are many shops of craftsmen and merchants, and especially of such as weave linen and cotton cloth.

Though undergirded by its economic success, Timbuktu's key role was cultural, as a crucible of learning. The difficulty of the journey to or from Timbuktu induced pilgrims and traders alike, once they got there, to spend months, even years, in the city before moving on.

In time, local belief held that, by studying the Qur'an or donating generously to Timbuktu's Islamic schools, one would be assured safe passage through the surrounding desert.

A rich account of Timbuktu's history and Islamic heritage has come to us through a series of chronicles, known as *tarikhs*, written from the mid-17th and through the mid-eighteenth centuries. These texts – some plain and undeviating, others embroidered with ornate rhetoric – help us slip into the world of Timbuktu in the Middle Ages. Here we learn of its great mosques, of its ruling families, of the eminent schools of literature and learning, and of its golden age.

Of these chronicles, none is more detailed or intricate than the *Tarikh al-Sudan*, or *History of the Sudan*. Written in 1653 by the city's most eminent scholar, 'Abd al-Rahman al-Sadi, the *tarikh* traces the history and society of Timbuktu from its founding until the time of writing. Al-Sadi's work is so reliable, and his descriptions so exact, that two hundred and fifty years after it was written the French journalist Felix Dubois used it as his guidebook. 'The author displays an unusual conscientiousness, never hesitating to give both versions of a doubtful event,' wrote Dubois in 1897.

The two major *tarikhs* that followed al-Sadi's were essentially less ambitious updates. The first, Mahmoud Kati's *Tarikh al-Fattash*, supplements al-Sadi's work up to the early eighteenth century. Kati lacks the astute insight of his predecessor, but his book does contain important information on the legal and administrative heritage of Timbuktu. The anonymous *Tadhkirat al-Nisyan*, or *A Reminder to the Oblivious*, is similarly thin in detail, and it in turn brings the history up through the mid-eighteenth century. The two latter chronicles frequently lapse into nostalgia and lament the decline of Timbuktu's fortunes.

Since its earliest beginnings, when the Tuareg would move down to the plateau each summer from the pastures of Arawan, Timbuktu has been dominated by its mosques. It is to them that the old city, with its triangular layout, owes its specific quarters – each with its unique character. Built literally of the desert itself, the adobe mosques of Timbuktu became famous throughout the Islamic world. They towered high above the sandy streets and afforded the city an impressively eccentric skyline.

The northern quarter, at the apex of the triangular city, takes its name from the Sankore Mosque. A great, tawny, pyramidal structure laced with protruding wooden support beams, Sankore was the bastion of learning in Timbuktu. Its imams were regarded with unequaled respect; its school attracted the noble and the rich as students. Indeed, mentors and scholars alike are said to have flocked to Sankore's *ja'iyyah*, or university, from as far afield as the Arabian Peninsula.

Here, surrounded by the Sahara's windswept dunes, students could concentrate their minds as nowhere else. And, as Timbuktu's fame grew in the Islamic world, Sankore became the most important centre of Islamic scholarship in Africa.

The eastern corner of the city was home to the much smaller Jami' al-Suq, the Market Mosque. Like many of the less grand mosques of

Timbuktu, it has fallen into disrepair, been enlarged or been rebuilt many times. The adobe construction, characteristic of sub-Saharan buildings weakens when it rains. Each year, after the winter downpours – if they occur – many of the city's major buildings must be patched up and reinforced, but it is unexpected thunderstorms that are the dread of Timbuktu.

The noted mosque Jami' al-Hana collapsed in a storm in 1771 and killed forty people. Local legend relates that, rather than being embittered by catastrophe, the residents of Timbuktu believed that God had been so stirred by the prayers from the mosque that he had whisked the congregants up to heaven at once.

When the grand caravan of Mansa Musa arrived on that scorching day in 1325, the sultan ordered the Granadan architect and poet Abu Ishaq al-Sahili, who had travelled with him from Mecca, to build a magnificent mosque – one far larger than any the region had known – in the western corner of the city. Its name, Jingerebir, is a corruption of the Arabic *Jami' al-kabir*, or 'the great mosque'.

Five hundred years later, in 1858, the German traveller Henry Barth wrote that the mosque 'by its stately appearance made a deep impression on my mind. [It]…includes nine naves, of different dimensions and structure.'

Giant and rambling, and one of the first mosques in Africa to be built with fired-brick walls, Jingerebir became at once the central mosque of the city, and it dominates Timbuktu to this day. In times of crisis, in years when rains failed and the Niger River had risen insufficiently or not at all in its annual, life-giving flood, the people of Timbuktu gathered at Jingerebir. Within the cool shade of its walls, the imam – who often doubled as the town's ruler – would lead his congregants in prayer.

According to the *tarikhs*, Timbuktu's religious leaders, judges and officials all tended to be graduates of the city's illustrious schools. In the city where the study of Islamic principles was regarded as of supreme importance, Leo Africanus found 'a great store of doctors, judges, priests, and other learned men'. This scholastic elite was underwritten largely by the city's business class, who themselves formed a considerable part of the student body. Especially at Sankore, it was also these scholars who provided energy and direction to civil administration, commercial regulation, legislation, town planning and architectural projects – in addition to maintaining a number of superb libraries. The ranks of the city's elite were limited, however: Six families have provided two-thirds of Timbuktu's *qadis*, or judges, during the last five hundred years.

By the mid-sixteenth century – the so-called golden age of Timbuktu – the city boasted well over one hundred and fifty schools, and the curricula were rigorous. The Islamic sciences formed the core of the academic syllabus, including Qur'anic interpretation (*tafsir*), the traditions of the Prophet (*hadith*), jurisprudence (*fiqh*), sources of the law (*usul*), and doctrinal theology (*tawhid*). Apart from the religious courses, students were also required to study grammar (*nahw*), literary style and rhetoric (*balaghah*), and logic (*mantiq*). Scholars focused on the way that a person should behave within the context of Islamic society.

Only when religious and linguistic literacy had been achieved was a student assigned to a particular mentor. The relationship between pupil and master often grew to be a strong one, and favoured students might work as *mulazama*, or private secretaries, to their teachers. As the community grew, an intellectual genealogy developed, similar to those acknowledged elsewhere in the Islamic world, that linked masters to pupils and those pupils to their own students. Strong academic and religious ties with other scholastic centers of the Middle East and North Africa linked Timbuktu to the rest of the Islamic world.

As the number of students increased, so did the fields of study available. Subjects such as history, mathematics, astronomy and cartography in time joined the wealth of courses available.

Although Timbuktu prided itself on the rigour of its teaching for even the youngest of pupils, visiting traders or travellers were encouraged to enroll while they stayed in the city. Thus many itinerant non-Muslim merchants were led to conversion in Timbuktu through encounters with Muslim scholars. Even older visitors could be assured that the city's scholastic community would educate them. Indeed, the people of Timbuktu were reputed to be so philanthropic that they would afford any visitor an education regardless of his means – maintaining that anyone who had endured the journey to their desert metropolis had earned himself a scholarship.

Likewise, those born in Timbuktu to humble families were guaranteed their education. So great was the fervour for Islamic learning that even the tailors of Timbuktu, among other craft guilds, founded their own centers of learning where instructors oversaw both the workshop and its college. In this environment, students worked as apprentice tailors while they were also instructed in the foundations of Islamic scholarship.

By the sixteenth century, Timbuktu is said to have had more than twenty-six establishments for tailor-scholars alone, many employing more than a hundred. Thus, these institutes also reinforced the city's role as a significant manufacturer of cloth.

At the height of the city's golden age, Timbuktu boasted not only the impressive libraries of Sankore and the other mosques, but also a wealth of private ones. One of the greatest, containing more than seven hundred volumes, was left by the master scholar Hajji Ahmad bin 'Umar. His library was said to have included many of the rarest books ever written in Arabic, and he copied and annotated a considerable number of the volumes himself.

The libraries of Timbuktu grew through a regular process of hand-copying manuscripts. Scholars would visit the caravanserais and appeal to learned travellers to permit their precious volumes to be reproduced. Alternatively, they duplicated texts borrowed from their mentors' collections, studying the material as they did so.

Al-Wazan, Leo the African, commented that 'hither are brought manuscripts or written books, which are sold for more money than any other merchandise.' As late as the close of the nineteenth century, Fèlix Dubois purchased a number of antique books in Timbuktu, including a copy of the *Divan of Kings*, a chronology of the rulers and events of the Sudan between 1656 and 1747.

Timbuktu's position as a principal staging point along the pilgrimage route to Mecca may partly explain why so many books were available. Even so, modern scholars are staggered by the sheer quantity and rarity of Arabic texts and poems proffered and composed in the city.

Of the books written in Timbuktu, a number are surprising in their scope. Ahmed Baba's biographical dictionary, for example, included the lives of notables from Arabia, Egypt, Morocco and Central Asia, as well as Timbuktu itself.

Of the city's scholars, none is more lionised today than Muhammad Askia, called 'Muhammad the Great', who reigned over Timbuktu for more than three decades in the late fifteenth and early sixteenth centuries. Regarded as the city's saviour, it was he who wrested Timbuktu from the infamous Songhoi ruler Sunni Ali in 1493. Ali was despised as one who undermined Islam by persecuting the scholastic class, efforts that earned him uncomplimentary entries in the *tarikhs*. Under Askia, however, scholarship and Islam were again revered and supported, and a new era of stability began that led to Timbuktu's sixteenth-century golden age.

Like any frontier town, the city also gained strength from the melting-pot of peoples who sought to make their lives within its walls. A mixture of North and West African tribes wove their unique ways into the framework of Timbuktu's culture.

The influence of the Songhoi people, for example, extended to the calendar, where Ramadan, the holy month of fasting, was popularly known by the Songhoi word *haome*, which translates, literally, as 'closed mouth'. The end of the Ramadan fast was known similarly as *ferme*, or 'open mouth'. Observance of the Ramadan fast has never been easy in Timbuktu, where the desert climate much resembles that of central Arabia, but the holy month has always been taken very seriously in the city.

Like Muslims everywhere, the people of Timbuktu were united by Ramadan. As the sun scorched down, or as the flour-fine Sahara sand squalled through the streets, the faithful would gather in the mosques, protected from the desert and enveloped in the simplicity of the adobe architecture, in order to renew their faith.

During Tyibsi, as Dhu al-Hijjah, the month which follows Ramadan, was called, feasting was in order. On the tenth day of the month, as pilgrims prepared to begin the taxing journey to Mecca, the men of Timbuktu would gather for special prayers, and the imam of Jingerebir would sacrifice a ram. Then everyone would hurry home, for a local tradition maintained that the first man to follow the imam's sacrifice with one of his own would be the first to ride into paradise.

With desert dunes surrounding it in all directions, and trapped in a severe and perfidious climate, the fact that fabled Timbuktu rose and prospered for eight centuries is remarkable.

But more surprising still is that Timbuktu's intellectual tradition remained largely intact generation after generation. Even during times of economic depression, caused by shifting caravan routes or spoiled crops, the community ensured that the Qur'anic academies survived.

Early in the nineteenth century, the young French explorer René Caille remarked that all the population of Timbuktu was apparently 'able to read the Qur'an and even know it by heart'.

With some sixty-six years later, when the French colonized the region, they recorded that some two dozen key scholastic centres still flourished in Timbuktu. Continuing to teach Arabic, Qur'anic doctrine and traditional lore, the schools had altered little in five centuries.

Now, as the desert creeps slowly southward all across sub-Saharan Africa, Timbuktu stands more isolated by sand and heat than ever. At the same time, in the city that captivated both West and East, some of the richest parts of the legacy of Islam lie only just beneath the city's baked-mud surface, waiting silently to be rediscovered, and perhaps reawakened.

Jinn Lore

THE OCCIDENT HAS NEVER FOUND it easy to grasp the strange netherworld of spirits that followers of Islam universally believe exist in a realm overlaid our own.

Although descended from an Oriental family with its roots in the mountain fortress of Afghanistan's Hindu Kush, I had been born and brought up in the West. I thought I knew the East. After all, I was well accustomed from childhood to understand the finer points of Arab etiquette, and I had been taught its tales, gleaned from *Alf Layla wa Layla, A Thousand and One Nights.*

That fabulous treasury of stories had introduced me early on to the extraordinary possibilities of a world peopled by invisible legions of Jinn. So when we came to live at Dar Khalifa, the Caliph's House, I felt as if nothing could surprise me.

How wrong I was.

From the first moment that we crossed the threshold, I realized that I was way out of my depth. The house had been empty for almost a decade. Whereas in the West an empty home might appeal to squatters, in the East there is a danger of quite a different kind. The unlawful occupants of our new home were not human, but superhuman.

The guardians who came with the property, as if through some mediaeval right sale, warned us from the outset that there was extreme danger all around. When I declared that we would be moving into the house right away to supervise the renovations, they laughed nervously – until that is they realized I was serious. Terrified, contorted expressions then swept across their faces, and they begged us to leave post haste.

The Jinn would not take kindly to intruders, they told me. For in the years that the house had been empty, it had become *their* home. Dare to trespass and they might kill us, the leader of the guardians declared. Irritated, yet willing to go along with them for the sake of respecting local sensitivities, I asked what to do. The chief guardian, whose name was Osman, swept his out arms wide, and yelled: 'You must hold an exorcism!'

Back in London I would have had no idea where to find an exorcist, let alone a troop of them. But Morocco is very different. It may be perched in Africa's North West's corner, just eight miles from the gates of Europe, but in many ways it is the deepest, darkest Orient.

And that is what is so appealing about it.

I asked around and, very soon, found myself in the old imperial city of Mèknes. According to all my informants it was the centre of exorcists. And they were right. A few minutes after my arrival I was offered dozens of exorcists from the Aissawa brotherhood. I negotiated a price for twenty, and the exorcist dealer threw in a further four of them for free. The only catch was that I was obliged to pay in advance.

A day or so later I arrived home and was greeted by the guardians' long looks. The Jinn were already exacting their revenge, they told me. A dead cat had been found in the garden with its head cut off. A tree had fallen in the wind and broken a window. And the maid, hired to look after our baby son, had run off screaming for no reason at all. I held out a hand at arms length and whispered confidently, 'Have no fear, the exorcists are coming.'

The guardians perked up.

They asked when exactly the visitors would arrive.

I shrugged.

'They'll come when they are ready,' I said.

My wife insisted I was mad to have handed over wads of money to exorcists I didn't know. She said she could hear them all the way in Mèknes, howling with laughter.

A day passed, then another.

I kicked myself to having been so ingenuous as to pay in advance. But then at that moment I heard the wild, whooping sound of men in high spirits, against a backdrop of grinding noise. A huge cement truck was inching its way down our lane. On the back were riding the exorcists, as if on some infernal chariot. I pointed at them and grinned, and the guardians grinned too.

Through days and nights the Aissawa wreaked their terrible work.

They slaughtered and skinned a goat at what they said was the heart of the house. As the person obliged to purchase the animal, I found myself naturally interested in how its execution would feature in the cleansing of my home of supernatural elements. When stripped of its skin, the carcass was beheaded, and its gallbladder swallowed by one of the group. The others slit open its belly and rifled through the organs, which gleamed like jewels in the candlelight.

One of the Aissawa then poured milk in all corners of the house, and another did the same with blood. Drums beat, and high-pitched homemade oboes wailed. The drumming grew faster and faster as the night wore on. And as it did so, the exorcists stepped into another plane, a kind of twilight zone of their own imagination.

They cut their wrists with knives and drank their own blood, then collapsed on the ground in trance. Yet more massed in a dark, damp room at the far end of the house. They barricaded themselves inside, killed chickens and drank more blood.

And all the while the drums beat and the oboes shrieked. I wondered if the walls would tumble down as they had done in Jericho.

I whispered sternly to the Aissawa leader that they could leave. He laughed, a wild hearty laugh, and I swear his eyes flashed red with fire. He would only quit our home, he said, when the Jinn had been sucked out of the walls and swallowed. I explained that my wife was growing impatient, and was uncomfortable at having the walls and floor strewn with freshly purged blood. The leader of the exorcists caught my glance in his. Widening his eyes in the most terrifying manner, he told me that he had never been in a house so consumed with evil spirits.

Then he asked for more money, and for another goat.

The next day, after brokering a deal which involved a handful of crisp hundred-dirham notes, the exorcists clambered aboard the cement truck. They rolled back down the lane and through the shanty-town to the open road. My wife gave me one of those looks that instilled pure fear. I bragged out loud that the house was now squeaky clean, that the last thing we ever needed to worry about again were Jinn.

In the years since, I have found myself living in a country where the belief in these normally invisible spirits is complete and unshakable. Jinn are described in the Qur'an, and they are a part of life for all God-fearing Muslims in Morocco and across the Islamic world. The Qur'an tells us that when God created Man from clay, he created a second race of beings – Jinn – from 'smokeless fire'. Jinn are not ghosts, that is they are not spirits of the dead. Far from it. They are living entities just like us. They are born, get married, and die just like humans. Some are good and others bad, some ugly, while others are radiantly beautiful.

Indeed, there are many tales of mortal men being wooed by the charms of voluptuous women, only to realize later that they are not human, but Jinn. The difference between us and them is that they have magical powers, and can decide when to be visible and when not. They can fly through the air, change their form, and are capable of magical feats of the most extraordinary kind.

The nineteenth century's fascination with *The Arabian Nights* saw the deeds and misdeeds of Jinn enter Victorian drawing-rooms. The creatures slipped into Western communal folklore through the tales of Aladdin, Sindbad and others, mixed in with epic quests, treasure, flying carpets and enchanted lands. And through the endless adaptations for children, and all the Hollywood renditions, Jinn became known to us all.

But gone was the Oriental imagery – the sly, ferocious race that lives among us, replaced by a comic jumble of towering, yet quite loveable creatures, who go by the name of 'genies'.

Anyone who's spent any time in the Arab world, knows the difference between Hollywood's depiction and that which is found embedded deep in local culture.

Living in a country like Morocco, where belief in Jinn is all-pervasive, provides situations such as the ones we faced at the Caliph's House. It brings an extraordinary level of cultural possibility that simply doesn't exist in the Occidental world. Imagine it: that all around you there may be invisible spirits, sitting, standing, laughing, chatting, cackling, crouching on the floor. Some of them are minute, while others tower hundreds of feet into the air. The more you think about it, and live with it, the more appealing the idea of Jinn becomes. And the longer you live in a place where everyone believes, the more you find yourself believing, too.

Long before I moved to Morocco, I had searched for a readable book about Jinn and their world. But there wasn't one. When I asked friends who were scholars in Islamic culture and tradition, they recommended barely readable texts written by academics for academics. Years passed. Then, through a kind of magic that was from the realm of Jinn themselves, Robert Lebling contacted me out of the blue. He spoke of a work, a great labour of love, which would reveal to the West all it needed to know about Jinn.

My prayers had been answered.

The boundaries of Lebling's work surpassed by wildest dreams. The books' scope exceeds simply listing stories of Jinn taken from Islamic texts and Arab folklore.

Lebling has left no stone unturned in his enquiry, roaming through traditional Eastern literature as well as the modern media, in search of anything which gives us a better understanding of Jinn and their world. The result is a truly extraordinary masterwork, a treasury within itself that can be consulted at random, dipped into as a bedside book, or read from cover to cover in a fabulous feast for the imagination and the enquiring mind.

Through its pages, we learn that the belief in Jinn is certainly Pre-Islamic, and that there are various distinct forms of these creatures. The Qur'an devotes an entire Sura to them, a form of life that is inextricably linked to the cultural and religious tapestry of Arab and Islamic lands.

Lebling details clearly how followers of Islam perceive the realm of Jinn, what the Prophet Mohammed said about them, and how regional and geographic divide has shaped them within local culture. An entire section is devoted to the study and appreciation of Jinn by geographic location – through Morocco, Tunisia and Egypt, to Arabia and Palestine, Turkey, Iraq and Iran; as well as through Nigeria, Malaysia, Zanzibar and beyond.

We learn that the Arabic word for 'crazy' – *Majnun* – comes from the same root as the word 'Jinn', suggesting that a deranged person is possessed in some way. And that Jinn are believed to lurk in wells and lavatories, in addition to their haunting empty buildings, such as our home. Space is given to King Solomon, the one human who could control Jinn through the magical ring he wore.

And Lebling describes the extraordinary encounters between those of us created from clay and the others, shaped from smokeless fire. These include examples of humans whom have married Jinn unwittingly, and others such as the fourteenth century Moroccan magician, Muhammad ibn al-Hajj al-Tilimsani, whose work *Suns of Lights and Treasures of Secrets*, provides a spell for anyone wishing to seduce the daughter of the White King of the Jinn.

Legends of the Fire Spirits provides a transparent window into Arab and Islamic society that is more usually clouded over, opaque to all except Arabists and scholars of Islam. The subject is one known to Muslims, embracing a belief that stands at the heart of the Islamic faith: but one that until now has been largely misrepresented and misunderstood in the West.

As for life at the Caliph's House, all is not well.

One of the guardians recently almost severed his hand while sharpening an axe in the garden. Then, last week, the maid tripped and cut her foot badly, and on the same day the swimming pool turned an eerie shade of yellowy-green.

The guardians have been imploring me to hold another exorcism. The very thought of it fills me with anxiety. Most of all, I don't know how I'll break it to my wife. But, as all my friends assure me, everyone knows that even the best exorcism has to be renewed once in a while.

N.B. *Legends of the Fire Spirits: Jinn and Genies from Arabia to Zanzibar*, by Robert Leibling, I.B. Tauris 2010.

Jma el Fna

PLAYED OUT AGAINST a backdrop of vibrant cultural colour, the late Marrakech afternoon is like nothing else on Earth.

The souqs are packed with bargains, bustle, and with people cloaked in hooded *jelaba* robes. Stacked up are bundles of wool carpets from the High Atlas, dazzling brass trays inscribed with the names of God, baskets of dried damask roses, mounds of pungent incense and sulphur, and endless shops, each one crammed with treasure from the remotest reaches of the desert.

For all the wonders of the medina though, it's the great square of Jma el Fna that I find the most tantalizing spot of all. It lies at the heart of real Marrakech, the city of snake charmers, the *crème de la crème* of the Exotic East.

Most people hurry across it fast. Pause too long and you're sure to be sucked in deep. But to me that's the true magic... being pulled down through the layers like a man floundering on the ocean waves. Allow yourself to be free, and you glimpse the many facets of this mesmerizing stew of humanity.

The Halka: A circle of people stands in the darkness, shoulders pressed together tight, necks craning forward for a view... a great green parasol looming over them, and me as I push in closer. The outside world gradually fades away and then...is shut out. The sense of anticipation growing, palpable and electric.

I'm being sucked in... through the rows of onlookers to the source of this frenzied, primal rhythm. I'm descending back through time... to when this place, Jma el Fna, was no more than an oasis in the desert. Suddenly, I break into the centre of the circle, walled by shadows and men's faces, illuminated by the jolting, jarring flame of a gas-lamp. It's like the meeting of a secret fraternity.

One of the ancient fondouks behind Jma el Fna

A water-seller in Jma el Fna

In the middle of the halka – the circle of souls – leaps the riotous silhouette of a man, a violin grasped tight in his hand, the crowd gripped by the wild strains of his instrument. As he turns into the light, I catch his features… bearded, tight curly hair, smiling eyes upturned to the stars. Raw, energetic, hypnotic… a Moroccan Jimi Hendrix, a Berber master musician.

First Impressions: Anyone who's ever been to Marrakech remembers the first time they stepped onto the frenetic expanse of Jma el Fna. For me it was a searing afternoon back in June '71. I was four years old. My fingers were pressed tight in my father's hand, my eyes blinking in the dazzling light.

Despite the heat, the square was crowded beyond belief. There were snake charmers and tumbling acrobats, medicine men in Toureg robes, blind men and water-sellers, madmen and doped out hippies crouching in the shade.

Stumbling forward through the waves of people, I was mesmerized. It was as if every man, woman, and child on Earth was right there. A seething stew of humanity set in random motion.

Watching over it all like a sentinel – the minaret of Jma el Fna itself, the mosque of the annihilation, the mosque of eternity, the mosque at the end of the world.

Over the years, and especially since I moved to Morocco, I have returned to Marrakech again and again, and always find myself criss-crossing the square, usually heading for shade of the ancient medina, whose twisting lanes stretch out behind it in a great secret labyrinth.

Soaking it up: My father used to say that the only way to absorb the atmosphere was to close your eyes. 'Listen to the sounds that go unnoticed,' he would tell me, 'and breathe in the smells that the nostrils try to filter out… concentrate, and the reality will reveal itself.'

It's a lesson that's never failed me. And whenever I venture into Jma el Fna, I do as he suggested, and find myself transported to a space on the edge of the imagination, a cross-section of medieval Morocco that's as real today as it's ever been… but one whose true form is truly elusive.

Facts and figures: My father, who was from Afghanistan, would scowl when I would ask for facts and figures... when I begged to be told how big the square was, or when it was laid out.

'You've been brainwashed by the West,' he would say. 'To understand Jma el Fna you must cut away Occidental thinking, release your mind, and absorb the place from the inside out.'

Zigzag: For my father, the zigzag approach was the only way to understand something. 'Throw yourself in at the deep end,' he would say, 'run free, bouncing around like a billiard ball on the baize, and you'll build up an accurate picture, a little at a time.'

Forty years later, and I'm back in the middle of the square, ready to step out, to zigzag. I'm itching to feel the waves of energy, to seek out the invisible, and to hear the sounds that are muffled to even the sharpest ears.

Day/Night: Just like the halkas, the circles of joy and entertainment, which are born and die through the day and the night, Jma el Fna is a place without a beginning or an end. It's a circle of life, with its peaks and lulls, enacted from the first rays of dawn to the last strains of night.

Every day. *Every* night.

Fishing for drinks: Every time I visit the square there's something new, a display of fresh ingenuity. This time it's the man over there with scarred hands and a limp. For the last half hour he's been laying out spiraling rows of plastic bottles, warm fizzy drinks. Everyone's wondering what's going on. He's already pulling a crowd and he's not even begun.

Jma el Fna is all about picquing the crowd's curiosity, and one way to do that is to keep them guessing. When they can't stand it any longer, he unfurls a clutch of homemade fishing rods, long bamboo staves, dangling strings with what look like curtain rings on the ends. The local preoccupation with fizzy drinks, and eagerness for a bargain, has made it an instant success.

Secret Police: Everyone says that the square's crawling with secret police. Like a separate group of invisible performers, they're masters of disguise, watching every hand, purse and pocket. The entertainers, healers, and food sellers all claim to know who's who. But they're not telling me. It's one of many secrets here, I suppose, I'll have to decipher for myself.

Tourists: The tourists stick out because of their pasty white skin and their clothing, but most of all because of the way they reel forwards between the halkas, enthralled by it all. Some of them are grinning, others scowling, all clicking photos instead of watching what's really going on.

It's as if they're desperate to penetrate what is a secret society. Some of them think they've actually done it, that they've been accepted into the folds. But they never quite manage. They're oil on the water. And although they can get mixed up for a moment, they separate out as they're washed forward through the crowds.

Earning Marrakech: These days it's far too easy to get to Marrakech. Budget airlines touch down at the new international terminal day and night, from across Europe and beyond. Waves of tourists emerge and, like moths to a flame, they're lured by the mythical reputation of Jma el Fna, the heart of Marrakech, the heart of Morocco.

Feel the fire: It's all too easy in a way. Until quite recently you had to struggle through the desert to get here. Sweat, thirst, heat, and even delirium. But you arrived changed by the journey, ready to receive something so magical that language can hardly convey. If I had my way, you'd still have to reach Marrakech by foot, for there's no better way to soak up its core than as a wayfarer, ripened by travel.

Cigarette sellers: Some square-dwellers are almost invisible as they slip nimbly through the crowds. But you hear them. A fistful of coins jangling as they approach, an open packet of cigarettes, sold one at a time to anyone needing a nicotine fix.

Medicine-man: As the afternoon light peaks in intensity, a row of healers lay out their stalls in a line on the ground in a corner of the square. Drawing a crowd, they reel off numbers and cures. Dressed in billowing indigo robes, embroidered with gold, turbans crowning their heads, they claim to heal any disorder – of body or mind.

Their dusty old quilts are packed with wares: ostrich eggs and stork feathers, tortoise shells, dried reptiles, great lumps of sulphur, antimony and chalk. Phials filled with murky grey liquids, dried damask roses, aromatic seeds, and swathes of shocking pink silk.

Of all those making their living here, it's the magico-medicine men who are doing the briskest trade. Customers hurry up one by one. They spit out the name of an affliction, in no more than a whisper… a rash, an eruption of sores, a need for revenge on a neighbour, or the yearning for a son.

The healer nods, his fingers conjuring a cure from the treasure chest of ingredients before him. His sales' patter is unbroken as clients and onlookers stand spellbound. He wraps the mixture in a twist of paper, hands it over fast, and snatches the customer's coins into the voluminous folds of his robe.

A desert lizard emerges from under the same robe, head held high, a string around its waist attached to its master's finger. It blinks, as if in approval of the transaction.

Dentist: Nearby, in the shade of the mosque, is a dentist, sitting on a stool… in front of him a platter overflowing with human teeth. He's got small darting eyes, a checkerboard smile, and confidence in his skill at bringing even the most severe toothache to a swift end. Whatever the condition, the treatment appears to be the same… a quick open air operation with a pair of rusted iron pliers, and a plug of grubby cotton wool to stem the flow of blood.

Henna women: It's true that most of those who make their living in Jma el Fna are men. But look around and you realize there are professions reserved exclusively for women. They are the sorceresses and fortune tellers. And cast an eye through the square during the quiet hours of the afternoon and you see the henna women perched on stools under parasols. As soon as they spot a pallid foreigner, they hold up their henna-filled syringe and grin.

A catalogue of pictures is at the ready… decorated hands and feet. Squat on a stool for a minute or two, hold still as the hand grasping the syringe weaves its magic, and you've been initiated into the ancient sisterhood of Marrakech.

Snake charmers: There's no noise so alluring, so utterly hypnotic as the *rhaita*, the snake charmer's flute. A cliché maybe, but a mainstay of Jma el Fna, a backbone of sound and sight that bewitches tourists and locals alike.

Long before you reach the square, you hear its piercing tone. Riotous, fearful, yet somehow tamed, it cuts like a laser beam through the interminable din of the traffic, and the clip-clop of horses' hooves.

Draw near, enchanted by the rawest streak of sound, and the serpents are knocked from their rest beneath a clutch of circular drums. Dazzled by the sudden blast of light, a pair of spitting cobras rear up, poised to strike. Despite the heat, the snake charmer's wearing a thick woolen *jelaba*, a ragged strand of calico wrapped around his head. And around his neck a water snake, its tongue licking the afternoon heat, a desert accessory.

Food Stalls: Just after the *muezzin* calls the afternoon prayer, dozens of iron carts are propelled forward from all corners of the square. Like gun carriages made ready for war, they're positioned precisely on the east side of Jma el Fna, and unloaded. Cast iron struts and staves, pots, pans, tables, benches and stools, are knocked into place.

These days the food stalls are fed by electricity, illuminated by bare bulbs, bathing the diners in platinum light. As soon as you draw near to the battery of stalls, the hustlers galvanize into action. They're paid to entice anyone with a few coins going spare, to eat at *their* stall.

Fingers jabbing at the hodge-podge of dishes on offer, they can recount the menu in any language you chose – there's sheep brains and lamb on skewers, octopus, squid, and fried slabs of fish, tripe, goat's head, snails, all of it washed down with miniature glasses of hot sweet tea.

Denzil Washington: King of the Hustlers is a burly fresh-faced man of about thirty, who goes by the nickname 'Denzil Washington'. Venture anywhere near his food-stall, Number 117, and he careens forward with a laminated plastic menu at the ready. Like the other hustlers, he's skilled in working out where you're from, long before you utter a word. This sixth sense, which must have evolved over centuries, makes the difference between survival and extinction.

Change: Travel back and forth to a place you love and it's the change you notice first. It hits you side on, blurring your memories. Sometimes when I visit the square, I cry out in rage at the creeping gentrification. For me, Jma el Fna should be stuck in time, unaltered ever… a Peter Pan destination.

But the wonderful thing about the square is that change is quickly assimilated or undone. Here, nothing is set in stone. Efforts to introduce boundaries of any kind are thwarted by an ancient system far more powerful than the authorities who clamour for change.

A few years ago the orange juice sellers were corralled into a row of mock calèche carriages. I jumped up and down in ire when I saw them for the first time. But these days I realize that they have a place, and that it's the content which is important, rather than the container itself.

Boxers: Another halka is forming. In the middle stands a rough-looking man with a woolly blue hat, a week's growth of beard on his cheeks, and the end of a cigarette screwed into the corner of his mouth. He's got a heap of third-hand boxing gloves beside him, and he's cajoling anyone to come forward and try their luck.

As soon as the crowd senses action, their numbers swell. More and more people are turning up, the atmosphere stoked by a hardened accomplice in a flame-red tracksuit. He's coaxing people to throw coins down onto the ground. He'll let the fight start when there's enough cash in the ring. The dirhams come slowly.

In one corner there's a desperate looking contender, with a broken nose, ragged *jelaba*, and back-to-front baseball cap. In the other, a handsome teenager in a Barcelona football shirt. He's got curly greased back hair. They raise their gloves, spar for a moment, but the fight's short-lived. The youngster dodges a few swipes, then quickly abandons his hopes and his gloves.

But now, a young woman steps forward, puts on the gloves. I can't believe it. Neither can the audience.

The secrets of Jma el Fna are only revealed to the patient, and to the observant. Turn up day after day and you'll find the same girl stepping forward into the ring and strapping on the gloves. She's the ring-master's daughter and, like the other boxers, she's in on the deal.

Gnaoua: The roots of Jma el Fna sink deep down into the sand beneath the entertainers' feet. The place may now be paved over but it's a square of desert, an oasis with a sacred soul. Most of all, it's African, the vast expanse of sky above, boiling with cumulus clouds, a reminder to anyone who doubts it.

And of all the life-forces that pour through you in the square, the truest and most vibrant of all is surely the Gnaoua. A brotherhood of African troubadours, dressed in brightly-coloured desert robes with cowrie-shell hats, they're forming a semi-circle now.

Great iron castanets, clattering like cymbals. Their rhythm gives the square its endless beating pulse, day and night. The sound is more like a cohort of warriors heading to battle, than a troupe of musicians touting for tourists' change.

Appeal of Jma el Fna: Pass a little time in the square, and you begin to see that it's peopled by ordinary Moroccans. It's not a place for the bling bling set or the nouveau riche. *They* steer well clear, preferring the fashionable cafés of the new town.

Yet Jma el Fna's great enduring appeal is that it turns no one away. It's an ancient entertaining machine, a healer, a listener, a giver of sustenance, and a friend.

Flautist: A flautist has entered the square and sits without fuss in the centre, playing his wooden pipe, as at ease here as a shepherd on a mountainside. Hunched in his dark blue *jelaba*, the crowds move around him, unsure whether to dwell or linger, the cacophonous nature of the space pulling them in different directions, looking for other circles to join.

He plays, oblivious to the surrounding throng, his cap on the ground, upturned and coinless. He plays a tune which, to my ears, could have been played here a thousand years ago… as the camel caravans paused *en route* for sustenance and entertainment. A timeless witness, he plays and plays but no coins come.

Blind Musician: It's true that some of the entertainers rely on their hustling skills to get by. But there are players with extraordinary talent as well. As evening slips into night, an old blind musician, with a microphone strapped around his neck, twists up the volume knob on his amplifier, and begins to play. He's not doing it for the money, but because the square is his sweetheart, his theatre, his home.

Pin-striped Healer: The business of a specific halka tends to be clear from a distance. Glance at the faces of the audience and you see it right away, reflected like candlelight in a mirror. Most of the time entertainers keep the atmosphere jovial, because humour leads to laughter, and laughter leads to generosity.

But some performers have a far graver message. The darkest of all on this night is a man in a black wool pinstripe suit. He has a huge beard, like a great black inverted candyfloss. He's missing his front teeth, and his creased face is gripped with an almost maniacal expression.

He's ranting on about Jinn, the spirits that Muslims believe exist in a parallel world laid atop of our own. The subject is greeted with terrified looks, especially when the pin-stripe healer starts spewing numbers – the alphanumeric *Abjad* system, linchpin in a magician's repertoire.

Row of Blindmen: Jma el Fna has its own telegraphy. It knows about you long before you know about it. A row of blind men begging for alms are alerted of my presence by a woman sitting on a stool nearby.

She calls to them, explaining that I'm recording them. They stand up and, staring directly at me with wide glassy eyes, wave their sticks. Commotion ensues and suddenly confusion and ill temper reign in a corner of the square. But the pervasive natural rhythm of el Fna soon restores order.

Bike Boy: Fleeting moments in the dark: a boy before me is suddenly pushed down to the ground on his bicycle by an older girl. She makes sure she hurts him, and is then gone, away into the night.

Storyteller: The storytellers (or *hakawatis*), draw the largest of all the crowds even if their own numbers are dwindling … when they are out, their halkas are lined with listeners, both old and young.

Recounting tales from *Alf Layla wa Layla*, *A Thousand and One Nights*, and other favourite collections like *Antar wa Abla*, they tap into a communal obsession for the fantastic.

The best storytellers are good businessmen as well. They know when to stop their tale on a cliffhanger, appealing for a few coins before they go on.

Like so much of what takes place at Jma el Fna, the stories are understood by few foreigners, as they're recounted in Darija, the Moroccan dialect. The tourists might take pictures of the crowd, but they don't penetrate… or receive the ancient message being passed on.

Order: Spend some time soaking up the atmosphere through all the senses, and patterns begin to emerge. It's part of Jma el Fna's own form of magic, an alchemy that transforms disorder into order.

Fears for the Future: I used to worry that the square would one day be destroyed, built over, its revelers disbanded. But now I see how impossible that would be. As a cornerstone of life, Jma el Fna is somehow indispensible to Marrakchis, as vital to them as the air they breathe.

Zigzag Conclusions: Standing in the ocean of people, circles forming, flourishing, and dissipating likes ripples all around, I'm reminded of my father's words, that the best way to understand the square, and to experience it, is the zigzag way… zigzag back and forth for long enough, and you're touched by the sorcery of the place… from the inside out.

Pass through it long enough and it begins to pass through you.

With the Dalai Lama at his home in northern India

'Little Lhasa', the Dalai Lama's home at McLeod Ganj

Little Lhasa

A CLUSTER OF TIBETAN LAMAS stand in the street, gorging themselves on juicy *momo* dumplings.

In the temple behind them, many more are prostrating towards a large statue of Buddha, while still more circumvent the compound, spinning prayer wheels clockwise as they go. All around, the streets teem with stalls selling Tibetan jewellery, embroidery, music and food.

At first glance you might be fooled into thinking you were in the back streets of Lhasa, the Tibetan capital. But this Buddhist community is far from there, in the northern Indian state of Himachal Pradesh.

Fifty years ago, when Chinese forces streamed across the border, the Dalai Lama, Tibet's spiritual leader, slipped over the mountains in disguise, along with his most trusted supporters. He sought sanctuary in India, where he was permitted to reside near the small hill station of Dharamsala. It's been his home for half a decade, and has become an outpost of homeland away from Tibet. The community, known locally as 'Little Lhasa', is a place of pilgrimage for Buddhists the world over.

Driving up to Dharamsala, the road zigzags sharply, twisting and turning back on itself, one precarious bend following tight on the heels of the next. Either side of the tarmac, lush vegetation looms up, the trees and creepers alive with langur monkeys, butterflies and brightly coloured birds. As my taxi ascended, reaching cloud level, the greenery all around seemed to change, the conifers replaced by fabulous jungle plants and ferns.

I had arrived by over-night train from Delhi, which pulled into the sleepy station of Pathankot a little after breakfast. The drive up to Dharamsala took about two hours, most of it spent with my begging the driver to slow down. Wide-eyed and grinning, he spun the wheel easily through his hands, recounting the close calls that had so nearly claimed his life.

The Dalai Lama's community is not actually based at Dharamsala, but a little further up the hillside, at McLeod Ganj. The incongruous place name, derives from Sir Donald Friell McLeod, a nineteenth century Governor of the Punjab. Set at six thousand eight hundred feet, the hill station enjoys spectacular sweeping views over the plateau below. Once favoured by the British, it offered a cool refuge from the ferocious summer heat of New Delhi.

As soon as you reach the outskirts of town, you see lamas strolling about, and wizened old Tibetan women, walking with canes, their legs hidden beneath striped aprons. From the first moment you arrive, the sense of tranquility hits you face on, as if the burdens of the outside world have somehow melted away. There's irony in this, of course, because the several thousand Tibetans who make their home at McLeod Ganj do so because they're unable to return home. Their struggle against the Chinese occupation of Tibet has been all about non-violence, after all.

Every year, hundreds of ordinary Tibetans travel in secret over the mountains to Nepal, and across into India, on a pilgrimage to Little Lhasa. For the first time in their lives they are permitted to celebrate the life of its most famous resident, the Dalai Lama. This religious freedom must come as a tremendous relief, for merely speaking his name in their homeland is a crime.

Many of the foreigners who arrive at McLeod Ganj stay for weeks, or even months, residing in the little guest houses and hostels found in the back streets and lanes. They fill the cafés on the main street, sipping green tea, chatting about Buddhism and the Dalai Lama's teachings, or browsing the stalls for bargains. It's not uncommon to find celebrities there as well. Richard Gere and other Hollywood A-listers are quite well known to the locals. Yet, unlike elsewhere in the world, when they come to Little Lhasa they are left alone.

Having visited Tibet a few months earlier, I had travelled to Mcleod Ganj in the hope of seeking an audience with the Dalai Lama. Two months before setting out to India, I had corresponded with His Holiness' office.

I had heard that a private meeting is near impossible, a result of his packed programme and frequent travels. After all, there's a never-ending line of world dignitaries hoping to meet him.

Fortunately for me, there had been no last minute travel plans. His Holiness' private secretary asked me to present myself at the main monastery in McLeod Ganj, called Namgyal, the afternoon after my arrival. Following an informal chat, and being looked over, he told me to return the next morning at ten a.m.

While waiting in the office, I was surprised how many dozens of tourists casually drop in, optimistically hoping for a spur of the moment rendezvous with the Dalai Lama. They are all politely turned away.

Having passed through airport style security, I was taken up to a private meeting room; and, after a short wait, was ushered down a long corridor into His Holiness' study.

It's always weird to see someone face to face who you know so well already – or, at least, someone you think you know. But, in this case, it was strangely comforting. Dressed in his trademark maroon robes, and wearing sturdy brown lace up shoes, the Dalai Lama shot up, and ushered me to a sofa.

In the three quarters of an hour we spent together, chatting about the situation in Tibet, and our shared affection for yaks, he struck me as someone utterly at peace with the world around him. Unlike anyone else robbed of their country, his pacifist approach was astonishing. But it isn't to say he was ready to give up the fight for his homeland.

As a writer, he asked me several times, to do all I could to draw attention to the plight of Tibet, and to remind the world of the situation for his people.

On the evening of my audience, I was sitting on a low wall in McLeod Ganj, thinking about it all, when an old Tibetan woman staggered up, and rested herself there. She had plaits, was dressed in the traditional apron, and looked about eighty-five. I asked her if she had lived there long. She looked at me hard, her eyes watery with age.

'I came here across the mountains with his Holiness,' she said. 'That was fifty summers ago. I was young then, and strong.'

I asked if she had ever returned back to Tibet. She shook her head slowly, left then right.

'The soul has left our country, and who can live in a place without a soul?'

Cheryl Mason with her Samburu husband and members of his family

Cheryl with her mother-in-law and sister-in-law in Samburuland

Love in the Desert

NESTLING AMONGST THE HILLS of Samburuland, in central Kenya, the tiny village of Bawaa goes about its daily life.

Women fetch water on their heads; young boys tend the herds of cattle; and a group of warriors preen themselves, as the sun blazes down from the expansive African sky. It seems as though nothing in this tranquil setting has changed in centuries. But then, without warning, a shrill cockney voice – radiating from a square-shaped hut – shatters the afternoon calm.

'Dikola! Come 'ere and tell me what the 'ell's goin' on!'

A slender, lean Samburu warrior, with a rather downcast expression, moves nervously over to the hut. Inside, encased by windowless cow-dung walls, a handful of Samburu women are seated. Each is bedecked with a great collar of traditional bead-work. At the centre of the group crouches a chubby, blonde woman with an East End accent and a sun-roasted complexion.

Meet Cheryl Mason-Lekimenju, the newest member of the fearless Samburu warrior clan.

Cheryl hit the British headlines when she left her three young children to marry Dikola Lekimenju, a Samburu warrior and part time tribal dancer. The couple had met while Cheryl was on a package holiday to the Kenyan coast. After being granted a visa, Dikola – who's ten years Cheryl's junior – was forced to leave the UK by the Home Office. It suspected that the Samburu had married merely to qualify for a British passport. Determined not to be parted from this, her third husband, Cheryl accompanied Dikola to his tribal village. The unlikely couple now lives within the remote Samburu community of Dikola's birth – encircled as it is by a rugged thorn stockade to ward off lions.

As Dikola takes his place on the floor beside his bride, his mother begins the lengthy business of making tea. Her shaven head, its face creased with age, melt into the darkness of the one-roomed hut. With care, she pours a precious calabash of cloudy brown water into an aluminium pot. The vessel is placed on a makeshift hearth in the middle of the room. Then, with the strike of a match, the neat bundle of kindling catches. The flames illuminate other life forms hiding within the room. Three little children are playing in the shadows, along with a nest of new-born puppies, and a clutch of hungry pecking chickens.

But the pride of place belongs to Cheryl Mason-Lekimenju who, squatting uneasily, rubs her hands with an unending supply of Superdrug wet-wipes. As she does so, her aged Samburu mother-in-law looks on in bewilderment. One senses that, in these conditions, no amount of wet-wiping could bring true hygiene.

A few drops of milk are squeezed into the cooking pot straight from the cow's udder. Then a handful of tea leaves are sprinkled into the bubbling brown water. And, as the dense blue smoke begins to billow sideways from the fire, Cheryl drops her beloved wet-wipes and begins to choke. No one takes any notice, except for Dikola's elderly one-eyed father, Loperecho.

Grasping a spear in his right hand, he pierces a hole in the dung wall. Fresh air wafts in through the instant window. Moments later, Cheryl is sipping her tea, trying as best she can to settle back into her new lifestyle.

The Samburu village which Cheryl now calls home, is a million miles from the respectable middle class existence that she left behind. Surrounded by customs, climate, and dangers, that are all unfamiliar, she's trying her level best to adapt. But the transition has not been an easy one.

For those not used to the hardy routine of Samburu life, the discomfort, boredom, and constant bouts of illness, can easily be too much to bear. The stress on Dikola, the swarthy warrior – ever present at Cheryl's side – has been equally great. Once the favourite son, his family are confused as to what exactly's going on. They wonder what the future with his cockney bride will hold. A man of few words at the best of times, Dikola mopes about with his head hung low, perhaps pondering how he got into such a peculiar situation in the first place.

Cheryl's is the tale of a woman who, trapped in her second loveless marriage, traded in her young children, husband, belongings and home, for the tall dark warrior of her fantasy. Vilified in the tabloid press for abandoning her two sons – Stevie, thirteen; Tommie, eleven – and her angelic daughter, Chloe, four – Cheryl maintains that her own traumatic childhood explains all the irrational behaviour.

In a book, entitled *White Mischief*, she reveals the intimate account of her journey from a high-rise in Bromley, to a *manyatta*, (group of cow-dung huts), in Samburuland.

White Mischief, a cross between a Mills & Boon romance and a psychologist's casebook, is peppered with italicized flashbacks to Cheryl's abusive childhood. The text paints a picture of abuse that was by any standards severe. Cheryl claims to have been molested by not only her natural father, step-father and mother, but by her sister and first husband as well.

For Cheryl's three kids, the separation from their mother has been filled with anxiety.

'The children have lost faith in me,' she says in a rather surprised tone, 'especially the middle one, Tommie. He's suffering from chronic depression. The boys have told me that there have been periods when Chloe's cried solidly for three weeks, calling out my name. And, there have been times when she sees a woman in the street who looks similar to me and she's clung onto her, screaming "Mummy! Mummy!"'

The fact that their mother is six thousand miles away from home, living with a semi-nomadic blood-drinking tribe, has brought raillery from the boys' classmates.

'My children have been ridiculed at school,' continues Cheryl as she lists all the damage that the relationship has done. 'They're told, "Oh, your mum's got a Masaai warrior in a tent in the garden"; or, "Your mum's gone off with a black man." But they never complain to me. They've been absolute gems.'

Communication with the children, who are living with Cheryl's second husband, Mike, is all but non-existent.

'I'm waiting for them to contact me,' she gasps, cleansing her hands with another wet-wipe. 'I used to phone them regular, by reversing the charges once a month or so. But now I'm leaving it to them. I left them some aerogrammes but, as yet, they haven't written.'

Throughout her life Cheryl has yearned to escape.

That escape finally came in the form of a package tour, on which she was accompanied by an elderly friend. The journey, to Mombasa, on the Kenyan coast, was blissful. And, it was there, while staying at a beach hotel, that Cheryl first set eyes on the timid tribal dancer Dikola Lekimenju.

The mother-of-three was captivated from the outset by the warrior's sleek form, his enormous brown eyes and amiable character. They spent every waking moment together, as Cheryl slowly entered the warrior's world. She learned that he had six siblings, that he belonged to one of Africa's most fearless tribes, and that he had killed his first lion at seventeen – but that he hated killing.

'Dikola is very gentle,' says Cheryl defensively, 'imagine what it's like to be told to kill animals if you don't want to. And Dikola didn't want to.' Performing in traditional tribal dances at tourist hotels, or selling trinkets on the beach, gave Dikola a break from the slaughter – which accompanies a warrior's life, and a profession he so despised. Every few months he would return home to his village to give his earnings as a dancer to his family.

On one such journey northward, Dikola asked Cheryl to accompany him. Her first impression of his humble cow-dung hut – one step below a mud hut – was that it resembled 'a hollowed out Oxo cube'.

'At first I kicked up a right stink,' remembers Cheryl, 'shouting 'I'm not going into no bush!' But the more I didn't want to go, the more he asked me to. We finally arrived at the *manyatta* in the late afternoon, having walked the twenty-six kilometres from Maralal, the nearest small town. The family were very hospitable though. They were lovely – gathering around to kiss my hands. I don't think they really understood what I meant to Dikola, or how far our relationship would go. The first night was so uncomfortable and really cold.'

Sleeping on the hut's main bed – a rough, hide-covered platform, without blankets – the couple huddled to keep warm.

The passages of Cheryl's book, describing her interminable abuse as a child and adolescent, are suddenly replaced by romantic texts of the steamiest variety. *'For the first time in my life'*, she writes, *' the desire to make love came with animal passion… I was a woman with sexual feelings and carnal desires… we made love five times in those first three hours. Making love in the African bush stripped away all inhibitions, made it the most basic and essential of all functions… I had asked God not to allow me to be pregnant and we would make love for hours on the floor of Dikola's hut.'*

The passion, it seems, only ended when Cheryl's digestive tract became infected from the local Samburu cuisine.

'When I first became very ill with streptococci,' she whispers softly, hinting that sickness has been frequent, 'Dikola's mother gave me a potion made from some sort of tree bark and roots, with a bit of honey in it to cut some of the bitterness. When they had boiled it up, it was put in the ground. Dikola fed it to me a spoon at a time. The Samburu don't like letting out their secrets, so I don't know quite what it was, except that it made my urine go red.'

Now certain that this was no mere holiday fling, Cheryl was ready to put her infatuation for Dikola before all else. In the months that followed, she returned to Kenya twice, to the dismay of her husband and deep sadness of her children. Then, having broken it to the kids that she was in love with an African warrior, Cheryl asked Mike for a divorce, and set about getting Dikola to emigrate to England. A tabloid newspaper helped financially in getting the young Samburu a passport and ticket. A few weeks later – when Dikola slipped into Britain on a tourist visa – the media frenzy began.

The first days in Europe together were spent locked in a hotel room in the custody of the tabloid. The pair were hounded by the paparazzi wherever they went. Dikola was encouraged to pose in full tribal dress beside London's famous landmarks. He might have wondered why, but there was no time to answer questions.

As soon as one photo session ended, another began. One fashion shoot, held at a prominent studio, had the warrior dressing up in couture tuxedos. Another had him posing in full tribal regalia and war-paint with Cheryl's children, at their Isle of Wight semi.

Fleet Street's finest had a field day. Cheryl's second husband, Mike, strained to protect the children from the media glare. After being introduced to Dikola for the first time, he was reported as saying, 'it is odd meeting someone who is sleeping with your wife. But what do you say to a man who has killed a lion with his bare hands?'

The first thing Cheryl's mother knew of the relationship was when she saw her daughter's face splashed across the tabloids' front pages. The two had not communicated for over three years.

'My mother kept saying, "there's no way my daughter would get involved with a black man",' recalls Cheryl, 'she was sure that the whole story had been made up. When she found out that it was not, she called me up and said sarcastically, "Well, aren't you a clever girl then?!" Later, I took Dikola to see my grandmother – just before she died. She told me that I was sordid and awful for leaving my kids and such a sweet man like Mike.'

When Cheryl was sixteen, she had a tattoo 'shaved' from her shoulder in an excruciating operation. The motif of a swallow, bearing the word 'Mum', was designed two years earlier – before Cheryl's long-running feud with her mother had begun. Aware that his new bride would not be tattooed again with readiness, Dikola requested they both have their right breasts tattooed with each other's name.

Meanwhile, newspaper hacks and film crews from across Europe – and beyond – devoured the story. They couldn't believe their luck. But little did they know... the best was still to come.

Cheryl and Dikola suddenly revealed to the world their intentions to marry. And, on fourteenth February, St. Valentine's Day, the couple rolled up to Newport's registrar's office in a borrowed 1927 Bentley. Standing tall in his traditional Samburu finery, Dikola braced himself against the cold. Beside him Cheryl posed for photographs, wrapped in a simple knotted red cloth, her body adorned with exquisite African jewellery. The media rubbed their hands with glee. It was as if Crocodile Dundee was marrying Shirley Valentine.

Cheryl regrets the way that she and Dikola have been treated by the press.

'I blame the media a lot,' she says in a bitter voice. 'We have been severely abused. The worst is that everyone's always saying we must have made a fortune out of all the publicity – I wish!'

Public ridicule, unpleasant as it was, may have been the more palatable consequence, from all the international attention. Anxious to show that permanent residency isn't automatic when one weds a British citizen, the Home Office ruled that Dikola would have to return immediately to Kenya.

'Dikola is my husband!' Cheryl exclaims in an impassioned cry, 'I'm English and have English children: the Home Office just can't do what they're doing. Of course we will win!'

Her anger at the Home Office and the press is largely rooted in the way her latest husband has been portrayed as a simpleton.

'Dikola isn't a primitive – he's got a brain! I want him to have a chance in life... I'd like him to have the opportunity of doing a few open day training schemes in England, to see what he likes best.'

In the meantime, Dikola is practising the 3Rs with a view to securing a good job in Britain when (and *if*) he gets residency. A brief education from missionaries as a child complemented his tribal training in hunting wild animals and herding the family flocks.

Since fleeing back to Kenya from Britain, immigration troubles have continued to torment the Lekimenjus. Incensed that a Kenyan citizen has been expelled from the United Kingdom, some politicians in Kenya are pressing for Cheryl to now be thrown out of the country, in a tit-for-tat expulsion.

'If London's immigration officials found the couple's behaviour unacceptable in that country, who are we to give them sanctuary here?' Mr. Mbugua, a prominent Kenyan politician, was reported as saying. The political calls for Cheryl to be banished back to England, have reverberated through East Africa's press. While numerous editorials have demanded justice and revenge. The 'Lekimenju Affair' – which has been simmering away – is escalating into what may become a full-blown diplomatic fracas.

Seemingly oblivious of the international furore they have stirred up, Cheryl and her warrior sit on a hillside just outside Bawaa village. As mosquitoes buzz about in the cool evening air, the couple watch the sun go down.

'I can't live without Dikola,' says Cheryl suddenly, brimming with romantic verve. 'I've never felt that about a single person in my life. I can even live without my children – I know they'll survive – but I can't live without Dikola!'

At her side as always, Dikola rolls his eyes as Cheryl continues another exuberant declaration of her love. 'He may not be romantic in the English sense of the word,' she says, 'I've never had a gift from Dikola – except for a few warrior beads – but he shows his love in other ways. And he's proved to me that he doesn't just see me as a ticket out of Kenya. He only wants to be in England because I want to be there.'

The couple would have liked to have had children. But, after going through three caesarean births, Cheryl says that another pregnancy would be life-threatening. It's a point that irks her, as she believes Dikola would have been a better father than her previous husbands.

'I don't regret the kids I've got,' she says, 'but I do regret the husbands I chose. I wasn't ready to have kids – I was blackmailed into having children by my first husband. Then the second marriage happened because Mike came along and the children needed a father, more than I needed a husband. Shortly afterwards, Chloe was born.'

Cheryl is thought to be the first white woman ever to have married a Samburu. She says that she's the only one in history to be honoured by being given a Samburu name. It is 'Nicmarie', meaning 'good woman'. A few other European women have taken morans, warriors, as lovers. But, in most cases, the liaisons were short-lived.

'All the white women I've met who have tried to make lives here have failed,' says Cheryl. 'Most of them meet, as we did, at the coast. Me and Dikola are the only ones who're still together. The other women see the relationship as an escape. It usually ends with the European thinking that the warrior was making use of her.'

One of Cheryl's acquaintances – an English woman in her sixties – had a twenty-year-old Samburu boyfriend. She bought him expensive gifts, and built him a fine concrete house over the hill from Bawaa village. When she left, the young warrior was scorned by the close-knit society.

'Another English woman, called Pauline,' recalls Cheryl, 'left her husband for a young man from this area. She was sixteen stone and forty-four years old. One day I got a package of beads and stuff the boy had given her, together with an anonymous note. It said that Pauline was dead, and asked if I could inform the boy and his family. I found out soon after that Pauline, who had got back together with her husband, had written the note herself. She wasn't dead at all. She was just tired of the affair!'

Like the other white women who come to Samburuland, Cheryl Lekimenju finds herself spending most of the time with the men-folk. A woman's role in African village life is a subordinate one.

'Women here do everything!' says Cheryl angrily. 'They don't have a life. They build the houses, collect the firewood, have the babies and raise the children. And they're treated like second rate citizens from the day they're born. It's lucky that I don't speak *maa*, the Samburu language, because I'd tell them to rebel!'

Most men dislike being told what to do by their wives and, in Samburuland, an over-dominating wife is a source of great embarrassment. As night falls over Bawaa, Cheryl's hard-edged tones can be heard over the nest of huts. Dikola, who seems to be a little more hen-pecked every moment, chaperones his English rose between the cow-dung homes of the village. The threat of wild animals is all around. Leopards come in the night and kill the goats; lions come during the day and kill the cattle. Blind to the dangers which surround her, Cheryl chirps on in the piercing voice that the community has come to know so well.

'Dikola married me in my culture,' she says matter-of-factly. 'But I haven't yet wedded him in his culture. Dikola's younger brother won't be able to marry, until we have been wed in a Samburu ceremony.'

A dedicated romantic, Cheryl wants the tribal wedding ceremony to be held on St. Valentine's Day. Dikola understands the relevance of the date, but his family have never heard of St. Valentine. To the Samburu – most of whom don't have calendars – one day is much like any other.

'I'm not looking forward to the Samburu wedding,' winces Cheryl restlessly, 'because they wrap the bride up in an oily goat skin. I'm not quite sure what the actual procedure is, except that the groom's mother shaves off all his hair, saying that he's passing from a warrior and becoming a responsible husband.'

The outlandish wedding ritual may sound harrowing to Cheryl. But it ought to be the least of her worries. For, in Samburuland, a bride is expected to be circumcised. Samburu circumcision techniques – performed as a matter of course on men as well as women – are regarded as the harshest of their kind. Dikola's mother and sisters (all circumcised and proud of it) are eager to get a knife to Cheryl's private parts.

'Usually the woman is circumcised when she is a child,' says Dikola's half-brother, Lmakayo, grinning broadly. 'But sometimes, the circumcision is done just before the marriage… even on the wedding day itself.'

Cheryl, who – perhaps unwisely – takes the calls for her circumcision lightly, wants to see the operation modified or outlawed altogether.

'Samburu women believe that their daughters won't find husbands,' she says, 'unless they've gone through the agonizing surgery. They just hack away blindly in a dark hut. A lot of girls die because of un-sterilized knives. The woman doing the cutting doesn't know what to remove, so she cuts out the whole lot. I bet that if you threw chicken blood all over the hut, and got the woman to scream, the men would think that a circumcision had been done!'

Dikola's one-eyed father, Loperecho, sits outside his hut, contemplating his family's predicament. One senses an air of despondence hanging over the old warrior. Like most in the community, you get the feeling he would have preferred Dikola to have chosen a nice Samburu girl, and taken *her* as a wife. A family is disgraced if the favourite son leaves to live somewhere else. And the Lekimenjus sense that Dikola will soon leave them. To have one's son go off to a distant land with a strange English woman – who's neither circumcised, nor a Samburu – is depressing. But, for Dikola's elderly father, there's a far more pressing worry.

In Samburuland, the father of the groom is expected to pay a dowry to the bride's family. No one else can pay the dowry – generally eight cows and two sheep – on his behalf. Loperecho, who lost most of his livestock in a drought several years ago, is concerned as to how he will raise the bridal gift. In line with customary protocol, he expects that Cheryl's family will soon contact him for the required head of livestock. But, procuring the animals – which won't be easy – is only half the problem. The real worry for Dikola's father is that he will, according to tradition, have to make arrangements to transport the animals to Cheryl's own 'hillside' – in England.

N.B. *White Mischief*, Summersdale Press, 1996.

Memoir of a Torture Jail

I SCANNED THE ROOM. It was arranged for torture.

There was a rack for breaking feet, a bar for hanging a man upside down, rows of manacles, straps and batons, and pliers for extracting teeth.

There were syringes with used needles, smelling salts, a medical drip, electrocution equipment, and dried blood strewn over the floor and walls.

Exactly where this dreadful place was I still do not know – I arrived and left in military blindfolds. All I do know is that it was near Peshawar on Pakistan's northwest frontier, and it is run by Islamabad's military intelligence.

I was arrested while travelling in Pakistan, just after the London bombs, and I was held for sixteen days, along with my two-man film crew, David and Leon Flamholc. We were heading overland from India to Afghanistan to research a documentary about a massive lost treasure of the Mughals.

From Peshawar our plan was to head down the Khyber Pass to Kabul, the Afghan capital. But I suggested a detour to find the house of a distant relative. As we searched, David videoed me, hoping to capture the reunion with old relatives. Suddenly a military police officer, armed with a sub-machinegun, strode up. He took our passports and the camera and led us to a military post.

We said we had not filmed anything sensitive and the atmosphere was calm – at first, anyway. They admitted there were no signs in English prohibiting filming but said there was a sign in Urdu, which none of us could read. They rummaged through our luggage, asked questions, and said they were waiting for a senior officer to turn up.

After about four hours, he swept in.

His tone was abrupt. He said we were being detained and had no right to call our embassies. We were blindfolded, our hands chained behind our backs, and led to a truck at gunpoint.

After a short drive we arrived at a medical installation. We were stripped and examined, still chained and blindfolded. Just to lose one's vision is the most terrifying thing. The doctor told his assistant to prepare sedatives. It was a terrible moment. I crouched, waiting for the prick of a needle which, thankfully, never came.

Fearing I was about to pass out, I fought hard to take deep breaths. I was sweating so heavily that my blindfold was drenched. Through a tiny gap I could make out blurred details of the room: resuscitation equipment, manacles and a pool of fresh blood on the floor.

Suddenly, we were bundled back into the pick-up and driven at high speed to an interrogation unit. We spent the next thirty-six hours in a military dungeon – a large, cavernous cell with bare walls and a concrete floor. Armed soldiers stood at the door.

A plain-clothes officer interrogated. At first he emphasized that we had committed grave crimes and would have to pay the price. But after watching the video footage, however, he changed tack, agreeing that there was nothing wrong.

'Then why are you charging us?' I asked.

'You are not charged,' he replied.

'Then can we go?'

'No, I must write a report.'

'How long will that take?'

'Days, perhaps weeks.'

It became clear that I was being held on suspected terrorism charges. As a British citizen of Asian Muslim origin, I was suspected of being part of the world of suicide bombers, religious schools and Islamic fanaticism.

At ten p.m. on the second night we heard the sound of keys.

The cell was opened by a pair of towering plain-clothes officers. I noticed that the chains and blindfolds they carried were different from those of the military police. It seemed that we were being passed to another agency.

We were led to a jeep and driven through the streets of Peshawar, then out of the city and down a bumpy dirt track. My overwhelming fear was that we were about to be shot in the back of the head and dumped away from town.

Eventually the jeep braked.

I heard an iron gate open and we jerked in over what felt like a cattle grid. One by one we were then dragged out in chains and held squatting on the ground. Behind my blindfold I could smell jasmine and hear a man moaning in the distance.

We were led calmly into a cell block and isolated in solitary confinement cells. Mine was about two yards by three, with a concrete floor and no furniture of any kind. There was a rough lice-ridden blanket, a strip light that was never turned off, a squat lavatory and a hosepipe.

The walls were bare white, covered in graffiti, written mostly in faeces and blood – much of it in English.

I could not sleep, nor see what was happening beyond my cell. But there were the sounds of men weeping and what had to be the screams of others being tortured. The fear of being taken out and shot was constant, especially in the first days. Nobody outside would have known; nobody had a clue that we had been taken away.

The next day I concluded that we were being held by military intelligence. The guards, who were all dressed in plain clothes, refused to give their names. One, a young man who brought me water, said the unit was known to them as 'The Farm'. He told me that keeping calm, and telling all I knew when interrogated, was the best way of staying alive.

My colleagues, Leon and David were in cells nearby, but speaking to each other was forbidden. When I needed the hosepipe to be turned on I would shout so the guards could hear me.

Late on the second night a guard came to my cell with chains and blindfold. I called out to David and Leon that I was being moved. They told me later that they thought I was being taken out to be executed.

I staggered down a long corridor and was pushed into a chair. A voice said that if I told the truth I would not be harmed but that I'd be in danger if I lied. I was so frightened that I felt weak and nauseous.

And the fear brought sweat. But it wasn't normal sweat. It was mixed with adrenalin, and stank like cat pee. For all the washing, I couldn't get it off my body.

That first night, I was interviewed for three hours.

The questions ranged from my family to my knowledge of Islam, explosives and weaponry, my work as a writer and documentary maker, as well as on how much money I earned. They were also preoccupied with the fact that my two colleagues were Jewish – something which I had never really thought about.

My fears were increased when, after several nightly interrogations, the blindfolds were untied. It was then I saw an array of bloodied torture instruments, and the central drain. The implication was clear. Horrified, I was returned to my cell.

As the interrogations went on, I explained my life and details of the books I'd written. Recounting it all piece by piece, I realized how complex it all must have sounded. After all, I am of Afghan and British ancestry, brought up in Britain, married to an Indian, and living in Morocco – and my passport has stamps from dozens of obscure countries. Every answer seemed to provoke another slew of questions. One young interrogator in particular drove me crazy with his inane questioning.

Night after night he grilled me.

Eventually, during a long session one night he unlocked the handcuffs. I rubbed my wrists. As the questions continued, me staring into blinding interrogation lights, I reached forward and grabbed the interviewer's face – digging my fingernails into his cheeks. Rather apologetically, he admitted that he was only a trainee.

The next night a colonel took over the interrogation. When I told him how grim the food was, he promised to send me some food from his own home. But he never did. On the second night, he asked if I could help get his son into Canadian university to study forestry. I remember almost smiling at the absurdity of the question. Blindfolded and chained once again, I replied that I could certainly have a go, but that in my current situation it was going to be difficult to help.

During the days I felt myself slipping into a kind of madness. Solitary confinement has an astonishing effect on the mind. The trick was to stay calm and keep myself occupied. I spent hours working out how to break free. But trying to escape would have been instant suicide.

Then I spent days and nights retelling myself all the stories I'd ever heard, playing them on the whitewashed walls as if I were in a psychotic form of cinema.

I forced myself to drink huge quantities of liquid to compensate for all the sweating, and spent the days in fitful sleep, worrying about my wife and two children who I had left in Mumbai, wondering when and how the outside world would begin to miss us.

Time and again I was interrogated, usually between midnight and about 3 a.m. Sometimes I was blindfolded and at other times not, but I was always chained.

One night I got a peek into other cells.

In one I saw two Afghan men crouching on the concrete floor. Both had long black beards. A guard said they had been there for months. Another prisoner was kept in a cell painted with black and white spirals to drive him mad.

The interrogators refused to let me contact my wife or the British embassy. One night I boasted that news of our incarceration could not be hushed up. The interrogator told me that two weeks earlier an American helicopter had strayed across the border from Afghanistan and strafed a truck, killing twenty-seven women and children. He said news of the atrocity had never got out – that anything could be covered up in Pakistan.

After about a week, however, I persuaded the young guard to leave a message for my sister-in-law in London, stating that my colleagues and I were alive.

I did not know that my family had assumed we had been kidnapped – or that my sister Saira Shah, known for her documentary about Afghanistan, *Beneath the Veil*, had jumped on a flight to Pakistan to try to find us.

The days dragged on.

I found that the best way to stay upbeat was to see the absurdity of it all. And there were moments of grotesque humour. One night I was stamping around the cell killing cockroaches. In the background I could hear the wild wailing of a man being worked over in the torture room. The guard came to my cell and ordered me to stop making so much noise. He said I was keeping the others awake.

There were also elements of touching humility. Late one evening a guard came to my cell. I was wearing just boxer shorts because of the summer heat. I started putting on my shirt, assuming another interrogation session was about to begin. He waved for me to relax and stuck his fist through the bars.

In his palm were three juicy pineapple cubes for me.

Then, after sixteen nights' detention, a guard turned up at four a.m. and clipped our fingernails, the clippings taken for DNA testing. It seemed a rather high tech for a place without even Internet. Then our bags were brought to our cells and we were told to check nothing had been taken, then and ordered to sign a document confirming that we had not been tortured. An officer from the Pakistani Civilian Intelligence Agency stepped from the shadows.

An hour later we were sitting in the VIP lounge of Peshawar airport as the civilian officer apologized for the military's 'heavy-handed' treatment. It was explained that we were being flown to London via Abu Dhabi and that we had no choice.

The officer informed me repeatedly that there were no charges against us, and that we would be welcome to return. I hope so. Despite the ordeal I remain a great admirer of Pakistan and long to walk in its mountains as a free man.

Arriving at Heathrow airport, we were met by the British Secret Service.

'All right lads?' said their leader, as he took us away for a debriefing. 'Sounds like you've 'ad a damned hard time out there.'

After answering his questions in an interview room, he escorted us to the arrival area. Just before we walked through, he said: 'No goodbyes if that's OK. I'm just gonna slip away. Best if you don't turn round. Just keep walking.'

Since my release I find myself often thinking of the solitary confinement cell where I spent so many days and nights. I can remember the smallest detail of the place. The graffiti, the stench, the sound of the industrial-sized fan which was switched off for just one hour a day, to allow the mechanism to cool down.

But most of all, I wonder.

I wonder who's in that concrete box now and what's going through his head.

Morocco's Alpine Hideaway

THINK OF MOROCCO, and a treasure house of tradition comes to mind.

It's a land of medieval medinas with their maze-like streets, of fabulous Almohad and Andalucían buildings adorned with intricate mosaics, and of unending beaches running along the Mediterranean and Atlantic shores. A crossroads *par excellence*, it's where the Arab world meets the African and the Berber. But best of all, Morocco is a land that never fails to surprise in the most enchanting and alluring way.

Less than an hour's drive from Fès, is the small town of Ifrane. Developed as an Alpine-style resort by the French during their Occupation, it is one of the Kingdom's most unexpected and precious delights.

The drive from Fès to Ifrane, set high in the fir forests of the Atlas Mountains, begins with olive groves, and with roadside stalls selling honey and pomegranates. Then, as you progress upwards, the food stalls give way to others, where villagers tout fossils and nuggets of quartz, mined in the Atlas.

The road passes fields in which sheep and goats graze, in a land once farmed by the Romans – they grew vines there. Eventually, after a thousand twists and turns, you reach the snowline, with the little town of Ifrane a little further beyond.

Surrounded by nature trails and hiking routes, and packed with cafés, Ifrane surprises all first time visitors – whether they be Moroccans or from farther afield. Covered by a thick blanket of snow through much of the winter, the town is quite European in feel.

There's none of the detail so readily associated with Morocco – no arched doorways, no mosaics, or geometric friezes carved into plaster-work. Instead, Ifrane is a haven of sloped Alpine roofs and timber frames, set against a backdrop of woodland. It's straight out of Chamonix.

In the central square there's the scent of chocolate-covered crêpes and the aroma of log-fires burning. The only tell-tale sign that you're in Morocco are the flowing *jelaba* robes, worn by many to keep out the winter chill. And the storks. Their voluminous nests crown too many rooftops to count, and are more Moroccan than almost anything else.

At Café La Paix, a throwback to the days of the French era, I met a retired American couple, George and Gene. They had perma-tans, perfect teeth, and told me both at once that Morocco was their greatest love.

'We come twice a year,' said Gene. 'After spending a few days in Fès, we come up here to Ifrane.'

'It's a kind of therapy to balance the frenzy of the Fès medina,' added Harry.

I asked if he skied. Harry thumped a fist to his thigh. There was a metallic sound.

'Duff leg,' he said. 'Korea's to blame.'

We sat in awkward silence for a while – Harry lost in the memories of youth, Gene applying lipstick liberally to her oversized smile, and I staring up at a pair of storks robbing twigs from another pair to build their own nest. The birds were all filled with a wonderful enthusiasm, as if they couldn't quite believe their luck. And, looking around, I could see the source of their zeal.

Ifrane is a mountain sanctuary like no other.

Much favoured by Hassan II, the former King of Morocco, the town has long hosted royalty, and is fêted for its celebrity associations. A champion of the outdoors life, Hassan II would spend months at a time there, moving his royal Court into the mountains when he tired of the capital, Rabat. With its long perimeter fence, the royal palace is in pride of place on the road towards Azrou. In the days of the former King's rule, a constant stream of dignitaries would make their way up to Ifrane to be received at Court.

A great many of his VIP guests were accommodated at an imposing Alpinesque chalet set on a promontory just above the town. This mixture of royal guesthouse and luxury hotel grew a little tired in recent years. But, after six years of work, not to mention a fortune spent on it, Hotel Michlifen Ifrane – owned by King Mohammed VI – has risen like a phoenix above Morocco's own Alpine backdrop. With the finishing touches complete, the hotel has reopened to visitors once again.

The Michlifen is one of the cosiest and most luxurious travel hideaways in the Kingdom. Inspired by the simple architecture of the Alps, it's a sanctuary of natural pine panelling and of dressed stone walls, of painted Scandinavian wood, sculptures and antique furniture.

The hotel's main lobby is vast but informal, filled with dazzling mountain sunshine by day and understated mood-lighting by night. The exposed stone pillars, the bare wooden floor, and the deep leather couches, give a sense of the American Rockies, rather than the Moroccan Atlas.

While the décor maybe Occidental, the service and warmth are definitely Moroccan. On weekends the hotel is filled with families who arrive mostly from Casablanca and Rabat. As elsewhere, the national obsession with doting over children certainly reaches Ifrane's snow-covered peaks.

Visiting with my family, I tracked my little son down to the kitchen, where he was being indulged by the chef with a pot of chocolate and a spoon. And my daughter spent an entire afternoon playing checkers with the barman whom, I noticed, always let her win.

A stone's throw from the hotel, laden in snow, the main square of Ifrane was alive with locals and with visitors through the short winter days. Students from the Al-Akhawayn University pack the cafés. Established through an *entente cordiale* between the Saudi Arabian and Moroccan Royal Families, the University is one of the most prestigious in Morocco. All around, there were storks building messy twig nests high on the rooftops, and children darting between the poplar trees down near the lake.

In dazzling sunshine, we set off on a hike through the forest.

The small town of Ifrane was soon well behind us, the snow crunching beneath our boots. We walked for miles, weaving a haphazard path between the firs, pausing every so often to hurl snowballs at each other. There was silence, except for birdsong, and the muffled cries of children down in the valley below.

After two hours of hiking, we came to a clearing where a family were gathering sticks. Their faces chapped from the wind, their hands bleeding from thorns, they seemed startled at seeing us. The husband dropped the branch he was holding, and raced over to greet us.

Welcoming us all to that part of the forest, he asked after our health in the prolonged salutations of Moroccan mountain life. His wife and daughters inched forward gingerly and kissed my wife and children.

Minutes later, we found ourselves invited to share their midday meal. No amount of excuses could curb their overwhelming hospitality. As we tucked into a feast of lamb *tagine* and fresh-baked bread, a fire was lit to warm us, the family throwing on all the twigs they had gathered that morning.

'The children must eat!' the husband exclaimed again and again, picking out the best pieces of meat and passing them to my little son and daughter, 'because children are a gift from God.'

I asked how the winter had gone.

'The snow's been deep this year,' said the man, 'and that's good because more people come and ski.' He paused, wiped a hand over his mouth. 'I have lived here my entire life,' he said, 'I was born in a little house just over there, as my own children were. And I must tell you there is something that I don't understand.'

'What?'

'Why people do want to go up and down all day on skis? It just makes no sense at all!'

In the afternoon we drove to the resort of Michlifen, after which the hotel in Ifrane is named. We reached it through an unending fir forest, lost in the mountain crags of the Atlas.

Although far less organized than European resorts, it has an old world charm that's been lost through commerciality from much of Europe. Hauled up the mountainside by a simple lift system, skiers were slaloming their way downhill with differing degrees of style. What amused me was the complete absence of pretension. It was as if no one was looking at anyone looking at them. And, for challenged skiers like me, there's nothing so precious as the feeling that no one's bothered about how many times you fall.

Huddled along the road were local people with sledges, clusters of used ski equipment for hire, and even horse-drawn sleighs.

While standing at the side of the road bartering for a pair of tenth-hand skis, I got talking to an aged Frenchman. He said he could remember the old days when Ifrane was packed with the chic European crowd through the winter season.

'You should have seen it,' he said a glint in his eye. 'We used to drink Pastis on the square, and eat fondue until late in the night, washed down with a nice Muscadet.'

I asked if Ifrane had lost its magic. The Frenchman waved a finger at me hard.

'Non, non, monsieur,' he replied, 'it's better than ever.'

'Are you sure?'

'Of course it is. Take a look around you! The French never would have permitted such *joie de vivre* as this!'

Morocco's Pirate Realm

RELOCATE FROM A CRAMPED East End flat to a haunted mansion, in the middle of a Casablanca shanty-town, and you can't help but slip into the Moroccan Twilight Zone.

It's a world conjured straight from a child's imagination – a realm of Jinn and exorcists, of dazzling colours, exotic foods and unending possibility.

During the years we have lived here, we have descended down through the interleaving layers of Moroccan society to its very bedrock. In that time I have become preoccupied with the Morocco that tourists rarely glimpse, the one that lies just beneath the surface, waiting to be discovered by anyone ready to receive it.

Every day Europe's budget airlines ferry tourists back and forth, depositing them at the gates of a few key Moroccan cities – Marrakech, Agadir and Fès. Yet, the rest of the kingdom is left largely alone. So, stray a little off the beaten track, and the rewards can be immediate and quite extraordinary. And, as often happens in Morocco, the greatest treasures are where you expect them least of all.

I was reminded of this last week when my daughter, Ariane, came home and begged me to help with her pirate project. She's obsessed with Johnny Depp, and imagines all pirates to be bumbling caricatures, rather than the ruthless killers of today's African Horn.

Googling 'Morocco Pirates', she began a treasure trail which led right from our own door.

An hour's drive up the coast from Casablanca is the capital, Rabat. It's rather staid – orderly traffic, clipped hedges, and droves of diplomats. Across from it, nestled up on the windswept Atlantic shore is the small town of Salé. Most Rabatis like to stick their noses up at their down-at-heel neighbour. They regard it as sordid, squalid, a complete waste of time. I had bought in to the whole Salé-bashing syndrome, and found myself snarling at the mere mention of the name.

A pirate cannon on the battlements of old Salé

But Ariane insisted I'd got it all wrong.

She told a tale of a pirate realm worthy of Jack Sparrow himself, one where Robinson Crusoe had been taken as a slave. For eight centuries, she said, Salé had been a world centre of looting, pillaging, and of white slavery. The frenzied debauchery had reached its height in the 1600s, under the greatest marauder in the Barbary history, the infamous Jan Janszoon.

A Dutch freebooter, and former Christian slave himself, Janszoon made himself overlord of a pirate republic based at Salé. He waylaid many hundreds of ships across the Atlantic and the Mediterranean, possibly extending as far as Iceland and the Americas. In true pirate tradition, he sired countless children. His descendents are said to embrace a Who's Who of celebrity, including the Marquis of Blandford, Humphrey Bogart, and Jackie O.

Intrigued by this curious nugget of international pirate trivia, I bundled Ariane into the car and sped north.

Soon we spied the skyline of Rabat, all proud and stately as a capital city should be. Across the estuary, the syrupy yellow light of late afternoon gave a glow to the ancient walls of what was once the pirate realm – the Republic of Salé.

Even from a distance there was something bleak and piratic about it.

Gnarled volcanic rocks, breakers, wine-dark sea, and walls right out of *Treasure Island*. Approaching from along the coast, we found ourselves at an immense and ancient burial ground – tens of thousands of graves packed tight together, the head-stones lost in each other's shadows.

Unable to resist, we strolled slowly between the graves, the chill Atlantic wind ripping in our ears. Ariane said she could imagine the pirates sleeping there, cuddled up with their secrets and their treasure maps.

In the middle of the graveyard a fisherman was crouching with a long slim rod, and an empty paint can filled with fish heads. He was surrounded by cats. When I asked him about pirates he narrowed his eyes, nodded once, and pointed to a low fortress at the edge of the cemetery.

We went over to it.

Crafted from honey-yellow stone, the *Sqala*, as it's known in Arabic, was built into the crenellated sea wall, rusted iron cannons still trained on the horizon. A policeman was standing outside. He had a weather-worn face, watery eyes, and a big toothy grin. Ariane asked him about pirates. Before we knew it, we'd been ushered inside.

He led the way through a cool stone passage and out onto a rounded terrace, bathed in blinding yellow light. There was something magical about it, as if it were so real that it was fake, like a Hollywood set. The cannons there were bronze, lizard-green with verdigris, each one bearing a different crest.

'They were obviously captured by pirates,' said Ariane knowledgeably. 'If they weren't, the crests would all be the same.'

Staring out to where the water joined the sky, the policeman suddenly recited a poem about unrequited love. He said there was no better place in all the world to compose poetry than right there, and that poetry was his true love.

I asked if he'd ever heard of Jan Janszoon. He cocked his face to the ground beneath his feet.

'The dungeon,' he said grimly.

We went down jagged steps, along a vaulted corridor bored out from the stone, lit by shafts of natural light. Home to nests of stray cats, it was damp and smelled of death. The officer showed us a truly miserable cell which looked as though it had been quite recently used. His grin subsiding, he explained awkwardly that the last prisoner had been forgotten, and had starved to death.

'Was it the famous corsair, Jan Janszoon?' I asked.

The policeman shook his head.

'For him, you must go to the old city,' he said.

After sweet mint tea, and yet more poetry, we escaped with directions scribbled in Arabic, directions to the home of Jan Janszoon lost in the maze of the old city.

After years living in Morocco, I am no stranger to walled medinas, and have traipsed through dozens of them – often searching for a cryptic address. In that time I've learned to be thick-skinned when approached by hustlers laden with tourist wares.

Slipping through the Malka Gate, we prepared ourselves for the usual onslaught of salesmen and mendicants. But it didn't come. Instead, the silence was so pronounced that we could hear the children playing marbles in the labyrinth of lanes. Without waiting for us to ask, one of them led the way to the great mosque.

Built in the glorious twelfth century Almohad style, it's one of the greatest treasures in the kingdom, and one of the least known. The boy said there were seven doors, one for each day of the week.

Twisting and turning our way down the whitewashed lanes, we found a time-capsule of Moroccan life from a century ago. There were vegetables piled high on carts, and chunks of fresh mutton laid out on fragrant beds of mint; tailors busily sewing kaftans, mattress-makers and carpenters, brocade-sellers, and dyers hanging skeins of wool out in the sun. And, rather than any tourists or tourist kitsch, there were local people out shopping, bargaining for underpants and melons, pumpkins, wedding robes, and socks.

When Ariane showed the scribbled directions to the marble-playing boy, he led us to a spacious square, the *Souq el Gazelle*, the Wool Market. It was packed with people buying and selling used clothes and brightly-coloured wool. The boy said it was where slaves had once been sold, having been dragged ashore from captured ships.

Nudging a thumb to the directions, I asked about the home of Jan Janszoon.

The boy beckoned us to follow him.

Winding our way through the *Mellah*, the old Jewish quarter, the air pungent with kebab smoke and baking macaroons, we reached the crumbling façade of a building. Once plastered, the dressed stone was exposed, ravaged by the elements. A fig tree had taken hold and was growing out from the side, and the studded wooden door was falling to bits. The boy glanced at the scribbled directions and gave a thumb's up.

Ariane and I stood there in awe. We were on hallowed ground after all – at the home of the greatest pirate in Barbary history, the progenitor of Jackie O no less.

As the *muezzin* called the prayer, his voice singing out over the tiled rooftops of old Salé, I whispered thanks to Jan Janszoon and to his band of marauding corsairs. Through a special conjury of Moroccan magic, the Dutch-born freebooter had lured us through a keyhole into his own pirate realm, the Moroccan Twilight Zone, where nothing is ever quite what it seems.

Moulay Idriss

A MAN WITH A HEAVILY scarred face and a limp, sidled up and asked me to follow him.

I was standing in the central square of Moulay Idriss, Morocco's most sacred and sinister town, peering at a map. I asked the man what he had to show. He tapped a finger below his eye, and motioned towards a narrow alleyway. My curiosity piqued, I slipped after him into the cool shadows behind the main square.

At the far end of the alley there was a turn, followed by another lane, then another, and another. Realising that I was deep in the labyrinth, I called out, but the man didn't stop.

After fifteen minutes of trailing behind him, he tapped his eye again, and pointed to a door.

'What is it?' I asked in a timid voice.

'A secret.'

'What?'

The man nodded, pushed the door inwards, and led me into a dark building with a low ceiling. My nose picked up the scent of sandalwood, sparking a memory from childhood. I pushed open one of the shutters, while the man pointed at the floor. As light flooded in, I waited for my eyes to focus. Then I gasped in surprise.

Nestled on a cushion in the middle of a room was a large glass jar filled with what appeared to be olive oil. In the liquid was part of a human skull. It looked like it had been trepanned and was missing the lower jaw.

'Where did you get it?'

'In the ruins, near Volubilis. A farmer came across it in his field,' the man paused, and rubbed a thumb and forefinger together. 'It's for sale,' he said.

I didn't want to appear rude, but explained that I'd be in the doghouse if I went home clutching a trepanned human skull. Making excuses, and smiling as widely as I could, I retraced my steps back to the main square. As I tramped back out of the maze, I found myself wondering what kind of maniac would buy part of a skull from a total stranger, in a place that seemed to scare most visitors away.

Read any of the guidebooks to Morocco and most of them tell the same story – that Moulay Idriss, the ancient spiritual heart of the kingdom, is unwelcoming to tourists, and unforgiving to any planning on sleeping there. Living in Casablanca as I do, I have often overheard travellers in the ramshackle cafés down by the port recounting the myth: that only the foolish or the unhinged would be crazed enough to stay over in Moulay Idriss.

When I asked my Moroccan friends about the town, which was founded by the great grandson of the Prophet Mohammed, most of them smiled. 'It's a little secret,' one said, 'a way of keeping the very best for ourselves.'

Unable to resist the temptation any longer, I dropped everything and jumped into the car. I headed north, following the coast road, and was soon turning inland away from the Atlantic on the road which runs eastwards to Fès.

Many visitors tend to think of Morocco as a desert land which, of course, is true. But the kingdom is a realm of contrasts, and none is starker than the nut-brown farmland of the Saïss Plateau, where vines have produced wine since Roman times.

Barely two hours after leaving Casablanca, I was trundling through Meknès, one of the most impressive walled imperial cities of all. Following the signs north towards the Roman ruins at Volubilis, I caught my first glimpse of Moulay Idriss.

Blazing white against a cobalt sky, it clings to the mountainside like a cluster of limpets bleached by the sun. A huddle of green roofs near the middle, stands as a reminder of why foreigners have felt threatened until now. Within the shrine beneath the green tiled roofs lie the mortal remains of Idriss I, the founder of the powerful Idrissid dynasty, and the man who brought Islam to Morocco in the first place, twelve centuries ago.

It's easy to imagine Idriss I standing on the hillside, surveying the fertile plateau below, dreaming of a time when the new religion would be practiced by every man and woman between him and the horizon. He had fled the Abbasid Caliphate in Baghdad, and brought Islam to the Berber tribes, despite the disapproval of the Caliph, Harun ar-Rachid. After winning over the Berbers, and founding the city of Fès, Idriss I was poisoned, supposedly on the orders of the Caliph himself.

Each summer a *moussem* is held in honour of the founder of Islam in Morocco. Tens of thousands of pilgrims come from across North Africa, and beyond, to pay reverence at the shrine dedicated to Idriss I. The town of Moulay Idriss swells with visitors then, many of them covering the distance from his second capital at Fès, on foot. For the rest of the year, Moulay Idriss is almost silent, a landmark photographed from a distance by tourists as their coaches rattle up the road to Volubilis.

The Roman ruins there are no more than a couple of miles away. They boast some exquisite mosaic floors, triumphal arches, and capitals crowned by giant stork nests. Local children weave about between the tour buses, offering fossils they have dug from the fields, and splinters of quartz dyed ruby red with ink.

One of the reasons the tourists have always sidestepped Moulay Idriss is because of the general sensitivity of Islamic shrines. Non-Muslims visiting Morocco rarely have the opportunity of entering the mosques or other religious buildings. The exception is the great Mosque of Hassan II in Casablanca, which holds regular tours. The Qur'an and the teachings of the Prophet mention nothing about forbidding those of other faiths from entering holy Islamic sites – far from it.

The Prophet himself is known to have welcomed Najran Christians into a mosque at Medina, where they held talks and prayed together. The resolution to prohibit non-Muslims into mosques in Morocco was apparently a political one, introduced during the era of the French Protectorate. It's likely that the Governor, Hubert Lyautey, made the decision to avoid intruding upon local sensitivities.

Another explanation for the lack of visitors to Moulay Idriss may be been the shortage of reliable places to stay. After the high-end *riad*-style boutique hotels of Fès and Marrakech, lodgings in Moulay Idriss have always been far more modest and thin on the ground. Since the 'seventies, when the hippy trail linked Casablanca with Kabul, local people in the town have taken in the odd visitor, squeezing them into their communal guest rooms. Anyone offered to stay as a guest in a Moroccan home should take advantage, as the hospitality is second to none.

Fortunately, it's unlikely that things are going to change fast at Moulay Idriss, but there is change afoot nonetheless. Mike Richardson, an exuberant young redhead restaurateur, formerly *maitre d'* at London's prestigious Ivy Restaurant, is a partner in a tiny inn that's just opened its doors.

Boasting five guest rooms in all, Dar Zerhoune as it's called, has been renovated with painstaking care.

'It's about eight hundred years old,' says Richardson, 'which is nothing out of the usual for round here. The last thing on our minds is to turn the town into a tourist magnet, but we do want to encourage people to fall in love with Moulay Idriss as we have done.'

The main square of the town is ringed by arched arcades, in which locals hide in the shade, and barter for plastic buckets, cardamoms, and pastries dripping with syrup. The wonderful thing about the place is that life continues as it has done for centuries, and that no one's very impressed when a fresh-faced tourist blusters in. They get on with what they're doing – weighing out dried chameleons, measuring skeins of wool, tasting spices before they buy, and haggling for great domed *tagines*.

The pace of life must have been how things were everywhere at one time, before mechanization forced everything to go fast forward. I watched as an aged shopkeeper woke from his siesta, prayed, sipped a cup of tea, chatted to his neighbour, and lay down to sleep once again – all in the space of ten minutes. There was a sense of simplicity which Morocco's cities lost long ago. The danger with Moulay Idriss is that the longer you spend there, the easier it is to forget a world ruled by reality of paperwork, traffic jams and e-mail. Stay there too long and one might never be able to go home.

I moved from one café to the next, following the sun, drinking tea and dreaming of escape to such a tranquil place. From time to time a beggar would amble up. The café's owner would take a coin from his apron pouch and hand it over in the name of God. At the third café, the waiter slipped a glass onto the cracked vinyl tabletop, and raised the teapot above his head as he poured. With a cloud of steam billowing out from the arc of boiling liquid, he glanced at his wristwatch.

'It's almost dark,' he said in a whisper, 'are you not going to leave?'

I asked what he meant.

'Foreigners always depart Moulay Idriss before dusk,' he said darkly. 'They're frightened to spend the night.'

'Well, I'm staying,' I said defiantly.

The waiter scratched a thumbnail down his nose.

'You are very brave, Monsieur,' he said.

I drank more tea, and found myself talking to a pair of footloose backpackers from Auckland, their possessions in a fetid heap beside the table. The woman told me that they'd taken a communal Mercedes taxi from Fès to Mèknes, and then another up to Moulay Idriss. I asked how the journey was.

'It was the most terrifying ride of my life,' said the man. It was the only time he spoke.

I told them about the skull.

'He offered it to us as well,' said the woman coldly.

I asked if they were planning on spending the night in Moulay Idriss.

The man looked at the woman, and she combed a hand through her hair.

'After the ride here on the old road from Fès nothing could scare us,' she said. She then mumbled something about a quest for turquoise beads and they ambled away.

The waiter sauntered over again, poured yet more tea, and described the *moussem* held each summer.

'It's then that Moulay Idriss comes alive with people and dancing, and tremendous noise,' he said. 'All day and night there is the sound of voices, and the beating of drums. Thousands of people pour into the shrine, and the cafés are filled to bursting.' His eyes glazed over as he relived the spectacle in his mind. 'If only the *moussem* was every day of the year!' he exclaimed.

I sipped my tea, peered out at the serene square, and watched a group of boys playing tag in the dusk light. A dog limped into the middle of their game, curled up and fell asleep.

Then I smiled to myself, thankful that Moulay Idriss was exactly how it was.

Of All the Medinas in the World

IT WAS THE PROSPECT of the real world that first lured me to Morocco.

I was living in a pokey London flat, but spent very little time there. I would walk the streets angry and desperate – enraged at the exorbitant taxes and at the crippling kindergarten fees, desperate for affordable sunshine and for danger. The way I saw it, England had become a nanny state *par excellence*. Any problems and the system would pick you up and dust you down. I yearned for a place where the safety nets had been cut away, where ordinary people walked on a high-wire of reality.

Rachana, my wife, didn't share my lust for jeopardy. She clutched our toddler to her pregnant belly and ordered me to not be so irresponsible. Taking little notice of her concerns, I flew back and forth from London to Marrakech, where I had been taken often as a child. I remembered the droves of fire-eaters and snake-charmers in the Jma el Fna, the main square, and searched for a cosy little house to buy.

Unfortunately, just about everyone in Europe seemed to have already come up with the same idea. Prices for 'riads', courtyard houses in the medina, were soaring, with the influx of the Euro-jetset. Someone suggested to go house hunting in Fès. So I did, and eventually found a crumbling merchant's house there.

Colossal in size, it was owned by seven ghoulish brothers, each one greedier than the last. In Morocco, before you even get to the matter of the sale, you have to coax the owner to sell. I sat with them for hours, coaxing, cajoling, begging them to allow me to buy their home. Spitting out a fantasy price, they narrowed their eyes with greed. I leapt up and ran out shouting. In that moment I broke the first rule of the Arab world.

Never lose your cool.

At long last, we were offered a wonderful sprawling home in the

The glorious Rialto Cinema, one of Casablanca's Art Deco gems

coastal city of Casablanca. It was called Dar Khalifa, meaning 'The Caliph's House', and from the first moment I set eyes upon it, I was in love.

All I knew about the city, I had learned from the film. I expected it to be a showcase of the mysterious East, half-expecting Bogart and Bergman and be living it up at Rick's Café Americain. But instead I found a French-built haven of fabulous Art Deco buildings and palm-lined boulevards.

On the night that I took possession of the great notched iron key to the Caliph's House door, suicide bombs went off across Casablanca. I cursed myself for courting danger so openly, and feared for what Rachana would think watching the news at home. It was a terrible moment. A few weeks later she gave birth to our little son, Timur, and we moved to Morocco.

My father, an Afghan, could never take my sisters and me to his ancestral home in the Hindu Kush. It was always too dangerous. So, often in our childhood, the family station-wagon would be laden with tattered old suitcases, and we would all be lured inside. With our gardener at the wheel, we would drive south from the verdant county of Kent, through France, Spain, and would take the ferry over to Tangier.

The journeys were a chance for my father to reveal fragments of his homeland. As he would point out frequently, the cultures of Morocco and Afghanistan are remarkably similar – mountainous landscapes, Islamic customs, and fiercely proud tribal clans.

When we bought the Caliph's House, I thought we'd be finished with all the work in about three months. But at the start I had no concept of the elastication in North African time.

With no power tools or specialized equipment, work progressed very slowly indeed. And as for money – renovate a large house anywhere and you exceed original budgets many times over. I was forced to take out huge bank loans to pay the bills which were stacked two feet high on my desk. Having had no previous experience in renovating a house – large or small – I found it impossible to ever see the big picture. I would go around buying last minute details, when I should have been concentrating on the structure of the project, and all the tedious stuff like water and wiring that no one ever sees.

Buy a house in a foreign country and, it seems, that anything which can go wrong usually does. Our experience was no exception. The first weeks and months were beyond miserable. There was no electricity, water or furniture, and there were so many rats that our shoes were eaten in the night. We found dead decapitated cats in the garden, supposedly left by someone who didn't want us to live at the Caliph's House.

Then there were locusts, followed by a swarm of ferocious bees. After that a workman fell through a glass roof, and hordes of police tried to break down the front door. If in England you found a troupe of bobbies trying to batter their way into your home, you would probably ask them why they were there. But in Morocco the police are kept out at all costs. I quizzed one of the guardians as to why we were the focus of such police attention.

'Because the architect doesn't have permission to do the work,' he said.
'Doesn't he?'
'No of course he doesn't. In Morocco no one ever gets permission.'

The architect brought a trailer full of the most savage men I had ever seen. They had unusually-developed shoulder muscles and were all armed with sledge hammers. In a very short while they managed to smash down a large number of walls, ripping out wiring and water pipes as they went.

Then they ran off and the rain began.

Many weeks of stormy weather followed in which the architect was an infrequent visitor. The reason for this was that, as I later found out, I had broken the second rule of the Arab world – paying in advance. On those long windswept nights, I would huddle in a blanket on a green plastic garden chair and congratulate myself for having broken free from the cycle of school fees, zombie-commuting and triangular chicken tikka sandwiches. My friends in London, I would tell myself over and over like a mantra, weren't having nearly as much fun.

Eventually the architect's building team arrived.

They spent most of their time camped in our unfinished sitting-room brewing up enormous pots of chicken stew. When they did do any work it was during the short time in between their feasts and long naps. The construction phase was completed at a snail's pace. After that we moved on to laying the floors with handmade terracotta tiles called *bejmat*, and coating the walls in tadelakt, a Moroccan form of Venetian plaster, made from eggs, lime, and marble dust. The architect brought a team whose work was so atrocious that I fired them all in a fit of fury. It meant sacrificing all the money I had paid to the architect in advance.

There was no choice but to locate and then to deal directly with real *moualems*, the master craftsmen. Morocco has an astonishing number of cowboy craftsmen. For every thousand there are one or two true masters who have learned their skills by long and ruthless apprenticeship. Moualem Aziz was one of them. A great barrel of a man, his bulk poised above nimble feet, he was in charge of the floors.

Over months, his team brought magic to the Caliph's House. The only time he was caught out, was whilst laying a complex pattern of glazed tiles in the children's nursery. On reaching the final row they saw they had misjudged the shape of the room. Without so much as a murmur they lifted the entire floor, rotated it through five degrees, and laid it again.

Now that the house is restored, I watch my little son and daughter in the courtyards, splashing in the fountains, prodding their tortoises across the lawn. I understand now that the difference between absolute failure and total success is less than a hair's breadth. And I see that success is about endurance. Keep standing and you will get to the end. But most of all I see that a life without steep learning curves is no life at all.

Old Cape Town

ON MY LAST VISIT to Cape Town a decade ago I remember asking directions to the Company Gardens, from a homeless guy.

Standing on a street corner smack bang downtown, he was furled up in a nest of matted blankets. As he realized I was speaking to him, he did a double-take. Then his eyes slowly widened.

'They'll take ya shirt and ya shoes,' he said dreamily, looking me up and down.

'Who will?'

'The Banana-men will,' he said.

Unsure quite what he meant, I made a hurried escape, back to the plush Waterfront District from where I had come. In the years that passed, I've often found myself wondering about the dreaded Banana-men, and have come to conclude they were a fantasy conjured by a troubled mind.

Far less fantastic though was the very real danger lurking in Cape Town's historic heart. In the old days, it was a no-go-zone, where muggers preyed on the unsuspecting, and where you were likely to be relieved of far more than just your shirt and shoes.

But with time – and a massive injection of cold hard cash from both private and public funds – the city's magnificent colonial quarter has now been completely revamped.

And what a jewel it is.

Stretching out a few blocks in each direction, it comprises an assortment of old world architecture, most of it restored to perfection, and all of it spotlessly clean. Part of a colonial legacy, the buildings hark back to when the Cape Colony stood as a byword for bullion and diamonds, and for wealth on an unknown scale.

After decades of despair, it seems as though the good times are here again. And, in these glory days of Cape Town's Renaissance, there's

199

nowhere in the city quite so alluring to roam as the old downtown.

A good place to set off is from the corner of Wale Street and the pedestrianized St. George's Mall. On that intersection stands the old Reserve Bank of South Africa, a granite fortress and an erstwhile beacon of power. It's recently been given a painstaking renovation, and is now home to the Cape Town Taj Hotel.

Beyond it, on St. George's Mall, are a throng of bistros, bars, and cafés serving gourmet fare and fine wines from the Cape. There's an old-fashioned sense, a primness that makes you feel warm inside and genuinely fortunate at being anywhere near there at all.

A stone's throw away, on Long Street, I found an abundance of second hand bookshops and antique emporia packed with 1930s junk. It's a real treasure trove of a place. And, in a wildly vibrant backdrop of cultural colour, you can find every imaginable cuisine too – from sushi to Ethiopian *ngira*, and from Indian *thalis* to Brazilian barbecue.

Pace slowly down Long Street and you can't help but glimpse Cape Town's past. What affects me most is the utterly genteel quality of it all. There's a sense that this is where the seed of Cape Town fell long ago. Squint a little and, in the canary yellow light of afternoon, you savour the village feel beneath the bustle of city life.

A twist and a turn and you reach Adderley Street, where the shops are a little larger, but where the atmosphere is straight out of the 'fifties. Woolworths stands in pride of place – not a haven for the down-trodden, but a shelter of subtle sophistication. There's a wonderful flower market, too, on the east side of the street, the stalls ablaze with tropical blooms.

It might not look like it, but this main thoroughfare dates back centuries, to the time of the first Dutch settlers – who arrived more than three hundred and fifty years ago. A sanctuary of safety from the dangers of the unknown lurking inland, Adderley Street quickly became the commercial hub for the Dutch East India Company, what eventually became the thriving Cape Colony.

The most heartrending reminder of this time – one forged on servitude – can be found at the Slave Lodge, now housing a museum of culture. Over the years, many thousands of slaves were imprisoned there, a great number succumbing to the terrible conditions, malnutrition and disease.

In line with Adderley Street, are the celebrated Company Gardens, which I failed to ever find on my last visit. It's there that the East India Company's master gardener, Hendrik Bloom, laid out the first garden in 1652. At first it was vegetables and fruit that were grown, to sustain the droves of immigrants who had begun to arrive. As time passed, the gardens were turned over to medicinal and botanical species, and gradually became the idyll they are today.

For me, the most touching place of all in old Cape Town is St. George's Cathedral, on the north-east edge of the Company Gardens. It was from there that Archbishop Desmond Tutu led his peaceful protest against Apartheid, a demonstration of dignity.

Visit Cape Town and history is never far from your grasp. It lingers in the air, a scent on the breeze, an explanation of circumstance that shaped the Rainbow People. Stroll around the old downtown and it's impossible not to be affected by the trials and tribulations of the struggle. But, in many ways, it is the sense of triumph in the face of such adversity that makes the experience all the more poignant.

On The River of God

THE JUNGLE CANOPY hung like a tremendous emerald barricade, concealing us from our world.

There was an energy about it, a power, a sense of consciousness, as if it were watching our miserable procession, faltering ahead through the interminable undergrowth. For more than sixteen weeks we had been in the cloud-forest. Most of that time had been spent staggering inch by inch through the raging, waist-deep waters of the Madre de Dios River, the so-called 'Mother of God'.

My porters were broken men. They had all lost the skin on their feet, weeks before. Most were lame, plagued with chronic diarrhoea, and guinea worms, which bored out from the soft tissue of our inner thighs. There was dengue fever too. It turned strong men into whimpering wrecks, crushing their bones, and dessicating their flesh. During the long insect-ridden nights we would huddle under the makeshift tent, shaking like crack addicts going cold turkey.

As leader of the expedition, it fell to me to drag the porters forward whether they liked it or not. But men stripped of health and enthusiasm for life are a dead weight. They missed their wives and the comforts of their village, and lacked the raw ambition which kept me going. I could feel that we were close now – close to Paititi, the greatest lost city in history. Endure the unendurable a little longer and, I felt sure, the El Dorado of the Incas would soon be mine.

I was not the first to go in search of Paititi, and I fear I will not be the last. For five centuries, soldiers, adventurers, explorers and warrior-priests, have hacked through the Peruvian jungle on the quest of the lost city, the Holy Grail of exploration. Most of them have followed the same clue.

The theory is that, as the Spanish Conquistadores swept through Peru in the 1500s, the Incas retreated with their most prized possessions, taking refuge in the densest cloud-forest on Earth. There, according to legend, they constructed a new city, more fabulous than anything South America had ever known.

After first hearing the legend ten years ago, the corrosive allure of Paititi ran wild in my mind. Like so many before me, my motivation was founded on an overwhelming greed. Not for gold, but for glory. Discover a lost city and I would be transformed overnight from a humble traveller into the world's most famous explorer.

To have a real chance of finding Paititi, I would have to unearth clues in the chronicles of the Conquistadores. I read them, spending months trawling through library stacks – thousands of books, many written four centuries ago. The recurring name was Madre de Dios, the vast impenetrable jungle, east of the Andes, on the southern cusp of the Amazon.

But there comes a point when the library research must come to an end. You must draw a line, and begin the expedition in earnest. From the outset, it was clear that mine would have to be an expedition born of economy. My bank balance was pathetically dry. All I managed to withdraw for expedition gear was £200.

So I bought a copy of the free advertisement newspaper, *Loot*, spread its pink pages out on my sitting-room floor, and searched for equipment worthy of a budget lost city expedition.

Within an hour I had found an old Zodiac dinghy, a pair of used jungle Altama boots, two shovels, six canvas kit-bags, three tarpaulins and a pair of Chinese-made lanterns. With the money that was left, I went to a hardware store and bought some rubble sacks, the kind used by builders to carry gravel, and a few rolls of plastic bin liners.

Lastly, I went down to Safeway and snapped up their entire stock of six hundred Pot Noodles, charged to my credit card. Pervious experience had taught me that an expedition marches on its stomach.

Explorers like to pretend that they are a select breed of people with iron nerve and an ability to endure terrible hardship. It is true that exploration can entail much misery, but anyone can find some used gear, buy a cheap airline ticket, and set out on a grand adventure. You don't have to be Indiana Jones to go in search of a lost city.

In addition to being overloaded with unnecessary supplies, I felt that the big expeditions which had searched for Paititi had failed for another key reason: their arrogance. They considered themselves far superior to the indigenous tribes, the very people who know the jungle inside-out.

As far as I was concerned, in order to locate Paititi, I would have to become trusted by the people who made the Madre de Dios their home – the Machiguenga. After all, I reasoned, it must be very hard to lose a city, especially one as important as the El Dorado of the Incas.

I flew to Lima, along with the rubber boat, the jungle boots and the mountain of Pot Noodles. Then I took the local bus across the Cordillera, the mountainous ridge than runs down the country like the spine on a chameleon's back. At Cusco, the former Incan capital, I heard that six well-funded teams had recently entered the cloud-forest in search of the very same prize as me. One of them boasted a million-dollar budget, and every contrivance from chemical toilets to air-conditioned tents. They even had a military field hospital.

Undeterred by the modesty of my own expedition, I clambered aboard the worn-out bus which occasionally ran the route from the highlands, down into the jungle. At the start, the landscape was desolate, abandoned, a thousand shades of grey; but as we descended, the vegetation changed. Prehistoric flowers and bronze-green fronds gave way to bamboo and bromeliads, to waterfalls and acres of trees.

Where the bus ride ended, I hitched a lift on a truck full of pigs and, three days later, I was at the edge of the Machiguenga tribe's ancestral lands.

The first contact is always the hardest.

But a lucky break came in the form of an old man, called Hector. A dreamer and a Seventh Day Adventist, he too yearned to mount an expedition to find the ruined city. Yet his real value was in his close connections to the tribe.

Hector had no doubt that the lost city existed. He said there was a man, a tribal warrior called Pancho, who had stumbled upon the ruins long ago in his youth, while out searching for new hunting grounds. Pancho was the key. After weeks of coaxing Hector, he agreed to take me to meet the warrior.

Fine-boned and fragile, Pancho was at first reluctant to talk about the jungle or what secrets lay within it. We spent the afternoon at his hut, drinking gallons of warm *masato*, a vile white beer made from manioc, chewed by old village crones and fermented in their saliva.

As late afternoon slipped into night, I realized that Pancho's ambition

Pancho resting on the river's edge

A giant tapir's hindleg

was the mirror image of my own. While I yearned to find a lost city, overgrown and deserted, he yearned to go to a live city, bustling with life, and the cars he had never seen.

Missionaries had told him of wayward places called discos, where coloured lights flashed, music blared, and beer flowed; and they had talked of high-class brothels where large-breasted women would service a humble man's needs. Grinning, Pancho whispered that he would like to go to the city and taste the vice for himself.

We made a pact: if he could take me to the ruins of Paititi, then I would take him to Cusco.

The journey that followed was the hardest of my life.

We felled a copse of balsa trees and pinned the trunks together with homemade nails, carved from the wood of chonta palms. Rafts were the only craft that could ascend the rapids. The jagged rocks tore at our feet, crippling the porters, the freezing water sapping their strength. Each mile was a struggle, earned in sweat, sores and disease.

Each night I would rally the men, cajole them to face the dawn with the brevity and conviction of heroes. I would heap their plates high with food, and never eat until the last of them was full. After all, nothing was so important as the well-being as the men.

But, with each mile, their resentment grew a little more. At first they laughed it off, humoured me for my pushing them. And, as days became weeks, and weeks slipped into months, the mood changed.

All of a sudden, men who would have given everything at the start, regarded me with poisoned stares and hatred. It was then that I felt the greatest challenge. Not only did I have to talk myself into carrying on, but I had to drag the men along with me.

From a fireside armchair, in a home with central heating and all mod cons, the idea of searching for a lost city is appealing. But, spend months in the jungle with rotting feet and terrible stomach problems, infested with worms and shaking from fever, the glory of it all wears painfully thin.

And, as the weeks passed, I found myself questioning why anyone would want to set themselves such an insane quest, why I couldn't make do with a nine to five job like everyone else.

I dared not allow the men know my feelings though.

It sounds clichéd, but ground down by weeks of fever, by guinea worms and putrid sores, I came to know myself. More importantly, I developed an astonishing respect for the jungle and its delicate web of life.

The more I thought about it, the more I realized that finding Paititi was a death sentence for the jungle and the tribes. Within weeks the great trees would be felled, and package tourists would be trouping through. Pancho and his peers would be bell-hops in swish hotels before they knew it. I cursed myself for thinking of the fame and glory, and swore that even if I found Paititi, I would pretend I had never been there at all.

As for Pancho, he returned to the city with me, where he tasted vice, and saw the curiosities of our urban life. He drove in a car, watched television, ate ice cream, and even tried a cappuccino.

At the end of a week, he said he wanted to go home to his village. when I asked him what he thought of our world, he was silent for a moment. Then he screwed up his face:

'What a terrible, terrible place this is,' he said. 'I thought it would be a lot better!'

The next day I took Pancho back to the emerald forest. He shook my hand and grinned hard once we were at his village. I said that I hoped we would meet again. The great hunter smiled one last time.

'You know where to find me,' he said.

On the Skeleton Coast

STREWN WITH HUGE BLEACHED WHALE-BONES, shipwrecks, and the occasional human skull, Namibia's Skeleton Coast is one of the most desolate shorelines on the African continent. Known to the Khoisan Bushmen of the interior as 'The Land God Created in Anger', it's where the freezing waters of the Atlantic meet the scorched sands of the Namib desert.

Stretching from the Angolan border, at the Kunene River in the north, down beyond the diamond ghost-town of Kolmanskop in the south, the Namib is a vast swathe of undulating dunes. Far too dry to sustain much life, the flora and fauna found there have adapted, enabling them to glean just enough moisture from the ocean's fog that spills inland at dawn.

Venture to the Skeleton Coast, and you get the sense that nature is warding you away right from the start. There are bones everywhere, flotsam and jetsam, the crumbling hulks of wrecks, dead plants, and the footprints of infrequent desert creatures, all of them on the constant and desperate search for sustenance.

Hanging in the balance, a slim no man's land between life and death, I was reminded time and again by the struggle to survive. It was a point never more powerfully made than on my first morning on the Skeleton Coast.

I was moving clumsily across a towering sand dune which rolled down to the beach and into the foaming white breakers. There were no plants, no animals, no hint of anything alive, just the spectre of Death all around. As I took a swig of water from my flask, a male oryx came out of nowhere. Alone and weak from thirst, he stumbled down to the shore, tasted the salt water, and collapsed on the beach.

A great uncompromising chunk of Africa, Namibia is one of the last true wildernesses. It's a place where a few drops of water have at

A 1934 Hudson Terraplane, abandoned by diamond smugglers decades ago

A Himba woman at her stockaded village on the Skeleton Coast

times been far more precious than the diamonds that famously litter its coastal sands. Nonetheless, it's blessed with a stable government and decent infrastructure, something you can't say about a good many countries on the African continent.

Tearing south-west up from Antarctica, the trade winds of the Benguela system batter the shoreline night and day. No one knows quite how many ships they've swept onto the barren rocks of the Skeleton Coast. But, making your way southward, you spot wreckage every few miles.

There are the remnants of ocean liners and trawlers, galleons, clippers and gunboats – testament to the perfidious current and the unrelenting winds. The wreckage is only one piece of the puzzle, but one with which we all readily identify – the crushed remains a reminder of our own fragility.

The most infamous of the wrecks is the *Dunedin Star*. A Blue Star liner, it was washed ashore in 1942. Laden with munitions, crew, and a few paying passengers, the ship's rescue has gone down in history as a catalogue of error. A Ventura bomber and a tug-boat, both sent to help, floundered as well. Their wreckage can still clearly be seen. And a slew of other vessels with good intentions were unable to get close. Forced to turn around, they left the stranded survivors on the desert. Yet, amazingly, most of them were rescued in the end.

Not so lucky was the shipwrecked crew of an unknown vessel, washed up in 1860. Seventy years ago their twelve headless skeletons were found clustered together on the beach, along with a slate buried in the sand. It read, 'I am proceeding to a river sixty miles north, and should anyone find this and follow me, God will help him.'

The remains of the writer have never been found.

My guide, Gotfod, drove us towards another wreck a little further down the coast. A quiet man with oversized hands and a wry smile, he'd made sacrifices to be there. His wife and family lived so far away that he only saw them a few times a year. The Skeleton Coast is no place for family life.

Slowing the Land Rover, he cocked his head out towards a twisted heap of rust and old iron chains.

'That's the *Suiderkus*,' he said darkly, 'a trawler wrecked on her maiden voyage forty years ago. Every time I pass it, there's a little less left.' Gotfod glanced towards the rocks. 'Sometimes I wonder how many ships have met their end here,' he added pensively. 'The wreckage disappears over time, but the ghosts are left.'

It's not hard to imagine the elation of a shipwrecked survivor clawing his way to shore, only to be confronted by a new terror – yet another ocean stretching north, south and east, an endless barrier of dunes.

Shifting constantly, the mighty mountains of sand are born when a few grains collect around a nest of quick-grass. Gradually, the little mound gets larger, kills the plant, develops into a dune, and roams the desert for eternity.

Not far from the mortal remains of the *Suiderkus*, at Möwe Bay, is surely the word's most remote police station. It's so cut off that the handful of officers rush out at the sound of an engine. They man a tiny museum, filled with remnants of wreckage, bones, and more bones. Inside are human skulls, and life-vests from Japanese whalers, the sand-worn figurehead from an ancient galleon, delicate wooden balustrades, brass cannons, rigging and sea-worn chains.

Walk along the lines of skulls outside, and you're reminded once again that the Skeleton Coast is a place where Death looms large.

But there is life, too.

Travelling down the shoreline, we came upon a huge colony of Cape fur seals. There were thousands of them. Jet black and glistening, they were basking on the rocks like mermaids, or slipping easily into the freezing Atlantic waters to feast on the schools of sardines.

And, on the beach itself, Gotfod pointed out canine footprints circling the putrefying carcass of a humpback whale – covered in ghost crabs. No one's quite sure why, but dozens of such whales have been beached in recent months. The only consolation is that their death means life for others.

'See how the black-backed jackals have been trying to get through the whale's thick hide,' Gotfod mumbled, pointing to teeth marks in the leather. 'It'll take a few more days before the rot softens it for them.'

We veered over dunes as high as any on earth, the sands roaring as the Land Rover descended. Then, jolting from side to side, we cut a path inland up a rock-strewn canyon.

Again, Gotfod nudged a hand to the distance. He was pointing to a straggly windswept plant, called *Welwitchia mirabilis*. Found only in a few areas of the parched Namib, it's a living fossilized tree. Despite its humble profile, with a wide trunk that reaches no more than a few centimeters in height, individual specimens live for a thousand years or more.

Having crossed a moonscape of cracked grey mud and many more dunes, we reached the first place with any real vegetation. There was even the odd puddle of water.

Gotfod insisted it was actually a riverbed.

'It's the Waruseb,' he told me, 'but it's dry most of the year. 'We're in the rainy season now, that's why the oryx are here.'

Watching us from a distance, were a dozen or so of the antelopes, their straight tall horns rising like lances above them. Their innate curiosity must surely keep their numbers down. After all, there were predators around.

Grinding a path eastwards, Gotfod gave a thumb's up, and almost grinned. He'd picked up a track. We progressed past a lone male ostrich, and a herd of springbok, who pronked away in all directions at the sight of us. Then, turning slowly to the right, Gotfod applied the brakes.

Touching a finger to his lips, he motioned out the window.

Twenty feet away, a dead oryx was lying on its back, blood dripping from the nose. It had just been killed. Craning his neck, Gotfod pointed again. A lioness was panting in the shade of a thorn bush, taking time to cool down before devouring her kill.

As we sat there watching, a desert elephant suddenly stormed up, blasting itself with a trunkful of dust to keep cool. Caught off-guard, the lioness retreated into the bush, vexed, but unwilling to attack a creature so many times her size. After a tense few minutes, the elephant rejoined the rest of the herd, trampling through bulrushes nearby.

Like the other creatures found on the Skeleton Coast, the elephants have adapted to the desert climate. Able to endure days of thirst, as they roam vast distances in search of sustenance, they can even cross the towering dunes. And, when they reach a dry riverbed like the

Waruseb, they use their tusks to dig down, creating pools on which the entire food chain feeds.

Lured by the wilderness, and by the chance of spotting rare desert elephants, a few intrepid tourists make their way to the Skeleton Coast each year. It's just about as remote as any tourist destination on earth, but one that pays fabulous dividends.

Visitors tend to fly in by Cessna for a few days, and stay at one of the handful of lodges. Lost in an expanse of rolling dunes, these rely completely on the air-link. All food and supplies are flown in, and everything – from garbage to dirty bed-sheets – are flown out. Only the fresh water supply is local. Beyond precious, it's fetched by tractor at a borehole thirty miles away.

Apart from the odd tourist, the only other people to be found are the nomadic Himba. Adorning their bodies with ochre and butter, to protect from the ferocity of the sun, they have spent centuries roaming the Skeleton Coast and nearby regions. It's thought they migrated from East Africa, and there's proof of this in their language – it contains some Swahili.

Gotfod took me to a little Himba encampment some way inland from the shore. Surrounded by a crude stockade, much of it topped with thorns, the hamlet was well defended against predators from outside. Hailing from the Herero, sister tribe to the Himba, Gotfod could speak their language.

'The Himba venerate their ancestors,' he told me, pointing to a sacred fire. 'They keep it burning in the centre of the community and they never allow it to go out.' His smile suddenly vanishing, he added: 'Please make sure not to pass between the dead tree and the fire.'

'Why not?'

Gotfod seemed uneasy.

'Because it will make them sad,' he said.

The oldest man in the community beckoned us over. His neck hidden in a mass of beads, a woolly hat pulled down over his head, he was grinding snuff in a metal tube.

'In the droughts the lions get hungry and try to attack us.' he said. 'One came last year,' he said slowly; 'it jumped over the stockade and ran round and round. We were frightened. After all, there were children playing on the dead tree.'

'Did you kill it?' I asked.

The old man grimaced.

'We're not allowed to kill lions any longer. It's against the law.'

'So what did you do?'

'We made a great noise and chased it away!'

For the Himba, the temptation to embrace modern life must be very real, if only as a way to escape dire poverty. Their sister tribe, the Herero, were converted by Christian missionaries a century and more ago. Many of them have their own houses and plenty of possessions. Herero women still sport colourful home-made dresses, reminiscent of those worn by the Victorian missionaries who brought them the word of Christ.

Travelling by ox wagon, the Afrikaans-speaking Voortrekkers travelled from the Cape Colony into the interior, and up Namibia's Atlantic Coast. They converted and conquered as they went, settling lands with European ranching methods.

Their ancestors are still found throughout Namibia, especially in the remote desert realm of the southern Namib. Proud of their ancestry, many of them now work with tourism, especially at Sossusvlei, where the massive red dunes are found.

Taking its name from the baked mud pan, dry for all but a few days each year, the dunes draw visitors from all corners of the earth. The highest soars to three hundred and eighty metres. Tinted red by the high iron content, it glows almost crimson at dusk.

Reeling over an eternity of dunes, scorching hot, fine, loose sand, I reached a second pan known as 'Dead-vlei'. Like something out of a sci-fi film, it was peppered with the remnants of a wind-seared forest, encircled by dunes. The gnarled trees there are said to be more than six centuries' old, relics of a time when there was more water and less sand.

A little further to the south, at the small town of Aus, I came across Piet Swiegers, whose ancestors have made their home in southern Africa since the seventeenth century. Passionate about Namibia, Piet makes a living by showing off the country's raw beauty to others.

Wild desert horses are one of the marvels found on his family's land. More than two hundred of them in total, their numbers rise and decline depending on the rains. They're thought to be descended from horses set free by soldiers during the First World War almost a century ago. As with everything else, they cling to life in a place where day to day survival is in itself an achievement.

Another curiosity on the farm is the bullet-ridden 1934 Hudson Terraplane. The rounded bodywork now russet-brown with rust, it was supposedly the getaway car of diamond thieves, shot at long ago by police.

The story might sound farfetched, and anywhere else it would be. But Namibia is a land of diamonds like no other. And a stone's throw from Piet's farm is the greatest testament of all to diamond fever.

Known as Kolmanskop, it sprouted up as a prim German town a century ago, in the middle of the Namib. There were diamonds everywhere, many of them on the surface, allowing prospectors to simply crawl about on their bellies to find them.

Over millions of years, the gems were flushed into the Atlantic from the Orange River in Namibia's south. Then the Benguela current forced the diamond-bearing sands ashore, forming the Namib desert.

The result was that easy pickings of the high quality stones led to plenty of instant millionaires. And overnight fortunes brought luxury.

There was a power station and tramway, a casino, a skittle hall, a Champagne and oyster bar, and an ice factory, a theatre, restaurants, and a huge hospital equipped with Africa's first X-ray machine.

But intense mining saw boom lead to bust.

Abandoned in the early 'fifties, Kolmanskop is today a ghost-town. Sand dunes fill the houses now, the paint stripped away from the walls, blow-torched by the wind.

In one of the buildings down near the tramway, I found a torn scrap of photograph. Black and white and burned on one side, it showed a young German couple, in Sunday best. They were straining to look serious as people used to do when posing, the tramway sign 'Kolmannskuppe' behind them. Like everyone else, they must have left when the diamonds were all mined out.

But there are still plenty of the precious stones nearby.

Kolmanskop is located within the restricted diamond zone, known as the 'Sperrgebiet', an area of more than 10,000 square miles.

Managed by De Beers, entry is forbidden, and it's under armed guard round the clock.

Twenty minutes' drive from Kolmanskop, the neat little German town of Lüderitz gives a hint of how life at the ghost town may once been. Although located on the coast, it was constructed about the same time, and with the same Teutonic attention to detail as at Kolmanskop. There's a sense that the glory days are long gone, a faded grandeur and irresistible melancholy.

Basking in the genteel glow of mid-summer light, Lüderitz was once gripped by diamond fever, too. The boom began when, in 1908, a station-master on the diminutive Aus to Lüderitz railway line, spotted something glinting between the tracks. Quietly, he staked out a claim, made a fortune, and lost it, before dying penniless.

At the town's Kegelbahn, the century-old skittles hall, the descendants of diamond miners and Voortrekkers bet over beers and hardwood balls on a Thursday night. Among them, Alexi, a Russian trawlerman, who was washed up in Lüderitz years ago. Downing his beer in one, he ordered another, then peered out at the street.

'Perhaps I'm crazy to live here,' he says all of a sudden. 'It's just as well if I am, because a little madness helps you to bear the silence of the Skeleton Coast.'

Giraffe on the savannah of the Kwandwe Reserve

Ostrich Hats and Model T's

IN A BIZARRE QUIRK OF HISTORY, it was the Model T Ford that spelled the end of ostrich feather hats.

Awash with great billowing plumage, the bonnets had been at the height of fashion during the Edwardian age. They were much admired when worn in equally-fashionable open-topped limousines. But, with its small doorway and cramped interior, Mr. Ford's economic Model T meant that fashion had to take a back seat. The result – the collapse of South Africa's burgeoning ostrich trade, and bankruptcy on an unimaginable scale.

But, almost a century on, and the former farmlands of South Africa's big bird business are at last witnessing a come back. This time round the ostriches roam free, along with a full gamut of wildlife, on land where the only shots taken today are through long lenses.

It's five a.m., and I'm furled up in a wool blanket, perched on the back of an open-topped Landcruiser – fretting because my Blackberry's lost the signal. All I can think of is how my bloodstream needs caffeine, and how a day without e-mail will take months to set right. But then, suddenly, there's a muffled cry against the first rays of silvery African light.

I glance up, squint uneasily into the middle distance.

Fifteen feet from where I'm crouching, still clutching my Blackberry, is a massive bull elephant. He's looking at me disapprovingly, ears flapped forward, tusks bowed down, as if he's about to charge.

The world slips into sharp focus while my adrenal glands prepare for fight or flight. As someone who spends his life mollycoddled by technology, and rather meaningless luxury, I realized right then how separated I'd become from the brutal reality of the natural world.

For me, nature is something you watch on the Discovery Channel, or on the evening news – as you learn how much more of it's been savaged to make way for the Blackberry realm that is my home.

My ranger guide, a South African version of Crocodile Dundee, called Brendon, fishtailed the vehicle out of harm's way a moment before the tusks reached their target. Sighing with relief, we continued on the morning game drive, and on our quest for lion cubs.

Nestled in the wilderness of the Eastern Cape, one hundred and sixty kilometres from Port Elisabeth, Kwandwe is one of a new breed of private game reserves. A great lure from the beginning has been that the region is malaria-free. Once populated by a full compliment of wildlife, it was 'settled' by white farmers in the 1830s, ringed with fences and farmed for ostriches. Regarded as little more than vermin, the original fauna was picked off for trophies and for sport, leaving a decimated animal population.

The original settler and his family worked the land and are buried beneath it. Beside their graves is another – oversized and angular – the farmer's favourite horse. In one of the lodges there's a faded sepia print of the family's Edwardian generation. Sitting to attention, dressed in the Sunday best, the women are all sporting the fabulous ostrich hats that brought them such wealth. But when the bottom fell out of the ostrich business, the farmers' own world collapsed.

For much of the twentieth century, the farmsteads lay silent. Then, following a dream, naturalist Angus Sholto-Douglas, who manages the reserve, was approached by an American investor. The rest is history. Over a decade, they bought up nine farms, encompassing more than twenty thousand hectares, and prepared them to receive wildlife once again.

'It wasn't so simple as trucking in animals and letting them get on with it,' says Angus. 'Painstaking planning was necessary to check the kinds and quantities of animals this vast property could sustain.'

Long before the first creatures arrived, two thousand miles of fencing had to be removed, along with telephone lines, water troughs, dangerous machinery, and the odd farm building. The result was a wilderness, returned to its natural state, a landscape unblemished by Man.

The foliage, known as 'succulent thicket', was in good shape and ready for the food chain. Gradually, over months and years, the animals were reintroduced.

Taking care to ensure they were as unstressed as possible after the drive, they were held in bomas, huge pens filled with trees and foliage –

in which they could spend weeks getting used to their new environment.

Herds of elephant, Cape buffalo, hippos, giraffes, and six rare black rhinos were introduced early on, in a Noah's Ark of creatures. Then came the cheetahs, the lions, the brown hyenas and the leopards. The carnivores had plenty to support them – oryx, eland, zebra, gemsbok and springbok, all of which graze on the grassland and scrub.

With the aid of a tracker, perched in a hot-seat mounted on the vehicle's bull bars, Brendon takes great care to give the animals their space.

'This is their home far more than it is ours,' he says, 'and it's critical that we don't do anything that will impact on their world.' Pausing to steer up an abrupt incline, he adds: 'I once saw a tortoise on its back out here. It was struggling to turn over and was about to become a predator's lunch. I flipped it over and, by doing so, I changed the order. I think about it even now. Because I allowed a tortoise to live, a predator may have gone hungry.'

At Kwandwe you can't help but be touched by the order of natural world, and by the humans who strive to maintain it. On a continent where the animal kingdom is under constant threat, there's a sense that in this small corner of Africa great achievements are being made. Yet despite all the work, poachers still succeed in their dastardly work. Last year more than three hundred South African rhino were killed illegally, the black market value at their horns put at about £35,000 for a single kilogram.

Without doubt the way forward, the new breed of private game reserves, like Kwandwe, offer low impact safaris in which you're far more likely to see animals rather than other tourists.

In addition to the balance of nature, the Kwandwe reserve has ensured another all-important balance – that of the local community. A number of small villages are found on the reserve, and those who live in them are at the heart of life. Some are employed as staff in the lodges, or as rangers and trackers, while others are involved in community projects. One endeavour is gathering the traditional knowledge of medicinal plants from the elderly, and recording its wisdom for generations to come.

Spend a few days watching animals in their native habitat, and you begin to forget all about the pressures of e-mails and the Internet. Even a diehard Crackberry addict like myself couldn't care less about the world I'd left behind. My priorities had changed. After a couple of days all I could think about was seeing lions and their cubs.

On the last morning, with only minutes to go of the final game drive, Brendon Crocodile Dundee spotted fresh paw prints in the dust. Risking his life, the tracker clambered onto his hot-seat and, through a sixth sense of his own, led the way.

Minutes later, we came upon them.

A pair of lionesses in the early morning light, a nest of honey-yellow cubs scampering about beside them. It was one of those moments that gets etched onto your memory. And I hope it will stay with me always.

As we turned quietly round to head back to the lodge, I mumbled prayer of thanks to Henry Ford. After all, had he not come up with the Model T, ostrich hats might still be in vogue, and the magic of Kwandwe might never have been conjured at all.

The People of the Cloak

SINCE THE FOUNDING OF ISLAM, almost fourteen centuries ago, one family has remained at the centre of the Faith.

Revered by all Muslims, and bound by rigid codes of conduct, this clan has been responsible for the spread and diffusion of Islam. In times of uncertainty, such as these, its members have the solemn duty to speak out and steer the religion back to its true path.

Throughout the Islamic World, they are known simply as 'The People of the Cloak'.

Lying on his death-bed, the Prophet Mohammed urged his closest followers to gather around. He would soon quit the mortal world, he said, but before departing, he wanted to bequeath to them the two most precious things in his possession: The Holy Qur'an, and his *family*. This second part of his legacy may have seemed strange, but it is one which has preoccupied the Islamic World ever since.

Often known in the East as The People of the Cloak, Mohammed's immediate family and their descendants, are revered by all Muslims, whether they be Sunnis or Shi'a. No other family commands such respect or devotion, nor has any other had such a dynamic bearing on the Islamic World's religious, political and cultural development.

A great number of the Prophet's direct descendants have been people of astonishing ability. They have ruled as Caliphs and Kings, have excelled as philosophers and mathematicians, as poets, men and women of *belle lettres* and geographers, as warriors, military tacticians and, of course, as celebrated religious scholars. Others have been leading Sufis, members of the Islamic brotherhood of mystics.

The Prophet's direct descendants are bound by a rigid verbal code of obligation. Raised to excel in everything they do, they are taught that achievement is of paramount importance: that they must uphold the pillars of the Islamic Faith, perform acts of anonymous charity, and lead by their own example. Most important of all, however, is the development of a sense of 'selflessness'.

The People of the Cloak are believed by Muslims to embody the purity and virtues of the Prophet Mohammed himself. To them, his family carries this purity in their veins, the very bloodlines of the Prophet. Such sanctity, it is believed, allows the People of the Cloak alone to recognize the revelations hidden in the teachings of the Qur'an: teachings to which ordinary men are blind.

But this integrity comes at a price. Members of the Prophet's close family are expected to live exemplary lives, according to an ancient framework of conduct and obligation. This states that in striving for modesty they must never be boastful or ostentatious, and that they must stand apart from all other men. The emphasis is on honour, chivalry and, above all, on generosity – especially in performing acts of anonymous charity.

This code binds the clan to uphold the true message of the Islamic Faith, and to speak out against misrepresentation. In times such as these, when deviant factions seek to 'hijack' the religion, its members are expected to act as a mouthpiece for moderation.

Mohammed's family have been associated with the spread and development of Islam since the faith's conception almost fourteen centuries ago. Indeed, it was a conflict over the succession after the Prophet's death, which led to the only major sectarian split in Islamic history. The dramatic result was the Shi'a minority dividing from the Sunni majority.

In the years after Mohammed's death, religious scholars collected every scrap of information about his life; and thousands of people who had known the Prophet, however briefly, were asked to recount his acts, aphorisms and teachings. Known as the 'Hadith', these fragments are regarded as sacred in themselves, ranking second only to the Qur'an in the reverence with which they are held. They are underpinned by the belief that, as a completely pure person, Mohammed's every action can be taken as a lesson in Islamic behaviour.

The Hadith forms the extraordinary framework by which Muslims can be reminded of the true path. Covering virtually every conceivable area of life, it stresses modesty and moderation, good manners, high ideals, and decent behaviour towards the ill-fortunate. The Hadith can act as an invaluable guide for non-Muslims, too. If in doubt about on how to behave in an Eastern land, search the Hadith, follow the Prophet's example, and one is unlikely to go wrong.

The Hadith's scope is astonishing: ranging in scope from charity to the treatment of animals, from cleanliness to marital law, and from usury to self-control.

It is from the Hadith that The People of the Cloak are said to derive their name. The story goes that while staying at his daughter Fatima's house, Mohammed complained of tiredness. Hearing this, his daughter fetched a fine camel-wool cloak and laid it over her father. The Prophet's face is said to have lit up and 'shined like the full moon'. As he lay there, his grandsons, Hassan and Hussain, arrived and asked if they might join their grandfather beneath the cloak. They did so, as did Ali (Mohammed's son-in-law) and lastly, Fatima herself.

When all five were under the cloak, the Prophet prayed to God, beseeching Him to keep his flesh and blood untainted. Speaking through the archangel Gabriel, God confirmed the purity and the importance of the Prophetic line.

Mohammed's clan, the Hashemites, are regarded with respect by Muslims as, to a lesser degree, is the Quraish, the wider tribe to which the clan belongs. But it is the descendants of Mohammed's closest relatives – those who lay with him beneath the cloak – who are held in highest esteem. Sometimes simply known as 'The Five', they are respected by both major branches of the Muslim Faith, by Sunni and Shi'a alike.

According to Islam, Mohammed was descended from the Prophet Abraham; and like him, he sought to rid his community of idols, to transform it into a monotheistic society. He was selected by God not as a son, but as a messenger. Whilst the Islamic Faith reveres Abraham, Moses, Jesus, amongst other Biblical prophets, it asserts that they were just that – prophets. According to Islam, Mohammed was the last Prophet.

His daughter Fatima is regarded with extraordinary reverence, especially by the Shiites, because she was married to Ali.

When Ali's own father lost his fortune and became impoverished,

Mohammed took him in, he himself having been cared for as a child by Ali's father. Then, when Mohammed was called by God to be His messenger, Ali was among the very first of his converts. Remaining loyal throughout his entire life he even, as the story goes, slept in Mohammed's bed to impersonate him on the night that the Prophet made his famous flight to Medina. It was this allegiance, his loyalty which the Shi'a believe has automatically entitled Ali and his descendants to be the leaders of Islam.

Born to Fatima and Ali, Mohammed's grandsons – Hassan, and his younger brother, Hussain – were forced to acquiesce to the rule of the Umayyed Caliphate who succeeded their father.

The sectarian split within Islam, which divided the religion into two main branches – Sunni and Shi'a – is often likened to the Protestant-Catholic divide in the Christian Church. Whilst the Christian split didn't take place until over a thousand years or so after the death of Christ, the Sunni-Shi'a rift happened within a lifetime of the Prophet's death.

Most importantly, the division of Islam took place not for doctrinal reasons, but because of succession: and the question of which members of the Prophet's family ought to succeed him. Western observers on Islamic themes often tend to neglect this point. There is no better way to understand the Sunni-Shi'a division than to study The People of the Cloak's role in the early years of Islamic history.

Upon Mohammed's death, the leaders of the fledgling Muslim Faith gathered to decide who would be the Prophet's political successor. Following a heated debate, Abu Bakr was elected the first Caliph (literally, 'Successor') in Islam. But Ali, Mohammed's son-in-law, who had not been present at the meeting, later protested that he ought to have been considered. Whilst Ali did swear allegiance to Abu Bakr, however, and eventually became the Fourth Caliph of Islam in 656 AD, the damage had been done. His followers, known as Shiites, came to insist that only members of the Prophet's family can lead the Islamic faith. It is their belief that Ali's lineage is the truest line to follow and that only members of Ali's family may lead. The Shi'a call this dynasty *Ahlul Beit*, 'The People of the House'.

The Sunnis, by contrast, believe that any right-minded Muslim can be named as a Caliph, or a leader, although they too regard descendants of the Prophet with unequalled reverence. Sunnis accept the Prophet's instruction that a person ought not to be taken merely on birth but also on his own merits. This theme, enduring through the development of Islam, raises the question as to whether Mohammed's family enjoys privileges which it has not earned.

By the close of the eighth century, the Shi'a branch of Islam had begun to develop its own clear doctrines: rejecting, for instance, the tradition of the Hadith, and instead collecting their own doctrines, and interpreting the Qur'an in substantially different ways from the Sunni tradition. This key divergence in the interpretation of basic Islamic values came about directly as a result of allegiance to The People of the Cloak.

While Sunni Islam has no well-established hierarchy of priests, the Shi'a employ titles such as *Ayatollah*, and its clergy wear distinctive religious dress. The Shi'a revere a line of Imams – the word means literally 'Leader' – all of whom had Ali as their ancestor. Different groups of Shi'a stop at different Imams in Ali's family tree – regarding theirs to be the final true guide – and, accordingly, these Shiite subgroupings are known as 'Fivers', 'Seveners' and 'Twelvers'.

The People of the Cloak, this inner circle of Mohammed's family, were largely responsible for the extraordinary speed with which the new Islamic Faith spread East and West. For, when the Prophet sent his closest relatives out to preach the Word, he placed absolute trust in them: certain that they would not corrupt his message nor be swayed by the spoils of war. Whilst Islam was still confined to the Arabian peninsula at the time of Mohammed's death, within a century it had spread as far east as Persia, and as far west as the Atlantic shores of Morocco.

After the conversion of Arabia, and the subjugation of Syria and Jerusalem, Islam spread like a wildfire into the east: sweeping into Mesopotamia, Armenia, Persia, Afghanistan and Samarkand. At much the same time, the new Faith swept westwards, through Egypt, across North Africa and up into Spain. The fall of Toledo in 712 AD completed the conquest of Iberia's Gothic kingdom. But Islam didn't stop there. It conquered Sicily and, for a time, pushed on into southern France.

In the centuries after Mohammed's death, Islam developed from a fledgling religion, into a structured political and cultural force, in which the Prophet's family became interlinked with a sequence of Islamic dynasties, or Caliphates. Under some of these, the sciences and the arts were patronized, although others fostered nothing but nepotistic avarice.

Whilst the Sunnis, who make up about ninety per cent of all Muslims, believe that the Prophet died without naming a successor; the Shi'a maintain that he *had* named his chosen successor: his son-in-law, Ali. The Sunnis hold the First Caliphate in very high esteem, while the Shi'a therefore despise it, except for Ali, who was the last of its four Caliphs.

On Mohammed's death, his father-in-law Abu Bakr was elected to lead Muslims with the title *Khalifa*, or 'Caliph'. In Islam all men are to be regarded as equal and therefore, strictly speaking, this means that there is no convention of a monarchy. The Caliph's role was to act simply as a guide, ensuring not only that the Islamic Faith remained pure, free from distortion, but also that it continued to spread.

Abu Bakr was the first in a line of four Caliphs, each of whom was elected upon his own merits, and none of whom founded a specific dynasty of his own. After Abu Bakr came Omar, then Othman, and eventually Ali, all four of whom were advisors and close companions during the Prophet's life. Like him, they were all also warriors and military tacticians, and were committed to spread the mission of Islam.

The Abbasids were Hashemites, tracing their ancestry through the Prophet's uncle, Abbas. When their dynasty replaced the Umayyeds, it regained the Islamic leadership for the Prophet's family, for the Umayyeds (who preceded them) had not been People of the Cloak. The Abbasids reigned for five hundred years, until overthrown in the Mongol invasion of 1258 AD.

The Abbasid Caliphate concentrated not on the spread westward, as the Umayyeds had done, but pushed East – towards Persia – moving their capital to the new city of Baghdad; and promoting not just Islam, but the sciences, the arts, and trade as well. Under leaders such as al-Ma'mun and Harun ar-Rashid, Islam entered its golden age. The era saw the Islamic World grow larger and increasingly diverse, with wildly differing ethnic groups meeting and mingling as equals for the first time.

Taking their name from Fatima, the daughter of Mohammed through whom they were descended, the Fatimids were a strong Islamic dynasty, with a sphere of influence that dominated much of North Africa and Arabia. Their leadership lasted almost two centuries, from the middle of the tenth century.

The Fatimids were a distinct movement in that they were not Sunnis, but of the minority Shi'a branch of Islam and, as such, they totally rejected the co-existing Abbasid Caliphate, with its capital at Baghdad. Their view being that only Ali's descendants could hold the title of Caliph, they saw their role as being to destroy the Abbasids and install a Shi'a Caliphate in their place.

The descendents of The People of the Cloak have, over centuries, radically affected the Islamic societies in which they lived. Their combined contribution has led to developments in the religion itself, as well as in areas of the sciences, literature, and the arts. Indeed, for The People of the Cloak, nothing is so important as scholarship. For this reason one finds that many of its members, who have been revered as kings or military tacticians, have excelled in literature and the sciences.

A selection of important figures from the Prophetic family:

Jalaluddin Rumi

The greatest Sufi mystic and poet, Jalaluddin Rumi was born in Balkh, Afghanistan, early in the thirteenth century, and died in Turkey, where his mausoleum can still be seen at Konya. Regarded not only as a scholar of extraordinary intellect, he was also a man who embodied the Sufi code of 'selflessness'. His epic literary treatise, *The Mathnavi*, which runs to more than twenty-six thousand couplets, is considered to be one of the most important of all Sufi texts. Rumi's scholarship spanned many disciplines, ranging from mathematics to botany; indeed, seven centuries before the birth of Charles Darwin, Rumi even published a paper on evolution in the natural world.

Following his death, Rumi's disciples continued to study his work, from the centre they had established at Konya. There they established the order of *Mawlawiyah*, which involves a form of trance-induced dance. They are known in the West as 'Whirling Dervishes'.

Al-Idrisi

At the height of its expansion, Islam was spreading at lightening speed. As its message moved both east and west, a geographical understanding developed, charting new peoples and far off lands. Born in 1100 AD, Al-Idrisi was the brightest light of his new Arab interest in geography, travelling widely from his birth place in Ceuta, (the tiny Spanish enclave in northern Morocco), through North Africa, much of Europe and as far as southern England. Eventually, he settled in Sicily, where he became an adviser to the Norman King, Roger II.

It was in the Sicilian Court he produced his greatest geographical work: *Kitab nuzhat al-mushtaq fi ikhtiraq al-afaq* ('The Pleasure Excursion of One Who is Eager to Traverse the Regions of the World'). Accompanied by a silver planisphere, upon which was depicted a detailed map of the known world, Al-Idrisi's monumental work was translated into Latin and other European languages in the years after his death. It formed the basis for all European geography of the age.

Harun ar-Rashid

Harun ar-Rashid, the celebrated Abbasid Caliph, is known in the Occident largely because his kingdom was immortalized in *A Thousand and One Nights*: a collection of tales that will give a European audience a wide variety of Arab folk heroes, including Ali Baba, Aladdin and Sindbad. Under Harun's Caliphate, folklore and storytelling did indeed flourish, along with science, and the arts.

Harun himself was infamous for touring his kingdom by night in disguise to see first hand what his people wanted, and what they thought of his rule; and whilst his court brimmed with wealth, pomp and grandeur, Harun ar-Rashid himself strived for knowledge. Under his Caliphate, Baghdad reached unsurpassed heights of scientific development.

Al-Ma'mun

The illegitimate son of Harun ar-Rashid, Al-Ma'mun succeeded his half-brother Amin as Caliph of the Abassid dynasty; and it was under his patronage that the very greatest era of Islamic scholarship took place, centred at *Beit al-Hikmah* – 'The House of Wisdom' – which Al-

Ma'mun established at Baghdad in 830 AD. Dedicated to gathering and translating ancient books, the *Beit al-Hikmah* was staffed by not only Muslims, but by Christians, Hindus, Jews and Buddhists. Its single aim was to make all the knowledge of the world available in the Arab language. With time, these translations ensured that many of the Latin and Greek texts were preserved during the European Dark Ages.

Among the scholars attached to the House of Wisdom was the legendary astronomer and mathematician, Al-Khwarizmi, whose works introduced 'Arab' numerals and the science of algebra to Europe.

Saladdin

With a name that translates as 'Righteousness of the Faith, son of Joseph, son of Job', Saladdin Yusuf ibn Ayyub was the feared adversary of the Christian Crusaders. In the West, his name is equalled in notoriety only by that of Harun ar-Rashid.

On July 4, 1187, aided by his own military good sense and by a phenomenal lack of it on the part of his enemy, Saladdin trapped and destroyed an exhausted and thirst-crazed army of crusaders at Hattin, near Tiberias in northern Palestine. So great were the losses in the crusader ranks in this one battle, that the Muslims were quickly able to overrun almost all of the Kingdom of Jerusalem, relieving the Franks of their eighty-eight-year hold on the city. In doing so, Saladdin established himself as the Sultan, forming the Ayyubid Dynasty – which encompassed much of modern Egypt, Syria, Yemen and Palestine.

Mir Sayed Ali

Regarded as the greatest Persian miniature painter of the sixteenth century, Mir Sayed Ali was born in Tabriz, and travelled to India at the invitation of the Mughal Emperor, Humayun. Leading the work at the Imperial atelier – first in Kabul, and then in Delhi – he oversaw the production of a series of gigantic paintings in the miniature style. The series is on an epic scale, running to more than fourteen hundred individual illustrations.

Mohammed ar-Razi

A celebrated alchemist and philosopher, as well as becoming the greatest physician of the tenth century, ar-Razi's work was translated widely into Latin (in which he himself was known as *Rhazes*), where it formed one of the bases of Western medicine. His two most acclaimed medical works are the *Kitab al-Mansuri*, which he authored in honour of the ruler Mansur ibn Ishaq; and the *Kitab al-hawi*, the 'Comprehensive Book', which surveyed Greek, Syrian, Indian and early Arabic medicine. In addition to these two voluminous works, ar-Razi wrote dozens of medical treatises, among them an important paper on smallpox and measles which was translated into Latin, Byzantine Greek and many other languages.

Abu al Faraj al-Isbahani

Born into a Shiite family in the tenth century, al-Isbahani claimed descent from the Prophet through Ali. Also a descendant of Marwan II, the last Umayyed Caliph of Syria, al-Isbahani was a celebrated scholar of both literature and music, best known for the *Kitab al-Aghani*, his monumental 'Book of Songs', which provides a wide body of information on early Islamic music and musicians.

Selim I

Nicknamed *Yavuz*, 'The Grim', Sultan Selim I was largely responsible for the way in which the Ottoman Empire rose to become the predominant Muslim dynasty of their time. Although Selim I, his antecedents and descendants, have claimed direct ancestry to the Prophet, most modern scholars dispute their lineage.

Responsible for securing and holding onto one of the most formidable realms the Islamic World has known, the Ottomans were also great patrons the arts, using their phenomenal wealth in the service architecture, calligraphy, metalwork and ceramics.

Visitors to Istanbul's Topkapi Palace can view a mesmerizing array of objects created for the Sultans. These include a cluster of relics brought from Egypt by Selim I, and amongst them are one of the Prophet's hairs, one of his teeth, his mantle, and even his footprint.

The Mahadi of Sudan

Born the son of a Sudanese boat-builder who alleged descent from The

People of the Cloak, Mohammed Ahmed ibn Abdullah, or the 'Mahadi', as he became known, was a messianic figure set on the reformation of Islam, on returning it to the pure Islamic values practised by the Prophet.

In some Muslim circles (most notably those of the Shiite branch) there is a tradition of a last messiah who will appear and lead for seven or eight years in a final golden age, before the end of the world. The most recent such messianic figure to achieve prominence in the Islamic World, the Mahadi of Sudan, called for revolution in 1881 against the Egyptian administration which, at that point, controlled much of Sudan.

Sweeping through Sudan, the Mahadists gained popular support among ordinary people. When they came up against the Egyptian army, which was led by a British colonel, they slaughtered all ten thousand of them and marched on to Khartoum. The famous British commander General Gordon was then dispatched to the Sudanese capital to put an end to the Mahadi's revolt. Gordon and his troops were butchered, allowing the Mahadi national control. Five months after throwing out all colonial forces, however, the Mahadi suddenly died, and his once-powerful movement disintegrated.

Ibn Saud

As a child, Ibn Saud's family lost their ancestral lands near Riyad on the Arabian Peninsula, and were forced to flee to Kuwait, impoverished. Ibn Saud yearned to regain his family's dignity; and, as soon as he reached manhood, made a daring attack on the opposing Rashidi fortress, killing their leader. Over the next years he continued to wage war against the Rashidis. By 1924, he was victorious, having regained not only his ancestral lands, but adding to them the entire central Arabian and the Hejaz regions, which controlled the holy city of Mecca.

A leader of burning charisma, Ibn Saud himself was drawn from the Wahabis, who espouse a puritanical interpretation of Islamic values. Regarded as a leader of rock solid ability, he is viewed as a man whose personal course was charted with great deliberation.

Jan Fishan Khan

The great nineteenth century Afghan warrior and statesman was among the most adulated warlords in Central Asian history. With a name which means 'He Who Scatters Souls in Battle', Jan Fishan Khan is largely remembered today for helping hundreds of British women and children to escape the siege of Kabul in 1842: one of the greatest acts of humanity during the days of the British Empire. It was a feat that astonished the British, as much as it enraged the Afghan people.

Hussein of Jordan

King Hussein of Jordan was, arguably, one of the greatest modern adherents to the ways of The People of the Cloak. Born into the Hashemite line, his family had been guardians of Mecca for a thousand years until the establishment of their own kingdom in the 1920s. A spokesman for the voice of moderation within Islam, Hussein spent much of his political career battling against fanatical Islamic forces within his kingdom and the region. In 1958, his first cousin – the Hashemite King Faisal of Iraq – was butchered by Republican soldiers in a coup.

Surviving more than a dozen assassination attempts (including having his eye drops poisoned), Hussein soon became an effective bridgehead between East and West. On his death in 1999, his powers as monarch were transferred to his eldest son, Prince Abdullah, who continues Jordan's Hashemite line.

Aga Khan IV

Prince Karim Hussain (otherwise known as 'Aga Khan IV') is the head of the Ismaili community. Half English by birth and schooled in Switzerland and at Harvard, he is recognized as a member of the jet-set elite: seen on the Côte d'Azur as often as he is in the Islamic World.

But the other side of the Aga Khan's activities – namely his devotion to charity – is less well publicized. His philanthropic foundations have built schools and hospitals in a range of countries, especially in East Africa and south Asia. The Aga Khan's current project of establishing a large Islamic museum and centre in London, is seen as aimed at drawing the West's attention to the moderate side of Islam, and the religion's rich cultural tradition.

From the earliest days of Islam there has been a grave temptation to invent fraudulent ancestry, linking a weak heritage to the Prophetic line. All kinds of people have been guilty of this practice – most notably an array of powerful Caliphs who have ruled over the Middle East and, more recently, a wide range of Arab leaders.

Harun ar-Rashid is said to have gone to great lengths to ensure that his genealogy reflected not merely the Prophet's tribe, but his clan. The Ottoman Sultan Selim I was equally ambitious, and sponsored only genealogists who would agree to link his own name to that of Mohammed.

Fraudulent claimants are more common today than ever before, hailing from every rank and corner of the Islamic World, and ranging from destitute beggars to national presidents.

The irony is that *bona fide* People of the Cloak are brought up to despise misuse of their heritage. For them nothing is so deplorable as bragging about their ancestry, or using it to achieve commercial ends. It is for this reason that a great number of the Prophet's ancestors refrain from using their hereditary titles, or ever mentioning their lineage at all. The fact that the family condemns the use of such titles for personal gain, makes fraudulent or misguided members all the more visible.

The Sufis are probably the most misunderstood group within the Islamic community, and their brotherhood is interlinked with the lives of The People of the Cloak. Regarded with awe throughout the Islamic World, their mystical fraternity is said to keep alive a secret knowledge. The most celebrated Sufi of all was the Prophet himself. His teachings – together with the codes of behaviour by which he lived – are entwined with the values held sacred by his line.

True Sufis believe that their brotherhood came into being long before Islam, and that consequently they are not bound to that Faith. But at the same time, many leading Sufis – including the most famous, Jalaluddin Rumi – have been People of the Cloak.

Central premises of Sufi life are the principles of 'selflessness', introspection and of anonymous charity: the very same ideals held so sacred by the Prophet's descendants.

Some say that the Sufis were the precursors to Freemasons, others that they take their name from the woollen coats they once wore (*suf*, meaning 'wool' in Arabic), as they shunned silks and finery. But as far as real Sufis are concerned there is no merit in tracing their history, or deliberating on why they are called what they are. Instead, they prefer to spend time bettering themselves and striving towards their own form of inner enlightenment.

With the expansion of science and the arts in the early Islamic era, many Sufis put their minds to solving mathematical problems, while others studied artistic techniques, medicine, architecture, alchemy and other magical sciences. Their symbols can be seen in many disciplines to those who know where to find them. Nowhere is their message so strong as in their literature.

Western society has only in recent years begun to understand the phenomenal clarity of Sufi perception, the psychology of which stresses that the mind must first be ready to receive knowledge. One of the techniques employed to this end is the use of humour, which Sufis believe frees the mind, allowing it to absorb. To comprehend Sufi knowledge one must also be trained to understand a secret language, known to Sufis as 'the Hidden Tongue'.

Literal translation of Sufi words or encoded terms has caused almost unbelievable confusion in the West, especially in the transmission of this secret lore. Sufi texts, many of them written by The People of the Cloak themselves, are misunderstood because their deeper allegorical meanings – which are clear only to the Sufi fraternity – are taken too literally by outsiders.

Complex methods of encryption used by the Sufi orders come in many forms, the most famous of which is the *Abjad* system – an alpha-numeric substitution cipher – frequently found in Sufi literature and all forms of their art.

It is almost impossible to overemphasize the importance with which ancestry is held in the Middle East and North Africa. As has already been stressed, the Prophet Mohammed's is regarded as by far the most important lineage of all. Ancestry is an Arab obsession, and virtually everyone can recount the names of their forebears, often dating back a dozen generations or more.

With the focus always on achievement, The People of the Cloak are ruthless with regard to genealogy. At the birth of a male child, they usually only mark its name in pencil. If the son becomes a person of merit and accomplishment, only then will his name be written over in ink. If the individual achieves nothing significant during their life, however, the name will be erased and forgotten.

When introductions are made in the East, mention is frequently made of a person's famous ancestors or noble bloodlines. For the Westerner, these extended deliberations over ancestral lineage can be perplexing. It is a process which dates back to Arabia's tribal past, and which is held as important today as it was centuries ago.

Spend a little time in the East, and one begins to sense who is (or claims to be) of noble ancestry. As well as *Hashemi* and *Quraishi*, you find the names *Fatemi* and *Hussaini* – descendants of Mohammed's daughter and her son, Hussain. The latter two are especially revered by the Shiite community.

In addition, there are ancestral titles available for members of the Prophet's family to use, should they wish to do so. These include *Sayed*, which means 'Prince'; *Sharif*, meaning 'Noble'; and *Amir*, meaning 'Commander'.

Rachel Pendergraft and other members of the Knights of the Ku Klux Klan

KKK Barbie and Ken dolls

Queen of the Ku Klux Klan

RACHEL PENDERGRAFT WAS PRESENTED with her first set of hooded robes even before she could walk.

Her earliest memories are of midnight ceremonies, of cross burnings, and oaths sworn in allegiance to the Ku Klux Klan.

Bought up in the very bosom of the Klan, Rachel is widely regarded as the most powerful female member of the KKK in America today. Hailed as a 'Grand Dragon', she is the only woman to sit on the Grand Council of the Knights of the Ku Klux Klan. With her smooth talk, good looks and designer wardrobe, Rachel Pendergraft is the new face of America's most feared secret society.

The door swings open to room 117 at a run-down motel somewhere in east Tennessee. Rachel Pendergraft stands in the frame, grinning widely, as if she understands the importance of first impressions. She is buxom, blonde, and fair-skinned, with large hazel eyes and thick fuchsia lipgloss. Dressed in a tailored navy suit, with a cream blouse, dangly gold earrings, and sensible shoes, Rachel Pendergraft is the opposite of what you might expect.

The motel room is cluttered with vanity cases, Italian outfits and children's clothes. Rachel's daughters stare into a TV screen, giggling at cartoons. Charity, aged three, and Shelby, who is almost two, have long golden locks and alabaster complexions. Like their mother, they are dressed in their Sunday best. At first it seems like any other motel room in America's Deep South: flowery wallpaper, cable TV, and vinyl-covered chairs. But look again. Hanging in one corner are two sets of white silky robes. Hooded and with face-veils, the full-length gowns bear the black stripes of high rank.

Stacked beside the hooded gowns are other clues: boxes filled with T-shirts and badges, banners and bumper-stickers, bearing the inimitable initials 'KKK'.

But the Ku Klux Klan has re-thought its dogma, sharpened its image, become eco-friendly, and is learning to play the media game.

Perhaps the biggest change of all is their new focus on welcoming women to the society's leadership. Gone is the foul-mouthed, grubby Klan of the past; gone too are the calls to take up arms. The Klan has a new message: *Merchandising, Media, Massive Power.*

The KKK no longer organizes lynchings, it holds coffee mornings instead.

'When we were kids we used to go to Klan picnics and barbecues,' explains Rachel, in her southern lilt. 'Everyone at school knew that I was in the Klan and that my dad was a member. I didn't have any black friends when I was a kid – but I did know a Mexican girl once. We weren't close though. She understood that I belonged to the Ku Klux Klan.'

Rachel pauses as Charity squirms up onto her lap.

'I'm really dedicated to the Klan,' she says, 'I'm committed because I care about the future of my children. I love my people because they're white, I love my kids because they're white – and I'll love my grandchildren 'cos they'll be white.'

'You must understand,' she bursts out energetically, 'we don't *hate* black people, we just *love* white people!'

This sound bite is the all too familiar new face of the Klan.

It rolls off the tongue smooth as silk. No neo-Klan interview would be complete without it.

'We haven't changed our attitudes,' Rachel confides, as she inspects her long, manicured nails, 'but we're perfecting our image, making it sharper, and working on our professionalism.'

Rachel Pendergraft and her father, the veteran Klansman Thom Robb, run the largest and oldest Klan group in the United States. Known as the Knights of the KKK, the faction realizes that the only way the society can become a national force again is by changing its spots. The group's radical programme of change has been greeted with rage from the die-hard Klan fringe. Indeed, the Knights, or '4K' as they're commonly known, lost about half their members when the reforms began.

Undeterred by the defection of Klansmen, Rachel and her father have encouraged their members to disrobe at public functions, to tone down their anti-ethnic rhetoric, and to embrace women members as well.

Marc Caplan of the Anti Defamation League in New York, feels that although the restructuring might be unpopular in the short term, it's well thought out.

'Women were always the weak link in the hate movement,' he says. 'The women, who were traditionally forbidden to attend male Klan meetings, held the men back. When, in recent years, they became fully integrated, everything changed. Women have the daunting role of indoctrinating children with Klan belief: and kids are the future of the Ku Klux Klan. The KKK is a brand name like Coca Cola, everyone has heard of it,' cautions Caplan, 'but unlike Coke it's not a registered trademark. Anyone can call themselves "Ku Klux Klan" and that's very damaging to the KKK's image.'

Back in Tennessee, Rachel is working on drawing in other bright young women like herself into the society.

'We have a lot of single women in all age groups,' she says, 'some are lawyers, others are businesswomen, students and office workers. Women make up about forty-five per cent of the Klan. When I was single, I converted my husband, Scott, who's a professional screen printer. He wasn't a KKK member when we met, just a nice young guy with the same white Christian values as me.'

Rachel and Scott are bringing up their children according to the code of the KKK. But, Rachel insists, she isn't weaning them on Fascist propaganda.

'I don't say "nigger" around the house,' she says grinning again, 'I try not to put down non-whites when I'm with the kids. And when I go on a Klan trip I tell Charity and Shelby that I'm going to speak out for other little white children just like them.

'It's so important to instill in one's kids racial pride when they're as young as possible,' she continues. 'White kids in the US have been given a guilt trip for long enough, just 'cos they're white. We're developing a Youth Corps programme for American youngsters between twelve and seventeen. This is a special area that we've got to concentrate on.'

Rachel and her father recently bought a hundred acres of land in the Ozark Mountains. The site, which is to house the new national office, will accommodate a Youth Klan Training Camp, as well as a KKK two-year leadership school.

'We're working on nurturing leaders,' says Rachel, as Charity plays on her lap with her Barbie doll, dressed in its designer Ku Klux Klan robes. 'We're like any business. If you have a message you need well turned out people to appeal to the masses.'

And it's the masses that Rachel and the Knights of the Ku Klux Klan are working on. Shying away from the militant image of the old days, the Knights have set their sights on national leadership.

'I think we're going to see our organization becoming a major political force in this country,' says Rachel earnestly. 'The Klan has a sensible, sane approach to the turmoils of America, and women have a central part to play in the new Ku Klux Klan.'

Rachel Pendergraft stops midstream.

She glances at Charity and Shelby as a lump gathers in her throat. Then, ever so softly, she whispers in a faltering voice:

'I see with all sincerity that the Klan will sit in the White House. I mean it sincerely. I believe a Klansman will lead the nation within the next twenty-five years. I could never see a black man in the White House, he wouldn't belong there. The White House is white. It was built for a *white* leader!'

The rise of women in the Klan during the 'twenties is thought to have begun after they were given the power to vote, in 1920. When the Ku Klux Klan was at its height, there were an estimated three million Klanswomen in the United States. Known as *Kleagles*, the women developed their own Klan groups, which were set quite apart from those of the men. Ironically, when suffrage was granted, women began to focus on their own differences.

The roots of Ku Klux Klan go back to 1865, and the end of the American Civil War. Donning ominous white hooded robes, the original Klansmen hoped that their gowns would give them a supernatural aura. Taking its name from the Greek *kuklos*, meaning a 'circle', the Ku Klux Klan first came to life in a small wooden shack in Pulaski, a remote town in east Tennessee. In homage to the founders of their order, the Knights of the KKK return to Pulaski once a year. They return to honour their ancestors and to preach their reworked message.

On a stormy day in mid-December, Rachel Pendergraft leaves her motel room. Bundling her daughters aboard their rusting olive-green van, she joins the Klan convoy heading for Pulaski and the Homecoming.

Advertisements in the local press announce: *Hey Kids! Come see Santa Klaus * Souvenirs * Krafts * Kountry Music * Klowns * Bagpipers * Have your picture taken with a robed Klansman.*

As the rain pours down, the convoy reaches the centre of Pulaski. Ashamed of the town's sordid legacy, the people of Pulaski have stayed at home. The mayor has no power to refuse the Klan its right to demonstrate.

'Until a couple of years ago,' he says wearily, 'they used to yell "Nigger Out! Nigger Out!" and do Nazi salutes as they marched. They wanted to change the street names to things like "Ku Klux Klan Boulevard" and "KKK Hill". But worst of all is hearing people from other communities referring to Pulaski as "The Klantown".'

Once at the main square, Rachel and her associates set up stalls and Ku Klux Klan bunting. As Klansmen appear from the woodwork, the new face of the Klan is put on view. Merchandising and public donations form the basis of the Klan's funds.

'We have hot-dogs, nachos, T-shirts and baseball caps,' says Rachel, unloading a stack of brown boxes. The merchandise is aimed to present the friendly face of the new Klan.

'Klan Kitsch', as it's known by non-Klansmen, comprises of KKK ball-point pens, badges which read 'Klan Kids Kare'; T-shirts with slogans such as 'Racial Purity is America's Security'; KKK Barbie dolls, and ceramic hooded Klansmen with eyes that glow red in the dark.

The current issue of *The White Patriot* newspaper, a monthly publication written and edited by Rachel Pendergraft, is passed around. Inside, along with articles telling Klansmen not to kill 'Negroes' or to pedal drugs, is a section enticing you to become 'a friend of the Knights of the KKK'. For this, you have to remit a small fee and sign a form declaring 'I am an Aryan and not of racially-mixed descent. I am not married to a non-white, nor do I date non-whites'.

On the right side of the square, a batch of hot-dogs are being cooked up by a grey-haired Klanswomen. Like many present, she's dressed in the new politically-correct uniform of the Klan: black tie and white shirt, its front peppered with badges. She sports a KKK baseball cap as well, embroidered with a robed klanswoman and the slogan 'girls in the hood'.

Rachel turns on a recording of the German Nazi Youth song *Tomorrow Belongs to Me*. Her smile turns to a look of disappointment as her father whispers something in her ear. Unfortunately, he tells her, the Klan bagpiper won't be attending, on account of the fact he lost a finger in a fight the night before.

Standing over a stall selling hooded KKK Barbie dolls is Anastasia Robb, Rachel's sister-in-law.

'I made the Barbie robes myself,' she winces. Aged just nineteen, Anastasia, who has been married to Rachel's brother for a year, is a new recruit and already a diehard Klanswoman.

'The Klan's the main part of my life now,' she says resolutely, 'I've never had any close minority friends. I always knew that I wanted to marry an Aryan man and have Aryan children. When I became a member of the Klan my family was apprehensive at first. They had mixed feelings. Although they're not members, they're supportive.'

Anastasia, an intelligent, blonde all-American girl, is glad she joined the Klan when she did.

'Women are important members of the KKK,' she explains, 'as the Klan becomes more liberal it's attracting more and more women who see its message as the future they want for their children.

'It's important for kids to be involved. They should come to rallies. The media steers them in the wrong direction and gives them stereotypes. Children come here and learn what the Klan is all about. They learn about our white Christian heritage.'

Rank and file members of the Klan continue to arrive from across the country, pouring into Pulaski's main square. Although attendance is hindered by the terrible weather, dozens have travelled thousands of miles to come *home* to the birthplace of the KKK. Shelley Watts, fifteen, whose family has made the three-day drive from Utah, has come with her parents and five sisters.

'We're Mormons,' she says. 'The Mormon Church doesn't like us being members of the Klan, but the KKK is a very important part of our family. I want to stick up for the white race, and when I have children I'll bring them up to be members of the Ku Klux Klan.'

As the Klan's Homecoming gets underway, anti-Klan groups monitor the proceedings from a distance. Pat Kelly of *Neighbours Network* looks on through binoculars from the far end of the square.

'Much of the hard day to day work is done by the women', he says, 'they tend to get on with running the organization while the men sit about talking. But don't be deceived, the women don't have an equal voice with the men. The Klan claims that it puts women on a pedestal, but that's far from the truth. What we're seeing increasingly is the attitude that "my skin colour is my nation". This may be one of the new "female" effects on the Klan. We're also seeing a severe drop in the average age of a Klan member: most are in their late teens or early twenties.'

Back at the T-shirt stall, Cheri, a middle-aged lady from New Orleans, is trying to find a KKK sweatshirt in her size. 'I'm the new kid on the block,' she says through a southern drawl. 'Although I always wanted to join up, I've never had the courage to become a member until now. I'm super-patriotic: I care what happens to America! I saw a Klan advertisement on cable TV. Now I'm a member and I'm going to recruit all my friends!'

Thom Robb, Rachel's father, saunters about ensuring that everyone is buying enough hot-dogs. Short and rather mousey, in a dark suit and shabby raincoat, he has struggled hard to bring the Ku Klux Klan up to date. In the past he called for the execution of gays and the shooting of illegal immigrants, but now, like his daughter, he's careful to be PC.

Robb rose to power when his predecessor was thrown in jail for trying to overthrow the government of Dominica. As leader of the Knights, he ditched the designation 'Imperial Wizard', preferring 'National Director', and has striven to clamber aboard the political bandwagon.

'We de-robed on our marches,' he explains in his articulate manner, 'because we wanted to identify with the American voters. We still wear robes at our private cross lightings because they're part of tradition, in the same way that a judge wears a powdered wig to court.

'My two sons and Rachel are very much involved in the Klan,' he says. 'Women have an important part to play in the KKK. We all have the same thing to lose – our white heritage. Remember that the majority of American voters are women. We must therefore appeal to women and appoint them to high levels of leadership.'

The de-robing of Klansmen was seen by KKK-watchers as an insane move. An undercover police officer, ensuring orderly behaviour, notes that the robes were always popular with the Klansmen.

'Once you go public you lose the allure,' he says, 'you forfeit the mystique, and lose the people who are attracted by that. Stephen King said that you should never open the closet door all the way, or you'll see the zipper up the monster's back.'

When the hot-dogs are all gone, the Knights of the Ku Klux Klan prepare to march around Pulaski. Rachel gathers the children together, hands out KKK banners, and helps arrange the Klansmen ten feet apart. Orders are given that they are to march in silence. There are not be no racist slogans.

In absolute silence, the men, women, and children of the Klan march around the deserted streets of Pulaski. Some of the young generation clutch Klan flags and others balloons. At the head of the entourage is Rachel Pendergraft.

Walking on her right is the KKK Santa Klaus.

As the Klan marchers reach the house where their organization was born, they pause. Rachel's face swiftly loses its characteristic, yet often forced, smile. With cold eyes, and an expression that could break glass, she raises her arm in a Nazi salute.

Beside her, Santa Klaus does the same.

Remembering Sir Wilfred

THE FIRST TIME I MET Sir Wilfred Thesiger, he was sitting in the shade of his porch in Kenya's remote Samburuland, drinking piping hot tea.

The porch was attached to a shack, which looked as though the great English explorer had built it himself. It clung like a limpet to the side of the hill. The temperature was touching forty-five degrees and Thesiger was wearing a pair of thick twill trousers and a tweed jacket with tatty elbow-patches and a tear down one side. He was staring out dreamily at the zebras slumped under the thorn trees down in the valley below.

The noise of my final ascent up over the crags, panting and wheezing, caused him to turn slowly and to peer down. Narrowing his eyes, he shaded a wrinkled hand to his brow, and called out, 'You're fussing like an old woman, what's wrong with you?!'

My first visit to Thesiger's home began a friendship that lasted until the explorer's death at ninety-three. It was a friendship of mentor and pupil, one that I value higher than any other of my life. Almost twenty-five years have passed since the afternoon I turned up in the Kenyan desert, and first set eyes on him, sitting there in tweeds. I was nineteen and was in need of raw encouragement, waiting for the order to seek out a path of my own

Thesiger was born a centenary ago, his life reflecting the stark hardship of the desert world in which he made his home. He is remembered as one who chronicled regions of Africa and the Middle East that hadn't changed in centuries, documenting them in the nick of time – before they were reshaped forever. And he is remembered as an icon, the kind of man who endured the unendurable without any fuss, and refused to tow a politically correct line.

These days he's regarded as an almost mythical character, someone unapproachable… the kind of lofty figure who's cast in bronze and put

With Sir Wilfred Thesiger, at his home in Kenya's Samburuland

on a plinth somewhere posh.

But, for me, Sir Wilfred was never aloof or distant in any way.

He was warm and caring, with a shockingly mischievous sense of humour, and the ability to inspire – not in a limp way, but deep down to the marrow of your bones.

His was inspiration right out of the *Boy's Own Annual*.

As he told me again and again over the years, by my age he had already been invited to the coronation of Emperor Haile Selassie of Abyssinia. After the pomp and grandeur of it all, he set off to hunt lion in the land of the Dannakil, a tribe who wore the testicles of their slain victims around their necks. He was still little more than a schoolboy himself. But death-dicing travels among the Dannakil in the Afar desert, paved the way for a life of exploration, a life unbounded by the expectations of others.

After Eton, Thesiger went up to Oxford. It was there that he won a Blue in boxing, and acquired the profile that was in many ways to become his trademark. It was best described in Eric Newby's classic travel narrative, *A Short Walk in the Hindu Kush*: '...and Thesiger himself, a great, long-striding crag of a man, with an outcrop for a nose and bushy eyebrows, forty-five years old and as hard as nails...' That meeting between the two extremes of English traveller was in the wilds of Afghanistan – yet it is for his travels in Arabia that Wilfred Thesiger is best known.

Following active service with the fledgling SAS during World War II, he spent more than five years with the nomadic Bedouin of the Arabian peninsular. He once told me that, from the first moment, he decided the only way to live with the Bedu was to do so without any compromise. He would live as they did, enduring levels of harshness that have become the thing of legend.

Along with them he twice crossed Rub al Kali, the fabled Empty Quarter, developing bonds of kinship that were far more important than anything else. Indeed, he would say that without his companions, a desert crossing would have been a meaningless penance. It was for the kinship alone that he travelled.

As a travel writer, I know too well the pressure which burdens one of getting a commission, the cold hard cash that will pay for the next great journey. But the wonderful thing about Thesiger's writing is that it came about years later, almost as an after-thought. He never intended to write about the years with the Bedouin, and only did so when his mother and the respected publisher, Mark Longman, begged him to do so. The critically acclaimed *Arabian Sands* followed, and was first published in 1959. It established Thesiger as one of a kind – the last of the Victorian gentlemen-explorers.

After Arabia, Sir Wilfred travelled to the marshes of southern Iraq. The lure was at first the prospect of a little duck shooting. He stayed in the marshes for years, returning once in a while to his mother's flat in Chelsea's Tite Street, where Oscar Wilde had once made his home. Again, only after leaving the marshes, and the life he so loved there among the labyrinthine waterways, he published *The Marsh Arabs*, in 1964.

As one who had known the rugged beauty of Arabia, and traditions that had been moulded by the desert terrain, Thesiger was understandably critical of the change that seemed to follow on his coat-tails. No long conversation with him would ever be complete without periods of silence, in which he was transported back to his youth – to the world of the Dannakil, the Bedouin, and the Marsh Arabs. In the same way, no cup of tea in his company was quite complete without him snarling at the 'infernal combustion engine', or exclaiming that cars and aeroplanes were robbing the world of all diversity.

It wasn't only motorized vehicles of which Thesiger disapproved. He despised anything mechanical. Towards the end of his life, he returned to England to live at the top-floor flat on Chelsea's Tite Street that his mother had bought during the Blitz. I used to go over a great deal, thrilled that I no longer had to traipse up to the shack in Samburuland to see him.

One summer afternoon we were sitting in silence over mugs of weak tea. Sir Wilfred was ninety, and had become a great deal more frail. He enjoyed just sitting in his old armchair, in the company of another. I always felt it were as if we were squatting around a campfire in the desert, the two of us lost in our thoughts.

Something stirred me to break the silence.

I spat out an idea that I hadn't thought through very well – said I was thinking of cycling from London down to Cape Town.

Thesiger looked up, squinted over at me hard, wiped his eyebrows away from his eyes. 'Sounds like nothing but a stunt,' he said coldly. I choked out an explanation, insisting that it was all about meeting people along the way. The great explorer winced, sipped his tea pensively. Then he seemed to rise up out of the chair, his lanky form looming over me like an executioner. 'On a bicycle you won't meet anyone or see anything at all!' he barked. 'You'll be going too fast! If I were you, I would walk it.'

I breathed in deep, and championed the idea. 'Walking, yes, I'll walk it,' I said nervously. Thesiger seemed pleased. He almost smiled. I asked if he had any advice, advice for walking. Sir Wilfred touched a long index finger to his lips and sunk back into his chair,

'Get yourself a good pair of army boots,' he said.

Romantic Travel

IF MOROCCO IS A LAND of romance, then its heart is surely the remote Berber village of Imilchil, without doubt the most romantic place I have ever been.

Nestled in the Atlas, it lies beyond the Gorge of Ziz, in a wild and unforgiving frontier of narrow passes and sweeping mountain vistas.

Once each year, in September, a festival is held in which the young are permitted to choose a spouse for themselves. In a realm usually confined by tribal tradition, the would-be brides and grooms are free to pick whomever they wish to marry.

Dressed in roughly woven striped black robes, jangling silver amulets and amber beads heavy around their necks, the girls stream down from their villages. There's a sense of frivolity, but one tempered with solemn apprehension, as they approach the doorway to a new life.

Reaching the village square, they catch first sight of the grooms. All of them are dressed in white woollen robes, their heads bound tight with woven red turbans, their eyes darkened with antimony.

The betrothal festival owes its existence to a legend, itself a blend of love and tragedy, a kind of Moroccan *Romeo and Juliet*. The story goes that, forbidden to marry, a couple who hailed from feuding tribes, drowned themselves in a pair of crystal clear lakes called Isli and Tislit. (One version of the tale says the lakes in which they drowned were made from their tears). So horrified were the local people at the loss, that they commenced the annual festival.

No one is quite sure when the tradition began, but everyone will tell you that the marriages which follow betrothal there are blessed in an almost magical way.

The first time I visited Imilchil almost twenty years ago, I met a young couple, Hicham and Hasna. They had met, fallen in love, and been betrothed, all on the same morning. They were glowing, their cheeks flushed with expectation and new love.

Last year, when I visited Imilchil again, I tracked down the pair. They look a little older now. Hicham's hair had thinned and his face was lined from a life outdoors tending his goats; and Hasna looked fatigued. But then she had given birth to six children, four of them boys.

As we sat in the darkness of their home, a wooden shack nestled in a copse of poplar trees, I asked them how the years had been.

Hicham looked across at Hasna, and smiled.

'On that day all those years ago,' he said, 'I became the happiest man in all the world. And each day since has been conjured from sheer joy.' He glanced at the floor. 'Do you want to know our secret?' he asked me bashfully. I nodded. Hicham touched a hand to his heart. 'To always remember the love of the first moment, the tingling feeling, the first time it touches you, and the first moment your hands touched.'

A few days after leaving Hicham and Hasna at their home in Imilchil, I reached my own home overlooking the Atlantic, in Casablanca. As I stepped in the door, my two little children, Ariane and Timur, ran up and threw their arms around my neck. They both asked where I'd been. I told them about the winding mountain roads, the Berber villages, and the Gorge of Ziz. 'And what did you bring?' they asked both at once, straining to look sheepishly at the ground.

'I brought you a secret.'

'What is it, Baba?'

'Always to remember the feeling of tingling love,' I said.

A courtyard guest house at the Royal Mansour, Marrakech

The Royal Mansour, Marrakech

In Morocco, real news isn't spread through the papers, but on whispers in the wind.

That was how I first learned of the Royal Mansour, the latest in top-notch grandeur on the Marrakech hospitality scene.

Our maid had heard from her brother, and he from his wife's cousin's friend, that a palace was being constructed, one that would put shame to almost anything else ever created by Moroccan artisanal hands. Years passed, and I quite forgot hearing of the rumour. Then, one morning recently the whisper came again:

'It's opened,' said a low voice.

'What has?'

'A palace fit for a king.'

In a city that's hemorrhaging hotels, the Royal Mansour is set apart by its sheer decadence. Slipping in through the gates, set into the ancient honey-coloured city walls, is like lifting the veil on a fantasy, one that's usually off limits to mere mortals.

The first thing that hits you is the scent of jasmine piercing the evening air. It's as overpowering as the silence. A handful of carefully positioned staff glide up without making any noise at all. They greet you in whispers, and offer the refreshment served in the desert to travellers – succulent dates and cool buttermilk. Then, only when you are ready, they lead you to your quarters, through a labyrinth of jaw-dropping opulence.

Wherever you look, every inch of every surface is adorned with exquisite workmanship and textures – acres of intricate zellij mosaics, hand-sculpted plasterwork, cedar ceilings, and geometric painted wood. The furnishings are equally lavish, including fabulous Suzani embroideries from Bokhara, suede cushions and throws, and miles and miles of silk.

At the heart of the hotel is a central courtyard open to the sky. Hanging like an ivory medallion above, is the full moon; fabulous bronze lamps suspended below, each one in itself a true work of art. All around there are Andalucian cabinets crafted in Cordoba, lovely mosaic and marble fountains, and Damascene banquettes, inlaid with fragments of mother of pearl. And the entire fantasy is bathed in the kind of hush that simply doesn't exist elsewhere in Marrakech.

This being the Royal Mansour, there's no clumsy bell-hop lumbering ahead with your luggage. Rather, the hotel's impeccable manager escorts you himself to your quarters, making equally impeccable small-talk as he goes. Everyone you pass greets you by name, and exudes a warmth, as though they are genuinely thrilled to meet you. It is the feeling of real celebrity, as if you're Mick Jagger and that, as soon as your back is turned, the staff rush off and call their friends to boast that they've seen you in the flesh.

Desperately trying to suppress all delusions of grandeur, you follow the manager into an Andalucian courtyard. It's filled with the sound of trickling water and with fragrant trees, all of them laden with perfectly ripe fruit – pomegranates, oranges and mouth-watering dates. And, eventually, you arrive at a medina, a mirror of the old city in miniature.

Instead of rooms or suites, you are taken to your very own *riad*, a three-storey building set around a colonnaded courtyard. As you approach, the door opens magically inward. A manservant steps silently from the shadows. Coutured in flowing robes, with a turban crowning his head, he asks permission to serve you vintage Champagne. Oh, the hardship of making such difficult decisions.

Miraculously, your luggage has already arrived, and the genie-like steward, has unpacked. Whatever your wish, he's already anticipated it, as if trained in mind-reading as well in hospitality. But the most extraordinary thing of all is how he, and everyone else, comes and goes invisibly, without ever stepping in or out through the door.

The Royal Mansour is a pleasure dome of magic, but none of the wizardry is more amazing than the great secret that makes its illusionary realm possible. For, beneath the entire property – laid out over eight acres – is a vast maze of secret tunnels, worthy of a James Bond villain's den. A city in itself, it houses vast kitchens and warehouses, laundries and staff quarters. And, plying the wide subterranean passages, is a fleet of brand new golf carts.

Morocco is a land of tradition, and one where the tradition of royal patronage dies hard. The king is almost expected to champion projects that will keep the ancient crafts and traditions alive. In the 'nineties, the present monarch's father, Hassan II, constructed a colossal mosque in Casablanca. Bearing his own name, it stands at the western edge of the Islamic world. Having reigned for a decade, King Mohammed VI, conceived the Royal Mansour himself, and directly oversaw every detail of the project.

Built from scratch in less than four years, twelve hundred *moualems*, master craftsmen, were called upon to do the best work of their lives. For each of them the challenge was all the greater because they were working directly for their king. And it's this point which has ensured that the Royal Mansour isn't just another plush address to stay in Marrakech, Morocco's ultra chic desert retreat.

'We have strived to create a landmark of Moroccan culture,' says sales manager Soufiane Berrada, 'through architecture, hospitality, cuisine and art, all of it in one place.' Leading me on a tour, he points out details hidden from view, like the high tech air cushion heating system that allows the central courtyard to be open to the sky even in winter.

In the cigar lounge he shows me a cabinet of rare Cognacs, including an unopened bottle of 1888 Armagnac Laubade. On the wall above it, hangs a fabulously intricate bronze appliqué frieze, crafted by the British-born Moroccan artist, now so celebrated that he goes by his first name alone – Yahya.

We step through to the library. As I wonder aloud why there's a giant telescope in the middle of the room, the manager presses a button set into the marquetry, and the cedarwood roof slides silently away.

Of the fifty-three *riads*, arranged in clusters, as they are in the actual Marrakech medina, most are two- and three-bedroom, with private salons, dining rooms, swimming pools, kitchens and roof-top terraces, from which you can glimpse the snow-clad Atlas mountains. There's a *Riad d'Honneur* as well, a palace in its own right, with two pools, gardens, private spa and underground cinema. Former French President Jacques Chirac and his wife were in residence during my stay, the *riad* guarded by dozens of swarthy men in black.

After two days and nights of the high life, I found myself back on the street, the mayhem of Marrakchi traffic frothing all around. I felt like Maruf the Cobbler from *A Thousand and One Nights*, whose desert palace had appeared by magic, before vanishing in the blink of an eye.

As I crossed the street to get a bus, I smiled to myself. After all, what would luxury be if it were not tempered by a little hardship from time to time?

Subcontinent of Miracles

THE AUDIENCE WAS QUAKING WITH FEAR.

The man standing before them was astounding, even by Indian standards. Stained in greasy black paint, his body adorned with mysterious symbols, his hair was matted with dirt and his eyes fixed in a maniacal stare. He had four arms, a vile protruding tongue, a golden filigree crown on his head, and a garland fashioned from human skulls hanging over his chest. In one hand was a cleaver dripping with blood, and in another was clenched the head of a butchered enemy.

The crowd of three hundred Bengali villagers edged backwards as the demonic figure addressed them. But, as I soon realized, their apprehension resulted not from fear, but from expectation.

For the deity was about to perform a miracle.

Whispering cryptic incantations, the avatar – a devotee of Hinduism's bloodiest goddess, Kali – rubbed a thumb and forefinger together six times. Moments later, a plume of smoke was spiralling up from his fist. The villagers glanced at each other with wonder.

Then the godman performed his second feat.

Stepping over to an urn of boiling oil, he plunged one of his four arms into the pot. There was no time for applause. Wasting no time, the *sadhu* gargled a mouthful of secret liquid from a clay cup, pulled a red-hot poker from his ceremonial fire, and stuck it into his mouth. As before, he seemed oblivious to the pain and, as before, the throng of villagers clamoured with delight.

Traipse through the Indian countryside for long enough and you're sure to cross paths with an avatar, like the Kali deity, who was weaving his magic in a small village two hours west of Calcutta.

Like him, thousands of others are making a good living as mystical advisers, healers, resolvers of disputes, dispensers of knowledge and as entertainers, all rolled into one. India's illusion business, booming as

A Kali devotee, West Bengal

Young Shiva devotees, near Calcutta

never before, hasn't enough godmen to go round. From Assam to Mumbai there are vacancies for anyone who can put on a good solid miracle performance. The main, if unlikely, reason for the sharp growth of the profession is Harry Houdini.

All but extinct in the West, Houdini's magic is alive and thriving across India. In the greatest cities and smallest villages alike, his magical feats are performed daily as miracles by godmen, India's mortal incarnations of the divine. Remembering Houdini only for his straitjacket and handcuff routines, we tend to forget he was the pioneer of modern stage magic as well as escapology.

Houdini's vast repertoire of magic has migrated east and taken root in India. The explanation lies in the magician's chest of formidable ingredients. For the majority of Houdini's magic – and that of many other nineteenth-century illusionists – was based on hazardous chemicals, the likes of which are hard to come by in our safety-conscious society.

Ask at a British pharmacy for ferric chloride, ammonium salicylate or mercuric nitrate, and you risk being reported to the police. But visit the smallest Indian bazaar – far from the 'nanny' states of the West, and you can snap up oversized tubs of even the most noxious compounds at bargain basement prices. The result: godmen and avatars, sages and *sadhus* are drinking nitric acid, sucking red-hot pokers, eating glass, spitting fire and even levitating.

The four-armed, cleaver-wielding godman in West Bengal might have impressed Houdini with his dexterity and showmanship, if not with his originality. For each of the supposed miracles was developed by the great American maestro himself.

The *sadhu's* fingers must have been treated with a solution of yellow phosphorus and carbon disulphide, which smokes on friction. And a cup of lime juice had doubtless been poured into the urn of oil. The citric juice sinks to the bottom and foams up at a low temperature, as if the oil is bubbling. As for the red-hot poker, the Kali godman had surely swilled his mouth with liquid storax, which absorbs the fiery poker's heat.

Far from taking pleasure in the new popularity of his tricks, Houdini must surely be spinning in his grave. Whereas he always claimed that he was performing nothing more than skilful feats of illusion, India's godmen are passing off their tricks as genuine miracles.

In his latter years, Houdini tried to debunk those whom he said pretended to have supernatural powers. He devoted an entire book to exposing his near-namesake and former hero, Robert Houdin.

But not all the miraculous feats one comes across in India can be attributed to Houdin. Some favourites are far older. Many *sadhus* know how to turn water into wine, and how to transform a rod into a snake.

Indeed, the 'rod to snake' illusion is said to be the oldest of all.

It was witnessed by Aaron at the court of the Egyptian pharaohs (Exodus vii, 10–12). The snake is cooled, then pulled straight between outstretched hands. The magician's thumb and index finger are clamped onto the reptile's head. Fearing that a gigantic predator has caught hold of it, the snake goes rigid – like a rod. Only when it is cast to the floor does it revive and slither away.

Other feats were developed more recently, most notably by Uri Geller. Indian swamis and godmen have, it seems, just learned how to read sealed envelopes and to bend spoons with mind power.

As India's brotherhood of godmen swell in number as never before, a small band of devoted men and women have vowed to expose them through public humiliation. Touring the country in a battered old van, they demonstrate how the tricks are done.

Dipak Ghosh is a leading member of India's Rationalist Movement. He has seen it all and is keen to tell how Jesus fed the five thousand, how a godman levitates, and how Uri Geller bends spoons.

'You cannot underestimate these fraudsters,' he says. 'They're hoodwinking people of their life savings. It's nothing more than common theft. Some are certainly excellent stage magicians, but they have no miraculous powers. With a few rupees they can purchase supplies of chemicals that will last them for months. They're becoming more devious every week. Worst of all is that new deceptions are being thought up all the time.'

Mr. Ghosh may have declared all-out war on the avatars, but it appears that he's fighting an uphill battle. India is a land where belief in miracles and the supernatural is a way of life.

Not long ago, I met a man in the small town of Solapur, known as 'Goadbaba' to his friends – which means 'Mr. Sweet' in Marathi.

Goadbaba is one of a new breed of illusionists.

He shook my hand and asked me to lick it. To my surprise, my palm tasted sweet. He touched a chair and a spoon. I licked them. Both tasted very sweet indeed. Goadbaba said that he had mysterious magical powers. He asked me to take him to London so that he could gain an entry into the *Guinness Book of Records*.

Some time after our meeting I learned the secret of the godman's Midas touch magic. It was *Sweet 'n Lo*, a sachet of which he had rubbed onto his hands.

An elderly villager about to receive the miracle fish cure, Hyderabad

Moments after the live murrel fish has been thrust down the patient's throat

Swallowing Live Fish

INDIA IS A LAND OF MIRACLES.

Godmen levitate or walk on water; oracles speak from mountainsides; effigies of elephant gods have even been known to spontaneously drink milk. But by far the greatest Indian miracle of all is revealed on a single day each year, a few hours before the first monsoon downpour.

Every June, at the first sighting of the Mrigasira Karthe star, about half a million people converge in a tiny whitewashed house in the old city of Hyderabad. They travel there from all corners of India. Frenzied, wheezing, and weary after the journey, they queue up to swallow live fish.

What's more, most make the trip three years in a row. Animal rights groups are apoplectic: but their pleas fall on deaf ears. For in Hyderabad swallowing a live fish is part of a mysterious 'miracle cure' – for asthma.

The free miracle remedy is handed out by the Gowds, a modest, impecunious family whose home is embedded in the labyrinth of narrow lanes and back streets that make up Hyderabad's old city. The current generation is continuing a tradition that began more than a century and a half ago.

With Indian cities as polluted as any others in the developing world, asthma is an ever more menacing problem. Spend a few days in Old Delhi, Calcutta or Mumbai, and you can find your chest tightening as if crushed by rogue elephants. Every year tens of thousands of Indians are diagnosed as asthmatics, the majority of them are children.

And, while the local pharmaceutical industry offers cost-price drugs for all, many are suspicious of the temporary relief that Western medicines provide. Why use an expensive inhaler all the time when a live fish can be swallowed for a permanent cure? It's this straightforward thinking that brings asthmatics flocking in droves to the Gowds' two-room residence.

Rather than being appalled by the unorthodox treatment, Indian asthmatics can't seem to get enough of it. In the first week of June, special trains, buses and flights are laid on to ferry people to Hyderabad from the farthest reaches of India. Many stake their life savings to make the journey. Others bring their entire families for the expedition of a lifetime.

It has become a pilgrimage.

In a rare show of solidarity, Muslims, Buddhists, Jains, and Hindus from every caste, gather with their belongings. By the eve of monsoon, every hotel and guest house is full to bursting. Mosques and temples, wayside cafés, bus depots and railway stations are cluttered with asthmatics from far away.

Hyperventilating and bent double after the arduous journey, they spill onto the streets, waiting expectantly for the miracle. As word of the cure's efficacy spreads, politicians hurry to endorse the event, and businessmen volunteer to fund it.

Each patient clutches a transparent water-filled plastic bag. Like children with goldfish home from the fair, they hold them up to the light. The bag contains a speckled black murrel fish, an oily cousin of the sardine.

The fish vary in size: anything from three to six inches. The longer the better. Their beady eyes blinking innocuously, they swim about in the limited confines of the plastic bag. They may be wondering what's going on. But a murrel fish would have a hard time imagining the precise details of its fate.

When they get to the front of the queue each asthma sufferer hands over their plastic bag to a member of the Gowd family. First, the fish is removed from the bag. Then its miniature jaws are prized apart. A magical and foul-smelling yellow paste is stuffed into its mouth. And, as the patient sticks out his tongue, the fish, replete with ointment, is thrust down his throat.

There are less than twelve hours to go, for the star of Mrigasira Karthe will be in alignment at eight a.m.

Harinath Gowd, second eldest of the five brothers, sits in the tiny courtyard of the family home and casts an uneasy eye at the main entrance. The battered blue door bends inwards as the crowd presses against the other side. The old city's narrow streets are clogged with asthmatics for miles around. Most arrived days ago, for fear of missing the astrological timing of the event.

Harinath attends to last-minute arrangements. Two hundred kilos of the magical paste have been prepared, concocted according to a secret Ayurvedic recipe. Pujas, religious ceremonies, carry on around the clock to appease malevolent forces. The air, which is thick with incense, only aggravates the asthmatics' difficulties. Police are briefed in case of rioting.

The astrological tables are double-checked.

Rubbing his greying beard anxiously, Harinath Gowd reinforces the tattered door with a plank of wood.

'Every year more and more people turn up,' he declares. 'See how popular is this miracle of miracles.'

'It all started with my great-great-grandfather,' says Harinath. 'He was a very generous man. He was known throughout Hyderabad for his good deeds. During the monsoon of 1845 he saw a *sadhu*, a holy man, sitting in the pouring rain. The mystic was cold, hungry and abandoned by the world. So, my ancestor, Veerana Gowd, brought him here, into this house. He fed him and nursed him back to health. Weeks passed. Then, just before the *sadhu* was about to go on his way, he revealed the fish miracle to my forefather.'

Harinath pauses to recite a string of orders to his son.

'The holy man,' he continues, 'said that from henceforth the well in the courtyard would be full of magical water. And that it was to be used in making a special paste which was to be put into the mouth of a living murrel fish. The water, the ingredients of the paste, and the astrological timing together form the magic of the miracle. The *sadhu* said that my family was to serve a free cure for asthma on the first day of the monsoon. But if any fee was charged for the remedy, it would have no effect. Charge money, and the magic would be broken. That was one hundred and fifty-two years ago. True to our word, my family has never charged for the cure.'

Initially, word of the miracle antidote was slow to spread. In the first few years, asthmatics from the back streets adjacent to the Gowds' house turned up. But, as the years passed, more and more people heard of the miracle. And, as more tried it, word spread faster and further.

Two years ago about a quarter of a million asthmatics ventured to the Gowds' house to be cured. This year, an estimated five hundred and thirty thousand arrived.

In any other country, if half a million patients came to your house appealing for a miracle, the authorities would demand forms to be filled and permits to be signed. But in India, where miracle remedies are a way of life, things are more straightforward.

Watching a Hindi movie on television the night before, the five Gowd brothers seemed remarkably relaxed. Didn't it bother them that half a million asthmatics were pounding on their door? Or that the responsibility of stuffing several tons of live oily fish down throats would prove too difficult?

Shivram Gowd, the eldest of the brothers, stretches out to turn up the TV's volume, to drown out the frenzied groans of asthmatics out in the street.

'Of course we're not worried,' he says. 'Remember, this isn't a feeble allopathic medicine – but a miracle cure.'

The sheer number of patients demanding the unconventional prescription has meant that, in recent years, the Gowds have had to take on extra volunteers. More than five hundred of them, speaking every major Indian language and dialect, help to make sure that things go smoothly. Hundreds more hand out free drinking water and custard creams, donated by local businesses and charities. And, whereas sufferers were all once treated in the Gowds' ancestral home, special stalls are now erected in neighbouring streets to administer the physic to the maximum number over the twenty-four hour period.

The *sadhu's* directions ensured that the Gowds make no profit from their miracle cure. But, it is obvious that they enjoy being the centre of attention for one day a year.

'We are proud to help people in this way,' intones Shivram Gowd warmly, 'for the rest of the year we are humble toddy tappers.'

Would he prefer that the miracle cure be handed out on more than one day a year? Shivram Gowd pauses to take in the cries of the hopeful outside. Then rolls his eyes. 'No, no,' he whispers, 'one day a year is quite sufficient.'

All night, mantras are repeated over the great basins of mysterious yellow paste. Then, as dawn rises over the Mughal city of Hyderabad, a prolonged ritual begins in the confined courtyard of the Gowd ancestral home. The five brothers sit on a raised platform surrounded by their families, as their forefathers did before them. Dressed in sacred saffron robes, they bless the tubs of oily ointment. Out in the maze of winding lanes, the asthmatics and their families jostle about with restless anticipation. The miracle is near.

At the front of the queue is Krishna Punji, an aged farmer from Orissa. He pokes a wrinkled finger into a small plastic bag to check that the murrel fish, which he bought from a vendor the night before, is still alive.

'I've been here six weeks,' he announces feebly, 'I wasn't sure when the miracle was to be held. So I came a bit early. You see, I've got very bad asthma.' He lets out a deafening wheeze to prove his point.

At the stroke of eight, Harinath Gowd stuffs a pellet of the yellow paste into the waiting mouth of a murrel fish, and thrusts it down his brother Shivram's throat. The Gowds always start by taking the medicine themselves.

They swear by it.

Moments later, the battered doors of their home are pulled inward and the great tidal wave of sufferers surges into the courtyard. At its crest is Krishna Punji. He hands over his fish, opens his toothless mouth as wide as he can and, before he knows it, the three-inch speckled charcoal murrel fish is swimming towards his stomach.

The miracle cure has begun.

Crushed together, and filling every inch of the old city, the legions of patients squirm forward. Many bought their fish the night before. For those who didn't, hundreds of murrel fish dealers sprout up from nowhere. Every street urchin and miscreant are suddenly crying out 'Machhi! Machhi!', 'Fish! Fish!' The competition between sellers, who get their stocks from the Department of Fisheries, keeps the prices down. A standard-sized murrel (three to six inches) costs three rupees. The emphasis is very much on large. Everyone believes that the larger the fish, the better it will clean out the throat as it goes down.

'The wriggling of the fish is very beneficial,' calls Harinath Gowd, as he shoves his complete hand into a woman's mouth. She begins to choke because her fish is so large – almost seven inches long. A harsh thump on her back dislodges it. The murrel fish can be seen, frantically trying to swim backwards, towards safety. Engulfed by the waves of asthmatics, all holding up their transparent bags, Harinath Gowd again rams his fingers down the woman's throat. The seven-inch fish heads into the dark abyss of the patient's oesophagus, never to surface again.

If you recoil at the prospect of swallowing an oversized antibiotic, forget the Gowds' miracle cure. It's traumatic for the patient; and is no easy remedy to administer. Every step of the procedure has its own obstacles. When removing it from the bag, the fish tends to flail about and often falls into the mud underfoot. With the throng so tight, bending down to search for a lost fish is hazardous in the extreme. More cumbersome still is the business of levering the murrel's jaws apart and inserting the nugget of yellow paste. Even when this has been achieved, the creature has to be propelled head-first down the sufferer's throat. Administering the medicine a single time would be an achievement worthy of praise. But performing it half a million times in a day is a miracle in itself.

Every city, town and village of the subcontinent seems to be represented at the Gowds' tiny home. Buddhist monks, Assamese tribesmen, businessmen from Bangalore, Goans and Tamils, Pathans and Sikhs – all congregate together into a whirlwind of life; all frantic for the miracle. Many are gasping for breath, seized by asthmatic attacks brought on by the crush of bodies. Others scream hysterically as they are separated from their children. Every moment the turmoil heightens. The mob is compressed like liquid injected through a syringe.

Then, suddenly, it is rife with rumours. The stocks of fish are running out. The supplies of miracle paste are almost at an end. A stampede follows. Babies are clutched above heads to prevent them from being sucked down. Moments later, the half million murrel fish are not the only casualties of the day. Two elderly men are killed in the stampede, trampled underfoot.

For Anila Mathani, an Indian living in Singapore, swallowing a murrel fish is no longer a novelty. This is her third time.

'You have to take the medicine three years running to get permanent relief from asthma,' she says, holding up her carefully-chosen specimen. 'This year volunteers are handing out the cure in the streets around the Gowds' home. I will only take it in the house itself; and from the hand of one of the Gowd brothers. This is where the magic spell was cast; and it was here that the *sadhu* revealed that the miracle would work.'

Does she believe in the remedy? Anila Mathani nods vigorously. 'Of course it cures asthma,' she says. 'Three years ago I was confined to bed. My doctor said I hadn't long to live. Now look at me. Remember, Indians are shrewd people: do you think they would spend time and money travelling here if there was nothing in it?'

Diehard believers in the miracle cure follow a strict regime in the days after their appointment with the murrel fish. They restrict their diet to a list of foods prescribed by the *sadhu* in 1845. These include such comestibles as snake gourd, old rice, dried chillies, mutton, dried pieces of old mango, and milk which has been left with a piece of porcelain in it. On the fifteenth, thirtieth and forty-fifth days after the miracle, the patient is expected to swallow two extra pellets of the magical yellow paste.

Vegetarians have it easy. They don't have to swallow the fish but can consume the repellent salve in a mixture of molasses jaggery. But the Gowds frown on those without the will to gulp down a live fish.

With news of the Gowds' medication spreading throughout India and abroad, a regular stream of fraudsters have tried to capitalize on the miracle cure. Quacks and charlatans in every large city advertise a similar antidote on the same day each year. Most claim to be related to the Gowds. Unlike the five brothers from Hyderabad, they charge for the medicine.

'It's expected that fakes will try to make money from this,' says Harinath Gowd pragmatically. 'We have been offered millions of rupees by multinational drug companies for the formula, too. But we don't have any fear of the con-men, or of people copying our recipe through reverse engineering. They can copy us all they like, but we have one thing that they can never have – the magical blessing of the *sadhu*.'

As the multitude of asthmatics choke down live fish, supporters for the Society for Animal Rights, a local pressure group with modest support, stand on the sidelines. But their calls for an immediate end to the slaughter of innocent murrel fish go unheeded.

'Imagine what an agonizing end those poor little fish are having,' says Dilip Narayan, the society's spokesman. 'This is an act of primitive barbarism. It *must* be stopped.'

By and large, the medical profession is equally reproachful. Not because of the pain the murrel fish may suffer, but for the dubious effect that the cure has on treating asthma.

'This isn't miracle healing, but faith healing,' explains Dr. Madan Kataria, a respected Mumbai physician. 'People line up for hours and go through the traumatic experience of swallowing a live fish. Then they feel better. The improvement has got to be due to a psychosomatic effect.'

The Gowd family's miracle cure for asthma may be the laughing stock of the medical establishment. And it may sound like nothing more than mumbo jumbo to the rest of us. But it seems that the remedy could have a scientific grounding after all. Scientists at the Royal Prince Alfred Institute of Respiratory Medicine in Sydney recently published a possible cure for asthma. And it happens to be very fresh, oily fish. A study at the institute found that only fresh fish (canned fish, for instance, doesn't work) has anti-inflammatory properties. Oily fish such as murrel, which contain omega-3 fatty acids, can decrease the amount of inflammation in an asthmatic's airway.

Back outside the Gowds' ancestral home, the local police officers have given up trying to keep control. Pickpockets are busy taking advantage of the crowds. A contingent of Naga warriors is waging a full-blown military offensive to raid the stall dishing out free custard creams. But, worst of all, I find myself at the head of the queue.

I hand over the bag containing my four-inch murrel fish to Shivram Gowd. A blob of the vile miracle paste the size of a walnut is forced into the fish's mouth and around its face. The paste, which has the consistency of marzipan, has the smell of putrefying offal.

A bystander indicates for me to stick out my tongue. At the last moment, the fish and I exchange a troubled glance. The murrel seems to be demanding an explanation. Alas, I am in no position to start justifying the unusual treatment. What comes next is a new experience for the both the fish and me.

Having a grown man's hand lunging to the back of one's throat is deeply unpleasant. But it is nothing in comparison to the sensation of a live and terrified fish bearing fetid miracle ointment swimming down one's oesophagus.

Hour after hour, thousands of asthmatics receive the treatment. All through the day, the afternoon, and then the night. By six a.m. the next morning, the short-lived shanty-town around the Gowds' two-room house begins to break up. The pickpockets board trains for other cities. Balloon-sellers, beggars, and most of the half-million asthmatics have disappeared. By seven a.m. the fish merchants are frantic to get rid of their supplies.

The bottom had fallen out of the murrel fish market for another year.

Swiss Movement

As a travel writer I've specialized in gritty, fearful destinations, the kind of places that make a reader's hair stick on end.

I've waded through swamps, hacked through jungles, done my time in war zones and in mine fields, and in rotten, rat-infested sewers the world over. Never before though, have I been asked to drop everything and journey to a place of sheer idyll.

Not until now.

So when an itinerary came through for a jaunt around the Swiss Alps, I balked. It all seemed too good to be true. My wife said they'd sent me the wrong trip, and that I'd better leave before they realized their mistake. So I packed my bags and left, post haste.

The next thing I knew, I was at Zurich airport picking up my Swiss Pass. It allows unlimited travel on most trains, buses and boats within the entire country. The clerk was a slim, small-eyed man with three clocks laid out neatly on his desk. I asked about getting to Appenzell, the heart of Alpine country.

'There is a train leaving in three minutes, forty-five seconds,' he said precisely.

'Well, I'll never make that.'

The clerk narrowed his eyes. 'Of course you will, sir,' he said, 'this is Switzerland.'

Two minutes later, I was aboard a train so silent that, when it left the station, you could only tell it was actually moving by looking out the window. It didn't grate along the tracks, so much as glide.

Lulled by the sense of safety and the silence of the carriage, I fell into a deep childlike sleep. When I awoke there were hillsides all around, rolling like waves and overlaid with fields, their grass the colour of crushed emeralds. There were mountains, too, great grey crags looming down like broken teeth, some still tinged with snow.

At Appenzell I alighted, and found myself in the backdrop for an *Alpen* commercial. No bigger than a village, it was the kind of place I never quite believed existed at all. Prim little chalets with window boxes overflowing in riotous reds and pinks, exquisitely painted buildings, cuckoo clocks, cow bells, and perfectly squared stacks of firewood awaiting the winter freeze.

In dazzling light of late afternoon I drove the short distance to Weissbad, where a smiling farmer named Johan showed me his cows. As someone who lives in a world shaped by crude reality, I was at first skeptical. It was as if the whole place had been conjured as a kind of tourist fantasy. But, the longer I stayed there, the more I came to see that the orderly perfection and sense of contentment were utterly real. Farmer Johan's grin was always on his lips, even when my back was turned. And he wasn't the only happy one. His cows were simply beaming delight as well.

If the surroundings were out of an *Alpen* commercial, then the cows were surely extras from a *Milka* chocolate ad. They were spotless, pale brown, pretty beyond belief, and had oversized bells fastened on leather collars around their necks. As they roamed the lush pastures ruminating, they made a wondrous music all of their own.

Johan told me that happy cows made lots of delicious milk, that he thought hard before naming them, and that they were all his girls. 'This one is Lisa,' he whispered, cupping the head of one lovingly in his arms as she licked him, 'and this here is Carmen. She can be quite naughty sometimes,' he said.

After much talk of cows and after a taste of the local *weissbier*, Johan showed off his trophies and the wreathes he'd won for scything grass. It turned out he was a champion. When I praised this little appreciated Swiss skill, the farmer grinned until his cheeks dimpled. Then, as a way of changing the subject modestly, he showed me to my room.

In actual fact it wasn't so much as a room, but a barn. Instead of beds there were stalls filled with fresh straw. I got a flashback of the travelling hardship I'm more used to, and sighed contently. Johan demonstrated how to fluff up the straw to make a pillow. Grinning, he went out to check on the girls once more before turning in himself.

Early next morning, after a breakfast of cured ham and tangy

Appenzeller cheese, I pinched myself to make sure I wasn't dreaming. The hillsides were glazed in dew, cool morning shadows streaming over them like giants' cloaks. Johan had just finished milking the herd, and was cooing over them like a mother hen. He introduced me to another farmer, called Willi, whose ample white beard sprouted from a creased face, and whose hands were the roughest I can remember ever shaking. He spoke of the past, of his eighteen grandchildren and, then he told me about his own herd.

As I wondered how much more talk of cows and milk I could take, Johan took me along winding roads to the cable car. He pointed up to a distant crag and clicked his tongue. Squinting against the sunlight, I made out a straw-coloured building nestled there. Johan nodded, cackled with laugher, and hugged me goodbye.

Minutes later, I was floating up towards the mountains in the cable car, sailing high above a seamless mantle of bottle-green conifers. The gondola was packed with hikers, most of them locals, whose lives are nailed firmly to nature. There was an extraordinary sense of anticipation, as if being in the mountains was a love affair.

The gondola delivered us to sixteen hundred and forty-four metres and to Ebenalp, one of the highest points in all Alpstein. After watching a flock of paragliders arcing and pirouetting on the summer thermals, I toured caves where prehistoric bears once lived, and where their bones can still be found. Nearby, nuzzled into the rock, I saw a tiny chapel built by hermits, who for centuries sought sanctuary in the Alpine solitude.

The next day, the wheels beneath me were moving once again.

I had boarded the fabled Glacier Express at Chur, which bills itself as 'the world's slowest express train'. On the exterior, the sleek carriages were gleaming grey and fire engine red, while inside was washed in blinding light, streaming in through special side-lights.

Outside, an idyllic canvas of nature rolled by, peppered with picturesque little villages, silent beneath boiling cumulus clouds; rivers swollen from weeks of late spring rain, their waters the hue of aquamarines, sided by forests as thick as any.

A contrast to the cutting-edge carriages, the train's dining car was a throwback to the 1930s when it was built. It was compact and wood panelled, with floral velvet seats, brass fittings, starched table cloths, and wild flower posies arranged at each place.

The waitress, whose name was Elvira, was energetically polishing the silver. She seemed a little flustered at seeing me arrive for a late lunch. 'We have already catered for one hundred and twenty,' she said apologetically, as she handed me the menu, adding, 'the kitchen may be small but we prepare everything from scratch.'

Uncertain of what to order, I asked Elvira to do so for me, and was rewarded with one of the most memorable meals of my life. The dining car had the ambience of a well-loved gentlemen's club, its cuisine – presented silver service – was worthy of any gastronomic pleasure dome. There was Salsiz sausage and veal paillard, *bouillon aux crêpe en lamelles*, platters of Alpine cheese, and a wine list that would make the most pedantic sommelier proud.

Leaving the Glacier Express at Brig, I had a lump in my throat.

All I could think of was about clawing my way back to the dining car, for another meal under Elvira's conscientious watch.

In most other countries, changing trains tends to be a sordid ordeal of waiting and of discomfort. You hang around for hours, switching platforms at the last moment, charging up and down, overstuffed cases dragging clumsily behind. But in Switzerland, things are very different. It's a land in which rail travel is still a genteel pursuit, one of enjoyment rather than of endurance. The station masters are well-dressed and courteous, the platforms clean, the efficiency of the system as reliable as an Oyster Perpetual. It explains why the Swiss one meets off the beaten track sometimes appear alarmed at how the rest of the world grinds on.

In the afternoon I reached the Alpine village of Kandersteg, a favourite with the British since Victorian times. Set in a monumental amphitheatre of peaks, ridges and jagged stone bluffs, it's far more rugged than the sweeping farmlands I had encountered at Appenzell.

I took a cable car up to the magnificent Lake Oeschinensee, whose azure waters mirrored the sky. The setting was lovely, abundant with wild flowers and lizard-green ferns, with soft, moist moss, lichens, the air thick with bumble bees and marbled white butterflies.

At the water's edge I met an American woman in a wide-brimmed hat. She was searching for tiny wild orchids, and had one of those smiles that sticks in your mind. She told me that she'd been coming to Kandersteg every year on the same day for four decades. 'My fiancé proposed right where we are standing,' she said. When I asked if he was with her, her smile faded. 'He died in Vietnam,' she said.

In the days I spent at Kandersteg, I found myself reflecting on the courtesy of almost everyone I encountered. However rushed or busy, there was always time for good manners. In Swiss villages, complete strangers greet each other as they walk past. Men still tip their hats, and people live in a well-honed system with do-as-you-would-be-done-by at its core. When taking a train, there's none of the usual fear that your belongings will be pinched if you slip to the loo. And, when you get to the loo, you find it immaculate, because the last person left it how they would want to find it themselves.

The journey north-west to Lake Lucerne involved three trains and a paddle steamer in a single afternoon, each one running on a schedule as precise as Swiss clockwork. I found myself flinching at the thought of ever travelling in any other country again. More worryingly, it was beginning to seem as if an on-time world was quite a normal place to be.

Set on the western edge of the lake, the town of Lucerne is as placid as the waters in which its medieval buildings are reflected. Rust-brown tiled rooftops, church spires and onion domes, its skyline is a credit to Swiss style and to diehard values. Thankfully lacking are the rows of grotesque package hotels which tend to accommodate tourists on a grander scale elsewhere.

Like everything else in Switzerland, when it comes to tourism, the emphasis is on quality rather than quantity. As a visitor you feel fortunate at being allowed in at all. It's rather like peeking under the curtain to see a play for which all the tickets were long since sold.

The lake and the town exist in harmony, each one respectful of the other. And, gliding across it like princesses dancing at a ball, are the steamers. Although built in 1901, the one I climbed aboard looked brand spanking new, and was christened Wilhelm Tell. One of five such vessels plying Lake Lucerne's gleaming waters for more than a century, its mechanism was a marvel of the Victorian age. Pistons heaving up and down, it ushered me gracefully past swans and pedalos, around the zigzag margins of the lake. As we moved slowly forward, I glimpsed a handful of fabulous chateaux poking out from between the trees high above the waterline – homes of the super rich.

The steamer pulled up at Weggis, little more than a hamlet. Having been thanked politely for my custom, I clambered off. Then, as the sun set, long shadows waning into night, I took a meal in the Weggiser Stübli.

A fragment of Swiss life from antiquity, the wood-panelled salon had escaped the ever-threatening need to renovate. With portraits of the hamlet's leaders looming down, I dined on *bratwurst* and *bauernrösti*, washed down with a glass of crisp Les Murailles.

Seated at the next table was a wizened old man who looked as Swiss as Toblerone. I half thought he might break out yodeling any moment. Raising his glass of Riesling, he caught my eye.

'We ought to keep it secret,' he said with a smile.

'Do you mean the food, or the wine… or the Stübli itself?'

The man sipped his drink, thought for a moment. He frowned.

'All of it,' he said. 'Let's keep it all to ourselves.'

Tetouan

THE CHESSBOARD WAS SO OLD and battered that you had to guess which squares were white and which were black.

The pieces were worn too, hand-carved from driftwood by my opponent, an old sailor named Abdel-Latif. He was wizened and frail, and had one of those blinding white denture grins that gives nothing away. Especially when he was lining up an attack.

We both opened with our pawns, breaking only to sip our *café noir*. I felt confident and somehow powerful, certain of early victory. But then, just five moves in, the old seaman's queen swooped down, and knocked my king on his side. The dentures parted no more than a crack.

'Checkmate.'

Abdel-Latif tapped a fingernail to the tabletop, indicating that his winnings were due. Like everyone else who frequented the hole in the wall café, in a lane off Tetouan's souq, I knew the rules.

Once the makeshift capital of Spanish Morocco, the sleepy town of Tetouan, a stone's throw from Morocco's Mediterranean coast, is one of café culture, long siestas, and Andalucian charm. It's a place forgotten by tourists, who make a beeline for Tangier, or the Imperial cities of the Moroccan hinterland. Inexplicably, they have always bypassed Tetouan, a whitewashed treasure trove of history, one that nestles between the Mediterranean and the Rif.

For me, it's the ultimate de-stress destination. There's nothing quite so wonderful as wasting long afternoons there. Bathed with Lotus Eater listlessness, I like to amble from café to café playing chess, a rough straw hat shading the blinding summer light. Tetouan is the kind of place that seeps into your bones, gently coaxing you to forget what you imagine to be reality.

But it wasn't a desire to relax, or even my love of chess, that lured me to Tetouan last week. It was a quest. I wanted to track down the military barracks outside town where Franco had rallied his troops before the Spanish Civil War. I had seen a picture – faded sepia – Franco standing on a mound, haranguing the *Guardia Mora*, his personal cavalry regiment, the Moroccan bodyguards. They were dressed in fabulous Moorish costumes, capes slung over their backs, turbans crowning their heads, rifles tight across their chests.

It took me no more than an hour to locate the barracks. Abdel-Latif the chess player had whispered the way. He said he could remember as a child seeing the fascist dictator himself parading through the town, his horsemen charging before him like harbingers from Hell. I'd told him about the sepia photograph. His acrylic teeth had grinned.

'There has been change,' he said.

And there certainly had. The long barrack buildings were derelict and black with grime, their roofs caved in, the doors torn away. The parade ground was overgrown and forlorn, waist-high with tinder-dry grass, through which wild peacocks roamed.

At the far end of the quadrangle I made out the mound where Franco had stood almost eight decades before. Abdel-Latif was quite right, there had indeed been change.

Later, in the afternoon, dazzled by blinding pink bougainvillea against stark whitewashed walls, I bumped into the chess player again in the Mellah, the old Jewish quarter. He was staggering home, tracing a line through the shade, one that he made twice daily, back and forth from the café in the souq.

'To know Tetouan, you must know Spain,' he said slowly, clicking the tip of his cane down on the flagstones, 'and to know Spain you must know Tetouan.' I asked if the Andalucian motherland could still be found there. Again, he grinned. 'You will find it hiding in the details,' he said.

And Tetouan is all about detail. It's bewitching and ubiquitous. You see it in the glorious tiled façades of the Hispano-Moorish architecture, and in the wrought iron arabesques, in the contraband from Andalucia that fills the shops, and in the way the young women tie their hair.

What I like best about Tetouan is the small-town feel, the sense that life carries on and no one's looking, a life conjured by ideal simplicity. There's none of the hustle and bustle of city life but, instead, a serenity, one that almost touches melancholy.

On a corner, just off the main square, Place Hassan II, a farmer was selling three goats and a sickly-looking lamb. Across from him, I found a boy standing with gleaming chips of painted amethyst cupped in his hands. And, next to him, a cluster of old men. They were touting moist cream cheese and parasols, cigarettes, and Spanish postcards from before the War.

I asked them if tourists ever strayed to their town. Two of the men shook their heads. But the last, a hunched figure in a thick camel-wool *jelaba* robe, cocked his head towards the square.

I looked round, and spied an Englishman standing there. I knew he was English because he was wearing those dull red trousers that the English wear on their holidays. He had horn-rims, a pallid, almost fearful expression, and a brow streaming with sweat. With nothing else to do, I went over and struck up conversation.

The Englishman said his name was George, explained that he lived in Guildford, and that his wife had got them the deal of a lifetime on a holiday home, bought online. I congratulated him on discovering Tetouan.

He tapped a finger to his nose.

'Better keep this one to ourselves old boy,' he said.

I'm not quite sure why, but George seemed unwilling to melt away into the shadows after our brief conversation. I turned towards the souq, and he followed. Down through narrow telescoping lanes, packed with wares – yellow *baboush* slippers and wool *jelabas*, golden kaftans and silk brocade, fresh meat, powdered henna, rose water, and *savon noir* for the hammam. And, like all the truest medinas anywhere, there were underpants and fake Reebok running shoes, wooden spoons, pots and pans, and wooden sieves dyed pink.

With every stride, I could feel George behind me, plodding forward in my footsteps. Just as I wondered how I might slip away, he sponged a giant polka-dot handkerchief over his cherry-red brow, and invited to see the villa he had bought. I accepted, and we drove south for twenty minutes, the slim ribbon of potholed tarmac shaded by olive trees.

The sun was low and the shadows long by the time we arrived. George pointed to an expansive clutch of villas and apartments, all of them whiter than white. He said you could get a villa there for next to nothing. We trooped out of the car and, a minute later, were in his sitting room, his wife was fussing around us. She took out a bottle of Bombay Sapphire and poured three enormous drinks. We clinked glasses. George from Guildford then made me swear a solemn oath not to publicize Tetouan in any way.

'The last thing we want,' he said, draining his gin, 'is this little scrap of paradise going to the dogs!'

Seated centre, Amjad Ali Shah, Tahir Shah's great grandfather, with his government at the familys' principality of Sardhana.

Nawab Jan Fishan Khan

The Afghan Notebook

ON THE MORNING OF HIS DEATH, my grandfather placed a tattered notebook in a brown manila envelope, sealed it with packing tape, and mailed it from his home in Tangier, to my father in Tunbridge Wells.

He must have stopped at the post office on his way up the hill to Gran Café de Paris, where he took tea late each morning, and where he was regarded as an eccentric by the other clientele.

An hour later my grandfather was dead, knocked down outside his house by a reversing Coca-Cola truck.

It almost seems like too much of a coincidence that the old man would have passed the notebook on to his oldest son on that of all mornings. After all, he had guarded the journal's contents his entire adult life, updating it meticulously over the years, and had kept it secret from even his own family. Perhaps he had had a premonition of some kind, or had foreseen that his skull was about to be split open outside his small villa on Rue de la Plage.

Whatever the sequence of events that caused him to mail the slim package to England that morning, the important thing was that the notebook got away. As for my grandfather's other possessions, most of them were stolen by his treacherous maid, Zohra, who had waited years for her master's death. She ran off to the mountains laden with all she could carry, and was never seen again.

The death that morning closed a life wildly rich in diversity, the kind that is almost impossible to summarize in a line of words.

My grandfather's name was Ikbal Ali Shah. An Afghan by ancestry, he had been born in northern India, the son of a Nawab, the Muslim equivalent of a Maharajah. His father presided over a Princely State named Sardhana, presented to our family by the British Raj a century and a half ago.

Unwilling to spend his life ruling ancestral lands in India or others

284

in Afghanistan, my grandfather set sail for Scotland to study medicine. He arrived to find Edinburgh gripped by the Great War. While helping the War effort he met Morag Murray, known within the family as 'Bobo', the daughter of a well-known member of Edinburgh society.

They fell instantly in love and eloped to the Hindu Kush.

My grandfather was a polymath. He was the author of more than seventy books, a diplomat and scholar, an adviser to half a dozen heads of state. But far more important to him than any of these things was the prospect of pursuing a quest, and the overwhelming desire to have what he always referred to as 'an interesting life'.

He spent years on the trail of the Yezidis of Iraq, the so-called 'People of the Peacock Angel'; and made long expeditions through Tibet, Turkey, the Arabian peninsula and the Sudan. But none of those pursuits matched his secret obsession, the details of which he kept in the Afghan Notebook.

After more than forty years of marriage, in August 1960, my grandfather lost his beloved Bobo to cancer. He was a broken man, and vowed that he would never return to any place they had travelled together.

That was how he came to live in Tangier.

After the funeral, he packed his belongings in an old sea trunk and journeyed to Morocco, where he rented a small but well proportioned house on Rue de la Plage.

At the time of his own death, in November 1969, I was less than three years old. My great sadness is that I never really knew him. We had been taken to see him at his villa a few days before the accident, presented so as to make him proud. My sisters were dressed in silk kaftans embroidered with gold, and I was trussed up in a camel wool *jelaba*, my miniature head crowned in a giant turquoise turban. I can just see it, a blur of memory.

As a child, my grandfather was an irresistible figure.

I would beg to hear the stories of his expeditions, his encounters with warlords, mystics and kings. My father would recount the tales, often tingeing them with a vein of disapproval, as if he regarded his own father as irresponsible.

'You cannot understand what it was like,' he told me one day as we sat on the lawn of our home at Tunbridge Wells. 'He would suddenly stand up at breakfast and order us out of the house, saying we were to leave our toys and all our things. Possessions, he would insist, were for the weak, and we were becoming far too attached. So we left everything, just walked out, and started afresh somewhere else.'

'He was a nomad,' I said.

My father regarded me hard, groomed his moustache with his hand.

'He was a maniac,' he replied.

My father's eagerness for stability explains our childhood in Tunbridge Wells. Odd trips to Morocco injected us with cultural colour, and proved there was a real world out there, somewhere. Throughout my youth, the Afghan Notebook lay in a box file, waiting to be appreciated. My father knew about it, of course. He had opened the brown manila envelope, perhaps had even scanned the frail pages, before burying it in a tomb of forgotten paperwork in his secret cubbyhole.

I have a feeling he knew I would one day find it, and it would begin a journey, leading me to seek out people and places I would not have encountered without it. The fact he didn't destroy the notebook or give it away, suggested he wanted me to take up the search – the search for the greatest lost treasure in history.

The Treasure

By the mid eighteenth century Mughal India was like a ripe fruit ready for the plucking. The Mughal Emperor Mohammed Shah had turned his back on his armed forces, and preferred to occupy his time with his harem and the arts. His coffers were overflowing with riches – diamonds the size of apples, emeralds, rubies, silver and millions of gold coins.

Word of the Mughals' fabulous prosperity spread on the wind, and reached the ears of Nadir Shah, Emperor of Persia. The son of a shepherd, Nadir had built an empire on a bedrock of ruthlessness. The idea of seizing the wealth of Mughal India – which had been amassed over centuries since the time of Babur – was too much for him. Without delay, we planned an attack, and sent spies to infiltrate the Mughal Court. Then, with a massive army at his side, he rode eastward across Afghanistan and up the Khyber Pass into northern India.

At the Red Fort, Emperor Mohammed Shah relaxed in his harem, oblivious to the fact that the might of the Persian army was about rewrite history. North-west of Delhi, at Panipat, Nadir made camp. While his sixty thousand soldiers recovered from the long journey from Persia, he sent word to the Mughal Emperor, demanding reparations. In one of the greatest miscalculations in Asian military history, Mohammed Shah sent a pathetically small force to rebuff Nadir Shah at Panipat. The outcome was slaughter, with the Indian force being decimated.

The battle proved Nadir's genius at warfare. Aware that camels are the only creatures without a blatant fear of fire, he ordered for his camel cavalry to be trussed in pairs, with a dais in the middle. On each dais a fire was constructed, onto which was thrown camphor. The clouds of pungent smoke sent fear into the Emperor's ranks. His cavalry and elephants beat a frenzied retreat.

After his victory at Panipat, Nadir Shah took his time. He could have marched onto Delhi immediately. But instead he decided to send word to Mohammed Shah, ordering him to prepare for the victor's arrival. When the messenger arrived at the Red Fort bearing the encoded communiqué, the Mughal Emperor was stupefied. He had expected Nadir to sweep into his capital, and begin a whirlwind of looting. Lulled into a false sense of security, Mohammed Shah ordered for Delhi to be festooned with decorations. He had the great Lahore Gate of the Red Fort flung open and, when the Persian ruler arrived on a caparisoned elephant, he welcomed him as a brother ruler and a guest.

While expressing amity to his fellow Emperor, Nadir wasted no time in pressing for reparations to pay for the cost of transporting his army and staff from Persia to India and back. He demanded a million rupees' worth of precious gems and gold. Mohammed Shah protested, declaring that he could muster only a fraction of the amount. The Mughal Emperor withdrew into his state apartments to consult his advisers. And for three days, Nadir toured the Red Fort. Such was the opulence that Nadir was struck dumb by what he saw.

Historians suggest he was about to demand extra reparations from Mohammed Shah, when fate gave him a godsend. Although the Mughal Emperor had commanded his people not to attack the Persian army, a high-ranking officer was knocked down and killed in Chandni Chowk, the nearby silver market. Using the event to his advantage, Nadir gave his soldiers permission to attack for six hours.

By sunset the streets of Delhi were running with Indian blood. Tens of thousands of innocent civilians had been slain, their homes burned and looted, their wives and daughters raped. As the Mughal Emperor was being briefed on the carnage, Nadir Shah hammered on his door. He said that the price of his compensation had just risen nine-fold. Mohammed Shah was to pay nine million rupees at once, and annual reparations thereafter. If he did not, his entire Court would be beheaded, and the Emperor himself would be subjected to a far slower, more painful death.

The seals to the Imperial treasure magazines were broken, and the royal stables were opened. The wealth amassed through generations of Mughal dynasty was laden onto twelve thousand horses, ten thousand camels and a thousand elephants. Mohammed Shah, it is said, was wailing in his private apartment, distraught at the loss.

At that moment Nadir Shah arrived to bid his host farewell. Before quitting the Mughal Court, Nadir it is said removed his simple turban and offered it to Mohammed Shah. It was common for monarchs of the time to exchange headdresses as a gesture of fraternity and goodwill. The Mughal Emperor's face turned crimson.

He had no goodwill to give.

Fearing death if he did not comply with the Imperial etiquette, he carefully removed his own silk turban and presented it to his victor. But there was another more important reason for his anger.

Concealed within the folds of cloth was his most prized jewel of all – the Koh-i-Noor diamond.

The Caravan

At dawn on the hundredth day following his march into Delhi, Nadir Shah led the treasure caravan out from the Lahore Gate of the Red Fort, westward, towards Persia.

Never in history could there have been a sight like it – thousands upon thousands of camels, elephants and horses, heaving under their burdens. Nadir not only stripped the Mughal capital of its wealth, but its finest craftsmen, too. His great army of veteran warriors, and his harem, were joined by thousands of stone masons, carpenters, jewellers and swordsmiths.

It's said that the caravan's entire length took three full days to pass a fixed point. The danger of starvation was very real for such a moving force, as few towns would possess enough food to feed animals and men. For this reason, Nadir ordered for flocks of sheep to be herded along with the train, as well as sending messengers to have encampments ready with animals along the way home. The pride with which the Persian emperor departed Delhi is easily imaginable. He was king of the world, the richest monarch in history, a man of unparalleled wealth and power. But, unfortunately for him, others nearby were already conspiring to relieve him of his new responsibility.

The caravan snaked its way north-west out from Delhi towards the fertile farmlands of what is modern Pakistan. They reached Lahore, a city famed for its scholarship, and pressed on westward, down the Khyber Pass into Afghanistan. With such an immense caravan to control, Nadir Shah must have been aware of the danger. The threat of having the hoard of Mughal India poached from his grasp was all too real. Nadir was obsessed with security, for himself, and for the treasure. Each night, along with his most trusted generals, he planned out the route the caravan would take through the badlands of Afghanistan, to his homeland, Persia. And, each night, his most trusted generals would then plan how best they could execute their master, and relieve him of his loot.

The history of Afghanistan fades in and out of focus.

At times it is little more than hearsay or myth. The difficulty for the historian is that Nadir covered his tracks, going to extreme lengths to hide his motives, and conceal his real strategy. He was a survivor, a tactician who had started off as a shepherd boy, and was now the richest ruler on earth. It seems that he split the caravan in two, sending part on a northern route to Persia, and part in a southern crescent through Kandahar. It is uncertain exactly when or where the generals unsheathed their swords and ended Nadir's life. But legend tells that it happened in a tented camp somewhere in the south, and that the fatal blow was made by the Persian Emperor's most trusted general,

Ahmed Shah Durrani.

With the death of Nadir, Durrani seized control of the treasure caravans, and shortly after, he called a *loyd jurga*, a meeting of elders from the Afghan clans. Such assemblies, which are still used today, named Durrani King of Afghanistan. He was twenty-three years old. In the following years, Ahmed Shah went on to sack Delhi again, and shored up the boundaries of Afghanistan. Establishing his capital at Kandahar, he planned out the future of the kingdom. But suddenly, he fell sick, struck down with cancer of the face. An Afghan legend tells how a soothsayer visited Ahmed Shah one night in his campaign tent. The woman foretold the future of the kingdom – that Timur Shah, Durrani's eldest son, would inherit, and would destroy all his father had established.

Terrified that his legacy would be undone, the dying king had his treasure storehouses emptied, and the immense hoard moved to a cave system somewhere in Afghanistan. There, it was concealed, in a series of vast chambers. So as to protect the location, Durrani ordered all those who hid the treasure to be executed.

For the last two centuries and a half, the whereabouts of the treasure of Ahmed Shah Durrani has been debated by generations of Afghans. Many have searched for it. More still have questioned whether it ever existed, or if it has already been found, by the British, or the Russians, or the Taliban.

The Fattening Rooms

FOR THE LAST SIXTEEN DAYS, Adele Mopoti, has sat on a low wooden bench in a thatched hut on the edge of her village, eating.

As soon as she's scraped up the last spoon of lumpy grey porridge, her grandmother barges in and hands her another bowlful. Once she's finished it, she will munch her way through a platter of cooked yams, and another heaped high with plantains. Then she will be permitted to sleep off the meal in the suffocating summer heat, before starting all over again at dusk.

Adele, seventeen, who lives in a small village on the Nigerian border with Cameroon, is being fattened up in an ancient ritual which has traditionally preceded marriage in south-east Nigeria. She is expected to eat between four and five enormous meals a day. The hope is that, once she emerges after a month, her body will be layered in a healthy cushion of fat. The thinking behind the so-called 'Fattening Rooms' has corresponded with customary values of the Efik and neighbouring tribes for centuries.

A stay in the rooms – generally no more than a thatched hut – have long been the last stop on a pubescent girl's journey to the altar. The residence is one part of a complex tribal initiation from childhood into womanhood. It's a place where one learns the responsibilities expected in the years to come, a time for solitary reflection, as well as an opportunity to get the body ready for years, possibly decades, of child-bearing.

In a land where excess food has never been easy to come by, a plump bride has always signified health, wealth, and hinted at the ability to produce numerous children. But the young generation of residents in the Fattening Rooms of Adele's village don't see the point.

These days, most of them have other things on their minds.

'I'm only here, to please my father,' says Adele as she pushes back her braided hair, 'he told me that if I didn't spend two months here, then he wouldn't pay for me to go and study in Calabar. I have dreams, big plans. I want to study to be a nurse. But at the same time I understand the importance of tradition. If I did not, I would have run away by now. As soon as I get out of the village, I'm going to lose all the weight I've gained. In the city people laugh at fat women, they make fun of you, saying that you're backwards, and from a village.'

Adele's best friend, Gloria, shares the scant room with her. They entered the hut at the same time, and spend much of their time talking, that is when they're not eating. Both girls are dressed in a *rappas*, a loose-fitting sarong, their feet bare. Unlike Adele, Gloria's legs are bound with shiny copper bracelets.

For the first two or three days you feel very pampered,' explains Gloria, 'our grandmothers come in with food all the time. They won't let us do any housework, or even do the washing. They tell us how nice we look, and that all the boys in the village are asking about us. Of course it makes you feel good! But then you start feeling disgusted with yourself, and bored... *so* bored.'

Gloria is cut short by a scratching at the boarded-up window. She giggles nervously. 'It's my boyfriend, he's not allowed to come in here,' she says. 'He misses me very much. And I miss him. But I can't see his face until I leave here. If I do, then my father will whip me, and our family's reputation will be ruined.'

Bending down, Gloria rubs her legs. It's a clumsy process, made difficult by the spiralling copper bracelets. When she is asked what they are for, she grimaces. 'They're like manacles that a slave wears,' she says. 'If I sneak out and meet my boyfriend, then my grandmother will hear the metal jangling, and she'll call out to my brothers. Then they will beat me, and when they have beaten me, my father will whip me.'

Gloria's grandmother is blind in one eye, but she watches out attentively for the two girls. She can't remember how old she is or when she herself was married. But she does know that of the ten children she gave birth to long, long ago, at least six are still alive. 'Maybe seven are still living,' she mumbles, correcting herself, 'the youngest son went away to Yaounde and never came back.'

The old woman, whose name is Walima, crouches outside the

thatched hut, stirring an immense pot of millet porridge. 'These girls are eating well,' she says as she stirs. 'But it's not their appetite's I'm worried about… I'm worried about their minds. They don't understand about duty now, and when you say anything to them, they think they know better than the customs.

'How can a girl know how to please her husband, how to care for him, how to cook for him, unless she has listened to the elders?'

Suddenly, footsteps can be heard from behind the hut.

With her one good eye, Walima moves her head about fitfully. 'There's been a boy coming here,' she rasps, 'if I catch him I'll have him beaten. Oh, the young generation have no respect for tradition. It will lead to the downfall of all we have.'

Tradition is something of incalculable importance to the Efik tribe. It is the traditions which have formed a basis to life, and have allowed vital knowledge to be passed down from one generation to the next. For millennia the Efik have been a farming people, tilling the land for maize and millet, fishing in the rich waterways of the Calabar delta. But now the traditions are under threat.

'We have talked and talked about what is right and wrong,' says Thomas, Adele's father. 'When my wife went through the *iria* initiation, she was so happy to eat the food her grandmother cooked for her and then, soon after, we were wed, and then the children were born. Adele wants to go and get educated and become a nurse. That's fine, but there's so much else for her to know. The *mbobi*, the fattening hut, is a place where she can learn much deeper information… information about people, about life.'

Across Africa initiation rites abound for both young men and women, all of them drawing a firm line between youth and maturity.

The *iria* ritual is different from many other initiations, in that it shows the community who is ready to be married, and just how beautiful they are. The fattening rooms are essentially pampering parlours, in which the nubile girls are indulged with food, attention and advice. One cannot overstate the significance of this last ingredient – the advice.

The elders dote on the beauty of their daughters, pointing out the growing layers of fat, but you get the feeling their attention is really on the wealth of information that the fattening rooms pass down. In a changing society, the information may be out of date, but it is ancient and tested knowledge.

Throughout the *iria* ritual, the elder women of the community guide the *iriabos*, the initiates. No one takes a keener interest in the proceedings than the girls' grandmothers. They take every opportunity to remind the young generation how things have *not* changed since the time they themselves passed through the ritual.

More than thirty years must have slipped by since Adele's grandmother was initiated, but she remembers the routine in astonishing detail.

'If you don't do everything right,' she says shrewdly, 'then the ritual will be worthless. Make a mistake, and a blanket of shame will descend not only over my family, but over the entire community.'

The *iria* initiation usually begins about five months before the fattening period. A group of girls pass through the rituals at the same time, bonding them together for life. The first step in the process is the cutting of their hair. A knife is sharpened ceremoniously, before being wielded by one of the oldest, most respected women. After that, the girls strip off their clothes, their bodies anointed with a paste of ash, ground indigo seeds and red camwood powder. Intricate geometric designs are scored into the paste, highlighting the girls' natural beauty, as well as repelling insects.

The second stage of the initiation is held on the morning of the entry into the fattening room. It involves the elderly matrons of the community inspecting the girls, scrutinizing their naked torsos, watchful for tell-tale signs of early pregnancy. Nothing is so important as for the *iriabos* to be seen to be chaste.

'The great danger is at that moment,' says Adele's grandmother. 'It is then that any mature woman can come forward and claim your daughter or granddaughter is not pure. Refuting such a charge is hard, and can only be done by a priest. I remember when I was an *iriabo* a bad woman with a grudge against one family said that their daughter had been immoral. A cloak of shame fell down on that family, and the girl had no choice but to drown herself.'

Then the girls are massaged with palm oil, and some of them have the spiralling copper bracelets, called *ikpalla*, wrapped round their legs. In some Efik villages, the leader of the community presents each girl with a wooden or paper tag, tangible proof of her purity. It's a sombre moment, similar in its portent to graduation at a western high school. With the entire village looking on in pride, the *iriabos* are ushered into the cramped huts.

During the confinement period, the girls are either alone, or in pairs. The last intention is for them to spend their time chattering. The period is intended for quiet reflection – mouths are supposed to be eating, not talking. Sometimes the rooms are hung with raffia, onto which are tied the bones of fish that the initiate has consumed: partly as decoration, and partly to show her ravenous appetite.

In the days that follow, the girls are massaged frequently with palm oil, and smeared with clay and ash. All the while, plates of food are ushered in – fish, millet porridge, cooked yams and maize.

Traditionally, the confinement period could last as long as a year. It was a buffer between puberty and marriage, and an effective way for girls to postpone married life. But these days the girls are anxious to escape the fattening rooms as quickly as they can, just as they are eager to make a break with the village. For most, nothing is so powerfully alluring as the draw of the city.

A hundred miles to the south of where Adele and Gloria are sitting, Constance is impounded in another fattening room, on a backstreet of the bustling town of Calabar. Unlike the others, Constance, aged eighteen, is eager to put on weight.

'I have been here for about a month,' she explains, 'and I will try and stay for another month or two. If I want to get married to a nice boy, I have to look my best, and boys here in Calabar like a girl with a full figure. I have seen the magazines from America... all those girls who look starved. That's so nasty. Oh, no, we don't want to look like that here in Calabar.'

Constance, who is of medium height, is doing well to achieve her ideal weight of ninety-five kilos. She is eating more food than she ever thought possible, all of it served up by her doting mother, Grace.

'In the morning I eat three or four large bowls of millet porridge,' she says, 'and then a bunch of bananas, and some boiled yams. At lunch I have more porridge, and a plate of fatty meat, potatoes, more yams, maize and some fruit. Then in the evening, I eat whatever is left in the kitchen.'

Constance's mother scurries around their three-room family house, attending to the cooking, giving orders to the younger daughter, who does the food shopping. 'We are pleased that Constance is putting on weight so fast,' she says. 'Yes, all this food is expensive, but we have no choice but to bear the expense. It's costing us about twelve thousand naira (£60) a month. We want our daughter to marry well, and for that we have to make sacrifices.'

Unlike many in Calabar, Constance's family was reluctant to send their daughter to one of the established fattening rooms operating in the town. Usually owned by women of vast proportions, they double up as beauty salons, where stern regimes dedicated to pampering are the norm. For Constance's parents, the commercial parlours were unnecessary, as they had space enough at home to turn a bedroom into a private fattening room for Constance. Then there's the issue of young male visitors. A recent scandal involving midnight parties has tarnished the reputation of one of the town's most established fattening rooms.

At home, the high-calorie diet has helped Constance gain weight fast. She's put on about eight kilos in a month. But another, darker factor has led to the rapid weight gain – steroids.

Like many Nigerian girls of her generation, Constance has discovered the little strips of pills, called *Easi-Gain*, which can be bought from chemists without a prescription. They make her feel hungry and sleepy, but they help her to put on the pounds extremely fast. And, like most other young women, Constance has no idea of the damaging effects of the pills.

'As a modern woman I am using modern methods to make myself more beautiful,' she says, reclining on the sofa. 'The pills are quite safe, and they are cheaper than all the food I have to eat to gain the same amount of weight. In any case, everyone is taking them.'

In a small office across town, a group of women is in the middle of a meeting at the, 'Women Guiding Women'. The walls of their headquarters are adorned with colourful posters, bearing slogans like 'THIN IS NATURAL' and 'SLENDERNESS IS NEXT TO GODLINESS'.

Leading the gathering is a woman called Ruth. 'Our aim is a simple one,' she says to the audience of new recruits, 'we go through towns and villages and teach women that moderation is good, and that gluttony is bad. You don't have to be the size of a whale to be happy with how you look.'

Ruth works part-time at WGW, an organization founded five years ago. It walks a fine line between traditional Nigerian rituals, like the fattening rooms, and the Western obsession of slenderness. As with many women of her tribe, Ruth spent more than a month being indulged with food before her marriage. After giving birth to four children, she realized that piling on the pounds for the sake of it wasn't necessary.

'Our society is changing fast,' she says, 'and as women we have to change with it. Our daughters need to be educated – taught how to use computers, not forced into fattening huts.' Ruth pauses in mid-sentence. 'There's a new danger in our society, though,' she says darkly. 'We hardly even know how dangerous it is to become. But news of it and its "magic" is spreading like wildfire.' As she speaks, she holds up a packet of pills. 'This is it... it's *Easi-Gain*.'

Back in their village, Adele and Gloria are sitting down to yet another high-calorie meal. A bulky pot of bubbling millet porridge has been carried in, and Adele's grandmother is dishing it out with a ladle. Two plates of bananas and boiled yams are standing at the ready. The two girls frown at the sight of yet more food. They're already full to bursting.

As she passes out the porridge, the old woman snaps: 'Eat it up, eat up, you lazy girls! If you stay skinny like that we will never find a good husband for either of you!'

The Favour Network

LAST WEEK ONE OF THE NEIGHBOURS near my home in Casablanca slipped a note under my door.

With almost toe-cringing politeness, he asked if I might introduce his niece to a friend of mine with connections in the art world. The girl, he explained, was eager to get an internship at a British auction house, but she was thin on contacts.

At first I wondered how the neighbour, a man I hardly know, had such good information on whom I know. But then I remembered that in Morocco everyone knows everything about everyone. They know how much money you make, the names and phone numbers that fill your address book and, most importantly, they know how you may be of help to them.

The matrix to pass on the minute details comes through the hierarchy of maids and cooks, drivers and guardians, who are relied upon by many to share each word that touches their ears. They know so much sensitive information that no employer in their right mind would ever fire them.

I sent a message to my friend with contacts at the auction house, and later advised my neighbour that his niece could be certain of an interview. The next day there was a knock at the door. I went and opened it, to find a delivery man straining under the weight of an enormous bouquet of exotic flowers. Having placed them on the table in the sitting-room, I sat back and smiled to myself.

It was a good example of the favour network in action.

You can't live in Morocco long without brushing into it. The favour network is all around, a blurred backdrop to life. In a culture based on connections and trust, the only way forward – or upward – is to rely on favours.

All Moroccans live with the same niggling fear: withdraw from the system before you've paid in, and the creditors will come calling. That was the reason for the pricey bunch of flowers – a fear that if the favour wasn't repaid at once, I would demand a favour in return. But as with the lure of instant credit in the West, there's always the danger of taking a favour that you can't pay back, and plunging into debt.

For anyone new to Arab society, the situation can be baffling. It's a kind of silent language. Everyone knows who has helped whom, and what strings have been pulled – now, yesterday, or a century ago. The slate is never wiped clean, because it's part of a system built on pride, written on an invisible chalkboard in the sky.

Our maid, Zohra, once told me of how her family's fortunes had been swept away in repaying a favour left owing by her great, great grandfather. I had asked why she simply didn't dispute the request.

She smiled.

'Do you not know about honour?' she said.

My father, who had been brought up in the East, drilled into my sisters and me his motto – 'Never owe anyone anything!' After moving to Morocco, I now understand his reasoning. He knew that, like Zohra, a family's security can be lost in the blink of an eye while striving to uphold its honour.

As a policy, I rarely ask favours. If I do, I repay at once and with abundant dividends. Equally, I have come to learn that only a fool boasts about whom he knows, or what contacts – or favours – he has in his arsenal.

The only difficulty is when someone pays into the system covertly, before turning up to be repaid in kind. In such situations, even the most astute expert must tread with care. The conditions are usually the same. First comes an absolutely over-the-top box of chocolates, a bottle of expensive aftershave, or perfume, just like that – out of the blue. In Arab society refusing a gift is tantamount to a declaration of war. So you have no choice but to accept. Once the gift has been received, you must respond with an equally lavish gift. If you don't, you can be certain that a request will be on its way.

If I'm unsure of how to act, I ask Zohra. She's an expert on the right etiquette. When I told her about the neighbour, the favour, and the flowers, she wagged a finger towards the door.

'Some people have no shame,' she said.

The Forgotten Women of Bhopal

TAKE A WALK THROUGH the narrow alleyways off the main road and you immediately know that something's wrong.

It's as if the spectre of death is hovering there, ready to speed away those who eluded it one December night, twenty-five years ago. Everyone bears the scars of that horrifying encounter.

Halfway down the lane, Ambereen Khan sits on a battered old chair outside her concrete home. Squinting through goggle-like glasses, she strains to make out the approaching visitor. Her body is emaciated, rigid with arthritis, her legs swollen, and her breathing forced. Ambereen could easily pass for a woman in her sixties, but she's just thirty-two.

If a cloud of poison gas swept silently across London or New York, killing thousands and crippling many more, we would expect drastic action and answers. The injured would be given relief, the bereaved would be compensated, the guilty parties prosecuted. And, once the dust had settled, Parliament would pass laws ensuring such a catastrophe never happened again.

But in Bhopal things are different.

To the outside world the city's name is still synonymous with a multi-national's incompetence. To the people who live there still, Bhopal stands for a far greater misfortune. In the back streets, a stone's throw south of the Union Carbide factory, they say that the lucky ones perished that night back in 1984. Those who survived have been dealt decades of pain, and the worst affected have been Bhopal's women.

On breathing the toxic gas, hundreds of them had spontaneous abortions. Many more pregnant women later had still-births, or babies which died after a few days of life. Yet thousands more were made sterile by the disaster. In Bhopal, congenital deformities are common to children born in the years since the toxic leak.

300

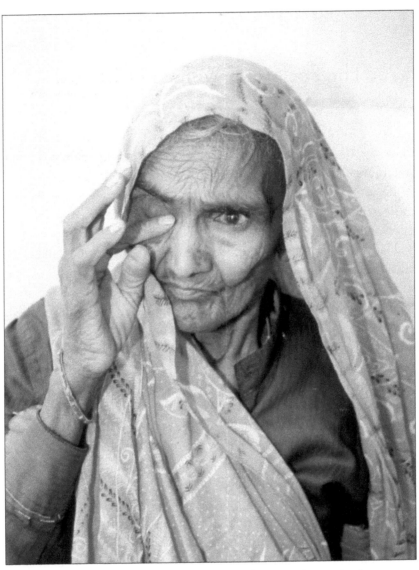

An elderly victim of the Bhopal disaster, waiting for her eyes to be examined

The day before the poison cloud destroyed her life, Ambereen Khan was preparing for her wedding to a man from a neighbouring town.

'As soon as his family heard about the gas leak,' she whispers softly, 'they forbid him to marry me. You see, people don't want to marry girls from Bhopal. They're scared that we will give birth to children with two heads.'

Ambereen was eventually married to a local man who had himself become handicapped by the calamity. The possibility of deformed children was never an issue though, for the gas had made Ambereen infertile.

'Now I am waiting to die,' she says resolutely. 'Look around... there's no joy here, only misery and death.'

As Ambereen pauses to rub her swollen eyes, I scan the street. She's right. There are no children playing in the long shadows of the afternoon, and none of the usual bustle of Indian back-street life. In the distance, a funeral procession carries a cheap coffin to a nearby Muslim burial ground. Walking solemnly behind, their eyes fixed at the ground, are the relatives of the tragedy's latest victim.

The area where Ambereen lives is called Jai Prakash Nagar. A predominantly Muslim area, it is home to hundreds of low-income families, most of which used to be casual labourers. They relied on their physical health to work.

A staunchly pious community, some considered the catastrophe to be a scourge sent by God. Accordingly, thousands refused to seek compensation but instead blamed themselves. Those that did seek justice – Ambereen and her husband among them – faced a steep uphill task. Most could not understand the paperwork needed to make a claim. Those who did receive a little money found themselves relieved of it by unscrupulous agents of the underworld.

But, for Ambereen and the women like her, some assistance is at hand. Twice a week, Aziza drops by to have a chat and make sure she's coping with the pain. Aziza, who's a health visitor from the Sambhavna Clinic, has to deal daily with the victims' anger and their sense of betrayal.

'They can't understand why their teeth are falling out,' she explains, 'why their eyes are bloodshot, why they're struggling for a single breath, or why arthritis is crippling them well before old age.'

After spending a little time with Ambereen, Aziza heads back to the clinic. Thirty women there are waiting to be treated. Dr. Rachana Pandey, sees each of them in turn.

'I had just graduated from medical school in 1984,' she says, 'and was at Bhopal's Hamidya Hospital the night of the gas leak. Words can't explain the scene. There were bodies everywhere. Every inch of space was covered with the dying and the dead.'

The doctor motions for the next patient to enter the surgery.

'My medical career has been devoted to helping those who were exposed to the poison gas,' she continues. 'We never thought that the suffering and death would go on like this. Women are getting their menopause decades before their time, children are suffering from stunted growth, while scores of others are mentally handicapped.'

Dr. Pandey smiles at the young woman who has come to her for treatment, suffering from chronic depression.

'Look at her,' she says. 'Her husband's been beating her because she can't conceive, telling her she's worthless, that she's a witch. No wonder she's depressed.'

The Sambhavna Clinic treats only victims of the Union Carbide seepage. More than a hundred a day flock through its doors and make use of its already stretched resources. Patients (eighty per cent of whom are women) are charged a small one-time registration fee, after which all treatment is free. The Clinic is kept afloat by donations, and was set up in the 'nineties with help from the British-based charity *Pesticides Trust*. There's an emphasis on Ayurvedic healing, on yoga, and on Western-style counselling – sharing experiences of that life-changing night.

The scale of the situation is enormous.

The hundred thousand female children who were exposed and survived are now at a child-bearing age.

'An additional problem,' explains Sarangi, 'is that women in this community aren't used to discussing such personal problems within their own families, let alone with others.'

While their bodies ache and burn with the effects of the gas, the victims' minds are haunted by the memory. Pick anyone at random and they'll recount their tale.

December 3rd, 1984 was a warm night. Most people had left their windows open. Shortly after one a.m., more than half a million people woke in terror, fighting for breath, their lungs. Their eyes streaming and, gasping, they leapt from their beds and ran into the streets.

'The gas came in a great fog, which wafted silently into the houses,' says one women. 'Outside there was a stampede. All around us our friends and relatives were dropping to the ground,' adds another.

At that moment no one could have known the awful truth: that a venting pipe at the Union Carbide pesticide plant had fractured, releasing a cocktail of eighteen toxic chemicals, including hydrogen cyanide and the deadly, unstable gas methyl isocyanate.

Unsure of what to do, thousands fled through the streets, charging directly into the path of the poison, over forty tonnes of which was being carried on the wind. Those who made it to hospital had little hope, as no one knew the cause of the disaster.

Morning brought a sobering scene of carnage. There were corpses everywhere. Families huddled together, mothers clutching their children, their eyes bulged, blood vomited down their chests. Hundreds of cows and dogs were dead, too, as were the birds, fallen from the trees.

The official human death toll that night was put at 5,325. But as bodies were scooped into massive pits so quickly, to prevent the spread of disease, no one's quite sure how many died. The real figure is probably closer to ten thousand.

Zenath was only a child in 1984. Now an adult, she's still deeply traumatized by the disaster.

'Everyone remembers,' she says gently. 'How can we forget? It's burned into our memories. We try not to speak of it, but it is always here inside us. My mother led my sisters and me to the mosque. We clambered over bodies to get inside, and we sheltered there, crouching down as low as we could. Around us people were praying, screaming, and they were dying. Everyone was blinded by the gas, everyone choking, desperately clinging onto life.'

Zenath would like to be married, but there's no money for her dowry. And, in any case, no one wants to marry a sterile woman. Not even in Bhopal. Her father, a watch-repairer, blinks through extra-thick lenses.

His eyesight is bad and getting worse. He's forced to concentrate on mending wall-clocks now, and soon he'll have to give that up, too.

Across town, at the Bhopal Eye Hospital, senior Surgeon Dr. Dubey is preparing to operate on his seventh patient of the morning. More than three hundred people flock daily to the hospital.

'Most of those who come here suffer from nebular cornea opacity,' he explains, 'it's like a cataract. Some were blinded totally, while others rubbed their eyes afterwards and went blind as a result.'

Dr. Dubey peers out of his first floor window. A line of patients snakes its way around the building. Most of them have their eyes bandaged. 'Look at that,' he says, 'I treat them as fast as I can, but each day dozens more arrive.'

Miriam is at the end of the line. A mother of three, she's blind in her right eye. And now her left eye is clouding over. She has constant headaches and can't walk very far these days. In the stampede that December night she was separated from her husband. She presumes he perished and was buried in one of the mass graves. Each of their children has illnesses resulting from the gas. Despite applying for compensation, the authorities insisted that Miriam had come from a neighbouring city, and was merely pretending to be a victim.

Every Tuesday, Abdul Jabar, a legal advocate, gives free help to women who were affected by the gas attack, in a park in central Bhopal. The founder of the *Bhopal Gas Victim's Association*, he sees that the ailing fill out the compensation forms properly.

'Had this tragedy taken place in the West,' he says, 'the factory would have been levelled straight away, but here people are too accepting. It's inevitable that there will be another "Bhopal". Indian factories haven't learnt from our example. It's just a matter of time. It could happen tomorrow.'

Thousands of women need Abdul Jabar's help. As they wait to see the man they regard as a saviour, they swap details of their illnesses. Those who come to Abdul Jabar's sessions need all the help they can get. Compensation for the Bhopal victims has become embroiled in one of the worst bureaucratic jams in Indian history, a nation famous for drawn-out legal actions.

From the very start, the signs were bad.

Union Carbide dragged its heels for years before paying up. Finally, they made a one-time settlement of $470 million to the Indian government – that was back in 1989. But, as a stream of people in Bhopal are quick to point out, the government is in no hurry to hand out the cash. Progressing at a snail's place, its system is still collecting millions of dollars in interest on money that hasn't reached those who so desperately deserve it.

Once the money was safely locked in the State's coffers, those making a claim were forced to queue up for days for a token which would permit them to get a claim form. Then began the convoluted process of claim courts and endless hearings. Victims need to attend as many as thirty hearings to have their claim considered. The only way to oil the wheels of justice is a seven hundred rupee bribe. But few people have that kind of cash.

The former Chairman of Union Carbide, Warren Anderson, is deeply unpopular in Bhopal as one might expect. His name forms part of a common slogan on walls around town – reading simply 'Hang Anderson'.

As he lives in quiet retirement in Florida, Union Carbide itself is eager to distance itself from responsibility. The Bhopal plant was, they say, owned by a separate entity Union Carbide (India), even though the American parent company is said to have owned more than half its stock. They protest, too, that the damaged venting pipe was sabotaged by a disgruntled employee.

Back in Jai Prakash Nagar, Ambereen's neighbour, Amina Beeh, pulls a scratched chest X-ray from a box and wipes it with her scarf. Like many of Bhopal's women, she's suffered for years from a catalogue of health problems, problems that are getting worse.

'My lungs were burnt, as if acid was poured into them,' Amina says. 'And I need regular treatment for a severe gynaecological disorder.'

Staring out at the former Union Carbide factory, Amina dabs her eyes. It's time for her medicine. Putting away her X-ray, she gulps down an assortment of pink and white pills. Then, she leans back into her chair, and sighs.

'Every day at this time I do this,' she says, 'I close my eyes and remember how different it used to be. I think of the faces of my family and all my friends,' she whispers, 'and I pretend the gas never came. For a moment I breathe easy, and I forget.'

A group of Guerrilla Girls protesting against the male-dominated art world

The Guerrilla Girls, calling for gender equality in art

The Guerrilla Girls

A PAPER TRAIL OF CLUES hidden at key points in downtown Manhattan leads you the basement chamber of a dilapidated office building.

The sect is distrustful of visitors and will go to any lengths to ensure security. Stone steps spiral down into the hide-out. A bare lightbulb hangs above a solid oak desk. And, reclining in a worn leather chair, disguised in a woolly gorilla mask, is Alice Neel, self-styled Guerrilla Girl.

New Yorkers pride themselves on their reputation of being impossible to surprise. They've seen it all. Businessmen roller-skate to work; exhibitionists run naked through the streets; and cow-girls do lasso tricks in subway trains. Weird fads come and go with the seasons. But few of the city's oddities and bizarre underground cliques stand the test of time… none have survived like the 'Guerrilla Girls'.

As plumes of vapour rise from the steam grates down in SoHo – Manhattan's artistic quarter – a gang of figures dart through the shadows back to their hideaway where their leader is awaiting them. Their faces concealed in snarling gorilla masks, this secret quasi-terrorist cell is New York's most belligerent feminist force. Scorning the male establishment, demonstrating against sexism in the art world, the band of die-hard feminists is known to all New Yorkers.

Formed a decade ago by a rebellious group of women artists, the Guerrilla Girls were galvanized into action by their disdane for what they regarded as New York's male artistic mafia. They pledged to harass, humiliate, and even to raid, institutions opposed to the cause of women artists.

The Guerrilla Girls have been honoured by feminists in the United States and, indeed, throughout the world. But, as their followers praise them, the Guerrilla Girls are mocked by many New Yorkers as the biggest joke in town.

Despite this, what began as a contest against Manhattan's misogynistic museums and art galleries, has now expanded to take in new themes. Today, the Guerrilla Girls' devotees say they battle to give a voice to those fighting against issues such as abortion and AIDS, rape and even female circumcision. As the scope of their battleground extends, the Guerrilla Girls encourage women in other cities, and in far off nations, to make use of their tactics and take up struggles of their own.

In a society where one's reputation is everything, the Guerrilla Girls have used humiliation as a terrorist tool. One night, lower Manhattan was plastered with thousands of simple black and white posters. The bulletins depicted no gruesome scenes, but instead listed names. The Guerrilla Girls' own unmistakable artwork – naming sexist galleries and their associated officials – became their calling card.

Each poster, which bears the characteristic stamp of ridicule, along with the honorary epithet *Conscience of the Art World*, rocked the art establishment from the start. New York's wealthy gallery district ran rife with rumours. Who were the Guerrilla Girls? How would they take out their fury? Were any of them – as the rumours suggested – famous artists themselves?

Overnight it seemed that feminism was back with a stylish, sleek and new bellicose face. During the 'eighties, when prices of art skyrocketed, as huge corporations began to invest in paintings and sculptures, very few female artists had their work represented by mainstream galleries.

Suddenly, the voice of female artists everywhere was visible. Refusing to reveal their identities, the Guerrilla Girls insisted on anonymity. This, they maintained, focused the limelight on their cause, and would not hinder their own artistic careers. The underground sect – who always wears gorilla masks when in public – takes the names of dead women artists. It was as if all the forsaken women artists from history were rising in torment from their graves.

As the great cultural bastions of New York tried to guess who the Guerrilla Girls were, the troupe hit randomly at gallery openings and shows. Gallery owners saw the attacks as a social conspiracy against them; many proprietors would not speak out for fear that their studios would be trashed. Rumours spread like wildfire – mingling with the facts – until it was no longer possible to distinguish actually how daring the Guerrilla Girls had been.

There are stories of galleries being daubed with slogans, of guests at grand society launches being trussed up with ropes, and tales of gallery owners having bottles of vintage red wine poured over them. And, as the art world speculated on the Guerrilla Girls, their spies, working at the city's artistic treasure-houses, helped co-ordinate battle plans – relaying information to the Girls' secret nerve centre downtown.

Among the main targets have been the most respected showcases of the art world, such as The Metropolitan Museum of Art, The Guggenheim and The Whitney. Demonstrations take different forms depending on the whim and fancy of the Guerrilla Girls. Sometimes they turn up *en masque* to cause havoc with the authorities, in other instances they plaster galleries and art museums with their lewd, hard-hitting posters. Always, they aim to deride the brotherhood of male gallery owners and dealers in control.

As their campaign gained momentum, gathering support from other feminists within the community, the Guerrilla Girls began to appear on talk shows and on lecture circuits: always appearing in primate masks. Prominent gallery owners defended the lack of women artists they represented, by saying that women were just 'less productive' as male artists. At the same time, they played down the extent of the Guerrilla Girls' infamous assaults.

For a decade New Yorkers have been divided over whether the *Monkey Women*, as they have become known, are a worthy cause, or just another clique on the lunatic fringe. 'If I ever got one of them in my cab,' says Lou Shrender – a yellow cab driver for thirty-two years, 'I'd rip off her mask and take her to the police station. They've got nice cages at the police precincts, just right for a gorilla. People are sick of the Guerrilla Girls: they play the media like a fiddle – everyone's frightened of speaking out against them for fear of being seen as sexist.'

Most gallery owners – like Pat Hearn of the well-respected Hearn Gallery – are careful to praise the cause of the Guerrilla Girls. After all, one's never sure where Guerrilla Girl spies are lurking. 'The Guerrilla Girls are no joke,' says Hearn. 'People take them very seriously in New York. I feel that their anonymity makes them a much more credible force. I, for one, would never try to find out who they really are.'

Alice Neel, self-styled Queen of the Guerrilla Girls, rests in the underground hide-out. The chamber is shaken every few minutes by a passing subway train. 'We want to make feminism fashionable again,' she says through the mask's set of snarling yellow teeth. 'It's for us to show that feminists are a broad spectrum of women – they come in all shapes, forms and colours. People used to think that feminists came in one style… that was the media's manipulation of the word "feminist".'

'Guerrilla Girls are anonymous because we want the issues we support to take centre stage, not individuals. The Guerrilla Girls are from a long tradition of masked avengers which include Robin Hood, Batman and Wonder Woman. I can't tell you how many of us there are – maybe there are a hundred, maybe a hundred thousand.'

Under the deep cover of their secret lair, the Guerrilla Girls plot their next moves. Like any revolutionary unit, they spend hours planning which institutions to abase, and the individuals to lambaste. For such an enraged feminist sect, no member of society is more loathsome than the white male.

'The majority of power is in the hands of white men,' says Alice Neel as she adjusts her gorilla head. 'Most gallery owners, dealers and art critics are white men. It's obvious that if you're a white male you see things in a certain way. Your vision – which is going to be a white male one… is therefore going to be limited.'

Despising the white masculine sector of society as they do, the Guerrilla Girls are careful to tow a diplomatic line at all times. 'We're not talking about eliminating white men altogether,' cautions Alice Neel, 'we're advocating an opening up of the field to let in other sensibilities as well. That's what the battle's all about!'

As well as being hailed as heroes by their admirers, the Guerrilla Girls are denounced by those they attack. 'We get a lot of hate mail,' says Neel, 'one guy wrote a long seething letter blaming us for AIDS. He went on and on that we were a bunch of dykes who were forcing women to hate men, and we were spreading AIDS to men as revenge.'

Over the first five years of Guerrilla Girl combat, New Yorkers witnessed a subtle and gradual shift in the art world. The major museums and plush galleries introduced exhibitions of female artists. But it's impossible to say whether the welcoming of more female artwork was a result of guerrilla tactics, or the effect of the current era of political correctness.

As the fans of the Guerrilla Girls insisted that their attacks were making headway, the masked feminist avengers made a dramatic shift of their own. 'With the onslaught of the first Gulf War,' says Gertrude Stein, Guerrilla Girl, 'we couldn't ignore the fact that President Bush's administration would go to war over oil. We knew that the Gulf War was very wrong. At the same time we realized that a lot of issues were affecting us as artists and women.' Within days, the wrath of women throughout society seemed to be voiced by the new and omnipotent Guerrilla movement. The white male-dominated art world took a deep sigh of relief, as the feminists in woolly masks turned their attentions to government.

A caustic campaign began against both the major American political parties. *The Monkey Women* blamed the Republicans for the breaking down of society: insisting that they were in some way responsible for female circumcision, breast implants, liposuction and even foot-binding. Observers – including many Guerrilla Girl followers – were confused by what the Republicans had to do with the ancient Chinese foot-binding. Opponents to their causes, contended that the Girls had progressed from the lunatic fringe to the asylum itself.

Another campaign hit hard at the Democrats for their policies on homelessness, on gay issues, rape and abortion. The Guerrilla Girls' prominent posters mock the establishment from every wall: (*Q. What's the difference been a prisoner of war and a homeless person? A. Under the Geneva Convention, a prisoner of war is entitled to food shelter & medical care*).

Every time New York's establishment is struck by a shocking act, the Guerrilla Girls' involvement is called into question. But, as the scope of Guerrilla Girl activities widens, a new and possibly devastating situation is taking effect.

Encouraged by the group's success, a spate of Guerrilla Girl impersonators have hit the street. Although discredited by the bona fide G.G. movement, the recent radical Guerrilla wave of rhetoric is threatening to undermine the original Guerrilla Girl triumphs.

'When the Guerrilla Girls started out they had the right idea,' says Mary Cassatt – leader of a Guerrilla Girl splinter group. 'But now they've gone soft… they get paid thousands for lecturing at colleges – they've lost their focus.'

Mary Cassatt and her faction of hardened Guerrillas operates out of a secret East Village location. 'We refuse to sell out like the founders of the movement have done,' continues Cassatt. 'If necessary we'll resort to violence – we have to get the message across to a new generation, and we'll do whatever it takes!'

Nearby, at her own secret den, Alice Neel – an original Guerrilla Girl – is wary of upcoming factions. 'New groups calling themselves Guerrilla Girls are sprouting up,' she splutters through the growling disguise. 'We encourage others to use our methods but to distinguish themselves from us and our own work. The Guerrilla Girls are inherent to New York… our habitat is SoHo.'

Los Angeles, Dallas, Boston and Phoenix have all spawned their own G. G. splinter groups. Dozens more have appeared around the world as far afield as Mexico City, Berlin and Melbourne as well. And, as the subversive masked feminist message spreads like wildfire, newer and more radical pseudo Guerrilla Girl units are being born.

Back in New York the original movement is challenging the system with ever more political rhetoric. And, as the neo-radical branches of the Guerrillas defame officialdom, the unique poster art of the Guerrilla Girls is being snapped up by collectors. In a strange and unlikely irony, those eager to pay top dollar for the sorority's art, are the New York Public Library, The Spencer and The Whitney Museums – all of which have been scourged by the Girls in the past.

The Khalili Collection of Islamic Art

DAVID NASSER KHALILI was born to collect.

As the son and grandson of dealers in carpets, lacquerware and other art in Isfahan, one of the greatest cities of ancient Persia and now Iran's second city, Khalili himself maintains that from age fourteen he dreamed of amassing one of the greatest art collections in the world.

It is a dream which took decades, a discerning eye and a fortune to realize, but a dream that came true nonetheless. The result, the Khalili Collection embraces virtually every known area of craftsmanship ever pursued in Islamic lands. There are illuminated copies of the Qur'an, rare manuscripts and miniatures, papyri, calligraphy, ceramics, metalwork, talismans and seals, carpets and textiles, gems, coins, glass, jewel-encrusted daggers and medieval armour, astrolabes, maps, padlocks, stirrups and even more, all of it packed in vaults and warehouses around the world, awaiting a permanent home.

In many areas, the Khalili Collection is regarded as world class. The illuminated copies of the Qur'an number more than five hundred, compared to the British Library's modest fifty, and they comprise one of the largest groups of fine Quranic manuscripts in private hands anywhere. The collection, that has grown exponentially since the early 1970s now lists more than twenty thousand items.

But all this is more than just a private indulgence. Nasser's ultimate vision is that the collection will further spur the world's appreciation of the artistic contributions of Islamic cultures. To this end, he insists that in his collecting he has not been 'mesmerized by objects made for kings and queens', and has attended also to the products of craftsmen made for everyday life.

Honorary curator of the Khalili Collection, Professor Michael Rogers, says Khalili's achievement has been to buy in areas in which there's been little interest to buy before. He's not merely interested in the beautiful or the exquisite, but in the curious as well.

'As a result,' Rogers says, 'the collection has shed a completely new light on practically every aspect of Islamic art. For the first time it will be possible to see the whole history of the cultures of Islam from the beginnings right up to the nineteenth century.'

The Khalili Collection, he adds, 'is far more systematic and historical in approach than the collections of either the Victoria and Albert Museum or the British Museum.'

David Khalili himself is soft-spoken yet confident, in the manner of one whose seemingly impossible success has come as no grand surprise to himself. Sitting straight-backed at his north London research centre, he tells a little of the story of his passion. Beside him, an expert works meticulously on the restoration of a tenth-century rose-tinted cameo-glass bowl.

'I grew up in Iran,' he begins gently, 'a country of Islamic culture which played a major role in the development of Islamic art. My father loved Islamic art, so I was brought up to appreciate it. Dealing in art and collecting is our family tradition; it was only natural that I should follow in my father's and grandfather's footsteps. I was drawn at first to Islamic lacquer. I was amazed by the quality of the painting and the absolute mastery that the craft required.'

In 1967, Khalili left Tehran bound for New York. Having earned a bachelor's degree in computer sciences, he was by the early 1970s ready to begin building on the foundations of his father's and grandfather's trade.

For any serious collector of Islamic art, the world's best marketplace is not in the Middle East. It is in London. During the centuries of Empire, a great many Islamic antiques made their way – legitimately and illegitimately – to England.

The thriving Islamic art market of the 1970s captivated Khalili. On trips from Iran, he began to frequent Sotheby's, Christie's and Phillips', the three leading auction houses at the time. His initial purchases were narrowly focused. From the outset, he bought Persian lacquerware, his first love in Islamic art, which, until the 1980s, was also regarded as undervalued. In 1978, when prices in much of the Islamic art market fell, setting off panic, Khalili kept on buying. This raised a few eyebrows, and earned the newcomer a measure of respect from London's established old-timers.

It was also in 1978 that Khalili, seeking to buy a gift, walked into a jeweller's shop on Bond Street. The woman across the counter was Marion Easton. Khalili proposed, and the two married later that year.

In 1980, they moved to London for good, and it was then that David Khalili began to buy on an unprecedented scale. Throughout the early 1980s, he bought and sold out of a gallery in London's fashionable Mayfair.

Many art dealers maintain that Khalili achieved the status and credibility of a serious collector upon his purchase of the fabled manuscript of *Jami' al-Tawarikh*, the 'Universal History' of Rashid al-Din, produced in Tabriz in 1314. Full of illustrations from the life of the Prophet Muhammad, it is widely considered the finest medieval manuscript ever produced in East or West. It was at the time the most expensive of its kind ever sold.

Khalili's low-profile, unassuming manner enabled him to purchase an enormous number of objects without attracting commensurate public attention. But by the mid-1980s, however, he was buying such sensational quantities, at equally sensational prices, that the art world began to run with rumours. Khalili missed no opportunity, and scooped up many of the finest pieces in every gallery and every auction house. He no longer focused entirely on Islamic art, either, and went on to create another important collection, Meiji-period Japanese art.

The most discussed – and least answerable – question of all was, where did Khalili get his money? On this point he has always remained silent, maintaining that it is his private affair. Khalili continued buying – and buying – and replied to the press in only the most general of terms: His wealth, he said, was the result of successful business dealings in sugar and coffee, on the options market, in real estate in the British Isles and abroad, and, of course, in works of art.

The announcement that Khalili was in fact purchasing for the Nour Foundation (the name means 'Light'), owned by the Khalili family trust, came as a surprise to many in the trade who had assumed all along that Khalili was actually buying on behalf of another collector.

Khalili had, after all, written a catalogue of the Islamic art collection belonging to the Sultan of Brunei. 'The Nour Foundation,' Khalili says, 'was formed many years ago by my father, to promote an understanding and appreciation of the great heritage of Islamic art.'

In the mid-'eighties, Khalili began work on a doctoral dissertation at London's School of Oriental and African Studies (SOAS). In 1988, he presented his research on eighteenth- and nineteenth-century Persian lacquerware, his enduring love in Islamic art. Like almost no other student before him, Khalili was able to study largely within his own collection.

Not long afterward, he underwrote a $1 million chair of Islamic art at SOAS and a research fellowship in Islamic art at the University of Oxford. The University of London named him an honorary fellow and appointed him to its governing body. Khalili found a donor to give $16 million for a new Islamic Centre at the University of London, which complements Khalili's endowed professorship, mounting exhibitions of Islamic art and provides a centre for research.

Today, Khalili is buying less and preparing more for the research and display dimensions of his collection. On this, he is straightforward: 'The plan has always been first to conserve and document the collection in its entirety, publish it, and then to house it in a museum.'

Almost every item in the vast collection has been catalogued on a scale befitting the collection's value. A single, overall catalogue of the greatest masterpieces was authored by Rogers, at the time that Khalili was Professor of Islamic Art at SOAS. But this volume was only a prelude.

A full series of thirty catalogues was produced, huge tomes that contained comprehensive scholarship and study. Directed not only to the academic and the collector, but to lay people as well, the catalogues include essays on particular themes in Islamic art. To assist him in organizing, drafting, and producing the catalogues, Khalili hired the world's leading authorities in each field of study. More than thirty specialists were contracted along with a full editorial team, an in-house illustrator, a photographer, and one of the world's most distinguished book designers, Misha Anikst.

In selecting scholars, Khalili comments, 'I am also keen on introducing new blood into the system. Some of the young scholars, many of whose names have not been familiar to most, have actually made valuable contributions to the catalogues. These will combine both scholarship with visual splendour.'

Produced in a large format on acid-free paper, the photographs were complemented with technical drawings, to reveal delicate details so characteristic of Islamic art. 'We are not cutting any corners,' says Khalili, 'but are aiming at the highest standards.' He adds that the books, published by the Nour Foundation in association with Azimuth Editions, cost far more to produce than the profits made by sales. Such subsidization, he believes, will give them the wider readership they deserve.

Dr. Julian Raby, general editor of the catalogues and lecturer in Islamic art at the Oriental Institute at Oxford, was taken by surprise by the scale of the publishing task. 'When I began,' he says, 'I didn't realize what I was taking on. I knew it was big, but didn't really have a sense of just how big. Indeed, I think there are only a handful of people working on the collection who do.'

Working closely with Khalili and designer Anikst, Raby has encouraged authors to highlight and emphasize what they, as individual art historians, are excited about in the collection. This spotlight approach, focusing on an object, a group of objects, or a particular issue, has resulted in a series of essays intended as a contribution to the scholarship of the subject. Since some of the catalogues consider overlapping areas of the collection, certain items will be studied from one or more viewpoints.

'Where the Khalili Collection differs,' Raby says, 'is that it's so large that it can be reconfigured in different ways. It's not telling a simple story. It has not got one simple vision. Two traditions determine the make-up of most private collections today. One is that of the connoisseur, with a few select items chosen for their aesthetic merit. The other is the philatelic approach, where the emphasis of the collector is on assembling complete series of objects. The Khalili Collection is remarkable in that it belongs, as it were, to the heroic age of collecting, for it combines both these traditions within an overall scheme of providing a synoptic vision of the arts of the entire Islamic world. What I particularly enjoy about the collection,' he says, 'are some of the more quirky, whimsical sequences. 'I said to one of the authors who is writing the *Science, Tools and Magic* volume, "We have some padlocks you might like to put into this part of the collection." He asked, "How many?" I said, "Three hundred and forty-seven!" Since then, it's grown by another six hundred!'

In addition to the catalogue series, the Nour Foundation embarked on a series of books focusing on specific areas of Islamic art. Entitled *Studies in the Khalili Collection*, this second series was aimed at students and academics. The first volume in the series, a supplemental study of thirty-six papyri titled *Arabic Papyri*, was published in 1992. Along with its main volume, *Letters, Bills and Records: Arabic Papyri From Egypt*, the book offers an unprecedented look at writing in the first three centuries of Islam.

Science, Tools and Magic covers astrology, astronomy, medicine and magic. Included was the collection's large number of astrolabes, globes, quadrants, scientific manuscripts and geomantic devices. In addition, it features practical items like padlocks, scissors, tweezers, spoons and weights and balances.

Since the written word is a central feature of Islam, calligraphy is of particular importance. Respected scholar Dr. Nabil Safwat says the volume on calligraphy 'has been written from the calligrapher's point of view.' It focuses on the collection's vast cache of exceptional calligraphic pieces. And, in a selection of accompanying essays, Dr. Safwat highlights central themes in Islamic calligraphy that until now have been almost unknown to readers of the English language – such as *muraqqa'*.

From the Arabic root *ruq'ah*, *muraqqa'* translates as 'patch', or a patch-work of pieces of exemplary calligraphy. Whether a complete volume or a single page, such manuscripts acted as calligrapher's source books.

The collection houses various examples of the finest *muraqqa'* ever made; pride of place goes to the so-called Royal Muraqqa' that combines the work of several grand masters of Islamic calligraphy – Shaykh Hamdullah, Hafiz Osman and Mehmet Rasim – on a single sheet.

In a third series of publications, the Nour Foundation also produced a selection of unabridged facsimile manuscripts. The first, says general editor Raby, was a reproduction of the work of the sixteenth-century Ottoman cartographer Piri Reis, whose 1513 world map included information derived from a map by Christopher Columbus that has never been found. Another provides a facsimile edition of the illustrated *Jami' al-Tawarikh* manuscript, the Universal History, which includes detailed studies of the miniatures as well as a translation and critical analysis of the text.

'Collecting,' Khalili says, 'is a fairly private activity. And it is my belief that, even if someone owns the greatest collection of art in the world, that collection is of no consequence so long as it is hidden from public view. There is a Persian proverb that is often used to decorate works of art: "Ultimately, all possessions are God's alone; we are but custodians."'

As chairman of the Nour Foundation, Lord Young of Graffham negotiated with the British government in the hope of establishing a London museum to house the Khalili Collection. The foundation's offer to lend the twenty thousand-piece collection for an initial period of fifteen years was met, however, with the skepticism.

In Britain there was no precedent for such a loan, and the cost of constructing a new museum was deemed too considerable. The offer was rejected.

All that is certain now, Khalili says, is that a museum will be built. But where is still a question. 'You will have a museum with more than twenty thousand items which have been fully restored, conserved, catalogued, photographed and published even before it has opened its doors. We will be giving Islamic art the credit it deserves, perhaps for the first time on this scale.'

And what a scale it will be.

The collection's Qur'anic manuscripts stretch from the first century of Islam until the late 1800s. Almost every type and subtype of Umayyad and Abbasid script categories is represented, often in rare complete manuscripts. Among them is the giant *Baysunghur* copy of the Qur'an, written for Timur Leng (Tamerlane) by the calligrapher 'Umar Aqta. The story goes that, in trying to impress the great Timur, 'Umar produced a copy of the Qur'an so small that it could slip beneath the signet ring of the great ruler. When Timur remained unimpressed,

'Umar went away and produced another copy, this one so huge it had to be wheeled into court on a cart.

The collection also houses the only copy of the Qur'an from twelfth-century Valencia known to be in private hands. Other copies of the Qur'an, originating from as far afield as Sicily and India, include one measuring a mere forty-seven by thirty-seven millimetres (1.85" by 1.45"), thought to have been written in fourteenth century Iraq.

As well as numerous astrolabes, the Khalili Collection houses some of the finest celestial globes in existence. One example was crafted by Muhammad ibn Mahmud al-Tabari in 1285 and 1286, and inlaid with more than a thousand silver dots indicating the major stars of various constellations. It is the original of an almost identical globe in the Louvre in Paris.

Khalili's Islamic coins number over eight thousand, forming one of the most voluminous numismatic collections of its kind in private hands. Nearly ten per cent of them are either unique or unpublished, and more than twelve hundred are gold. Coins appear from across the Islamic world, from Africa to Asia. Of particular interest are the earliest Arab gold coins from North Africa, which bear Latin inscriptions. Others include a rare Abbasid dinar struck in the year 750, two more Abbasid dinars issued by Harun ar-Rashid in 787 and 788, and a variety of exquisite gold Qajar tomans.

No less diverse is a wide range of figures and figurines. Fashioned to function as door knockers, incense burners, jugs, and other useful objects, they demonstrate that the prohibition of portraying figures in Islam has, historically, often been ignored.

Dr. Sabiha Khemir, the author of the volume entitled *Figures and Figurines: Sculptures of the Islamic Lands*, points out that the Qur'an warns explicitly against the worship of idols. One of the most intriguing figures in the collection is that of a kneeling, bearded man thought to portray the Seljuk ruler Tughril Beg at prayer. It was produced in Kashan, Iran, under the Mongols in the thirteenth century.

The ceramics' collection illuminates a thousand years of Islamic pottery. The two thousand items include an unparalleled collection of twelfth- and thirteenth-century Afghan pottery, rare Iznik pieces, early lustre-painted bowls and an extremely rare polychrome painted

Persian bowl from the tenth century, incorporating a representation of the Prophet's steed, Buraq.

The more than a thousand pieces of metal-work range from an early Islamic silver ewer in the Sassanian style to a rare thirteenth-century *jazirah* casket that once had an unusual combination lock, and an Ottoman silver fountain ladle dated 1577 or 1578.

Deputy curator of the Khalili Collection and co-author of the volume on Islamic metalwork, Nahla Nassar, says the metalwork collection 'emphasizes similarities'. So numerous are the examples, she says, that 'one can judge how a style has changed and developed' over time and distance.

Islamic weaponry in the collections ranges from the most elegant of daggers to an important group of early stirrups. 'The arms and armor in the collection,' says Dr. David Alexander, author of the collection's volume *The Arts of War*, 'include items as varied and widely separated as a Crusader sword from the Mameluk arsenal at Alexandria and an eighteenth-century cannon from the palace of Tipu Sultan at Mysore.' Of historical importance is the sword of the Sudanese warlord Ali Dinar, taken after his defeat and death in 1916. Alexander's volume includes discussions of the belt in Islamic culture, the use of talismanic shirts, the ceremonial drum, and the advent of gunpowder.

In complete contrast to the weaponry is the assembly of Islamic glassware. Through the three hundred pre-Islamic and Islamic pieces, one can trace the entire story of glass-making. The collection's cut glass and cameo vessels dating to the tenth and eleventh centuries are unequalled. With walls as thin as a tenth of a millimetre it seems miraculous that such pieces have survived the centuries at all.

Inspired as he was in childhood by Persian lacquerware, Khalili now holds the largest collection of lacquer objects in the world – more than five hundred penboxes, bookbindings, mirror cases and caskets.

It will take a substantial museum to do justice to the collection. Khalili wants that museum – regardless of the city in which it is built – to be a dynamic place, not just an exhibition hall of echoing footsteps.

Creating a fossilized museum is the last thing on my mind,' he says. 'There are millions of Muslims in Europe. A centre for Islamic art will work on different levels. It will show non-Muslim Europeans that their

Muslim fellow-citizens are heirs to a great tradition that deserves their respect. It will stop them thinking of Muslims only in terms of fundamentalists, terrorists and hostage-takers. It will also give European Muslims access to their own culture, and make them even more proud of it.'

'People from the forty-six Muslim countries have different traditions, and speak different languages. What unites them is their religion and the artistic heritage which was shaped by that religion,' he continues. 'It is true that until recently most scholars in the field were non-Muslims, but that's changing dramatically as Islamic countries wake up to the importance of their artistic heritage.'

'The moment has come for the "People of the Book" – Jews, Christians and Muslims – to speak openly to one another and to see clearly the close cultural, social, spiritual and intellectual ties that have existed among them for centuries.'

The Laughter Club

As DAWN BREAKS over Mumbai, a group of figures hurries through the morning shadows.

Moving without a word, they assemble silently at the middle of a field, not far from the city centre. Then, as the first rays of crisp morning light stream down, the gathering take their places for what is surely Mumbai's most mysterious ritual.

A distant clock-tower strikes seven a.m. and, as it does so, the congregation of seventy begin.

First, the members of the clan stand tall, hands above their heads. Then, in perfect synchronization, they start to smile. The smiles turn into giggles. The giggles become heavier sniggering. Moments later, the sniggering has become gut-wrenching laughter. By this point, a modest group of onlookers are exchanging uneasy glances. And, as they do so, the members of the secret league before them, are gyrating wildly – with arms thrashing, heads rolling, and feet stamping, in unison.

Meet Mumbai's most recent sensation: meet 'The Laughter Club International'.

Founded a year ago in north Mumbai, the Laughter Club meets each morning at fifty locations across the city. Its members believe that the most effective way of maintaining good health is by staying happy. And, they say, there's no better way to get healthy, than to giggle yourself fit.

In our drug-obsessed society, doctors who have endorsed the use of comedy as a cure, have themselves tended to become the laughing stock. But, the tide on 'Laughter Therapy' seems to be changing. At last, hospitals across Europe and America have begun to reassess the merits of happiness and humour to patients. Researchers taking a good look at other societies, have noticed that humour and health have always gone together.

We know that healing centres in ancient Greece were located near amphitheatres – so that patients could use comedy as part of their treatment. Research shows, also, that remote tribes – living as far apart as South America, Africa and New Guinea – have held special festivals of laughter to boost public morale. All the major religions have incorporated humour in their scriptures: realising that, as well as healing, mirth makes the student more receptive to absorbing key ideas.

Sanjna joined The Laughter Club at Mumbai's Hanging Gardens last October. A regular participant, she's found that the early morning laughter sessions give her a sense of exhilaration which lasts all day long.

'I know that laughing yourself fit sounds a bit unlikely,' she says with a grin, 'but there's no better way to greet the world each morning than by rolling about, and laughing at it!'

Like most in her group, Sanjna was introduced by a friend. 'When a pal told me about laughter fitness,' she remembers, 'I burst out in hysterics. It was the funniest thing I'd ever heard! So I came down and took a look. Before I knew it, I was hooked.'

Laughter Club International – which is spreading across India fast – was the brainchild of Dr. Madan Kataria, a respected Mumbai GP. His first session attracted just five members. The media was scathing, mocking what they thought was an insane idea. But within a week, Dr. Kataria had a following of one hundred.

A month later, membership was in the thousands, with Laughter Clubs mushrooming up all over Mumbai. The doctor's appointments' book is filled for months to come. And, across the sub-continent – from Calcutta to Calicut – people are clamouring for Laughing Clubs to be established in their cities.

'At The Laughter Club we're applying what's been know for centuries,' explains Dr. Kataria. 'Laughter makes a person feel great – it aids relaxation, reduces shyness and fights depression: but its benefits for far deeper. Scientific studies on humour show that a good belly-ripping chortle once or twice a day can do wonders for the body's mental and physical processes.'

Kataria points to Yogic texts – over five thousand years in age – which mention laughter as an effective method for breathing control.

'Laughter has been applied, almost like a tool or antidote, for millennia, he continues, 'yet it seems that we're just re-learning its powers now. But, perhaps more importantly, we are now understanding that the effects of laughter are multiple.'

A bout of hardy laughter helps increase the lung capacity and expels residual air. This is good for asthmatics and those with bronchitis. People with high blood pressure and cardiac problems find that blood pressure levels are reduced drastically by the end of a twenty-minute session. Others claim that the laughter drill in the morning cures insomnia that night; or that their complexion improves from the increased blood circulation to the face.'

Mumbai, the birthplace of the Laughter Club, is a city that's adept at surprising. The thought of several thousand people meeting to guffaw their hearts out for twenty minutes at dawn, is strange. But stranger still is the fact that, at The Laughter Club International, joke-telling is prohibited.

'When The Laughter Club was founded we used to tell jokes,' intones Dr. Kataria, looking sombre for a moment. 'But we soon found out that we were experiencing problems. Some jokes cause dissent when they are aimed at fellow members of society. Others offend because they are dirty. 'But,' continues Kataria with a sudden look of worry, 'the main cause for the ban was that one day the supply of jokes may run out!'

Rather than ever face a world devoid of new wise-cracks, The Laughter Club dealt with the problem right from the start. Forbidding all one-liners (however hilarious), it taught people to laugh on cue instead. Research has proven that even 'artificial' giggles have beneficial results. So, Dr. Kataria decided to use synthetic laughter at the start of each session. This, he found suddenly gives way to genuine chuckling, and on to the belly-aching laughter we all know and love.

Another sunrise, and Sanjna is back at Mumbai's Hanging Gardens, ready for action. Her group – around eighty people – stands in a half circle. The atmosphere is cheerful. Some members break into laughter spontaneously, even before the 'workout' has begun. But, despite the intermittent giggles, there isn't a joke book in sight.

Suddenly, without prompting, everyone's clapping their hands together. This begins the concentration, and gets the laughers synchronized. The group leader speeds the clapping up. Then, he bellows 'Ho ho ho, ha ha ha', sounds which, those serious about their trade, believe are the key components of laughter. As well as acting as an artificial 'flux' from which genuine laughter can ignite, the prelude brings people out of their shells, helping them to relax. Seconds later, and with arms high above her head, fingers jarring wildly, Sanjna's grin erupts into a head-rocking frenzy of laughter. Her long plaited hair waves about wildly; and her gleaming white teeth flash, as her face turns deep crimson.

As the roaring waves of laughter begin to subside, the anchor person initiates the next routine. 'Giggling without making a noise. A favourite with Sanjna and her friends, it helps rekindle the real laughter. 'It looks so stupid to see someone laughing in silence,' whispers Sanjna, pausing for breath, 'it's like out of a silent movie – just watching everyone else is enough to make you roll about on the floor!' And, as Sanjna nears the point of collapse through hilarity, the leader moves on to the next exercise. Known as 'laughing with the lips closed', the technique is aimed at increasing the pressure on the lungs.

The exercise, which is recommended for asthmatics, ends with everyone coughing. 'It brings up all the mucus from your lungs,' explains Sanjna as she wipes tears from her eyes, 'you can feel the blood surging round your body and face – it's wonderful!'

With the exercise class nearing its twentieth minute, the laughers embark on their most strenuous routine – the 'free-style laugh'. A no limits, no holes barred technique, the 'free-style' encourages members to lift laughter to new heights. The eighty members, ranging from small children to octogenarians, suddenly seem paralysed with ecstatic happiness. Their guffaws, which can be heard far away from the park, attract a growing number of avid spectators. 'We're delighted when people stop and have a giggle,' says Shamoli, 'having a chuckle is where it begins. We may look like a scene out of a Hitchcock film, but so many people who stop to watch, end up joining The Laughter Club themselves.'

Shamoli, a nurse at a large Mumbai hospital, needs no convincing of the powers of laughter. 'Of course this isn't the panacea for all ills,' she continues in a shrill voice, 'but laughter is undoubtedly one of the best supplementary medicines for any kind of illness. The female members of The Laughter Club find that the exercises help reduce period pains, as well as keeping their skin supple and blemish free. Women take laughter very seriously – I think they take anything seriously that they have one hundred per cent belief in. Laughter is like a magic wand in our stressful lives…it puts a smile on your face and massages your internal organs at the same time!'

As The Laughter Club sweeps India, humour seems to be catching on elsewhere, as well. In Europe, where people are more prone to sneer rather than smile, happiness is catching on in a big way.

'Laughter is a cheap, ozone-friendly form of energy,' explains Robert Holden, author of *Laughter, The Best Medicine*. 'Since the 1950s well over five hundred medical research papers have been published on the medicinal value of mirth. And psychologists have presented over a thousand papers on the subject since the 1940s. Modern medicine and psychology are at last catching up with ancient schools of common sense!'

Holden, who founded the Britain's first 'Laughter Clinic', now trains over ten thousand health professionals each year. His courses, which stress the medicinal importance of happiness and laughter, preach that we should re-think our medical system. 'Hospitals tend to be cold, damp, characterless places with the stench of disinfectant,' says Holden, a man in an ever-jubilant mood, 'if we want people to laugh and smile, we have to do something about their surroundings first.'

The eminent cardiologist, Dr. William Fry, like Robert Holden, is outspoken about laughter. He believes that one minute of laughter is worth forty minutes of deep relaxation; and that one hundred laughs a day are equal to a ten minute jog. A real belly laugh, he says, exercises not only the heart and lungs, but the shoulder muscles, arms, abdomen, diaphragm and legs. And exercising the major muscle groups is only the start.

Fry's research has advanced the threshold of laughter therapy, by looking at laughter as a pain-reducer. Recent studies have shown that laughing – whether genuine or 'artificial' – pumps pain-relieving, stress-freeing, endorphins into the bloodstream. Hospitals of the future could well offer a choice between a dose of jokes and a shot of morphine. This may sound ridiculous, but it's already begun...

When Norman Cousins contracted a rare spinal disease, he was given a one in five hundred chance of survival. Cousins, the long-time editor of America's *Saturday Review*, decided that after years of prolonged pain from illness, he would give up on drugs. Instead he designed for himself a radical new course of treatment.

The regimen was focussed on laughter as a medical remedy. Whenever the pain became unbearable, Cousins instructed his nurse to switch on the video. He would watch his old favourites – Laurel and Hardy escapades, or the Marx Brothers movies – sometimes around the clock.

Cousins learned that five minutes of laughter would work as an anaesthetic, giving him up to two hours' of pain relief at a time. In the weeks that followed he quite literally laughed his pain away.

At his small office in the suburbs of Mumbai, Dr. Kataria is planning his next moves. The doctor, who has just heard of Montreal's Museum of Humour and Laughter, is keen to establish an Indian version in Mumbai.

But, perhaps, before that, he's eager that Laughter Clubs should be launched in Europe and the USA. 'We are getting calls from all over the world,' says Kataria, as the phone rings with another inquiry. 'Our clubs are simple – we don't use any expensive equipment... we don't even need to buy joke books... so we don't make any charges at all. How can we charge people to laugh?'

Glancing at a folder of press clippings on the Laughter Club, Dr. Kataria smiles with modest pride.

'The media who have now seen the popularity in laughter therapy were quick to mock it at first. The Laughter Club International, it seems, is saving the last laugh for itself.'

The Magic of the Ordinary

THE OTHER DAY a man approached me down at the port.

I was waiting for a friend, a friend who is always late. As someone who moved to North Africa from northern Europe, I find it near impossible to be late myself. Punctuality is quite unfortunately in my blood. So, whenever my friend and I arrange a rendezvous, I always spend half an hour or more glancing at my watch, fussing at his tardiness and at my inability to learn from the past.

While I was standing there, a little on edge, and a little irritated at what I imagined to be a waste of time, a short stout figure in a tattered *jelaba* staggered towards me. On his cheeks was a fortnight's crop of tattered grey beard, and on his feet were a pair of grimy yellow *baboush*.

When he was close, his face fifty centimetres from my own, he put down the basket of fish he was carrying, cleared his throat, and began to laugh.

As I had the time to make use of my curiosity, I smiled politely, and enquired what the man found so amusing. He didn't answer at first. He was too busy wiping his eyes. But then, taking his time, he pressed his hands together, palms followed by fingertips.

'To understand the extraordinary,' he said all of a sudden, 'you must learn to appreciate ordinariness.'

I asked what he meant by what seemed to me like a random remark. The man touched a calloused finger to his cheek. Then he smiled. It wasn't a big toothy smile, but rather one that was very gentle. It filled me with a kind of warmth, as if something unspoken was being passed on. For a split second I thought the first remark was about to be followed by another. But the man lifted up his basket by the handle, shooed away a pair of cats that were now sitting before it optimistically, and he strode off towards the old medina.

For an instant I considered going after him.

I sensed my weight shifting forward from my back foot. But then, in the moment before stillness became animation, my friend arrived. He spat out an excuse, something about his mother-in-law and a kilo of lamb, and we went for tea.

For an hour, as my friend rambled on about the challenges of his life, and as the waiter circled our table like a tired old shark, I thought about the man with the basket of fish.

I couldn't get him out of my mind.

At length, when our meeting was at an end, my friend and I exchanged pleasantries once again, good wishes for each other's families, and we parted. But I was on auto-pilot, because still, all I could think of was the man and the fish, and what he had said: *To understand the extraordinary you must learn to appreciate ordinariness.*

I have spent twenty years in search of the extraordinary. I've written books about my quests for it, and have made television documentaries about it too. I have ranted on to anyone prepared to listen about the glorious energy, the sheer intensity, of the unusual and the unexpected. I've risked my life in the mountain ranges of Afghanistan, and in the jungles of the Upper Amazon, and have surmounted all sorts of difficulties, on the trail of oddities and the bizarre.

Through each of those years, the extraordinary has been my currency, one that I have hoarded and squandered, and enjoyed with every breath. And in all that time, the months and years in celebration of the peculiar, I have never given any thought or time to considering the exquisiteness of the ordinary form. It had always seemed like comparing consommé to goulash, a delicacy unlikely to satisfy the appetite of a starving man.

But the stray remark at the Casablanca port changed my outlook in the most unexpected way. It coaxed me to appreciate a secret underbelly of ordinariness, a layer of existence so profound, that it is extraordinary within itself.

I have come to believe that we receive things when we are ready to receive them. Like seeds falling on arable land, the right conditions must be present for them to germinate and prosper. Our ability to appreciate takes place in very much the same way. We see, *really* see, when we are ready to, and not a moment before.

What I find so bewitching is the way the world slips you a jewel when it knows you are prepared to recognize it as a jewel. Equally, you could say there are jewels all around us, but ones that will only be activated for our particular perception in days and years to come.

The amusing thing for me is that, these days, glossy style magazines the world over devote acres of space to their fantasy of Morocco. It's a destination that's regarded as wildly exotic, rapturously appealing because it mirrors – or surpasses – our own imagination. But most of the time the media's fantasy doesn't reflect the genuine article at all.

To understand this extraordinary kingdom, you must understand the ordinary, and hold it tight to your heart. Three rusty chairs on a terrace by the sea, the shadow of a man moving quickly across warm tarmac, a fragment of graffiti on a mottled old wall: this is Morocco, *real* Morocco, the place those of us who live here yearn for when we are gone.

On my travels I have crisscrossed this country. I have visited desert shrines and mosques, palaces, bazaars and citadels. And in the wake of those journeys, I have regaled my audience with tales of colour and mystery. But I have never told them of the silent moments: a thousand meals alone with a worn old paperback, beaches naked of footprints, railway platforms in the rain. Such subtlety is rewarding beyond words if you can catch it, like a whisper on the wind.

This morning when I went to meet my friend, the one who's always late, I asked him something. I asked him to describe the beauty of his land to a person who had lost the power of their sight.

My friend thought for a long time before answering.

He seemed a little nervous, as if I were asking the impossible. Then he glanced out at the street.

'The real beauty of Morocco,' he said pensively, 'can only be seen from the inside out. Search from the outside in and you will never find the truth or the real beauty held within.'

The Mango Rains

I BELIEVE IN ZIGZAG TRAVEL.

Never has there been a route to anything more worthy than one which meanders through twists and turns. Over years and many miles I have tried and tested this zigzag approach, making use of the miscellany of material that presented itself along the way.

Of course, what's important is to be ready to receive.

Blink, and you miss the hidden signs. But, stay alert, be ready at all times, and the most magical rewards can be yours.

Never had the boon of zigzag travel been greater than in my search for the Mango Rains.

On a sweltering summer day an age ago, I was doing research in the back stacks of the London Library on the secret history of the Yezidis, self-styled 'People of the Peacock Angel'. It's a subject that has captured my attention for as long as I can remember, a family obsession – one that has led to all manner of escapades through five generations.

I was sitting at a low desk nudged up against the wall.

One eye was on the patterns of peeling green paint, the other on a rambling Victorian text about the Peacock Angel. I felt myself drift into a kind of psychotic state. Experience has taught me that this separation from reality is the perfect moment to grasp a path.

Rather than forcing my concentration back on the rows of hand-pressed type, I allowed it to meander. My gaze roamed over the shelves above me. Dusty leather bindings, gilt bands and faded script.

All of a sudden, and uncertain why, I reached up and picked out a book. It had brittle calfskin covers and smelled of faintly of beeswax. Opening it at random, I read:

The Mango Rains are an elixir all of their own. Some search their entire lives yet never have a hope of finding them. While others locate them without ever looking for them at all. Without having made a search, those who arrive too easily misunderstand the true essence of the treasure they have found. The best way to come upon the Mango Rains is to never stop looking and to question everything that passes before the eyes.

The book didn't reveal much more on these elusive rains, except to say that there was the chance to find them anywhere on Earth – so long as the searcher was prepared to recognize them.

For months, I dropped everything and scoured a dozen libraries for any mention of the Mango Rains.

I learned that the people of Suriname regarded them highly for the way they assisted in ripening the mango crop. And, I came to understand that the Portuguese in Goa had claimed they alone could cure those ailing from venereal disease.

As ever, my library research proved one thing: that the only way to reach conclusions was to abandon the books and set off on the open road.

I travelled through Africa and Europe, through the Americas, Asia, and beyond. While on these journeys I wrote about the people I met, and the situations in which they found themselves. Ever fascinated by observation, I found myself ripened, my rawness chapped by a new education, a kind I never thought possible. And, the more seasoned by travel I became, the more I wrote, and the more perceptive I found my observation to be.

Best of all, one horizon gave way to another, and one journey led to a dozen more.

On the savannah of the Rift Valley, I met a Samburu warrior. He was tall as a tree, his nimble form covered in bright beads and scarlet skins.

I asked if he had ever heard of the Mango Rains.

He led me to his village. It was a day's walk through scrub and long dry grass. When we got there, he took me to meet his grandfather, a man so old his body seemed somehow petrified.

My question was whispered into his ear.

After a long while, his eyes opened half way and he blinked.

'Does he know?' I asked.

The young warrior whispered again. And, this time, the wizened old man spoke.

'The Mango Rains are the Devil's work,' he said. 'Continue to search for them and Death will be your end.'

Undeterred, I set out again, roaming the world.

A chance encounter in Tokyo, led me on a trail that took me to heat-baked Alice Springs. And that journey ended at Manaus, in the Brazilian Amazon. The great city built on the fortune of the rubber barons was a wild rumpus of a place.

In a backstreet bar, not far from the opera hall in which Caruso played, I met a Swiss anthropologist called Frédérique. Sipping a gin and tonic thoughtfully, he told me the Mango Rains were a figment of Man's communal fear.

I asked what he meant.

'What I mean is that you should leave the Amazon. Follow your nose and never doubt.'

'But I have been following my nose,' I replied. 'That's how I ended up here!'

The Swiss wiped a hand to his lips.

'Very good,' he said, 'but believe me, there will be plenty more bounces before the rubber ball comes to a halt.'

Years of travels came and went.

Destinations with names I couldn't pronounce, and food that challenged my digestive tract. And all the while, I searched for the elusive Mango Rains.

Then, at dawn one morning I was walking along a beach on Mexico's Pacific Coast when, quite suddenly, it began to rain. It wasn't the heavy rain of a monsoon, but a gentle drizzle. Best of all, it was fragrant and had the scent of exotic fruit. I breathed it in deep, as if the smell were somehow healing me from the inside out.

As I was standing there, bathed in what seemed like a stream of perfection, a petite woman approached me. She had a postal sack slung over her shoulder, and was going down the beach picking up plastic bottles.

I felt a little embarrassed. But the woman seemed to understand. She laughed, a crazed maniacal cackle of a laugh.

'It's good!' she exclaimed.

'Yes, yes, it's wonderful,' I said.

'It's sent by God. Rich or poor, it's sent to us all.'

I nodded eagerly.

The woman began trudging towards a plastic bottle half buried in sand. Some distance from me, she turned her head and called out, 'Thank God for happiness! Thank God for these Mango Rains!'

The Mother Teresa Bandwagon

A HUNCHED FIGURE weaves his way through Calcutta's unending gridlock traffic.

Suspended from his neck is a broad tray, brimming with the usual assortment of tempting novelties with which to entice choking motorists. But instead of peddling fluorescent pink toothpicks or bottles of homemade rat-poison, the hawker is offering far more sought-after merchandise.

His tray is teeming with the latest in Mother Teresa kitsch.

Statuettes and baseball caps, ash-trays and candlesticks, calendars, alarm-clocks and cartons of incense: all bear the unmistakable, saintly image of a frail woman in a white sari with a royal blue hem.

Mother Teresa may be dead, but her spirit lives on, and her name is more strongly linked with Calcutta than ever. But, just as Princess Diana's legacy is awash with souvenir mugs and signed margarine tubs, Mother Teresa's memory is falling victim to her adoptive city's notorious blend of ingenuity. Everyone in Calcutta, it seems, from shoeshine boys to politicians, is clambering aboard the Mother Teresa money-making bandwagon.

In a bustling corner of central Calcutta, big plans are afoot.

S. S. Gupta, the city's former mayor, is busy co-ordinating elaborate schemes – all with a distinct Mother Teresa bent. A bulky, round-headed man, he defines his devotion to the cause in a silky, vote-winning voice:

'I met Mother Teresa many times when I was mayor – I even had my photograph taken with her,' he says. 'Now that she's dead, I have founded an organization called the Mother Teresa Memorial Committee.' He pauses to spit a mouthful of paan into a bucket beneath his desk. 'We want to mark Mother Teresa's first death anniversary in a special way. When Mother became a Nobel Laureate she became an icon of the world. As such, she belongs to us all!'

Mr. Gupta's committee is striving towards numerous big-budget goals. It plans to confer an annual honour – the Mother Teresa International Award – on a person who selflessly aids the needy. It is lobbying for Park Street, Calcutta's central thoroughfare, to be renamed Mother Teresa Sarani. And a Mother Teresa souvenir publication, replete with innumerable deluxe advertisements, is in preparation.

But of all Mr. Gupta's plans, the last is the most ambitious. A vast bronze statue of Mother Teresa has been commissioned by the committee and is under construction. If Mr. Gupta has his way, the towering effigy to Calcutta's most famous adopted daughter will be installed on a plinth in the centre of the city.

Across town at Mother House, the headquarters of Mother Teresa's Missionaries of Charity, there is unease at the committee's plans. The Missionaries have reason to be anxious. Within hours of Mother Teresa's death, the Sisters' planned funeral proceedings were hijacked.

Instead of a dignified burial, attended solely by the Sisters, the event was turned into a media extravaganza staged by Calcutta's Municipal Corporation. Mother Teresa's casket, which was carried upon the very gun carriage used in the funeral of Mahatma Gandhi, was borne for eight miles through the streets of Calcutta. Never before had the city seen such a panoply of red-turbaned Rajput soldiers, immaculate Gurkha warriors, celebrities and statesmen.

Sister Nirmala, Mother Teresa's successor, is too preoccupied with paperwork to pay much attention to Mr. Gupta and his Committee. But forty years of pupilage under the indomitable Teresa have taught her to be resilient and now, for the first time, she has spoken out.

'I completely disapprove of this committee,' she says, 'and of its having an office and a bank account. In her lifetime, Mother depended totally on divine providence and did not allow any fundraising whatsoever to be conducted using her name.'

Quiet and unassuming, Sister Nirmala appears to have all the qualities necessary to carry on Mother Teresa's work. She was born in Bihar state of Nepali parents, and only converted to Catholicism in her teens after watching the carnage of Partition. An early disciple, she joined Mother Teresa in May 1958 and has worn the uniform white and blue sari with a crucifix pinned to the left shoulder ever since.

She draws on decades of experience in missions deep in the Venezuelan jungle, in New York's slums, and in Calcutta. When not dealing with the administration of the charity's five hundred and fifty-nine missions spread among a hundred and twenty countries – Sister Nirmala spends much of her time praying at Mother Teresa's tomb. It is set at one end of the meeting hall at Mother House.

'Mother is not far away,' she says softly. 'She might have changed her residence from Earth to heaven, but I can feel her presence and guidance all around me.'

A year after her mentor's death, Sister Nirmala still seems preoccupied by the loss. 'My feelings for her death are still so fresh,' she explains. 'We knew that she could go any day, but when it happened it was a shock. She died at about 9.30 p.m. She had done a full day's work and had had dinner. We were all around her when she died. A doctor rushed in, but could do nothing to save her. She wanted to die in her house, in her room – in Mother House.'

Nirmala and all the Sisters are praying that Mother Teresa be canonized. 'I very much expect her to be made a saint,' she muses. 'We all pray for that. Mother wanted to become a saint – indeed she challenged us all to become saints, saying that it's a beautiful thing! For some it is a long process with many years of wait involved, but,' Sister Nirmala continues with a glint of expectation in her eye, 'for some, it doesn't take so long.'

If Mother Teresa is to be canonized, some of her belongings will have to be taken to Rome as holy relics. For now, her few possessions have been left in her bedroom exactly as they were on the night she died.

Not far from Mother House, in a dingy back-street office, sits Dilip Basu, the self-proclaimed king of Mother Teresa kitsch. No one could be more desperate to lay their hands on Mother's personal chattels than Mr. Basu.

'It's impossible to put a market price on these relics,' he fawns, stroking his scant waxy beard. 'There are private collectors in Europe and America with crores of rupees to spend on such items. The Sisters could give me a few of Mother Teresa's possessions and I would auction them to the highest bidder on eBay. The money would go to charity, of course.'

While his optimistic negotiations continue with Mother House, Mr. Basu has much else to attend to. His desk is cluttered with prototype Mother Teresa products and typed orders. 'Look at these!' he shouts, waving a fistful of papers, 'I'm having orders from all over the world… you see, everyone loves Mother Teresa!'

Mr. Basu's business is booming. Forty extra staff have been taken on at his factory to keep up with demand. A dozen of them are devoted to the most popular line of all – plaster Mother Teresa statuettes with Mona Lisa smiles. The ruthless commercialization of Mother Teresa's image may be surprising, but, as everyone in the small plaster knick-knack business knows, Calcutta is a world centre.

The future for Mother Teresa kitsch is looking rosy.

Dozens of new products are being developed at Mr. Basu's factory. The international market shows no signs of saturation. A spectacular range of new products for the coming year – including Mother Teresa soap flakes, shampoo, pencil-cases and lampshades. And the *pièce de résistance*: an embarrassingly low-quality rendition of a Mother Teresa Barbie doll.

RUBY

Largest star. 2475 carats. The *Rajarathna* ruby from India, owned by G. Vidyaraj, Bangalore, India, displays an animated star of six lines and is cut as a cabochon.

Largest double star. 1370 carats. A cabochon cut gem, *Neelanjali*, also owned by G. Vidyaraj, displays 12 star lines and measures 7·62 cm *3 in* in height and 5·08 cm *2 in* in diameter.

The full international edition of the world's best-selling record book – for the first time in paperback.

G. Vidyaraj's prestigious *Guinness Book of Records*' entries

The Penniless Trillionaire

IMAGINE OPENING A CUPBOARD in your home and discovering a fortune greater than the United States' defence budget.

Is such instant and incalculable wealth only found in dreams or fairy tales? Perhaps so, or in India, where practically anything is possible.

G. Vidyaraj, an ageing and penniless farmer's son, lives in a rented flat in Bangalore, southern India. Born some sixty years ago into an impoverished farming family, he moved to the city in his youth to begin a career – determined to seek fame and fortune.

Now an old man, still penniless, and suffering from a catalogue of ailments, he sips a cup of green tea and tells the extraordinary tale of how he became one of the richest men on Earth.

A cautionary tale par excellence, it's a story in which an immense fortune has brought nothing but worries, obsessions, and envy from those all around.

'My ancestors were direct descendents of the Vijayanagaran kings,' Vidyaraj begins, in slow and precise English. 'Our family was once in the ruling class, and through the Jagirdar lineage their history goes back more than seven hundred years. Heirlooms were passed down from one generation to the next. Seemingly worthless objects, but nonetheless each was worshipped by our family for centuries.'

A special room was set aside in the farmhouse where Vidyaraj grew up. The strange assortment of icons, idols, and other objects that filled it fascinated Vidyaraj as a boy.

'My father used to worship those things in the puja room,' he recalls, speaking at a secret location in central Bangalore. 'Amongst the items there were four odd black lumps. On all auspicious occasions they would be taken down and worshipped with great reverence and devotion. Afterwards they would be hung up on the ceiling again.'

One generation after the next performed rituals in respect of the solid black lumps.

'Nobody knew exactly what they were,' continues Vidyaraj with a glint of excitement in his eye, 'indeed, they didn't even have any idea what they were made of. All that was known was that the lumps were very special. They were always protected and worshipped as religious and revered objects.'

The years passed.

Vidyaraj went off to Bangalore where he began his career as a legal advocate. He moved into a tiny apartment, where he still resides, above a post office in the centre of the city. He married, had four children and, after thirty-two years of practice, retired because of ill health. His life, like that of so many millions of Indians, was very ordinary. In no way had it prepared him for the astonishing events that were to come.

Vidyaraj had never been a religious man. He had after all left the village in search of an education and a professional career.

'My horizons were opened when I was educated,' he says, 'I was the only one in my whole family who had a real education.'

When at last his parents and his siblings were dead, Vidyaraj inherited the room filled with icons, objects and four black lumps. He remembers how he was far too busy and impatient to perform the pujas, the rites of devotion, necessary to keep the gods at ease.

Instead he shut the heirlooms up in a cupboard and forgot about them.

'My wife used to nag me for locking the relics away,' says Vidyaraj recalling her scolding, 'she has always been much more religious than me. To please her I agreed that we would take the artefacts and four lumps to the great temple of Nanjundeswara at Nanjangud, about a hundred miles from Bangalore. I wanted to donate the whole lot to the temple, as these were venerated religious objects.'

At the temple, Vidyaraj was met with a blizzard of forms and the bureaucracy.

'Being an advocate,' he says, 'I knew how to make an application, and that getting through all the red tape was not worthwhile. I had no intention to get permission from the High Commissioner just to donate some old heirlooms.'

So Vidyaraj took his family back to Bangalore. On the way his wife pestered again, insisting that the objects should be given to the local temple, as it was certainly sacrilegious not to invoke them at all. But Vidyaraj's mind had set to work and he had other plans.

'As we made our way home,' he continues, 'it struck me that the black lumps were very heavy. Perhaps, I thought they were made of *panchaloha*, an alloy of five metals that usually contains gold. If one fifth was gold, and was extracted, I would be sure to make some money. My wife was horrified at this thought, fearing retribution from such sacrilege and blasphemy. She pressured me not to melt down the lumps or change their shape in any way.'

The idea of the gold ready to be removed so easily, nagged at Vidyaraj's conscience. He tried to forget about it, but was unable to do so. Everything reminded him of the possible ore, the gold, the instant wealth. So one night Vidyaraj sent his wife and daughters off to the cinema and set to work.

'I embarked on an investigation,' he began softly, speaking in formal English moulded by decades of legal work. 'There was a thick black crust of soot and grime covering the lumps. I took an old toothbrush and a bar of soap and began to wash. I assumed I was washing metal. The dirt was so hard that only some came away. After a lot of cleaning with the toothbrush, I held the lumps up to the light. In one I could see specks of red, and in another blue specks. It was then that I realized that these were not metal, but minerals, and they might be very valuable indeed.'

For months Vidyaraj kept his discovery secret. He immersed himself in the study of gemstones from books and articles borrowed from a public library. Worries that word of his fabulous fortune would leak out dogged him.

He could trust no one with the secret.

'I thought,' he went on, 'if I took them to a jeweller that I might be hoodwinked and misguided. Such people might try to work for their own benefit. So I studied the geological sciences for a year or two.'

Through dedicated and gruelling studies, Vidyaraj learnt the elaborate experiments necessary to identify a precious stone. In the seclusion of his book-lined chamber he performed the vital tests. It was only then that he could pronounce with certainty the minerals' true identities.

Three of the stones were rose-coloured double-star rubies, the fourth – a colossal sapphire.

How did four of the world's biggest gems end up in Vidyaraj's cupboard? The most plausible explanation is that they were passed down through generations, from his supposed ancestors – the Vijayanagaran kings. For safe keeping the gems must have been dyed black, then covered in soot and dirt.

Vidyaraj began to fear more than ever for his safety and that of his family. Constant anxiety, overwork, and his diabetic condition hampered his health. But still he could confide his great secret in no one. So having read a little bit about lapidary, he bought a small hand-driven grinding wheel. In a darkened room at his home, he set to work with the grinder to remove the top portions of the stones himself.

'After some time each began to shine,' he recalls. 'Each exhibited star lines, and slowly they took on their individual shapes.'

For months Vidyaraj maintained his secrecy.

He would attend to his legal work by day, and study gemology by night. One by one he had the three rubies and the sapphire cut. Then he gave them names. And, over the few months and years, he announced their existence to the world. All the stones were cut in India. Vidyaraj himself admits deep regrets for rushing into having them cut. His knowledge, on how some of the biggest and most priceless gems in the world should be faceted, was very limited indeed.

The largest ruby in the world at the time, read Vidyaraj in the *Guinness Book of Records*, was the Rosser Reeves ruby of 138.72 carats, kept at the Smithsonian Institute in Washington DC. The smallest of his own rubies, he named Indumathi after his wife. Weighing two hundred and fifteen carats, it immediately earned an entry in the *Guinness Book of Records*. Vidyaraj amazed the geological world by producing the Indumathi first.

But he had far better specimens still to come.

His second great ruby, named Vidyaraj, after himself, was the next to be shown to the world. It weighed six hundred and fifty carats, having been cut from the original stone of 1,125 carats. He still grieves at the probably unnecessary loss in great weight when cutting. In height the stone measures about three and a half centimetres and, in diameter, more than four centimetres.

As for the whereabouts of the stones, it's anyone's guess where they are. Vidyaraj is keeping his lips tightly sealed, for fear that he'll be robbed. He says that the huge wealth in his possession has caused everyone he meets – even old friends – to view him with suspicion and greed.

But the biggest problem is not the way in which others covet his gems, but the fact that no one has the funds with which to purchase them. After all, the value of these gems is put at billions of dollars, a fact that seems to have escaped Vidyaraj himself.

'I am asking anyone with deep pockets to come forward and to make themselves known to me,' he says, sipping his tea. 'There are surely plenty of millionaires or billionaires out there who have enough cash. I am certain of it. What about the Arabs for example?' he asks. 'We all know how rich they are. They ask if you want cash, cheque or credit card.'

When asked why he doesn't simply cut the stones up and sell them off in bits, he screws up his face in alarm.

'Oh my goodness,' he says wearily. 'No, no, I could never do that.'

'But why not?'

'Because I would lose the *Guinness* entry of course!'

The Queen of Assamese Hearts

FOR THE LAST THREE DAYS the remote village of Mirza, in southern Assam, has been buzzing with anticipation.

The community, which is known for its tea plantations, is hosting Royalty. As the dank evening air fills with giant moths and fireflies, several senior members of the British Royal Family have been spotted parading openly in public.

Queen Elizabeth, Princess Anne, Prince Charles, as well as courtiers and Coldstream Guards, have caused quite a stir – after all the tiny village of Mirza is generally neglected by State tours. But, to the soft-spoken people of Assam, the Windsors are not the real draw. A far more famous celebrity has eclipsed the presence of even Her Majesty. Dripping with diamonds, and dressed in a shimmering silver wedding gown, a fairy-tale princess has arrived – Diana, Queen of Assamese hearts.

Take a closer look at the regal guests, and you begin to notice subtle inconsistencies. Her Majesty, Prince Charles and, Diana herself, can't speak a word of English. Their hair is jet black, their skin dark, and their costumes are not handmade. Few Assamese have met Royalty before, which may explain how the regal charade has gone undetected. But the distinguished visitors are not impostors, rather they're actors in the latest Assamese theatrical sensation *The Life and Death of Lady Diana*.

With an acting tradition stretching back more than four centuries, India's North-eastern state of Assam boasts some of the greatest travelling theatres in Asia. More than thirty touring companies crisscross the state, continually providing entertainment to villages where television and cinemas are still unknown.

The plays are celebrated for performing the great Hindu scriptures, along with passing on regional news. Until recently, Assam's theatre-going public had had very little exposure to Western drama. But all

347

that changed last year when the *Koh-i-Noor* troupe of players staged an epic, the likes of which Assam had never seen before.

Hauling a colossal plywood steam ship across the state, they dazzled one village after the next with their own theatrical rendition of *Titanic*.

Rival theatres searched high and low for another story, charged with passion and overflowing with grandeur, to match the astonishing success of the *Titanic* love story. The director of the *Abahan* travelling theatre, Hem Bhattacharya, considered his options carefully. '*Titanic* changed everything in Assam,' he says, 'before that, people were content with the myths we had been enacting for centuries. But now our audiences are far more demanding. They want new epics. I decided that we would put on the greatest tale of love ever known, even greater than *Titanic* – the story of Lady Diana.'

Mr. Bhattacharya wanted to capitalize on his people's inexplicable affection for the former Princess of Wales. For years, local newspapers had recounted the trials and tribulations of Diana's life in the most minute detail. It's an obsession that grips the entire Subcontinent, with dozens of original books about her in regional Indian languages.

Once Mr. Bhattacharya had begun research into the Princess' life, he dispatched scouts to all corners of Assam. 'They hunted for a woman to play Diana,' he explains, 'an actress with her grace and her inner beauty.'

Remarkably, the quest took only two months, in which hundreds of hopefuls were auditioned. One morning in May, Mr. Bhattacharya first set eyes on the radiant figure of Jubilee Rajkumari (literally 'Princess Jubilee'). Against all odds, he says, he'd turned up a woman so similar in looks that she might be regarded as Diana's long lost twin.

To our eyes, Jubilee's resemblance to the Princess may at first be difficult to discern. Aged twenty, she's a little on the homely side, with a round face, oversized hands, and swarthy complexion. But spend time talking to her, and one quickly realizes how she landed the part – it's her smile. Even when dispirited, she beams with blinding delight.

Once he had a Diana, Mr. Bhattacharya sought the other key players in the fateful tale. The Queen, Prince Charles and Earl Spencer, James Hewitt, Dodi Al-Fayed and Camilla Parker-Bowles, were all cast with Assamese clones. As strenuous rehearsals commenced, so was construction of an astonishing array of scenery and props.

In the travelling theatrical business, the difficulty lies in the fact that everything has to be lugged from village to village every four days. A thirty-foot backdrop of Buckingham Palace, crafted from plywood, looms down as the main symbol of Britannic majesty.

But the royal residence is just the tip of the iceberg.

There's Kensington Palace, too (inside and out), St. Paul's Cathedral, the Royal Yacht *Britannia*, three speed boats, a pair of helicopters, a jumbo jet, the infamous Mercedes, the paparazzi motorbike and Paris tunnel and, even the Eiffel Tower.

The day before the show, a white Indian-made Ambassador car charges through the outlying countryside whipping up enthusiasm. Battered speakers on the roof announce 'Lady Diana! Lady Diana!' Giant hoardings of the Assamese Diana in her most stylish apparel are dotted in key positions around Mirza. But the advertising is hardly necessary, as all the tickets were sold long ago. The insatiable demand has created a thriving black market.

Krishna Das is one of thousands of plantation workers who has staked his family's savings on a tout's tickets. He waves the four slips of yellow paper above his head. 'My wife and daughters are desperate to see the play,' he says, 'how could I let them down? This may be the only time my little girls will ever see Lady Diana.'

Across the street, final touches are being made to the stage, constructed on an area of waste ground at the edge of the village. A complex web of bamboo poles and ropes will keep the Buckingham Palace backdrop upright in the strongest winds. This is just as well, as the latest weather reports suggest that an Orissan cyclone is about to strike. An army of barefoot workers in *lungis* and string vests hurry about ensuring that the theatre is extra sturdy. Three thousand chairs have been laid out in rows beneath an enormous tent, with standing room for many more.

Sitting in the second row, Mr. K. Roy, the producer, is making calculations. Since opening in August, the play has been seen by more than two hundred thousand people in sixteen villages. As the one who stands to make the most money, Mr. Roy is keen to pack in as many seats as possible. The play, which cost about £2,000 to put on, is due to end in April. Although he waves away questions of profit, local rumours say Roy will have made as much as millions of rupees before then.

Backstage the preparations are well underway. Five trunks are unlocked and, with utmost care, the play's elaborate costumes are taken out. All Assamese theatrical productions are founded on two main components: extensive song and dance routines, and plenty of costume changes.

Lady Diana is no exception.

Prince Charles appears in four uniforms and three suits, while Diana sports a series of colourful cocktail dresses, gowns, and the resplendent wedding frock. Only the Queen is more modest, with a single glittering golden robe.

When all the costumes and Union Jacks have been ironed once and then again, and the miniature shrine's incense has been lit, the laborious make-up procedures begin. The drawback of using Assamese actors is that all visible skin has to be covered by a thick, blancmange-like grease paint.

Jubilee Rajkumari sits obediently before a naked lightbulb. A stern-looking make-up artist spatulas the salmon-coloured goo onto her cheeks.

'I felt so miserable when Diana died,' she declares, 'the whole of Assam mourned. People adored her. You see, she stood up against the Royal Family, and was a defender of women's rights.' Jubilee pauses as a spoonful of the make-up is slopped onto her hand. 'Lady Diana may have been a princess, but her marriage suffered from common problems, the kind which even ordinary Assamese women are faced with.' Jubilee breaks off as a voluptuous, fair-skinned young woman enters the tent. Thin as a rake, with high cheek bones and soft pouting lips, she winks at one of the male actors. Jubilee broods with irritation. For the luscious nineteen-year-old is none other than Likuma Sharma, *a.k.a* Camilla Parker-Bowles.

Until recently, Likuma, who's regarded as one of the great beauties of her generation, played basketball for Assam. She admits that although she's never seen a picture of Camilla, she has worked hard at mastering the part. 'Camilla is so misunderstood,' Likuma gushes, waving the make-up woman away, 'She's a loving, romantic woman who is *very* attractive to men.'

Outside, the audience is beginning to arrive. The atmosphere is electric. Hawkers are selling *paan*, popcorn soaked in ghee, and two-foot chunks of sugarcane. Wild dogs and cows amble about searching for food, against a backdrop of noise, a generator rumbling in the distance. The luckiest four thousand people in Mirza trample through the mud to the cavernous tent. Each ticket is inspected carefully because there are forgeries about. Everyone is dressed in their best clothes: women in saris, little girls in tutus and little boys in tight-fitting suits with matching bow-ties.

Tuning their eclectic range of instruments, the band is drowned out by the growl of the generator. In the dressing-room tent the cast is assembled. One at a time, they pause to pray at the shrine, and to gulp down a mouthful of *prasad*, a holy offering. The Coldstream Guards dust off their scarlet coats and scruffy nylon busbies, which resemble Rastafarian wigs. Jubilee stares into space, going over her lines. Earl Spencer whispers a joke to Camilla, who pouts seductively at the punchline.

The spectators all inside, the house-lights slowly go down, and community officials clamber onto the stage to give speeches. Assamese officials like nothing more than to give long speeches to a captive audience. Four thousand hecklers soon drive the politicians from the platform. Silence.

And then, the extraordinary play commences.

The Life and Death of Lady Diana begins with the screech of a car crash, and Diana's ghost (in a white night-shirt) roving around the stage. This gives way to a rollicking Cossack-like dance scene, in which the Coldstream Guards wave Union Jacks. The actors are virtually obliterated in pungent sandalwood smoke, which ascends in clouds from beneath the stage. As the routine reaches its climax, the prow of *Britannia* appears, bearing Charles and Diana, who are on their honeymoon.

All is blissful… but not for long.

Almost from the outset, Charles – portrayed as a friendly, but weak man – has eyes for another. Enter the steamingly seductive Camilla Parker-Bowles ('Bowles' pronounced 'Bowels'). Distraught by her husband's infidelity, Diana seeks comfort in the dashing, tender war hero, Major James Hewitt (pronounced by the Assamese palate as 'James Herriott').

Sitting in the drawing-room of Buckingham Palace, the Queen is kept abreast of the affairs by an obsequious adviser, not dissimilar to Mr. Bean. Her Majesty is strangely eager for the sordid details. She learns how Charles is cavorting around with a woman who has the body of a goddess; while the rather chunky Diana's being wooed by James Herriot (sorry, I mean '*Hewitt*'). Always caring, with a soft shoulder for the young Princess' head, Hewitt comes out as the real hero of the show. So much so that you begin to wonder whether the poor chap's been dealt a harsh hand.

But there's no time to ponder this…

The palace guards have been bribed by the unscrupulous anorak-clad paparazzi. Meanwhile, Diana has a blazing row with the Queen, and storms out of Buckingham Palace (the audience goes wild with delight). Her Majesty is anything but amused. Over at Kensington Palace, Diana assaults Camilla, who's strutting her stuff, waiting for Charles. More blue anoraks, as the press tries to get a look-in. A couple of quick dance scenes to lighten up the mood, before Diana capers about with a lost expression to delicate strains of a *sitar*. Realising that her marriage is over, she gives in to Hewitt's advances, agreeing to spend the night with him. The women in the audience whoop with glee… this is racy stuff, in Assam at least.

To his credit, the writer has kept away from Squidgy-gate, eating disorders, and obsessive phone calls, perhaps fearing that such material might not be understood in an Assamese village. A cynic might pick holes in the performance but, for my money, there isn't a dull moment. It's no less accurate than an amateur version of *The Mikado*.

After almost three hours, punctuated by power-cuts (one caused when a pye-dog chewed through the generator's cable), Dodi Al-Fayed slinks onto the scene. He whisks Diana away on a jumbo jet to the Med, where they career about in a speed boat. Then to Paris (with its Eiffel Tower backdrop), where the blue anoraks are waiting.

Backstage there's pandemonium as a cohort of workers heave Buckingham Palace and St. Paul's away, and position the Mercedes. Like the motorbike, it's attached to a trolley, and runs on bamboo rails.

Every now and again there's a shriek from the sea of dark heads, as anticipation spills over. The crash is coming, and everyone knows it. The Assamese can relate to nothing better than a bloodthirsty car crash. Their roads are a constant theatre of carnage.

Spotting Dodi and Di off-stage, the paparazzi take chase. The stage lights dim. The piercing sound of an engine revving fills the tent. Four thousand mouths gape open with expectation. A drum beats faster and faster. Cymbals clash together. Then, when we can stand no more, the Mercedes – its lights blinding us – shoots forward through a tunnel-coloured backdrop, and smashes onto its side.

The curtain falls.

Without a word, the people of Mirza slink away into the night. No one waits for a curtain call, or even applauds. When asked if this infers that the play has flopped, the producer shakes his head wildly from side to side. 'Are you mad?!' he bellows. 'It means they loved it!'

The Romance of Richard Halliburton

THERE WAS BETWEEN THE WARS a faint aperture of time in which great marvels were still to be found. These holy grails of travel were made reachable through new technologies, and by the boldness and grit of an intrepid band of women and men – a new breed of explorer.

Until then, travel chronicles had been dominated by the great nineteenth century adventurers. Mostly men, they were towering figures of Victorian celebrity – names like Burton, Barth, Livingstone and Stanley. Their accounts of subjugating natives, and hoisting the flag for colonial rule, were at best terse and at worst unreadable, by today's standards at least.

Great travel writing is all about evoking an atmosphere of adventure. But more than that, it's about story-telling plain and simple. Far too many works of travel have slipped into obscurity because the writing is lacklustre, dated, or downright dull. Trawl the shelves of the London Library and you'll find miles and miles of books that are all but forgotten. And many of them deserve to be left there – deep underground.

Yet from time to time you come across an author whose work is a beacon of originality. The American adventurer, Richard Halliburton, whose life was snuffed out at far too early an age, was one such writer.

Although his work has a small but devoted following, his books warrant a far greater readership – and are the kind of travel literature that have withstood the test of time, and continue to inspire the youth to achieve.

With the slaughter of the Great War over, the roaring 'twenties were a gateway to a new realm. Effervescent and frivolous, it was a time to assuage the pain of battle and to uplift the sunken hearts of armchair explorers the world over.

The result was a new kind of work – the birth of the modern travel book.

NEW WORLDS
TO CONQUER
By
RICHARD HALLIBURTON

RICHARD HALLIBURTON

With Numerous Illustrations

Richard Halliburton, whose name was known to all
Americans between the wars

Quests in their own right, these accounts were less about empire or life and death exploration, and more about engaging the reader through passionate description and a really good yarn.

On the eastern shores of the Atlantic, we like to imagine that to be a worthy adventurer you have to be an European as well. But nothing could be farther from the truth. Leading the field in this genre of new romanticism was a zealous young American named Richard Halliburton.

Born into a middle class home in Brownsville, Tennessee, at the start of 1900, Halliburton was a frail youth who suffered from a heart murmur. Despite an enthusiasm for the outdoors and for sport, he was confined to bed for months at a time in childhood, and even attended the legendary Battle Creak Sanitarium of self-styled nutritionist John Harvey Kellog.

Putting his clinical confinement to use, Halliburton devoured every work of geography and exploration available. Yearning for a time when he could break free, he longed to experience the wild lands of which he had read. A romantic through and through, he had been weaned on the Classics, a fabulous backdrop and a blend of fact and fantasy without equal.

Indefatigable, eloquent, and rip-roaringly upbeat, Halliburton was intensely alluring as a character. Soon after graduating from Princeton, he was well on his way to achieving the celebrity he so desired. Inspired by the intellect of Oscar Wilde, and the glamour of Rudolf Valentino, he was himself a dandy of the time. Impeccably dressed, exquisitely groomed, charming and ambitious, it's easy to imagine him as a player in *The Great Gatsby* world of the inter-war years.

For me, Halliburton's most intoxicating quality was the effortlessness with which he embarked upon a quest. Respectful, yet deaf to his detractors, he followed his gut, and used the media to his advantage right from the start. Certainly, the old guard wrote him off as whimsical, but Richard Halliburton was a man who grasped the pulse of the time better than almost anyone else alive.

The 'twenties were about recuperation, a return to the serenity of the Classical world that had been so obliterated from common culture on Flanders' fields. By understanding this – and by adoring it – Halliburton rose to astonishing fame. By the 'thirties he was a household name across America.

Daring, jovial, and eccentric, reports of his expeditions filled the news reels of the time, to the delight of a generation of youth. His *Boy's Own* style of adventure leaps off the page, the kind of writing that can't fail to enthuse, inspiring as much as it does entertain. Relying on fledgling aviation much of the time, and never fearful of terrible danger, Halliburton broke new ground, soaring high above wonders that other travellers had only skirted from the ground.

As far as he was concerned, the world was his giant playground, one still unscathed by mass tourism, political correctness, or industry. In this sunset of empire, the suave and fearless young Halliburton could do no wrong. Fêted by columnists and swooned over by adoring young women – and men – he was in a league of his own.

First published in 1928, *The Glorious Adventure* came hot on the heels of *The Royal Road to Romance*, an amalgamation of disparate travels through Europe, North Africa, Central Asia and the Far East.

In scope, *The Glorious Adventure* is certainly far less wieldy than any of the other Halliburton travelogues. By choosing Homer's *Odyssey* as his theme – his great childhood love – he embarks on a journey to the theatre in which Ancient Greece was played out. Lyrical, light-hearted and passionate without end, the book must have been a hymn to thousands of young men about to be hammered by the Wall Street crash of 1929.

His reasoning to leave is as spirited as the quest itself. He wrote:

Suddenly I became bored and impatient with everything I had and was: bored with people, bored with knowledge. I realized I didn't want knowledge. I only wanted my senses to be passionately alive, and my imagination fearlessly far-reaching. And instead, I felt I was sinking into a slough of banality. Adventure! Adventure! That was the escape; that was the remedy.

Seeking out the land of the Lotus Eaters, the Cyclops' cave, Circe's lair, and Mount Olympus, home of the gods, Halliburton satiates his need for adventure and his infatuation for the Classical world. Furiously fast-paced, packed with verve, at times it exhausts even the most devoted fan.

Enamoured by the life and legacy of the English war poet, Rupert Brooke, Halliburton seeks out his grave on the Greek island of Skyros. It was there the poet had expired in his prime from fever whilst en route to Gallipoli. But it was another English poet – Robert Byron – who provided the inspiration for the greatest feat of the journey. Following his lead, Halliburton succeeded in swimming the Hellespont, the brutal current almost drowning him.

Of the handful of books he published, there's one that stands out as a monument to the time in which he lived, as much as it is a chronicle of everything Halliburton stood for. *The Flying Carpet* is a rare and enthusing tale of *Boy's Own* bravado. It's one of those books that stays with you, not so much because of the intoxicating roll call of adventure, but because of the frantic sizzle of the tale.

Halliburton may have been thirty but he was gripped as ever by the raw enthusiasm of a twelve-year-old. Longing to once again be, as he put it, a 'footloose vagabond', he searched for an aeroplane capable of crossing deserts and jungles, oceans and seas. Without hardly any preparation, and almost no background knowledge of flight, he bought one on the spur of the moment – a Stearman biplane. Shiny and small, with an open cockpit, he christened it the *Flying Carpet*.

The only thing needed now was a pilot.

By a stroke of luck he was introduced to a young Stanford graduate named Moye Stephens, who was employed for flying passengers over the Rockies. Sharing the same lust for daredevil adventure, Stephens readily agreed to pilot them both on a circumnavigation of the globe – 'to all the outlandish places on Earth'. He was promised no pay, but unlimited expenses.

His only question was when they were to leave.

'In half an hour,' Halliburton replied casually.

And, pulling him to the door, they did.

The journey was the kind of feat that people are drawn to recreate today, but with a rigid safety net of support. And yet the alluring thing about Halliburton and Stephens' epic flight, was the absolute lack of safety, and the child-like zigzagging of wonders of the old world.

Flying by the seats of their pants, and with almost nothing in the way of preparation, the pair set off into the unknown.

Halliburton was dead set on visiting Timbuktu first. Lured by the mystery of the name and by its seeming inaccessibility, all he knew was that it was somewhere in Africa.

To reach it, they traversed the United States eastwards from California, headed south through Europe, and into the mysterious hinterland of Morocco.

Soaring high above the Atlas, they climbed to fifteen thousand feet, to avoid pot shots from the tribesmen eager to bring down a shiny little plane like theirs.

And, then, laden with extra fuel, they began the gruelling flight southwards, with the formidable dunes of the Sahara laid out in an ocean beneath. Warned time and again about sand storms, but taking no notice, they flew headlong into one after the next, their faces and the *Flying Carpet* rasped raw.

Causing immense excitement as it came to land at Timbuktu, the little biplane assured the two Americans immediate celebrity. They were received by Père Yakouba, the so-called 'White Monk of Timbuctoo' – the first of many intriguing locals they encountered.

Flying on eastwards, they reached the Algerian Sahara, where they were welcomed into the folds of the French Foreign Legion, at Colomb Bechar. Amazing all they met with acrobatics and tall tales of their journey so far, they flew back up to Europe.

In an era in which travel was far more leisurely an activity, they took off and landed where they liked, *when* they liked. Reaching Italy through the Simplon Pass, they made a beeline for Venice, where they spent a month.

Then they wondered where next. Halliburton wrote:

> Once more we unrolled our world map. Moye suggested Berlin. I voted for Malta. We compromised on Constantinople. A few hours later the Flying Carpet and its crew were in the air.
>
> Our first stop was Vienna. Then to Budapest – to Belgrade – to Bucharest – through storms, across plains, over mountains – on to Constantinople and the Golden Horn.

On and on they flew – across Turkey, down through the Holy Land, to Cairo and the Pyramids, over the Nabatean ruins of Petra, and eastwards over the great basalt desert to Baghdad.

The frequency with which they landed must have reflected the trying conditions of low altitude open-cockpit flight. Yet always gung-ho in style, Halliburton's writing brushes aside the air-sickness from what must have been rollercoaster flights.

But their eagerness to land was inspired, too, by a genuine delight in witnessing new realms. At a time when the globe was not yet homogenized by mass media and equally mass travel, Halliburton and Stephens observed first hand the last vestiges of the old world order.

And wherever they went, their celebrity status was enough for the doors of palaces, monasteries, and jungle longhouses to be flung open for them.

No one, it seemed, wanted to be left out.

In Baghdad, they took the young Crown Prince Ghazi up for a ride; and, in Persia, they carried aloft the daughter of the Shah, Princess 'Flower-of-the-Morning'. While there, they helped out the stricken German aviatrix, Elly Beinhorn, who was flying solo around the world, and had just arrived from Timbuktu. Aged just twenty-three, she was the same age as Stephens. She must have outlived all the other early pilots for whom longevity was at odds with their sport. She finally passed away aged one hundred, in 2007.

Halliburton was a great believer in the wonders of the world.

He understood that associating his expedition with great landmarks would guarantee the media exposure he so desired. Soaring over the Taj Mahal was a natural way to hit the headlines back home, as was the daring flight in the shadows of Mount Everest.

A devoted aficionado of George Mallory, who had perished on that mountain seven years before, Halliburton was desperate to do a fly-by in some kind of tribute. Risking life and limb, and almost freezing solid in the ultra-thin air, they managed, with Halliburton taking the first aerial shots of the mountain with his camera.

The episode is Halliburton description at its best. He wrote:

And then Everest itself, indescribably magnificent, taunting the heavens with its gleaming crown. Her precipice, her clinging glacier shield, her royal streamer forever flying eastward from the throne, her court of gods and demons, her hypnotic, deadly beauty... what incomparable glory crowns this Goddess Mother of all mountains!

Of all the characters and encounters, my very favourite comes a little further, once they had traversed Burma, Indochina, and arrived at the seething, steaming jungles of Borneo. There, they found the fabulously eccentric English aristocrat, the 'Ranee' Lady Sylvia Brooke, whose husband ruled Sarawak, a principality the size of Britain, peopled with Dyak headhunters. The author of a remarkable book herself (entitled *Queen of the Headhunters*), they took her up and did acrobatics over the jungles that were her home.

An astounding success, The Flying Carpet Expedition helped in making Halliburton a household name across the United States. The adventure supposedly cost him $50,000, but he recouped twice that in media deals – a huge amount for the time.

As his meteoric career progressed and, as he crisscrossed the planet, Richard Halliburton became one of the most travelled men alive. Always longing for adventure, one gets the feel he also longed to be remembered, cognizant of the fact it would take one slip up, or act of god, to end it all.

And, ultimately, Halliburton's daredevil brand of travel ran out of luck. Not yet forty, he had embarked on his most hazardous adventure – The Sea Dragon Expedition, in 1939. Having commissioned a Chinese junk in Hong Kong, he intended to cross the Pacific to San Francisco.

After a catalogue of teething problems, the craft set out. Three weeks at sea, and aloft mountainous waves, they sent their last radio dispatch.

Neither the Sea Dragon, Halliburton, nor the crew, were ever heard of again.

To disappear on the trail of a glorious quest is surely the secret dream of any travel writer. But to vanish in one's prime – with years of accomplishments still unfulfilled – is our great loss.

Richard Halliburton deserves the celebrity he so enjoyed, and to be remembered as an inspiration from the nascent age of modern travel. His was a time of good manners, genteel delivery and, most of all, of impassioned values. It was an era of biplanes, tramp steamers, and of vast open-topped vehicles, a world in which most of humanity had not yet been exposed to the trappings of the industrial age.

And, of course, all too soon, the technology that made such travel possible for one, made it possible for all – with a result of a homogenized global culture – something Halliburton would surely have despised.

As I see it, what he stood for was as important as what he achieved. A new romantic without equal, Halliburton's *joie de vivre* and gung-ho attitude was itself a catalyst that rallied a generation to go out and seek marvels of their own. And, as such, his legacy is not only poignant, but a tangible gift that continues to inspire today.

A contemporary of Hemmingway, the young Richard Halliburton had none of the melancholy and all of the passion. Brimming with charm, good looks and natural charisma, he was the kind of man to which both men and women were drawn.

While others were languishing on the terrors of the Great War, he was setting about making a name for himself by crisscrossing crumbling empires by any means possible. Making use of the media with impressive foresight, one can only imagine the heights he'd have soared to given the technology we all take for granted today.

To grasp Halliburton's celebrity, one must remember the time in which he lived. His playground was the world caught in a no man's land between the Wars. The British Empire still ruled the seas, ferocious tribes inhabited the immense African plains and the seething jungles of the Amazon and Borneo; and motor cars were a *jeu du jour* for tin-pot dictators, Maharajahs, and for anyone else with the means to afford them.

A pioneer, a trail-blazer, not to mention a media junkie, Halliburton understood the power of making a splash. In the vein of *Ripley's Believe It Or Not*, he tantalized his readers with jaw-dropping accounts of intrigue, exploration and awe.

His books are a cocktail of key ingredients. They have adventure in great measure, humour, and a smattering of history. But, more importantly, they give the reader the overwhelming sense that just about anyone could follow Halliburton's lead and embark on a madcap escapade just like him.

And, for me, that's the really great attraction of all his work.

A fresh young-faced layman with no technical experience, Richard Halliburton surfed a tidal wave of enthusiasm and good old get-up-and-go. He wasn't trying to impress with ground-breaking hypotheses, or by discovering far-flung lands. Rather, his writing was a sympathetic lens through which ordinary people could experience the extraordinary world in which they lived.

The Sanctuary of Lot

THE PEOPLE OF SAFI speak fondly of the stranger who came to live with them six years ago.

They tell of how the curious Greek man would sneak out of the town before dawn each morning. And they recount how he would amble about on a barren hillside all day for what seemed like no reason at all.

'Sometimes we would stand at the bottom of the hill and laugh at him!' chuckles Mohammed Abdul, a local trader. 'People came from miles away to watch him wandering about in circles in the blazing sun. As you know this is the lowest point of land in the world. It's damn hot here!' Mohammed's smile suddenly disappears. 'But', he says gently, 'who was to know then what the crazy Greek man was to find?'

Constantine Politis, an archaeologist from Athens, was first drawn to Jordan by its rich ancient heritage. Having studied archaeology in Greece, in the United States and in England, he spent years excavating in Greece, Jordan, Oman and in Liechtenstein. His overwhelming fascination has always been for the Holy Land and for the Levant. Yet despite the region's known Biblical legacy, Politis felt sure that more Old Testament sites were waiting to be unearthed.

So he spent many hours gazing at the fabled mosaic map of the Holy Land, at Madaba, in western Jordan. The map, located on the floor of the Madaba's Greek Orthodox Church – dates back to the sixth century AD – and provides the most accurate reference guide we have to the Holy Land in Byzantine times. The Madaba map, with Jerusalem at its centre, depicts the locations of over one hundred and fifty Biblical places.

As Politis stared at the soft pastel mosaic of ancient cities, of rivers and forests, he noticed something startling.

On the southern banks of the Dead Sea, above the Biblical town of Zoar, the map showed a small monastery – dedicated to the Biblical figure Lot. The retreat, which seemed to be perched on a mountain, had eluded archaeologists. Using the map and his Biblical knowledge as his guide, Politis went down to the ancient town of Zoar, which is today called Safi.

On a treasure hunt, he pressed on out of Safi for a mile or so. The Dead Sea was on his left and, on the right, was a mountain – the only one in the immediate area. And, as depicted on the Madaba map, there were date palms at its base. He was just a few miles from Qumran – where the Dead Sea Scrolls were found in 1947.

For the first time Politis ascended the steep scree slope, with its dramatic views over the Holy Land. He climbed halfway up the hillside and looked around. There was no monastery as the Madaba map had suggested.

But there was something else instead.

'I kept finding clues, incredible clues!' Politis exclaims as he remembers that first morning. 'There were mosaic cubes strewn about on the surface. But they weren't any old mosaic cubes, instead they were exquisitely fashioned – as if they had come from a palace. Then I started to find other clues – shards of fine pottery, fragments of sculpted stone, things like that. Remember that all this was halfway up a totally barren hillside.'

Intrigued, Politis had a hunch he was onto something – something very important indeed.

And, while the local people of Safi felt sure he was a madman, the archaeologist was certain there was more to the mountain than met the eye.

'I refused to let myself think the unthinkable,' recalls Politis. 'The obvious temptation – to link the site with the Prophet Lot – was too great. So, instead of jumping to hasty conclusions, I proceeded to get modest funding from the British Museum and from the Jordanian government, and I began to excavate.'

Engaging a team of workmen from Safi, and having been joined with a small international contingent of archaeologists, Politis began the laborious process of excavation.

'We named the site *Deir Ain Abata* – which means the Monastery of the Abbot's Spring', says Politis, 'you see there's an ancient freshwater spring at the base of the mountain.'

But despite the rather grand name they found no monastery. The initial work involved making a series of topographic maps and contour plans of the area, collecting shards from the surface, and so forth.

'Even in those early days it was certain that this was no ordinary hillside,' says Politis, 'Why were there so many luxury items? Why was so much effort put into building structures on such a secluded and precarious location? And why were there such high quality architectural pieces strewn about on the ground? Things just didn't add up. Of one thing we were certain: that this wasn't just another Byzantine fort or farmstead.'

Every schoolboy knows the story of Lot.

The tale, which is told in Genesis, recounts how God was angered by the depraved antics of the people living at two cities in the Holy Land's cities of Sodom and Gomorrah. Having sent angels to guide Lot – the one righteous man and his family – from area, God destroyed Sodom and Gomorrah with fire and brimstone. And, as every school child is well aware, Lot's wife defied the angelic instructions: she turned around and became a pillar of salt.

Genesis, chapter nineteen continues that Lot and his two daughters left the city of Zoar and sought refuge in a cave overlooking the Dead Sea, which is itself known in Arabic as 'The Sea of Lot'.

And, as the scriptures relate how Lot's daughters, fearing that they may never bear children, plied their father with alcohol and seduced him. Both became pregnant. From their offspring – Mobab and Ammon – many of the Arab peoples of the Middle East are descended.

Historians like the eminent Jordanian scholar Rami Khouri suggest a deeper reason for the rather sordid events, which are reported in Genesis.

'The Genesis accounts in the Bible,' says Khouri, 'were written in ancient Hebrew by Jews who were constantly fighting against the Ammonites and Moabites. Depicting the origins of their trans-Jordanian enemies in this manner may simply have been an extension of national combat – into the sphere of literary religious texts.'

Lot has been a popular Biblical figure since before Byzantine times, there being numerous churches, tombs and monasteries dedicated to him across the Holy Land. And, in more modern times there's been a fascination, too. In the sixteenth and seventeenth centuries well over one hundred important paintings were created by European artists, illustrating the famous biblical tale of Lot.

With the site carefully charted, Politis' team removed the topsoil and began the excavations. The first area to be tackled was a sizeable reservoir and elaborate water catchment system. The reservoir itself, which was surrounded by seven-metre walls, was once covered by stone arches and palm trunks – some of which were, remarkably, still in situ.

The discovery of the reservoir answered few of Politis' questions. Indeed, it raised further questions, and he became more baffled. Why should a large and sophisticated water system of this type have been built on such an abrupt hillside?

Seeking answers, Politis dug deeper.

Ancient ash deposits – when analysed – revealed the remains of creatures as diverse as fallow deer, goats and parrot-fish. This rich diet suggested that the community was anything but impoverished.

Other finds included dozens of oil lamps, drinking cups, marble bowls, inscribed stone jars, coins and glass vessels. But, the further the excavations went, the more bewildered Politis became.

'You can't imagine how we felt!' he exclaims, thinking back, 'I was tormented by the riddle. Why was there so much in a place so utterly barren? Then we unearthed a superb stone block inscribed in Greek invoking Saint Lot to bless Sozomenou. This was thrilling – it was the first decisive piece of evidence linking Lot's association with *Deir Ain Abata*.'

Looking back at the initial excavations, Politis is astonished at how unassuming he and other archaeologists had been.

'Eventually, working in the tremendous heat, hundreds of feet below sea level, we came across a large triple-apsed basilical church,' he says. 'The entire structure had been buried. There had been no hint that it was there at all. It was so exciting!'

But the findings which were to follow shocked Politis and his team far more than the discovery of the monastery itself.

'On one September evening we went back to our camp house,' remembers Politis remembers, 'and that night I had a strange dream. I know it sounds crazy, but I dreamt that the next day we would unearth a cave, perhaps the cave to which Lot and his daughters had fled?'

'The next day, we were startled by one of the workmen's cries. He had broken through the east end of the north aisle of the basilica, into a natural cave. Could this have been the holy grotto which the church was built to venerate? Then we found a stone inscribed in Greek which seemed to answer the puzzle. It called on Saint Lot to bless the builder of the church!'

Work continued at fever pitch.

The atmosphere was electric as the floors of the church were cleared – revealing their beauty for the first time in centuries. The first great mosaic, which lead to the cave itself, was decorated with a geometric design of stepped squares and diamonds. At the east end, in front of the entrance to the cave, was an inscription: also in Greek, naming Bishop Jacob as the Abbot of the monastery. It was dated 606 AD.

'Compared to the other mosaic floors at *Deir Ain Abata*, says Steffie Chlouverakis, the site's resident mosaic expert, 'the one outside the cave might seem uninteresting and ordinary: but for me it's by far the most extraordinary of all. Notice how the mosaic cubes themselves are perfectly uniform, and how the geometric lines run straight for many metres. This floor was laid by a master of his craft.'

In the chancel of the church another fabulous mosaic was unearthed. Adorned with vines, the frieze depicts a variety of animals, created with the fine pastel shades that are exemplary of the site. Many birds, a lamb, and a peacock, seemed to sleep for a thousand years or more at their vantage point gazing out across to the Promised Land.

Yet there was another mosaic floor – located in the nave of the church – which interested Politis the most.

'Its long Greek inscription,' he says, 'mentions several church and administrative officials by name, and describes the site as a Holy Place and the church as a Basilica. The mosaic text indicates that this was not merely a monastery, but a venerated place to which pilgrims would journey.'

With work on the mosaic floors progressing well, Politis and his team turned their attentions to the cave itself.

'The discovery of the cave made all those weeks of scratching about the surface worthwhile,' he laughs, 'I know people were beginning to think I was crazy – who knows, maybe I *am* crazy! Years spent on a mountainside like this in the tremendous heat and you need something to keep you going. First we found a few fine mosaic cubes, then the reservoir, then the church itself, and now the cave.'

The entrance to the cave, which had no door, was sided by plaster capitals – decorated with Maltese crosses and painted red. The lintel above the door was also adorned with a cross. To the right of the entrance Politis noticed several lines of graffiti etched into the plaster. The two main portions of graffiti are written in Greek and in Kufic Arabic.

'Inside the cave,' says Politis, 'we came across a lot of ceramic oil lamps. Initial excavations inside revealed a series of steps leading into a very small room paved with fine marble slabs. This natural cave, it seems certain, was chosen by the Byzantine Christians to represent the place to which Lot and his daughters sought refuge.

'But we were still dogged by questions. Why did the Byzantines decide to venerate this cave in particular? Was there any evidence that this Biblical story actually took place there?'

Politis was well aware that biblical episodes were often not recorded in writing until centuries after they had happened. This word-of-mouth passing on of tales must have distorted the facts. Yet Politis and his team felt confident that they might strike more valuable clues by excavating the cave itself.

Meticulous digging followed in the constricted space of the cave. Every few inches of removed soil, revealed more intriguing and older artefacts. First, a number of early Byzantine ceramic and glass oil lamps were found. The team dug deeper. They came upon early Roman pottery. Still they quarried deeper, and unearthed disarticulated human bones and pottery shards dating back to the Middle Bronze Age II (1750 – 1550 BC). These Middle Bronze Age relics fitted in historically with the thirty or so cairn tombs – which Politis had discovered dotted around the hillside. The evidence suggested that, during the Middle Bronze Age, a substantial community had occupied the area. Some scholars believe that this was the time of Genesis.

Inspired by the Middle Bronze Age finds, Politis excavated still deeper. As if peeling off layers of an onion, he came upon more wonders. Further down the team unearthed a quantity of Early Bronze Age I-II (3150 – 2850 BC) pottery and human bones. And, the most remarkable find at this level, was a complete Early Bronze Age jug with a dipper and drinking cups. Still deeper excavations – at a depth of three metres – revealed the earliest human occupation of the cave, dating back to Late Neolithic times – over eight thousand years ago.

The excavators discovered a number of freshwater mollusc shells inside the cave itself, perhaps suggesting that the cavern was at one time a spring source. The spring at the base of the mountain – which still contains several varieties of freshwater fish, molluscs and crabs – has survived since before the Dead Sea was 'dead'. The spring has been cleaned and been cleared of modern debris by the excavation team, who plan to turn it into a model aquatic park.

After the discovery of the cave, excavations advanced on other areas of the site. It was only then that the full extent of the monastic complex of Saint Lot became fully understood.

'We unearthed a refectory with long benches and a large stone oven,' reflects Politis, 'north of the basilica church. Then, further north still, we identified a pilgrim's hostel: inscribed with the name of its builder – Ioannis Prokopios.

'*Deir Ain Abata* seemed to be revealing one marvel after the next. We could never have hoped to find more areas of consequence. But, at that moment, we came across something of tremendous interest!'

The skeletons of well over forty individuals, mostly those of adult males, were unearthed. The remains – presumably those of monks – were found beneath the refectory floor in a communal burial chamber, constructed from a disused water reservoir. As the skeletons were exhumed and studied, it became apparent that one of them was that of an African, and at least one other was a woman.

'Then,' continues Politis, 'we unearthed five cist burials cut deep into the bedrock. They contained three young children, a foetus, and a newborn. If all these were buried before 606 AD of the monastery, their deaths may have been related to the Great Plague which ravaged the Mediterranean world from 541 to 570 AD.

Politis hopes that the site may in time become a model area of focus for visitors to Jordan.

'*Deir Ain Abata* has an ancient tale to tell,' he says, 'it has exquisite mosaic scenes, a heritage which stretches back ten millennia and, it has one of the finest views westward to Jericho.'

But what of future discoveries on the mysterious hillside overlooking The Sea of Lot?

'Well,' says Politis thoughtfully, *Deir Ain Abata* has revealed so many wonders to us. She has shown us her reservoir, her basilica church with its glorious mosaic floors, the cave – packed with its own artefacts, and the tombs. What could be next? I don't dare tempt fate, but finding the library of rare scrolls would be the icing on the cake!'

The Potala Palace, Lhasa

A pet shaggy goat, at a Tibetan nunnery

To Tibet

My contact had scribbled an address in Mandarin on a scrap of paper no larger than a postage stamp.

Nudging a thumb in the direction of a *hutong*, one of the labyrinthine alleys tucked away in downtown Beijing, he balked.

'Dealer very dangerous man. You go alone.'

So I did.

After zigzagging down telescoping lanes abundant with life, asking everyone who passed me, I eventually arrived at the dealer's den. I knocked apprehensively.

Much time passed, then the door slowly slid back.

A stocky waxy figure wearing only an eye-patch and a pair of fake Calvin Klein's was standing in the frame. He barked something angrily in Chinese. I held up the scrap of paper. The dealer's good eye glanced left and right subversively, and he yanked me inside.

The contact at my hotel had promised that the dealer could source just about anything – legal or illegal. Having travelled to Beijing to take the celebrated new train to Lhasa, I was getting desperate. Restrictions and astonishing passenger numbers, set against a backdrop of general Chinese railway mayhem, had made tickets a very elusive commodity. Weeks before, I had paid a huge amount of cash in advance to a Tibetan guide based abroad. Despite promising the earth, he hadn't been able to secure any seats, leaving me ticketless on the day I planned to travel.

Probing a hand down the front of his Calvin Klein's the dealer slid out a mobile phone, roared into it for a minute and a half, looked at me, then grunted hard. He whipped out the hand and rubbed thumb and forefinger together fast. I counted out a wad of money and left with nothing to show for it, except a smirk from the dealer as he slid the door shut.

Early that evening I had all but given up hope when an envelope was slipped silently under the door of my hotel room. It had dried blood on the front, and a crumpled railway ticket inside.

An hour later I was pushing through the crowds at Beijing's immense West Station. Oceans of people, most of them clutching sacks filled with their worldly possessions, were shuffling forwards away from the station, as if fleeing a natural disaster. Diving in, I pushed upstream, swimming against the current. And, after terrible difficulty, arrived at the gate of the fabled Lhasa Express.

Pushed up in a kind of holding pen, waiting to board the train, I could hardly believe that the journey I had anticipated for so long was at last about to start. Ever since I had heard of the Beijing to Lhasa railway opening four years before, I'd been desperate to get aboard.

Modern China is a land of tremendous engineering achievement, one in which the word 'impossible' simply doesn't exist. And the cherry on the Cake of Marvels is surely the railway line that spans the route from Beijing to the Tibetan capital, a journey of four thousand kilometres. Known locally as *Kien Liu*, the 'Railway to Heaven', it's something of which all Chinese are justifiably proud. But at the same time it's controversial, the easy access it provides for ordinary Han-Chinese to visit Lhasa, has made it yet another nail in the coffin of ancient Tibetan culture.

The frenzied hysteria of boarding was replaced by a silent serenity, as train T27 glided out of Beijing West precisely on time, at nine p.m. The majority of the passengers were Chinese tourists, eager for a glimpse at Tibet, a province that's become for them a kind of exotic Disneyland, and an extension of their own realm.

From the moment the train slipped through the suburbs of Beijing, to the time of its arrival at Lhasa, my fellow passengers galvanized into a ubiquitous routine: slurping pots of minute-noodles, gambling incessantly, sms-ing each other madly, slugging back small bottles of gut-rot liquor, chain-smoking in the corridors, gorging themselves in the dining car, and embarking on marathon sessions of mahjong.

For two days and nights a hard sleeper berth was my home. Across from me lay a woman whom I never saw move once. She was covered head to toe in sheets of tatty newspaper. An old English teacher from

Shanghai named Mr. Ma, on the lowest berth, said she was not to be trusted. He wouldn't tell me why, but instead spent most of the journey asking how I could help get his son into British university.

Other than some of the more peculiar dishes on offer in the dining car, the hardest thing to stomach on the Lhasa Express were the loos. They quickly became an obsession for all the passengers. Ten minutes from Beijing and every toilet was overflowing with excrement. Those of a fragile disposition took to bottling their pee, and leaving it furtively in the corridors.

Desperate for a clean loo, I roamed the train's entire length. Clambering from one carriage to the next meant hoisting oneself over the seat-less, their babies, and their bales of luggage and wares. Mr. Ma said those without seats were Tibetan, adding darkly that they were not to be trusted either.

In the middle of the train lay a kind of no-man's-land, three carriages of hard chair cars, a raucous day and night jamboree of Chinese college students. Seething with hormones and alcohol, iPods buzzing, they spent their time eyeing each other up, playing it ice cool.

Beyond them was the dining car with its ferocious waitresses and bowls of steaming pig-fat stew. And, beyond that, was the Promised Land – the soft sleeper compartment: piped musak, pristine toilets, miniature TVs, and all mod cons.

I got talking to a Chinese student said who her name was Jennifer, and that she was in love with Robbie Williams. I asked her about Tibet. She sighed. At first I mistook it for a sigh of affection, the kind she reserved for Robbie. 'Shopping in Lhasa very very good,' she said enthusiastically. 'Because Tibetans very frightened of us Chinese.'

By dawn of the second day, the train was ascending steeply. With the wheels grinding hard against the tracks all morning, the locomotive hauled us up to the highest point, the five thousand metre Tanggula Pass.

Now wearing a pair of silk royal blue pyjamas, Mr. Ma got a nosebleed that wouldn't stop. He looked as though someone had stabbed him through the heart. The woman across from him moaned she had a headache. Then she fainted. A minute later there was a gushing sound and we all perked up. The engineers had thought of everything, even pumping oxygen into the compartments through little nozzles built into the walls.

A railway journey gives a fleeting cross-section, a blend of blurred detail against a backdrop of gradual change. We live in a world preoccupied with cities, but it's the rural landscape that always stays so firmly in my mind. Modern China may be all about the urban, but it's the rural topography that's still the heartland. And what a vast, uncompromising place it is: boundless vistas of fields and lakes, little hamlets, forests, and great swathes of emptiness, save for the odd herd of sheep, or goats.

As the train rolled on towards Tibet, the scenery changed. The weeping willows, farmland, and screens of rustling poplar died away, replaced gradually by stark steppe, peppered with thousands of black dots – grazing yaks. And the closer we drew to Lhasa, the more wondrous the feats of engineering and technology – vast dams, power stations, tunnels, road-building and sprawling bridges, beneath great boiling cumulus clouds.

All of a sudden, Lhasa arrived.

Gliding into the station was like slipping into a military encampment on high alert. The platform was awash with stern-looking soldiers in camouflage, marching double-time, automatic weapons held tight over chests, eyes fixed on the middle distance. I watched as an American tourist, trying to take a photo of the station's name, was tackled for his camera. Photography was against the law.

As he said goodbye, Mr. Ma ordered me to beware of yak meat and of Tibetans, neither of which he said were to be trusted in the least. We shook hands, and he was gone.

Reaching Lhasa at last was for me itself a profoundly moving experience. My obsession for all things Tibetan began in childhood on reading Heinrich Harrar's classic, *Seven Years in Tibet*.

A champion skier and mountaineer, Harrar had found himself trapped in Tibet during World War II. His tale was later turned into a movie staring Brad Pitt. Unable to leave, Harrar was invited to become a private tutor to the young Dalai Lama. His writing paints a candid picture of a Tibet, a land quite untouched by the modern world. *Seven Years* is a time capsule of a book, illuminating in freeze-frame a way of life that changed irrevocably with the Chinese invasion sixty years ago.

Like everyone else watching the mountain stronghold from afar, I had been touched by the gentleness of the society and its Buddhist faith. Yet I had never quite imagined I would actually set foot in the place that has become such a symbol, much more than a simple destination.

Visiting Tibet is a subject plagued in misinformation, and surfing the Internet leads to all sorts of contradictory advice, much of it surrounding the compulsory Tibetan Travel Permit. Despite what you hear, you can apply for the Travel Permit yourself, although most people get theirs through an agency or a guide.

And the business of guides to Tibet is surely one of the great rackets of the international tourist game. Most visitors use one on their journey, although nothing at all says that you must have a guide. As it happened, the one I found online cajoled me into paying top dollar in advance. He turned out to be a crook, a Tibetan sharper forbidden to set foot in his own homeland. He ended up farming me out to a local guide for a small fraction of the money I had paid him.

To anyone interested, my advice is to get the permit yourself, and to wait until you reach Lhasa before looking for a guide, that is if you think you need one at all. Do-it-yourself Tibet pays great dividends.

You don't need to be an intrepid explorer to visit Tibet. I can hardly imagine an easier or more pleasant land to wander through. From the first instant, there's a sense that you have arrived at one of those golden destinations, the kind which changes the way a traveller sees the world. The few Western tourists I met there staggered about with a cloud-nine glow wrapped over their faces, as if they had won a jackpot.

The Tibetans are celebrated for their peacefulness and for their resilience, and it's that which visitors take away – the feeling that dignity prevails in the face of truly terrible adversity.

For those like me, preoccupied by Tibet, the reality is fascinating and at the same time disturbing. It's like looking at a picture through a kaleidoscopic lens. The picture's there, yet it's distorted. Ordinary life continues for the Tibetan people. They pray at the Jorkhang temple, with its gilded bronze roofs, prostrating themselves every few paces until they reach inside. They eat yak-meat *momo* dumplings in the backstreets of the old town, shop for rancid yak-butter, vegetables, and for second-hand clothes. And they make the pilgrim circuit clockwise around Jorkhang complex, spinning prayer wheels as they go.

All around them is the dark shadow and unflinching gaze of the Chinese system. There are soldiers on every street corner and at every crossing, many of them outfitted in riot dress, batons and shields gleaming in the late afternoon sunlight, tear gas canisters ready to be deployed. There are lookouts, too, on the rooftops, and even on the minaret of Lhasa's main mosque. Nothing is overlooked, neither by the soldiers, nor by the legions of spies mingling with the general populace. The heightened state of alert is the result of civil uprisings just over two years ago, unrest that left unknown numbers of Tibetan civilians and lamas imprisoned and dead.

Much of my time in Lhasa was spent standing on street corners, staring at the well-honed melody of life. On one street corner, a stone's throw from the Jorkhang monastery, a street seller stepped up and tried to interest me in a pair of immensely long brass trumpets, adorned with exquisite silver appliqué.

He was a short man, with large hands, and the kind of smile you can't quite forget. I asked him how I'd ever get the instruments home. They must have been twenty feet long. Without wasting a second, he collapsed the trumpets in on themselves, telescoping them down to the length of a shoebox. 'Now they are hand luggage,' he said with a grin.

The military lock-down is what you notice first, but dwelling on it would be to miss the bigger picture. And that is the dilution of Tibetan culture, the ancient circle of life. Everything Chinese is stressed and applauded, and anything Tibetan is frowned upon, ridiculed, and shamed.

The road signs are in Chinese, and many streets have been renamed, the stores are filled with Chinese goods, a great number of them staffed and owned by Han-Chinese, who are making all the cash.

In a suburb of Lhasa known as the 'Island of Love', I was taken to a swish art gallery in which an energetic Chinese lady was encouraging foreigners to part with large sums in the name of modern art, pieces including an enormous wooden phallus painted red. She stressed that most of the artists were Tibetan, and that major dealers were at that moment bidding for the works. She motioned to the door and, as if on cue, it opened and a scout from Sotheby's stepped in.

The local art market isn't the only one controlled by the Chinese.

Tibetan medicine was until recently celebrated in both East and West. But these days few pharmacies within Tibet practice the ancient techniques. Instead they dole out drugs mass-manufactured far away in China. The Tibetans endure it all, existing in a kind of limbo, a limbo that's slowly sucking their lifeblood away.

On one street corner in the old town, a farmer was standing with his yak. It looked very old, as if it were diseased. One of the shopkeepers saw me wondering whether the animal was for sale. He said to me, 'Have pity on this old man. Buy the yak, take it back to your own country and nurse it back to health.' I told him that I lived a great distance from Lhasa. The shopkeeper seemed worried for a moment. Then he said, 'If you buy the yak I will look after it for you.'

Spend a little time outside Lhasa, roaming around the countryside, and you do glimpse snapshots of a society that in many ways has hardly altered since medieval times.

Farmers and their families out in the fields winnowing the wheat, nomads in their smoky yak-wool tents pounding the yak-butter with giant pestles, a clutch of pilgrims pausing at crisscrossed prayer flags swooshing in the wind. The deafening sound of gongs and elongated trumpets shattering the silence of dawn.

While monitored through a network of spies and informants, the temples, monasteries and nunneries soldier on day to day. The Dalai Lama's photo and his name are conspicuously absent, although you quickly realize he's the one person on everyone's mind. The Chinese authorities have sought to incapacitate the system gradually, from the inside out. And to a large degree, they have succeeded.

Not surprisingly, it is within the Buddhist institutions that the lifeblood of the Tibetan realm remains most in tact. At Lhasa's Tsamkhung nunnery, prayer books are still hand printed on slivers of wood, as they have been done for centuries. And at the imposing Potala Palace, which looms down over the capital, lines of pilgrims pour ghee on the flickering lamps, their robed forms mingling with Chinese tourists, coutured head to toe in spotless Burberry. The contrast couldn't be more incongruous.

To enter the actual palace is to descend back in time, through the interleaving centuries of Tibetan life, a life bound unflinching to the calm serenity of Buddhist culture. It's not easy to say why the cramped halls of the Potala affect all who enter them as they do. As you trail through them, up narrow staircases, down sweeping corridors and through the many shrines, pungent with incense and smoke, you feel a part of something very ancient. It's as if you're being bathed in a thousand years of energy, left by supplicants whose names are lost, but whose devotion lives on.

And at a tiny outlying monastery on the road to Nagansey, I met an eighty-year-old hermit-monk crouching in a niche a little bigger than himself, carved out from the rock. He had been in there for three decades. When I held up a camera, he begged me to take the photo to freedom, to Dharamsala.

On one of my last nights in Tibet, I camped in a steep-sided valley, the verdant slopes grazed close by yaks. Either side of it was a glacier. They seemed to hang there between the crags, translucent ice, prehistoric and compacted, the colour of aquamarines. All through the night a freezing wind ripped down from the ice mountains, followed by hail and rain. My tent collapsed completely, leaving me in a wretched stew of tent poles, plastic sheeting and quilts. The driver and my guide, who had slept like kittens curled up in the van, split their sides in laughter when they saw me emerge at first light.

The driver mumbled something and cackled in delight.

'What did he say?'

My guide wiped a hand over his face.

He said, 'Only a moron would use a tent not made of yak wool.'

A mile or two away, atop a precipitous slope, with sweeping views of the plateau below, I came to the nunnery set beside a towering stupa and encircled by bronze prayer wheels. My guide had at first resisted making the steep climb on foot. Given the altitude, it was like staggering forwards wearing diving weights. I assumed his reluctance to be inspired by a dislike for physical activity.

But then, when we reached the nunnery – one that's on no tourist itinerary – I realized that my guide's apprehension came about for fear of the authorities. Even there, he said, we would encounter spies. And we did. One of the nuns, an old woman with a childlike grin and a shaven head, cocked her creased brow in the direction of a young man sitting in the shade of the central courtyard. When we were out of earshot, she whispered that she didn't care any longer, at least for herself. 'We close our eyes,' she said softly, 'and we are free.'

As dusk became night, one of the nuns cooked up a thick vegetable broth, and served it with *momo* dumplings and tea. In the distance there was the sound of a girl singing, a shrill ribbon of tone, mixed with the intermittent clanging of a yak-bell far away. I slept more deeply than on any night I can remember, huddled up on an old rope bed, a patchwork quilt pulled over me.

I was up at dawn, in time to see the nuns with their shaven heads take up their positions for the first chorus. Watching Tibet from a distance, through magazines and photographs, the ritual can appear stiff and even austere. But being there, at the heart of a nunnery as the first blush of sunlight warms the darkness, you can't help but be moved by the openness, the sense of real conviviality of it all.

As I was about to leave the nunnery, I saw a round loaf of home-baked bread sitting on a wall. I could smell it from quite a distance, fresh-baked and snug. Surprised that something so tempting would have been abandoned, I asked my guide whom it belonged to. He said, 'The nuns believe that charity should be anonymous, that you should give to benefit someone in need to help them and not to receive thanks. And that is why the bread is on the wall.'

As we descended down to the plateau once more, the villagers streamed out of their homes with pots, pans, whistles and drums. My guide pointed to the sky. It was darkening, as if night were approaching – a solar eclipse.

As soon as the moon slipped over the sun, the villagers banged their pots and pans together, and shrieked for all they were worth.

The only person not straining to frighten away the Devil was a Chinese official. He was standing in a doorway and looked very angry indeed, as if superstition was restraining progress. My guide started clapping his hands together hard. I asked if he too was trying to frighten the Devil and restore the sun. He turned to face the official and clapped even harder.

'That's right,' he said. 'If I do this for long enough, maybe the Devil will go back to his own home and leave us Tibetans in peace.'

Widows begging for alms in the streets of Varanasi

Where Widows Go to Die

BEFORE DAWN HAS BROKEN over Varanasi, India's holiest city, a procession of figures wends their way down to the Ganges.

Barefoot and cloaked in simple white saris, they move with slow, deliberate steps through the morning chill. Once at the margin of the sacred river, as the first rays of yellow light touch the mist, they cleanse their bodies in the dark waters of the Ganges. And, with the ancient city stirring to life behind them, the figures – a chain of women aged anywhere between twenty and eighty – stand in prayer. Each has the same invocation. They pray that God will see them, purged by the Ganges' waters, and they pray that He will grant them their single wish – sudden and immediate death.

Devika is standing at the centre of the group. Her features are refined, her face framed by an abundance of wet black hair. With eyes tightly closed and palms clasped together, she pleads to be lifted to Paradise. Like the other women, Devika, is in good health. At twenty-four, a lifetime stretches out before her. But, like the others, she too yearns for death.

Varanasi is home to at least sixteen thousand such women. Each of them lives in a state of self-enforced limbo, desperate for execution. For, Devika, and the group of women surrounding her, are widows.

Conservative Indian society affords no place for widowhood. As a wife, a woman was traditionally regarded as a chattel, property of her husband. With his death her life is without purpose

Widowhood is a relatively new phenomenon in India. The practice of *sati*, a grieving widow climbing onto her deceased husband's funeral pyre, traditionally put an end to the predicament of the surviving partner. But since the British made *sati* a criminal act in 1829, Hindu widows have lived as outcasts until their natural deaths. After the British law was passed, such women flooded to Varanasi, fabled 'City

382

of Light', most hallowed place in Hinduism. They believe that to die beside the Ganges in Varanasi is to guarantee *moksha*: the release from the eternal cycle of reincarnation. And, they say, with death all sins are annulled as one slips into Paradise.

Banished by their families and shunned by society, innumerable widows have turned to Varanasi since *sati* was abolished. Travelling from all corners of India, they begin a new existence: a life waiting for death. Scant sustenance is provided by pilgrims who flock to the city's three thousand temples, and by the handful of charitable hostels dedicated to them.

Take a stroll down the winding lanes that lead down to the Ganges and you see widows all around – stooping, praying, singing, or simply standing in silence. Most are dressed in plain white, or lightly patterned, saris. None wear *bindis*, the red religious mark on the forehead. None have *sindhur*, the vermillion dye worn in the hair-parting, sign of a married woman. Instead, they are expected to have their heads shaved once a month. For most, employment is out of the question. Traditionally equated with witchcraft, widows are reviled, resigned to begging for a living.

Some unscrupulous employers take advantage of the desperate widowed women. Paying wages far below the standard rates, they run sweat-shops in the dark back streets at Varanasi's Chowk. In one such alley, far from the temples and trappings of ritual, Devika crouches at a loom. Her hands are rough from work, her fingernails torn. Three years ago she journeyed to Varanasi from a village near Calcutta.

'My husband died seven years ago,' she says in a frail voice, as she pauses from her weaving. 'He was twenty-two years older than me and died of lung cancer. We were married when I was thirteen. After his death I found myself unwelcome at his ancestral home where we lived. His mother told me that I was cursed. She said that her son had passed away because of me, and she ordered me to leave right away. I wept very hard. I had nowhere to go. My mother-in-law sold my belongings and gave me enough money for a third class single ticket to Varanasi. She swore that if I ever returned she would blind me.'

Her hazel eyes staring in concentration at the floor, Devika cannot forget the ordeal that brought her here. 'When I arrived in Varanasi, it was as if I were a leper,' she continues. 'Ordinary people spat at me. Others shouted insults or crossed the street to pass me. Mothers whispered to their children "Don't look, she's diseased!" I begged at a temple dedicated to Kali. Gradually, I have learned how to survive. And the longer I spend, the better I understand.' Devika sponges a hand over her face. 'The widows who have lived here for many years are best positioned,' she adds, 'it's they who know where to stand to catch a pilgrim's eye.'

After eight months of begging, Devika was given a job at the weaver's shop. Emaciated and recovering from malaria, she now weaves blankets fifteen hours a day, seven days a week. Her wage of just forty rupees (50p) a day, is a third of the going rate. Every month she pays half her earnings back to her employer as rent for the small room she shares with two other widows.

'The work is hard,' Devika says stoically, 'but I thank God for giving me this chance. Each night I pray to Him to let me die soon. I know that He has heard my pleas. I know that He will take me soon.'

When asked if she would ever marry again, Devika looks confused at what must sound to her like a completely inane question.

'How could I wed a second time?' she asks in confusion. 'That's impossible. I am a widow.'

Although they have flocked to Varanasi only since *sati* was abolished, widows have sought refuge in the holy city for at least two thousand years. Teenage dowagers and those in their early twenties are not uncommon in Varanasi. Some say that widowed girls as young as eleven can be found eking out an existence in the back streets of the Chowk. Resigned to mourn until the end of their days, they live as beggars.

Like Devika, most believe that their span of life on Earth will draw to a close before long. But decades spent working for a pittance, or bowing with cup in hand, proves such anticipations wrong.

Sixty-three years ago, Gita Sarkar arrived by ox-cart at the City of Light, fleeing after her husband died of typhoid. She had dreamt of cleansing her soul in the Ganges, and yearned for a speedy delivery to Paradise. These days her face is aged, wrinkled like elephant hide, her body rigid with arthritis and wrapped in white. She spends her time at the dying rooms of the Bhavan Hospice. Gita, now eighty-two, was just nineteen when she arrived in Varanasi, newly-widowed and grieving. She had been married at ten. 'Long, long ago I was a wife, a mother and a daughter,' she says in a faltering voice, 'but when my husband expired, what was I to do? His family told me to stop eating – to simply starve myself to death. When I refused, they poisoned my daughter. I ran away and came here to Varanasi.'

As Gita tells her tale, the widow in the next cubicle is pronounced dead. Her slender corpse is wrapped in muslin and laid on the stone floor of the small chamber. There is no ritual, just the echoes of a drum beating monotonously in a courtyard outside. An oversized leather-bound volume is pulled open and the name of the latest deceased is entered in the crowded columns. Gita pauses for a moment from her memories in respect, and then goes on.

'When I arrived here all those years ago,' she says, 'most of the widows were so young, many of them little more than children. It was no surprise I suppose, after all most of us had been married as infants to old men. I prayed for death and expected that it would soon follow. But death has eluded me. Now nearly all those of my generation are dead. They have gone to heaven – they've been freed. I shall be with them soon.'

Next door, the body is prepared for immediate cremation. The hospice, which provides free accommodation for almost sixty widows, covers the expenses of the funeral. A simple cotton shroud is wrapped over the corpse, which is then taken through the winding streets down to the 'burning ghat' on the western banks of the Ganges.

Just enough firewood is weighed out log by log and a makeshift pyre is assembled. The cadaver is positioned, a few drops of sandal oil are sprinkled over it, and the consecrated flame is applied. Three hours after death, and the ashes of yet another widow are cast into the dark sacred waters. With it, another dream of *moksha*, entrance to Paradise, is attained.

Director at the hospice, Kunal Bashak, has attended too many cremations to remember. 'We try to ensure that these ladies – who are so hated by everyone – die with the dignity they deserve,' he says. 'Unlike other hospices in Varanasi, we only have space for those who are ready to die. When they come here, widows, often ask for their food to be stopped. Death comes quickly.'

Strolling about the lanes that form the great bazaar is Ravi Gupta, a short, bespectacled south Indian man. While others avert their gaze, to avoid eye-contact with passing widows, for fear of attracting the evil eye, Gupta greets Varanasi's mourning women.

For six years he has studied widowhood in Varanasi, and is a friend to them all. 'Don't listen to people when they tell you that widows no longer come here,' he says sharply. 'There are almost as many widows here now as after Partition. And, although pilgrims support most of them, more and more are being used as slave labour in workshops around the town. Young girls, married in childhood and widowed as teenagers, are being tricked into prostitution now as never before. A mafia controls the illegal workshops, the illicit trade, and force beggars to pay rent for their "patch".'

Gupta has petitioned for an organized government pension for each widow. 'Red tape and corruption prevent most women eligible to claim pensions from ever getting them,' he says. 'People still believe that widows are cursed or diseased; that even by simply speaking to them one will somehow get infected. Others are calling for *sati* to be re-introduced, defending the idea saying that it's tradition. It's not surprising that Indian widows are so desperate to die – they are being treated very unjustly!'

Balancing precariously on a slender concrete platform outside a cobbler's kiosk, Yaksha Mishra waves out to Gupta. The two have become good friends. Yaksha, sixty-nine, has lived on the slab – measuring two foot by four – since 1976. When it rains she furls herself up in a crumpled plastic sheet. And, when it is hot, she veils her head with the embroidered hem of her sari. The platform costs her ten rupees a month in rent – paid directly to the local *dada*, mafioso, as protection money.

'Yes of course I long to leave Varanasi and go to heaven,' she whispers narrowing her eyes, 'but for now life continues. I am comfortable with my situation. When people pull their children from the window as I walk by, I smile at them. Decades as an outcast has made me strong.' Yaksha pauses to accept a rupee coin from a passing pilgrim. 'Many of the widows who come to Varanasi torture themselves. They compete in their misery. One will cut her legs with a razor blade; another will walk across broken glass. And, although a widow who kills herself will not reach heaven, sometimes a woman is so dispirited that she will buy *zeher*, poison.'

As the evening draws to a close, there's the muffled clang of temple bells in the narrow lanes, bustling with priests and sacred cows. Squatting, forgotten against one wall of the passage, are a dozen widows. A middle-aged pilgrim sprinkles a handful of rupee coins to the line of outstretched hands.

'I am here searching for my own mother,' he says. 'She was banished by my *Dadi*, my paternal grandmother, when my father died suddenly in my childhood. I know there's almost no hope of ever finding her alive, but I come each year. People think I am mad to continue with the search. But how could I live with myself if she is here, living as a beggar on Varanasi's streets?'

Nearby, a handful of figures moves once again through the dispersing twilight towards the Ganges, their bare feet pressing into the soft mud of the riverbank. All clothed in white, they stand with their arms outstretched, their fingers splayed wide, and their eyes firmly closed.

As the ancient City of Light hides beneath a curtain of darkness behind them, the widows renew their simple and identical prayer to God.

Women on Death Row

WHERE HIGHWAY 231 crosses the Tallapoosa River in central Alabama, the sky is inky grey, the panorama cold and forgotten.

A ghostly silence hugs the landscape.

As the road ascends a low hill, you get your first view of the Tutwiler Prison for Women. Square watch-towers loom upwards from the compound, every inch of it encircled by electric fences and razor-wire. Locked down inside the jail's white-washed walls, Alabama's five most feared female inmates await their rendezvous with the electric chair.

Myth and misinformation surround America's women on Death Row – two thirds of them are white, ranging in age from eighteen to seventy-five. In more than sixty per cent of cases the victim was an adult male, most often an abusive partner.

Built in the late 'thirties, Tutwiler Prison has a cramped and ominous atmosphere, one stripped of any comfort. With its old-fashioned no-frills construction, the jail is free from the high-tech features common in more modern penal institutions. The long stone-floored corridors echo to the sounds of steel gates opening for a moment, before slamming shut. Like most of the nation's female prisons, Tutwiler incarcerates women convicted of petty theft, as well as others condemned for far more brutal crimes.

Turn right off the main passageway, where the general population is housed, and you come to an unmarked entrance. Without warning, the tempered-steel door opens from behind, swinging inwards. A pair of towering women guards in blue uniforms take the signatures of the visitors. There is a different atmosphere here.

Most striking of all is the silence.

Silence that is, except for the high-pitched screams of a deranged inmate. The bars of her cell are fitted with a fine lattice grate to prevent her from hurling faeces at the guards. As her delirious shrieks shatter the quiet, you move down the special corridor. This is the heart of Tutwiler, the solitary confinement wing of Death Row.

Linda Block sits on her bed in a cell at the far end of the isolation unit. With light grey hair, huge olive green eyes and chalky white skin, Linda, forty-eight, is the most recent woman to be sentenced to death in the United States. Dressed in the white prison-issue tunic, bearing the monogram of the jail, she glances around her windowless cell. The walls are a putrid yellow; the floor is bare cement. Linda's few possessions are kept in a battered cardboard box at the foot of her bed.

'I have been here since December,' she says in a calm voice. 'Before this I was a publisher, a pillar of society. I was known and respected across the country. I hadn't even ever had a speeding ticket. Then I shot a cop and everything changed.'

Before her conviction, Linda Block published *Liberatis*, a political magazine. Far from the sort of person you might expect to find residing on Death Row, she hails from the well-heeled end of society. More likely to be accused of white collar crime than murder, Linda's peers were shocked that a woman of such social standing could end up on Alabama's Death Row.

'Now I'm condemned to die in an electric chair,' she says. 'I'm regarded as the most heinous criminal of all. Being on Death Row is in itself a dead feeling. You are already dead to the world, to your friends, family and, especially, to the public. The state just hasn't destroyed the body yet.'

Linda spends a lot of time thinking about the incident that got her sentenced to death in Alabama's electric chair. A police officer died in the shooting. And, when a cop dies in the Deep South, there's enormous pressure to press for the maximum punishment – electrocution.

According to her account, Linda was using the telephone at a gas station in eastern Alabama when her husband, George, was approached by a police officer. When asked to show his driving license, he leaned into the car. Fearing that he was reaching for a gun, the officer pulled his own weapon. At the trial, the police contended that the gunfight which ensued was an act of naked aggression on the part of Linda Block's husband. As she was walking back to the car, Linda saw the officer and her husband exchanging shots.

'Whatever the reason, am I supposed to stand there,' she asks, 'and allow the cop to shoot my husband till he's dead?' Without wasting a moment Linda pulled her own revolver and began to fire at the officer as well. Amid the hail of bullets the cop staggered to his car and drove away.

'Just because a man puts on a badge,' says Linda, 'it doesn't mean he's superhuman. Nonetheless, we knew that we'd shot an officer and the mentality of the force would be crazed. If you shoot a regular civilian they'll come after you, but not with the ferocity as when they're hunting a "cop-killer".'

As they made their escape from the area, Linda and George hit a massive police roadblock. They thought then and there about committing suicide. But Linda was terrified for the safety of her ten-year-old son. He had been sitting in the back of the car all along. Only when she surrendered, did Linda realize that the cop they had shot was dead. Forensic evidence used later in court showed that it was probably her bullet that killed the officer. She and her husband were charged with murder. Both were sentenced to die in the electric chair, making them the only married couple on Death Row.

During the case that followed, Linda Block dismissed her lawyers and took on her own legal defense. Such an action is unprecedented in a death penalty case.

'When you hire an attorney,' she says, 'you're signing your life over to him. I fired my attorneys and did a far better job at defending myself than they had done on my behalf. When you are fighting for your life, you begin to understand what's important and what's not.'

Expecting a sentence of manslaughter or life without parole, Linda was stunned at hearing she was to die by electrocution.

'When the judge read the verdict,' she says reflecting, 'I sensed the blood drain from my face and I felt faint. I had been sentenced to death by the state of Alabama. But I forced myself to sit erect, to show no emotion, no response. I have become a master of self-control. I wasn't going to give anyone the satisfaction of seeing how much shock and pain they had inflicted upon me. Although I didn't expect to get death, I did not want life without parole. I had decided that if they were going to convict me, go ahead and let them give me the death penalty. At least then you get an automatic appeal.'

Linda Block's apathetic expression was seen by the press as proof that she was nothing more than a cold, calculated killer. She was transported directly from court to Tutwiler Prison.

'When I arrived here I was given a full strip-search,' she explains. 'It's the most dehumanizing process any woman could ever go through. I hated it and was extremely upset. In Alabama, men can be present at female strip-searches. The warden saw the expression on my face when I had to strip in front of all those people. She said to me "I understand how you feel. We're not doing this as a punishment... it's the rules. If you behave, we'll never do this again. Being here is punishment enough".'

'On my first night in this cell,' Linda continues, 'I lay on my bed and thought "My God, I have been sentenced to death... how on Earth did I get here?" The first few days were so depressing. Like most women, I cry when I'm depressed. I miss my son more than anything. We've changed his identity to protect him from the media, and he's gone to live with my mother. Being away from him is the greatest punishment of all.'

New Death Row inmates are put on a ninety-day probationary period in total isolation. Psychiatrists watch to see if they're adjusting to the rigorous regime. The initial short sharp shock determines whether the convict will survive the decade or more she's likely to spend at the periphery of death. During the three months of solitary confinement the inmate has almost no privileges and is isolated even from the other residents of the Row. Human contact is kept to an absolute minimum.

When the ninety days are up, the prisoner is permitted a little more interaction with the other Death Row women. They have opportunities to gather together in the chapel or in their own exercise yard. Misbehaviour of any kind results in severe discipline and the suspension of any privileges they have earned.

'At times the struggle is too much,' says Linda. 'And I've felt like writing a letter to the governor and telling him to sign the form to have me sent to the chair. But although I do get despondent, I've decided to fight my situation. My life is now a clock ticking away the minutes. Every moment is part of a race – a race to win my appeal and to win back my life. If I were to accept my situation then, psychologically, I would lose my fight.'

'For me, the most depressing two days were Christmas and my son's birthday. I don't dare reveal my depression to the guards as they'd put me on suicide watch. That's the worst thing that could happen. They take your sheets and blankets, your toothbrush, shoe-laces and even your soap. People wonder why there are so many suicides on Death Row. It's because Death Row is so drawn out. It's like having an axe hanging over your head day and night. It never goes away. You keep waiting for it to fall.'

Alabama's Women on Death Row are segregated from the general prison population, with whom they have no interaction. Three short blasts on the intercom indicate the rare occasion that a Death Row inmate is being moved.

'When I am taken out of my cell,' says Linda, 'my wrists are handcuffed behind my back. If I'm ever taken outside the building, my ankles are shackled. I still have scars from wearing leg-shackles while at court. When a Death Row inmate is taken through a main corridor, the whole prison is locked down.'

The other convicts are forced to stand behind special grates, watching the Death Row inmate with deep fascination, as if almost with a sense of awe.

'It gives the impression', she continues, 'that we're so dangerous to society that even our fellow prisoners must be protected from us.'

As Linda Block's case was going through the courts, the US Senate was passing the controversial new Crime Bill.

The death penalty is something of a magic wand for the American legal system: it pleases the voters, boosts prosecutors' careers and, conveniently, it disposes of the evidence. Spurred on by public anger at the escalation of violent offences, and the eagerness of politicians to make their mark, the Bill ushered in dozens of new capital offences.

'The Crime Bill,' says George Kendall, of New York's *Legal Defense*

Fund, 'was the largest expansion of death penalty crimes in the history of the United States. Before it was passed, there were only a couple of offences that carried a sentence of death. Now there are over sixty.'

As public pressure grows to execute violent offenders, hundreds of new female inmates are expected to find their way to Death Row. At present, forty-eight women in the USA have been sentenced to die for their crimes. Spread across fourteen states, they wait for their appeals to be used up and the executioner to summon them. Society's confusion over whether or not to kill its female killers, has resulted in Death Row's women lingering in incarceration for years.

Legal experts and lobby groups alike are predicting a long, gruesome spate of female executions throughout America's Deep South – known locally as the 'Death Belt'. With Death Rows filled to capacity, politicians and the public are baying for more regular executions of society's female murderers.

'Prosecutors work hard to de-feminize a female defendant,' says Professor Victor Streib of Cleveland University, 'Lesbianism is one factor often referred to in female capital cases. In the Deep South, especially, lesbianism is abhorred. A woman who's gay is more likely to get the death penalty than one who's not. Prosecutors try to prove that the crime was in some way "macho", performed by a monster. Then it's easy to sell the jury on the idea that the best way to get rid of a monster is to kill it.'

Empathizing with women who are to be executed is an impossible task. The only ones who can accurately understand what a sentence of death is like, are the prisoners who have had their own sentences reversed. Debra Bracewell, thirty-five, was the first woman in recent times to be sent to Death Row in Alabama. She spent three years on the Row before having her sentence commuted to life without parole. Now, working at the laundry room at Tutwiler, she's thankful.

'When I was on Death Row,' she explains timidly, 'I thought about God a lot. I would pray about five hours a day and spend the rest of my time reading the Bible. There was no one for me to speak to. I was very lonely. I've lived here at Tutwiler for sixteen years. But this is not my home. I would never call this place my home.'

For Alabama's five female Death Row inmates life is a routine of loneliness. Linda's day begins at 4.30 a.m. when breakfast, like all meals, is brought to her cell.

'This is the Row,' says Linda. 'No one's going to do you any favours – they do what's convenient for them, and feeding you in the middle of the night is convenient. Breakfast is grits and biscuits. I come from an affluent strata of society and was used to eating off nice china with fine cutlery. Suddenly, I had to get used to eating everything with a spoon. After breakfast I take a shower. I'm lucky to not only have the largest cell – it's about eight feet by ten feet – but I have my own shower as well. I spend the morning reading law books and working on my appeal. Then, at 9.30 a.m. lunch is served. Like most of the meals, it's a mixture of various kinds of starch. They purposely feed you a lot of starch in jail; it's cheap, makes you feel lethargic, slows brain activity and it's fattening. I'm a health food person, at least I *was* till I arrived here.'

'In the afternoon I do exercises in my cell, I do push-ups to keep limber. Sometimes I go to the chapel. As I'm in solitary I have to go when its free from other inmates. Most of the time I sit here at the small desk they gave me and I work on my legal defense. At 2.30 p.m. the "evening" meal is served... it's usually just like lunch: starch.'

'After dinner, there's no other food until breakfast. In the afternoons I read, write letters to my family or talk to the guards. Lights are turned out at ten p.m. Death Row is a routine of boredom, but I force myself not to let my mind go blank.'

Despite the isolation and harsh routine, the female prisoners take great pride in looking their best. Make-up has a special value for women in prison, often to the point of being used as currency.

'It's very important for women', says Helen Frick, an independent expert on the US prison system, 'to look and feel feminine. Jail robs women of so many effeminate things. A simple stick of mascara, a lipstick or pot of nail-polish boosts morale and helps the Death Row inmates in particular to feel like women again.'

When sentenced to death, women tend to deal with the captivity differently from men.

'They express their grief in their own feminine way,' continues Frick. 'There's little of the physical anguish so often shown by men who're incarcerated. Instead, women form tightly linked cliques – often with a mother figure presiding over the group. Women on the Row weep, pray and comfort each other when the existence becomes too much to bear. The bond between women sentenced to die is a strong one. Their unwavering support for each other helps them to endure the separation from their children.'

Tutwiler's general inmates are given activities and training to prepare them for the outside world, but as little time or money as possible is invested in Death Row prisoners. If they are ever allowed to do work for the prison, they are only permitted pay of only a few dollars a month. Most of the time women on the Row are locked up and left to themselves, in solitude.

'On male Death Rows,' says Helen Frick, 'there may be as many as three hundred inmates appealing their sentences, or awaiting execution. Some states have just one or two women on their Death Rows, which effectively assigns the prisoner to a life of solitary confinement.'

'Here in isolation,' says Linda Block as the screams of the insane prisoner echo through the hall, 'the solitude is deadening. I feel forgotten by the world. The loneliest feeling on Earth is being a woman on Death Row in America – particularly in the South where women are still regarded as the gentle flower of mankind.'

'It doesn't shock people when a man is sentenced to death, because men are considered more violent in nature than women. But, in the public's eye, women who have been condemned to death must be monsters – the antithesis of all that women are supposed to represent. As a woman on Death Row, waiting for the *Yellow Mama*, the electric chair, I am considered a traitor to my gender. Women like me are seen as an embarrassment to our nation. Society is appalled, yet confused. We may be despised, but the thought of killing a woman by electrocuting her is hard for most Americans. So we're ignored, the forgotten part of the prison system. We're never discussed and are rarely even thought of.'

In a state of limbo, America's women on Death Row exist to die. The method of their execution depends on the state they're in. Alabama only uses the electric chair. If executed, the women at Tutwiler, would be transported to the male Death Row at Holman

Prison. The state has only one electric chair. While many states now offer lethal injection, some still employ hanging, the gas chamber or, as in Utah and in some military court-martials, the firing squad can still be used. Lethal injection is becoming the preferred method of execution with authorities, primarily because it is cheap and reliable.

After a sedative has been administered, Potassium chloride is injected through and intravenous drip into each arm. There is no doubt that lethal injection, which was first introduced in 1982, is more merciful than the chair or the gas chamber. Executions by these other methods rarely entail sedating the condemned person. Both electrocutions and gassings have regularly ended in botched executions. The chair kills by sending two thousand volts surging through the body, causing the prisoner's eyeballs to explode as it does so. In some states, such as Virginia, members of the public can volunteer to watch executions. There are always far more volunteers than there are seats in the execution room.

Sitting in her cell, uncertain whether she is to die or live, Linda Block is adamant on how she would want to be killed.

'I'm violently opposed to electrocution,' she says resolutely. 'The chair is such an indignant method. If my case comes to it, I would opt for the firing squad. There is more dignity in that. If I am going to be killed for something that I feel I'm not guilty of, I want to be standing up when I die. I want to be facing my executioner, to die with all the dignity I can.'

'As far as the state is concerned women on Death Row are America's living dead,' says George Kendall of the Legal Defense Fund. The state wants to put no resources into them, except to keep them alive to kill them.'

Kendall has been present at a number of electrocutions in several states. He campaigns to have the chair abolished, along with the lurid, almost medieval trappings that accompany it.

'Electrocutions are horrific,' he explains, 'because you're literally cooking the person. They're always done in the middle of the night. First, the head and the lower right leg are shaved to ensure a good connection between the electrode and the skin. Shaving the head also prevents the hair from catching fire during the electrocution process.

Six burly guards place the inmate into the chair and tie down the straps. If the convict struggles, he or she has no chance of escape. An electrode cap is fitted to their bald head, and other electrodes are attached to the shaved right leg. After the inmate has been given the opportunity of making a last statement, a mask is put over their face so you won't see it contort as they die. Without any warning,' continues Kendall, 'the executioner hits the button.'

In recent years several of highly-publicized female capital cases have gone through the courts. The case of Susan Smith, who drowned her two children in South Carolina, shocked America. Three years before that Aileen Wuornos – the only woman regarded by the FBI as a serial-killer – was convicted for murdering at least seven men in Florida. But, as heinous crimes such as these steal the limelight, the majority of women sentenced to death are sent to the Row for killing their husbands after years of abuse.

Guinevere Garcia, thirty-five, a tall, slim woman with dark curly hair, was sentenced to Death Row in Illinois in 1992. Like many the Row's forgotten women, Guinevere's story begins in childhood. Aged only six, a male member of her family raped her repeatedly. The identity of the rapist was never disclosed in the trial. Guinevere was brought up by her grandmother after her own mother committed suicide when she was raped by the same man. At eleven years old she started to drink heavily; then at fourteen she was raped by five men. Not long after, she was forced by her grandfather to marry an illegal alien in a sham marriage. But it was her second husband, whom she had met while working as a prostitute, that she shot after his continual beatings.

Now resigned to the fact that she is to be killed by the state, Guinevere Garcia waits in Room Six of Death Row at the Dwight Correctional Centre – one of the country's most modern Death Rows. She has asked that her appeal be dropped and that she be executed as soon as possible. She waits for the pinprick of a needle puncturing the skin, for the lethal injection to end the purgatory.

Many of the women who have made it to America's most disreputable address claim to have committed murder out of fear. Such killings divide society. Support groups declare that dozens of women are killed each year for not fulfilling their abusive husbands' commands. But, particularly in the traditional heartlands of the South, pro-death penalty lobby groups stir the public's animosity. And when sordid crimes are involved, it's perhaps not hard to understand the calls for revenge.

The catalogue of crimes committed by women on Death Row includes the case of Deirdre Hunt. She was instructed by her boyfriend to kill a nineteen-year-old man in Florida. Having bound him to a tree, she shot three .22 calibre bullets into his chest. As she fired the semi-automatic pistol, fitted with a silencer, her boyfriend videotaped the killing. Then, as the boy lay slouched, gasping for breath, Deirdre Hunt is said to have grabbed him by the hair and shot him in the head with an AK-47.

In another case, Frances Newton – a petite, reserved woman from Houston, Texas – was convicted of shooting her husband and children (aged two years and seven years) while they slept. Newton, who was sentenced to Death Row, aged twenty-two, was found guilty of murdering her family in order to claim the $100,000 insurance policy.

In the second wing of Tutwiler Prison's Death Row, Warden Lobmiller is doing her rounds.

'I control the majority of things which occur in the lives of the Death Row inmates,' she says. 'I do not have a friendship with them. They are merely acquaintances. If one of the Death Row women was executed, I would not feel remorse: rather, I think I'd be happy for her. It might be shocking to say that – but if I was one of those individuals, that's what I would want.'

Like most women who have made it to the Row, Linda Block ponders death with meticulous attention.

'Being condemned to death is unlike any other feeling one could possibly experience,' she says. 'To await death as a convicted murderer is vastly different from knowing you are dying of a terminal disease. Dying of an illness is at least acceptable and prompts sympathy. At least that person will die among friends and family. They may not know the hour when death comes, but there is no dishonour in their passing.'

'There is a curtain of empathy between the women here on Death

Row,' Linda whispers, 'facing what few women will ever have to face. Only the strong can maintain hope and faith under these conditions. But I am a survivor. Even if I lose my fight, despite my best efforts, I will accept my fate with dignity.'

N.B. Linda Block was electrocuted on May 10th, 2002.

Debra Bracewell, former resident of Alabama's Death Row
© Melissa Springer

Index

Lightning Source UK Ltd.
Milton Keynes UK
UKHW010722271118
333052UK00004B/176/P